Law for Leviathan

Law for Leviathan

Constitutional Law, International Law, and the State

DARYL J. LEVINSON

OXFORD
UNIVERSITY PRESS

Oxford University Press is a department of the University of Oxford.
It furthers the University's objective of excellence in research, scholarship,
and education by publishing worldwide. Oxford is a registered trade mark of
Oxford University Press in the UK and in certain other countries.

Published in the United States of America by Oxford University Press
198 Madison Avenue, New York, NY 10016, United States of America.

© Oxford University Press 2024

All rights reserved. No part of this publication may be reproduced, stored in a retrieval system,
or transmitted, in any form or by any means, without the prior permission in writing of Oxford
University Press, or as expressly permitted by law, by license or under terms agreed with the
appropriate reprographics rights organization. Inquiries concerning reproduction outside the scope
of the above should be sent to the Rights Department, Oxford University Press, at the address above.

You must not circulate this work in any other form and you must
impose this same condition on any acquirer

Library of Congress Cataloging-in-Publication Data
Names: Levinson, Daryl, author.
Title: Law for leviathan : constitutional law, international law,
and the state / Daryl Levinson.
Description: New York : Oxford University Press, 2024. | Includes index.
Identifiers: LCCN 2023033278 (print) | LCCN 2023033279 (ebook) |
ISBN 9780190061593 (hardback) | ISBN 9780190061616 (epub)
Subjects: LCSH: Constitutional law—United States. | International law—United States. |
Constitutional law. | State, The.
Classification: LCC KF4550 .L475 2023 (print) | LCC KF4550 (ebook) |
DDC 342.73—dc23/eng/20230802
LC record available at https://lccn.loc.gov/2023033278
LC ebook record available at https://lccn.loc.gov/2023033279

DOI: 10.1093/9780190061616.001.0001

Printed by Sheridan Books, Inc., United States of America

Contents

Acknowledgments	vii
Introduction	1

PART I: LAW FOR STATES

1. Law Without the State	23
2. Law Versus Sovereignty	60

PART II: MANAGING STATE POWER

3. State Building and Unbuilding	83
4. Rights and Votes	111
5. Balancing Power	139

PART III: BAD STATES

6. Personal Morality and Political Justice	165
7. No Body and Everybody	194

CONCLUSION

8. New Leviathans	227
Notes	*245*
Index	*297*

Acknowledgments

This project began to take shape fifteen years ago at Harvard Law School through a series of conversations with Jack Goldsmith, which led us to run a workshop on international and constitutional law, and then co-author an article, "Law for States," 122 *Harvard Law Review* 1791 (2009). That work laid out some of the broad framing of the book, and large parts were incorporated in revised form into Chapters 1 and 2. While Jack is absolved of any responsibility for the results, the book would not exist without our formative intellectual collaboration and everything I have learned from him then and since.

I also owe special gratitude to another co-author and close colleague, Rick Pildes. Parts of our article "Separation of Parties, Not Powers," 119 *Harvard Law Review* 2311 (2006), were absorbed into Chapter 5.

In addition to much new material, the book includes other prior work that has been revised, updated, and recombined in various ways: "The Inevitability and Indeterminacy of Game-Theoretic Accounts of Legal Order," 42 *Law & Social Inquiry* 28 (2017); "Looking for Power in Public Law," 130 *Harvard Law Review* 31 (2016); "Incapacitating the State," 56 *William and Mary Law Review* 181 (2014); "Rights and Votes," 121 *Yale Law Journal* 1286 (2012); "Parchment and Politics: The Positive Puzzle of Constitutional Commitment," 124 *Harvard Law Review* 658 (2011); "Empire-Building Government in Constitutional Law," 118 *Harvard Law Review* 915 (2005); "Collective Sanctions," 56 *Stanford Law Review* 345 (2003); "Framing Transactions in Constitutional Law," 111 *Yale Law Journal* 1311 (2002); "Making Government Pay: Markets, Politics, and the Allocation of Constitutional Costs," 67 *University of Chicago Law Review* 345 (2000).

This body of work could never have been produced without the hands-on help, tutelage, and camaraderie of too many friends and colleagues to name, but I will single out Oren Bar-Gill, Gabby Blum, Clay Gillette, Richard Fallon, John Ferejohn, Barbara Fried, David Golove, Rick Hills, Dan Hulsebosch, John Jeffries, Pam Karlan, Mike Klarman, Bob Keohane, Lewis Kornhauser, Larry Kramer, Liz Magill, John Manning, Eric Posner, Daphna Renan, Ricky Revesz, Jim Ryan, Ben Sachs, Adam Samaha, David Schleicher, Mike Seidman, Scott Shapiro, Seana Shiffrin, Matthew Stephenson, David Strauss, Bill Stuntz, and Adrian Vermeule.

I am beyond grateful to a group of extraordinarily generous colleagues who read the entire book manuscript and offered extensive comments and suggestions: Adam Cox, Barry Friedman, John Goldberg, Don Herzog, and Emma Kaufman. At an earlier stage, several readers of the precis provided invaluable feedback that helped put the project on a better path: David Garland, Heather Gerken, David Grewal, and Trevor Morrison. For more focused help with particular chapters, I am indebted to Liam Murphy, Noah Rosenblum, Ganesh Sitaraman, and Jeremy Waldron.

Finally, thanks to Eve Bain, Sagnik Das, and Adam Littleton-Luria for lifesaving research assistance; and to my editor at OUP, Dave McBride, for patiently seeing the project through.

Introduction

For the past several centuries of Anglo-American legal thought, law has been paradigmatically understood as the product of the state. Operating through the legal and political institutions of its government, the state imposes law on the people who are its subjects. Over the same centuries, however, the state itself has also become subject to law—most prominently, international law and constitutional law, overseeing the external and internal conduct of the state, respectively. But systems of law for states necessarily work differently than systems of law by states for people. For one thing, law for states must do without a super-state or government standing above the state, capable of creating and enforcing law from the top down. For another, the state is a unique kind of legal subject, calling for different behavioral models, moral standards, and regulatory techniques than those developed for ordinary people.

It is precisely these differences that have long marked international law as a curious, and in many eyes dubious, form of law. Seeing a system of "law without government" operating according to a structural logic of "anarchy," skeptics have long questioned how international law can possibly operate with the kind of efficacy that is taken for granted in "hierarchical" domestic legal systems backed by the state.[1] Even those who are more sanguine recognize that, precisely because it is a system of law for states, international law must work differently from ordinary state-run legal systems.

Constitutional law is equally a system of law for states. Oddly, however, it has seldom been subject to the same doubts, or fully understood as different in kind from the paradigmatic legal system run by and through the state. As a result, constitutionalists have lagged, and still have much to learn from, their internationalist counterparts in coming to grips with the common project of making the state the subject rather than the source of law. By assimilating constitutional and international law as parallel projects of imposing law upon the state, and by highlighting the peculiarities of the state as a legal subject, this book aspires to close that gap, and to bring focus to *Law for Leviathan* as a distinctive legal form.

Seeing the State

What is Leviathan? To start, it is the creation of Thomas Hobbes, the first "modern theorist of the sovereign state."[2] The iconic frontispiece of Hobbes's eponymous work of political theory, first published in 1651, depicts the state as an "Artificiall Man,"[3] a kingly colossus looming over countryside and town, wearing an expression of beatific omnipotence beneath his coronated human head (of state).[4] Hobbes's arresting image of the state as a giant person remains deeply influential to this day.[5] Routinely personifying the state, ordinary citizens and sophisticated theorists alike speak of its interests, desires, and emotions, and hold it personally responsible for its decisions, actions, and obligations. As the book will go on to describe, even while calling into question the reality and utility of the states-as-persons metaphor, international law and relations have been deeply influenced by it.[6] Equally pervasively, but less self-consciously, constitutional law and its surrounding political theory likewise has been built around the anthropomorphized image of the state as a giant person.[7]

Yet the image of a personified Leviathan we carry in our heads is not the one Hobbes or his cover artist actually portrayed. A closer look at the frontispiece brings into focus the multitude of "natural" persons—as Hobbes distinguished them from the artificial person of Leviathan—whose tiny figures populate Leviathan's arms and torso, and whose collective identity Leviathan is meant to represent. To further complicate matters, Hobbes's head of state, drawn to resemble that of a real-life monarch,[8] is supposed to represent not the natural person of the king but the impersonal government offices in which sovereign authority has been vested. As the text of *Leviathan* makes clear, the power and status of these offices—the crown, as well as representative assemblies and other institutions of government—are independent of the persons who occupy them at any given time.[9] The modern state as Hobbes saw it is thus, in the words of Quentin Skinner, "doubly impersonal": "We distinguish the state's authority from that of the rulers or magistrates entrusted with the exercise of its powers for the time being. But we also distinguish its authority from that of the whole society or community over which its powers are exercised."[10]

This depersonified understanding of the state is true to both its historical development and the modern reality of its form and function. The state is nothing more, or more mysterious, than a particular approach to social organization and governance that has prevailed over the past several centuries.[11]

That approach is characterized by the centralization of lawmaking and enforcement in a governmental organization that, in Max Weber's famous definition, "(successfully) lays claim to the monopoly of legitimate physical violence within a certain territory."[12]

The modern state emerged in Europe starting around the turn of the second millennium, outcompeting families, feudal lords, cities, empires, and the church to become the dominant form of political order.[13] In its origin, the state was primarily a technology of warfare.[14] Confronted with the perpetual threat and reality of armed conflict, kings came to see that they could support large armies by extracting wealth and manpower from populations placed under their control and protection. Power over these nascent states was initially concentrated in the hands of a single ruler and his household—an absolute monarch. Over time, however, increasingly elaborate bureaucratic apparatuses were built up around the tasks of conscription and taxation. The infrastructure of the state continued to grow as rulers realized they could increase their tax base by creating a legal system and supporting trade. Governance capabilities initially constructed for fiscal and military purposes eventually found new uses, as the state began to provide additional public goods to meet the demands of its citizens and secure their ongoing cooperation. In exchange for taxes and loyalty, groups of constituents in some places insisted upon more direct control over government decisionmaking, giving rise to representative assemblies and the beginnings of democracy. Increasing control over the state by its citizens has pushed it to serve their welfare in more and various ways, by providing education, health care, economic support, and more. As the state has taken on new tasks, its institutional forms have grown ever more complex and impersonal. Bureaucracies, judiciaries, legislatures, and professionalized armies and police forces have long since superseded the personal rule of kings and their retainers.[15]

At the end of this line of development stands the modern state, with its bureaucratized and complexly institutionalized system of government and, in many places, democratic rule by broad segments of the population. This version of Leviathan looks nothing like an absolute monarch on steroids. Yet the personified image of the state is difficult to give up—in part because it is far from clear what picture or metaphor should take its place. The image of the state as a giant king declaring "L'etat c'est moi" is simple and intuitive. Writing about the British government in the mid-nineteenth century, Walter Bagehot made the case for the indispensability of royalty by arguing that, for most of his fellow citizens, monarchy was the only "intelligible" form of government:

> The nature of a constitution, the action of an assembly, the play of parties, the unseen formation of a guiding opinion, are complex facts, difficult to know, and easy to mistake. But the action of a single will, the fiat of a single mind, are easy ideas; anybody can make them out, and no one can ever forget them. When you put before the mass of mankind the question, 'Will you be governed by a king . . . or a constitution?' the inquiry comes out thus—'Will you be governed in a way you understand, or will you be governed in a way you do not understand?'[16]

The modern state is indeed more difficult to make intelligible.[17] For Hobbes and subsequent theorists, the state is an immaterial, abstract concept, standing for a group of people united by, and capable of acting collectively through, a system of government.[18] Such an intangible entity is hard to picture; the *Leviathan* frontispiece might be as good as it gets. That image, however, is too easily reducible to that of an oversized person. Imagining the state as a person—as a self-directed being with a life of its own—has led to a great deal of confusion about how states behave and misbehave and how they can be governed by law.[19]

Working through that confusion has been a central part of the internationalist project. Much of the theory of international law and international relations can be read as an extended interrogation of the Hobbesian metaphor of states as personified Leviathans—or, as Hobbes originally conceived it, of persons as mini-states. Hobbes's account of Leviathan's birth starts from a state of nature in which, owing to the absence of "a common Power to keep them all in awe," the population is subject to the perpetual risk of war "of every man, against every man."[20] This dismal picture of the state of nature for men is developed by analogy to the natural environment of states. Hobbes envisions states in the international arena "in the [] posture of Gladiators; having their weapons pointing, and their eyes fixed on one another; that is, their Forts, Garrisons, and Guns upon the Frontiers of their Kingdomes; . . . which is a posture of War."[21] Only the creation of Leviathan can save people from the fate of states that lack their own super-Leviathan and thus continue to struggle in an international state of nature.

Hobbes's comparison of states and persons—the so-called domestic analogy[22]—has been the starting point for the most influential theories of international law and relations.[23] International relations realists continue to embrace Hobbes's perception of world politics as an inherently anarchic domain populated by self-interested states pitted against one another in a competition for power and survival. Drawing a different moral from the analogy, cosmopolitan internationalists reason that the only escape from the international state of nature is a global Leviathan—if not a full-fledged world government, at least a robust regime of international law and governance capable of doing for states what states have done for their own citizens.

But theorists of international law and relations have also recognized that the states-as-persons analogy is, for many purposes, too simple an equation. Hobbes himself recognized the limitations of the analogy. Noting that "there does not follow from [international anarchy], that misery, which accompanies the Liberty of particular men,"[24] Hobbes never recommended the creation of a global Leviathan. Picking up on this line of thought, theorists of international relations have continued to make the case that international peace and cooperation can be achieved among states notwithstanding the absence of a super-state standing over them.[25] Precisely because "states are different kinds of agents from natural individuals," the neo-Hobbesian argument goes, they "can more peaceably coexist with other states" under legal and political conditions different from those necessary to create order among persons within states.[26]

As the chapters that follow will describe, the recognition that states are "different kinds of agents" has punctuated the theory and practice of international law and relations, serving as a counterpoint and corrective to the states-as-persons heuristic. Doctrines of state sovereignty that were developed on the model of personal autonomy have been challenged on the grounds that "[s]tates are not sources of ends in the same sense as are persons. Instead, states are systems of shared practices and institutions within which communities of persons establish and advance their ends."[27] Realist models of perpetual conflict and competition among states have been called into question by theorists who doubt that states can be usefully understood as self-interested maximizers of their own power with interests or wills of their own. Frameworks of international humanitarian law that derive principles of just war among states from the legal and moral rules regarding self-defense and harm to innocents that apply to ordinary people in "the familiar world of individuals and rights"[28] are tempered by the recognition that in many respects "[s]tates are not in fact like individuals (because they are collections of individuals) and the relations of states are not like the dealings of private men and women."[29] Assessments of the costs and benefits of international legal compliance for states are confronted by the complication that "states do not possess their own "projects and life plans" and do not "experience welfare or utility" because states are not, in fact, persons, but merely "vehicles through which [actual persons] pursue their goals."[30] For centuries, theorists and practitioners of international law have been attentive to the special nature and status of states and to the ways that legal, moral, and political frameworks of analysis designed around ordinary persons might be a bad fit for Leviathan.

One might have expected constitutional law, the second major regime of law for Leviathan, to follow a similar path. Sharing common origins in the rise of the modern state, constitutional and international law were originally conceived as conjoined efforts to regulate state power, internally and externally. For Hobbes and other early theorists of the sovereign state, what made these two regimes deeply similar to one another—and deeply different from ordinary, state-run legal systems—was their mutual aspiration to impose law on a creature that was supposed to be law's source rather than its subject.[31] Hobbes himself saw no possibility of accomplishing the self-contradictory project of legally constraining sovereign states that, by definition, could be subject to no greater power. Even if law for states could be something more than an oxymoron, it was far from clear how it could possibly work in the absence of a Leviathan standing above the state, capable of authoritatively specifying the content of law and enforcing compliance. Law *for* states, international and constitutional alike, confronted a set of unique theoretical and practical challenges that did not apply to, or had already been solved by, regimes of law *by* states, for ordinary people.

Yet constitutionalists have almost entirely lost sight of this unifying, Hobbesian perspective.[32] Indeed, most American constitutionalists would be puzzled if not appalled by the suggestion of any deep connection to international law. After all, constitutional law is supposed to be the ultimate expression of self-government by the American people and the foundation of our indisputably legitimate and effective legal system. International law, in contrast, is perceived by many in this country as a vehicle for foreign interference with American sovereignty and self-government, and a dubious attempt to cloak political power relations in the guise of law. Constitutional law, in short, is *real* law, securely embedded in and backed by the state. International law, floating outside of the state, is fake.

This misapprehension has stunted the development of constitutional thought. As the chapters that follow will show, many of the most persistent theoretical and practical difficulties of constitutional law follow from the inability of its designers and practitioners to fully appreciate that, in common with their internationalist counterparts, they are constructing a regime of law for states—using similar tools to solve similar problems, stemming from the substitution of states for persons as the subject of law. Rather than dismissing international law as fake, constitutionalists would do better to follow in its path, coming to appreciate the distinctive difficulties of imposing law upon Leviathan, and recognizing what Leviathan actually is.

Laying out that path is the project of this book. More ambitiously, the project is to bring together international and constitutional law to develop a unified theory of law for states—or, with apologies and credit to Hobbes, *Law for Leviathan*. Hobbes turned out to be wrong about the impossibility of imposing positive law on the sovereign state. As the development of international and constitutional law has proven, states can, in fact, be subject to law. But Hobbes was right to see that states could not be subject to the familiar form of law created and implemented by and through states for the purpose of governing the lives of ordinary people. Because Leviathan is different from an ordinary person, law for Leviathan must also be different. The chapters that follow describe the distinctive structural, functional, and moral features of that form of law.

What Follows

The rest of the book is divided into three parts and eight chapters. Part I ("Law for States") is about the basic structural differences between legal systems created by and for the state. From Hobbes through the present, law has been paradigmatically understood as a product of the state. The authority to make and enforce law stems from state sovereignty. And law is made and enforced by and through the institutional apparatus of the state: legislatures and courts authoritatively promulgate, refine, and disambiguate legal rules, while executive enforcement authorities, possessed of the state's monopoly on the legitimate use of coercive force, ensure compliance. Legal systems that cast the state as the subject rather than the source of law are, necessarily, different. In the absence of any super-state capable of subjecting Leviathan to law, it is far from clear how systems of law for states can replicate the normative, institutional, and functional features of a real legal system. Hobbes dismissed the prospect out of hand.

A long line of Hobbesian skepticism has continued to cast doubt on international law, emphasizing precisely the deficiencies that follow from the foundational absence of the state. Constitutional law is equally a system of law for states of the sort that Hobbes imagined impossible. Oddly, however, it has seldom been subject to the same doubts or understood as different in kind from ordinary, state-run legal systems. Part I of the book presents constitutional law as equally a regime of law for Leviathan, showing how, like international law, it has had to make do without the resources of the state it is trying to regulate.

Chapter 1 ("Law Without the State") describes the related challenges of legal settlement and legal enforcement. An effective system of law requires the validity and content of legal norms to be authoritatively specified and broadly complied with. If subjects are free to decide for themselves what the law is, or ignore it, then law will fail in its essential function of making its subjects do things they would not otherwise want to do. That is precisely the kind of worry that has long afflicted international law, as critics wonder why a global super-power like the United States would bow to a rule of international law that disserved its interests, rather than changing, disregarding, or interpreting it away. We might equally wonder, however, why a president of the United States would choose to abide by constitutional limitations that stand in the way of doing what he and a majority of the country believe would be best. When President Obama's chief counter-terrorism advisor made it known that the administration "had never found a case that our legal authorities ... prevented us from doing something that we thought was in the best interest of the United States to do," he was talking about constitutional law as much as international law. If ordinary domestic law, administered and enforced by states, can rely on enforcement by a "gunman writ large,"[33] international law and constitutional law, imposed upon states, both raise the question of why "people with guns obey people without guns."[34]

While constitutionalists have paid much less attention to these kinds of questions than their internationalist counterparts, the answers available to them are, unsurprisingly, similar. A lingering line of Hobbesian skepticism connects international realists with constitutional theorists who doubt that constitutional rules and rights serve as anything more than "parchment barriers," and who see constitutional courts as doing little more than ratifying the preferences of the politically powerful. At the same time, however, both internationalists and constitutionalists have also recognized the possibility—and plausible reality—of widespread legal compliance. International institutionalists and Madisonian constitutionalists have demonstrated how compliance might be a product of decentralized enforcement and cooperation by self-interested actors within the system. And international relations constructivists and like-minded constitutional theorists have highlighted the possibility that illegal behavior might become undesirable or unimaginable to actors who have internalized legal norms and institutions or been swayed by their legitimacy. Proceeding on parallel tracks, internationalists and constitutionalists are developing similar explanations of how law for states can achieve some measure of settlement and compliance even in the absence of a crown-wearing, sword-wielding Leviathan standing above.

Chapter 2 ("Law Versus Sovereignty") describes how international and constitutional law have negotiated the common challenge of state sovereignty. Accompanying and facilitating the rise of the modern state, the concept of sovereignty was conceived to justify the political authority of the state's government over its subject populations and, at the same time, to establish the autonomy and self-governance of states in the international realm. It is no coincidence that the international system of sovereign states, formally recognized by the Peace of Westphalia in 1648, took shape at the same time Hobbes was developing the concept of sovereignty in *Leviathan*. Sovereignty, as Hobbes and other early theorists of the state conceived it, denied the existence of any higher power standing over Leviathan—including the power of law, constitutional or international.

Even as these regimes of law for states have taken hold, they have been forced to wrestle with Hobbesian doubts. International law from its inception has struggled with the apparently self-contradictory project of attempting to impose law upon states that it simultaneously conceives as sovereign. The way out of this dilemma has been the foundational principle that sovereign states can be bound by international law only with their consent. But as the consent requirement has been stretched, strained, and selectively abandoned, skeptics have assailed international law as an illegitimate threat to state sovereignty. Recent waves of populist and nationalist resistance to globalism testify to the force of these criticisms.

Those who distrust or disparage international law, Americans in particular, often hold up constitutional self-government as the contrasting ideal. In fact, however, the Hobbesian understanding of sovereignty is no less a problem for constitutionalism. Indeed, reconciling constitutional constraints with a commitment to sovereignty has been the central challenge of constitutional theory since the American Founding. Following in the footsteps of international law, American constitutional law has attempted to solve the problem of sovereignty by invoking sovereign consent—relocated, for constitutional purposes, from the government to "We the People." The shift to popular sovereignty paved the way for law to be imposed on government. But this concept of sovereignty raised no less difficult questions about how the people themselves could be bound by constitutional rules and rights that conflicted with present-day popular will. The perpetual challenge of constitutional theory has been to explain why constitutional limitations on democratic decisionmaking serve not as constraints on popular sovereignty but as popular sovereignty's true expression.

Whether constitutional law's attempts to square the circle of sovereignty and legal obligation are any more convincing than international law's is open to debate. But the robust existence of these regimes of law for Leviathan might also lead us to question what is left, or worth preserving, of the Hobbesian conception of sovereignty. Sovereignty for Hobbes was grounded in the analogy of states to free and autonomous persons in the state of nature, who could only be subject to political or legal authority with their consent. Recognizing the limitations of that analogy, and the costs it has inflicted on the actual human beings who have for centuries struggled to overcome sovereignty, might lead us to suspect that the "artificial man" of Leviathan has created an artificial problem for regimes of law governing the state.

Part II ("Managing State Power") turns to the distinctive challenge of regulating state power through law and catalogs the array of techniques that have been developed for that purpose by international law and constitutional law alike. This part begins by replacing Leviathan with a different metaphor for the state: not an "artificial man," but a manmade technology. Like artificial intelligence or nuclear power, the technology of the state comes with enormous potential benefits for human welfare, but also the risk of catastrophic harms. One approach to managing such a powerful and potentially dangerous technology is to make and enforce rules about how it can be used. Another approach is directed at its *users*, selecting for trustworthy or well-motivated controllers and creating channels of accountability and influence over their decisionmaking. Yet a third approach, much cruder, is to limit the development of the technology in the first place, or dismantle it, sacrificing the potential benefits in order to avoid the downside risks. Constitutionalism makes use of all three of these strategies. But it has done so with too little understanding of how the different approaches to managing state power relate to one another and the trade-offs among them. Drawing on parallels from international law and relations, the first pair of chapters in Part II develop a framework for thinking about how best to build, control, and *un*build the power of the state.

Chapter 3 ("State Building and Unbuilding") starts with project of building state power. From the post–World War II Marshall Plan to the post-9/11 state-building projects in Iraq and Afghanistan, building stronger states and fixing failed ones has been perceived as a foreign policy imperative. Hobbes would have approved. A state that did not build and consolidate power was destined to devolve into conflict and civil war, returning its inhabitants to the state of nature, where life was "solitary, poor, nasty, brutish, and short." As history has painfully demonstrated, however, building stronger states comes with risks of its own, both domestically and internationally. Before embracing the Marshall Plan, the U.S. government had seriously considered Treasury Secretary Henry Morgenthau's "Program to Prevent Germany from Starting a World War III," which called for decimating and dismantling—*un*building—the German state. A similar ambivalence between building and unbuilding state power has been a pervasive feature of American constitutionalism since the Founding, when Federalist state-building ambitions met Anti-Federalist fears of distant and tyrannical government. The same arguments about the risks and rewards of state power, and the costs and benefits of building and unbuilding it, have run through contemporary debates over presidential powers, the administrative state, and constitutional federalism. On the home front, Americans have resolutely resisted Hobbes's advice, intentionally designing for ourselves a state built, if not to fail, at least not to fully succeed.

Chapter 4 ("Rights and Votes") considers the prospects for successfully controlling state power once it has been built, focusing on the two primary tools designed for doing so. As the technology analogy suggested, strategies for controlling power can be aimed at uses or users. Particular uses of state power can be specified or prohibited through legal rules and restrictions, protecting vulnerable subjects against abuse—the strategy of "rights." Alternatively, the users of state power can be selected or influenced through a system of politics that empowers vulnerable subjects to protect their own interests—the strategy of "votes." This simple way of assimilating rights and votes will be jarringly counterintuitive to many constitutionalists. Constitutional rights and political representation are conventionally cast as opposing forces. Theorists of political liberalism and justice tend to view rights as extrapolitical limitations on democratic decisionmaking. Constitutional lawyers, likewise, have been long obsessed with what they see as an inherent conflict between constitutional rights and democracy, or "countermajoritarian" judicial review and democratic majority rule. Internationalists, in contrast, have been more inclined to see political power and legal protections as working in parallel. The political techniques of international relations, leveraging diplomatic, military, and economic power, and the legal prohibitions, obligations, and governance regimes created by international law, have long been understood as joint and substitutable strategies for protecting the interests of states and their peoples against the threatening power of other states.

Constitutional law has much to learn from this perspective. Viewing rights and votes as comparable tools for protecting vulnerable groups against state power raises questions about why constitutional designers, courts, and political actors have chosen to press for one rather than the other, or for particular combinations. While rights and votes are broadly substitutable, they work in different ways, with characteristic advantages, disadvantages, and domains of feasible implementation. In some contexts, rights and votes function not just as substitutes but as complements: political power can increase the value of rights, and the other way around. Finally, rights and votes can both be understood as forms of political "voice" and compared to the alternative strategy of "exit,"[35] through federalism or outright secession. In fact, the sovereign state itself can be understood as a kind of exit strategy, shielding its citizens from power of other states, perhaps more securely than rights or votes ever could.

Chapter 5 ("Balancing Power") goes on to consider yet another approach to managing state power, one that has long been central to both international and constitutional statecraft. Proceeding from the premise that "power can only be controlled by power,"[36] internationalists and constitutionalists alike have looked to the balance of powers among and within states as a safeguard against hegemonic oppression. From Hobbes to Henry Kissinger, realist approaches to international relations have held that the best hope for stability and peace among inherently power-seeking, self-interested, and rivalrous states is to maintain a balance of power among them.[37] Internal to the state, casting the different branches and units of government as similarly self-aggrandizing entities pitted against one another in a contest of "[a]mbition ... counteract[ing] ambition," constitutionalists since Madison have converted the balance of powers strategy into a system of "checks and balances." In the constitutional arena as in the international one, competition among power-seeking Leviathans is supposed to create a self-enforcing equilibrium of balanced power kept safely within bounds.

Yet the constitutional version of balance of power, upon closer inspection, turns out to be deeply, and doubly, misguided. The first problem, long recognized by internationalists, is that Hobbesian realism cannot provide anything like a full account of state behavior. As institutionalists and liberals have emphasized, states cannot be usefully understood merely as power-mongering Leviathans pursuing their own interests in perpetual conflict. State behavior is driven by the interests of the actual people who control what the state does, and those interests often point in the direction of cooperation rather than competition. Constitutionalists have been slower to recognize that the same is true at the level of government institutions in domestic politics. Whether the branches of government will compete with one another or cooperate in the service of shared political goals depends on whether the parties and coalitions that control them are allies or rivals. That is why, in American politics, Madisonian competition between the president and Congress all but disappears during periods of party-unified government, and Madisonian checks and balances come into play only when the separation of powers coincides with a separation of parties.

An even more fundamental problem with the constitutional theory of power-balancing is that it has never been clear what beneficial function institutional checks and balances are supposed to serve. The international balance of powers among states is supposed to preserve peace and provide security by preventing a powerful state from attacking and conquering its weaker neighbors. There is no obvious analogy when it comes to the constitutional system of government, however. The kind of security that matters in constitutional law is the security of political interests and groups in society who need protection against domination by powerful rivals. But balancing power at the level of government institutions will do little to guard against that kind of danger. Constitutional law's concern with checking and balancing power would be better redirected to the distribution of power at the democratic level, among the various groups and interests that compete for control over these institutions. Madison's warning that "the accumulation of all powers . . . in the same hands" is "the very definition of tyranny,"[38] makes better sense as applied to the hands of actual persons than the metaphorical hands of Leviathan.

The moral of this chapter, and of Part II more broadly, is that constitutionalists need to look past the image of Leviathan as a self-directed being possessed of its own will, power, and will to power. They would do better to shift focus to Leviathan's subjects and controllers—the people who possess power *over* the power *of* the state.

Part III ("Bad States") considers the moral and legal frameworks used to assess and rectify state wrongdoing. For this purpose, as well, the state is commonly imagined as a personified Leviathan whose conduct can be evaluated, blamed, and corrected using the same metrics and methods commonly applied to real-life persons. Theorists and practitioners of international law and relations thus derive principles of just war from the legal and moral rules regarding personal self-defense; argue that states should pay reparations to the victims of wartime atrocities and climate change on the model of corrective justice; and blame and sanction states for violating rules of international law as if states themselves were wrongdoers and susceptible to punishment. Constitutional law treats government in all the same ways. The rights of citizens are designed to protect against the kinds of harms that concern personal morality and private legality; rights claims are adjudicated on a common-law model of corrective justice; and government institutions and officeholders are blamed and sanctioned as if they had personally misbehaved and could be made to pay the consequences.

Yet there is little reason to believe that normative frameworks developed to govern the conduct of ordinary persons continue to make sense when transposed to states and governments. As theorists of international law and relations have long recognized, Leviathan is nothing like an ordinary person, morally or behaviorally. Moreover, fixating on the pseudo-person of Leviathan risks ignoring the actual people who bear the consequences of their state's conduct. Neither of these points has clearly registered with constitutionalists, however. As this part describes, a plethora of problematic features of constitutional liability, ranging from the myopically libertarian cast of constitutional rights to morally and instrumentally misguided applications of group punishment, follow from constitutional law's unreflective personification of Leviathan.

Chapter 6 ("Personal Morality and Political Justice") makes the case that personal morality and legality are a poor fit for the state. In developing the analogy between states and persons, Hobbes was tempted to equate their moral and legal natures: "[B]ecause commonwealths once instituted take on the personal qualities of men," he was led to think, "what we call a natural *law* in speaking of the duties of individual men [becomes] the *right of Nations*, when applied to whole commonwealths."[39] Constitutional law has unwittingly followed the same path. The doctrine, jurisprudence, and adjudication of constitutional rights more or less duplicates the standard frameworks of personal morality and private legality, oriented around localized harms to individual interests and emphasizing negative responsibility and intentional wrongdoing. The upshot is that constitutional law focuses on discrete, small-scale harms to individuals while blinding itself to big-picture, systemic injustices, from racial and economic inequality and subordination to the degradation of democracy into effective oligarchy. And even the myopic rights that are constitutionally cognizable cannot be framed in any conceptually or morally coherent manner when they are understood on the model of harms inflicted by ordinary persons on one another.

Moral and political philosophers have taken a different view of state wrongdoing—and, not coincidentally, a view of the state as different from ordinary persons. Political morality pointedly demands that the state treat its citizens with equal concern and respect. Ronald Dworkin tellingly refers to this principle as the "special and indispensable virtue of sovereigns."[40] The virtue is special because it does not apply to ordinary persons, who are morally permitted to display greater concern for their own lives and the lives of people close to them than for the lives of distant strangers. Leviathan is morally special in other ways, as well. John Rawls begins his landmark *Theory of Justice* by identifying the domain of justice as the basic structure of society, comprising the major political and legal institutions of the state. Because the principles of justice do not apply to "individuals and their actions in particular circumstances," Rawls draws what has been described as a "division of moral labor."[41] The state alone is subject to the systemic demands of justice, while individuals are subject to a different set of more localized and limited legal and moral obligations in their personal lives.

It is this division of moral labor that constitutional law appears to have missed. In constructing a theory of justice distinctively suitable to the state, Rawls was working from the sound methodological premise that "[t]he correct regulative principle for anything depends on the nature of that thing."[42] Constitutional law's conceptual and moral failures reflect its inability to appreciate the distinctive nature of Leviathan.

Following on the question of how the wrongdoing of states should be assessed, Chapter 7 ("No Body and Everybody") addresses the question of who, exactly, should be blamed or punished for the state's wrongdoing. The formal answer provided by international and constitutional law is, Leviathan itself. But even if it makes moral or practical sense to hold the abstraction of the state responsible for wrongdoing, there is no meaningful sense in which the state itself can be punished or penalized. Sanctions pass through the immaterial body of Leviathan and land upon the real people who are Leviathan's subjects. That is true even in cases where most or all of these people bear no personal responsibility for the wrongdoing of their states or political leaders and have no ability to prevent that wrongdoing from occurring. For Hobbes, the citizens of a state are the collective "authors [] of every thing [Leviathan] saith, or doth, in their name," and perhaps for that reason should "own[] all [these] actions."[43] But contemporary observers of international law, seeing economic sanctions and missile strikes pass through the target of the state and land on innocent human beings, have not been entirely convinced. Some go so far as to describe international law as a "primitive" legal system, premised on collective responsibility and indiscriminate punishment of the innocent and guilty alike.[44]

Constitutional law is no less primitive in this regard, but it has proceeded oblivious to its own pervasive use of what are, in effect, collective sanctions. Pretending that governments can be made to pay for their constitutional wrongdoing, constitutional law ignores the fact that the costs are passed on to innocent citizens. Constitutional sanctions miss their target from an instrumental perspective, as well, failing to deter government from violating constitutional rights and even in some cases encouraging constitutional violations. As international law has learned the hard way, the image of an embodied Leviathan that can be blamed and punished too often masks the moral and functional consequences of legal responsibility imposed upon the state.

That image has distorted political and legal thought in other ways, as well. As Chapter 7 goes on to describe, the fiction of an embodied Leviathan that can be made to feel pain by dispossession of its money feeds perpetual fears of a Leviathan state, or Big Government, intent on engorging its girth or purse by swallowing up the wealth and resources of its subjects (who desperately try to protect themselves by "starving the beast.") This is not just political rhetoric; it is also the premise of public choice models of the state and constitutional attacks on the "empire-building" administrative state. In reality, however, just as states and governments have no intrinsic interest in avoiding the kinds of losses that sanctions impose, they have no intrinsic interest in growing richer or bigger. What matters to states, and what matters *about* states, is not their corporeal size, but the consequences they create for the lives of their citizens. Here again, fully seeing the state requires looking through the artificial body of Leviathan to notice the living and breathing persons inside.

The book concludes, in Chapter 8 ("New Leviathans"), by looking further beyond Leviathan. After a triumphant run of half a millennium since Hobbes, the state appears to be in some ways weakening, if not withering away. Increasingly usurping the state's functions are a proliferation of international, regional, and nongovernmental organizations engaged in "global governance." At the same time, the power of states to control their economies and societies has been challenged and rivaled by Big Tech and other multinational corporations, which have increasingly come to resemble privatized, nonterritorial Leviathans. As power flows to entities above and independent of the state, the historical processes of state formation appear to be running in reverse, eroding the Westphalian order. This final chapter explores what might be different in a world in which states have ceded power to these alternative governors, global and corporate. As far as the design of legal regimes goes, the answer may be, not so much. Nascent efforts to manage the power of global governance institutions and Big Tech firms have conceived of these bodies as new Leviathans and proceeded to draw upon the now-familiar tools for managing the power of the old-fashioned state. Even if the Hobbesian state is on the road to retirement, *Law for Leviathan* is likely to live on.

* * *

Before proceeding, it may help in setting expectations to mention several limitations on the scope and ambition of the project. The book unfolds by showing that a relatively familiar set of features and ideas thought to be idiosyncratically characteristic of international law, politics, and theory are, in fact, inescapably applicable to constitutionalism, as well. As a consequence, the book has more to offer, measured both by depth of engagement and original contribution, to constitutionalists than to internationalists, whose ideas are borrowed and used but not much improved. Despite that imbalance of intellectual trade, the hope is that the book's broader conception of the differences between law by and for states will be at least somewhat illuminating to legal and political theorists of all stripes. At the very least, internationalists might take some satisfaction in seeing how far they have advanced beyond their constitutional counterparts in clearly identifying and resourcefully negotiating the challenges of imposing law upon Leviathan. In this regard, at least, it is constitutionalism that has been more "fake."

Constitutionalists, for their own part, may be disappointed to discover that the book is parochially focused on *American* constitutional law and theory.[45] As the burgeoning study of comparative constitutionalism has highlighted, constitutional systems of law and government around the world vary along a number of significant dimensions—including the specificity, recency, and interpretive priority of constitutional text; the institutional configuration of the judiciary and its approach to judicial review; the basic architecture of the structure of government and the democratic process; the separation and division of powers among the branches and units of government; and the content and scope of rights. While some comparative observations are noted throughout the book, there is no comprehensive consideration of constitutional systems or ideas from other countries.

Having acknowledged that major limitation, a hubristic hypothesis is that much of what the book has to say about American constitutionalism will be true of constitutionalism in other countries, as well. All systems of constitutional law confront the same basic challenges of imposing law on the sovereign state; settling and enforcing law without the state and its ordinary governance apparatus; building, constraining, and otherwise managing state power using the same essential toolkit; and normatively assessing and effectively sanctioning political misbehavior by government and its collective constituents. Accordingly, a theory of law for Leviathan holds some promise for uniting not just international and constitutional law but also different systems of constitutional law with one another, even if that project is barely begun by this book.

Finally, readers of all stripes may be frustrated by the book's failure to offer conclusive answers to some of the questions it raises. What ultimately explains legal compliance in systems of international and constitutional law, and how much compliance have these systems actually achieved? To what extent have originalists, living constitutionalists, or internationalists succeeded in reconciling legal constraints with popular sovereignty, and is there any reason to care? Do realists, institutionalists, or constructivists have more to contribute to our understanding of state behavior and legal order? What particular balance of power among states in the international arena, or among groups and interests within states, should law and politics be trying to achieve? Is there any way of justifying collective obligations and sanctions that fall upon people just by virtue of their membership in a political community? What is the right approach to thinking about the moral agency or survival prospects of the state? Rather than trying to resolve such questions, the book is invested in showing how they arise in parallel in international and constitutional thought; stem from the common project of constituting and controlling state power; and cannot be definitively settled without coming to terms with what Leviathan is and what we want it to be.

PART I
LAW FOR STATES

1
Law Without the State

For Hobbes, law is definitively a creation of the state. Without the state—in the state of nature—law as we know it cannot exist.[1] Law, as well as justice, come into existence only with the birth of Leviathan and its distinctive capability to issue authoritative commands underwritten by legitimate sovereign authority and backed by supreme coercive force.

Hobbes's vision of law is far from obsolete. The paradigmatic conception of a legal system, to this day, is one that is run by and through the state. We have come to expect that authoritative legal rules will be promulgated by state-run lawmaking institutions such as legislatures, regulatory bureaucracies, or even dictators ruling by decree. We expect that ambiguities about how these rules should apply in particular cases will be adjudicated and resolved by courts organized in a hierarchical judicial system. We assume that subjects will be obligated to comply with the law, even when legal rules stand in the way of their interests or are imposed without their consent. And we are accustomed to seeing legal obligations backed up by an executive enforcement authority capable of coercing compliance, making use of the state's monopoly over the legitimate means of violence. In all of these respects, following Hobbes, we have become accustomed to viewing law as inseparable from the political and legal institutions of the state.[2]

At the same time, however, we have come to believe in the possibility of making the state not just the source of law but also law's subject. The premise of constitutionalism is that states and governments are constituted by law and constrained to act in accordance with legal rights and rules. That is also the premise of international law, which purports to create a legal framework recognizing states and governing relations among them. These dual systems of law for states—designed to organize and limit state power from the inside and from the outside, respectively—must somehow operate *without* the state. Law made for states seemingly must come from somewhere above or outside of the states that are organized and governed by it. And it must operate without possession of the political and legal institutions and capabilities of the state that are used to run ordinary domestic legal systems.

Law for Leviathan. Daryl J. Levinson, Oxford University Press. © Oxford University Press 2024.
DOI: 10.1093/9780190061616.003.0002

For Hobbes, the idea of law without the state was a logical absurdity. As the sole source of legal authority and power, Leviathan could not be bound by any law; it exercised legally limitless power over its citizens and interacted with other Leviathans in a lawless international arena. Following in Hobbes's footsteps, a long tradition of positivist jurisprudence, defining law as the command of a sovereign backed by the threat of sanctions, has denied the reality of any form of law not stemming from the state.[3] International law has been the particular target of positivist skepticism. The progenitor of the sovereign command theory of law, nineteenth-century legal philosopher John Austin, bluntly dismissed the possibility that international law could count as real law. In the absence of an international sovereign capable of issuing and enforcing the kinds of authoritative commands that counted as law, the very idea of international law was fictitious.

Today, few if any legal philosophers would join Hobbes and Austin in defining law strictly in terms of sanction-based, sovereign commands. As H.L.A. Hart persuasively argued more than half a century ago, what we recognize to be law can exist in the absence of commands, coercive sanctions, or an Austinian sovereign.[4] But from a functional perspective if not a jurisprudential one, Hobbesian skepticism about systems of law without the state lives on. Hart himself had doubts about whether international law should count as a full-fledged legal system (as opposed to a "primitive" one), in light of the facts that it "lacks a legislature, states cannot be brought before international courts without their prior consent, and there is no centrally organized effective system of sanctions."[5]

Doubts along these lines are widely shared. Seeing a system of "law without government," skeptics question how international law can possibly operate with the kind of capability that is taken for granted in domestic legal systems backed by the state.[6] The absence of any centralized lawmaking authority or mandatory adjudicatory body means that states cannot be bound by international law without their consent. A "voluntary" system of law cannot force states to act against their self-interest, solve collective action problems, or prevent powerful states from having their way in the world. Even where states have consented to legal obligations, moreover, the content of these obligations is often indeterminate. A further impediment to binding states through international law lies in the difficulty of determining what the law actually is. Lacking a centralized legislature or a court system with mandatory jurisdiction to specify and clarify the content and application of legal norms, international law is said to suffer from irremediable uncertainty and disagreement. States are left free to interpret away their international obligations. Or to simply ignore them. The international legal system's most damning deficit is the absence of any centralized enforcement mechanism—like a global military or police force—capable of coercing recalcitrant states to comply. The monopoly over the means of violent coercion that empowers states to enforce their own laws leaves the international legal system with no resources for similarly coercing states.

These peculiar characteristics have led many to conclude that, as a matter of both form and function, international law is not just a distinctive species of law but a deficient one. Constitutional law, in contrast, has been largely immune from such doubts. Conceived as the overarching framework for, and thus inseparable from, the familiar domestic legal system, constitutional law seems securely internal to the state. Constitutional law is perceived to be not voluntary on the part of government but a mandatory, non-negotiable obligation imposed through a proto-legislative enactment and amendment process. The meaning of constitutional rules and rights is authoritatively specified by the constitutional text, and ambiguities in textual meaning are authoritatively resolved by a hierarchical judiciary empowered to say what the law is and to enforce it against government officials, who are hardly free to ignore constitutional obligations. In all of these respects, constitutional looks much more like the paradigmatic state-run legal system and less like ineffective, institutionally deprived international law.

The contrast has not always been so clear. Hobbes viewed constitutional law and international law as structurally identical, seeing both as futile efforts to impose law on, and without, the state. Hobbes's positivist successors perceived the same commonality. Austin sharply distinguished ordinary domestic law, conceived as the command of the sovereign backed by force, not just from international law but also from constitutional law, dismissing both as merely "positive morality" rather than law "properly so-called."[7] Hart's most penetrating critique of Austin's command theory of law was likewise based on the fact that constitutional law, like international law, cannot be reduced to the command of a sovereign state, but instead serves as a constraint on the sovereign state. If constitutional law counts as real law, Hart argued, then so too should international law—leveling up rather than leveling down.[8]

This chapter makes the case for putting international and constitutional law back on a par. Viewed from a Hobbesian perspective, constitutional law shares all of the functional challenges of international law—challenges inherent in any regime of law for and without the state.[9] Upon closer inspection, processes of constitutional lawmaking and interpretation are much less decisive than they might appear, leaving constitutional meaning unsettled and up for grabs. As in the international arena, powerful political actors can often bend constitutional law to serve their interests. And to the extent constitutional law does not serve their interests, there is no constitutional enforcement agent capable of coercing them to comply. The same worries about uncertainty, contestation, and weakness that have afflicted international law might well be directed toward constitutional law, as well.

Consider a seemingly straightforward, and highly consequential, legal question: When can the United States, and the U.S. president as commander-in-chief of the armed forces, use military force abroad? The international law version of this question turns on the U.N. Charter, which is supposed to prohibit the "the threat or use of force against the territorial integrity or political independence of any state," in the absence of U.N. Security Council authorization unless the use of force is in self-defense against an armed attack.[10] Yet this legal constraint on the use of aggressive force, if taken at face value, has been violated hundreds of times (and counting) since the Charter's enactment in 1945. The United States, for its own part, has not let the Charter stand in the way of bombing Yugoslavia together with NATO allies in 1999, invading Iraq in 2003, or striking Syria in 2017, among other instances of unauthorized military aggression. Like other apparent scofflaws, the United States has defended the legality of its actions in creative ways, interpreting the Charter to permit anticipatory or preemptive self-defense, invoking a customary international law exception for humanitarian interventions, or inferring implicit Security Council authorization. Even in cases where these arguments seem dubious or entirely ad hoc, the international legal system has no court or other authoritative adjudicatory body with the power to state definitively what the law is. And, of course, the international legal system also lacks any centralized enforcement capable of coercing militarily powerful nations like the United States. As former high-level Justice Department lawyer and now law professor, Jack Goldsmith, describes the situation, "The frequent violations of the U.N. Charter, its uncertain impact on the practice of states, the ease with which humanitarian intervention exceptions are made, and the lack of courts or an executive agency 'above' the treaty to interpret and enforce it, lead many . . . to wonder whether the document really functions as law."[11]

But as Goldsmith goes on to emphasize, we might wonder the same thing about constitutional law. The constitutional legality of U.S. military actions, including those in Kosovo and Syria, as well as the wars in Korea and Vietnam and the ongoing war against terrorism, has been endlessly debated without any authoritative or consensus resolution. Some constitutional lawyers, scholars, and government officials believe that the president can unilaterally decide to fight a full-fledged war without any authorization from Congress, or even in the face of congressional disapproval. Others believe quite the opposite, that the president can do nearly nothing without Congress. The constitutional text has done little to resolve these debates: the relevant words and phrases ("declare war," "executive power") are interpreted in drastically different ways, reflecting second-order disagreement about interpretive method and the relative priority of text, original understanding, historical practice, and other (arguable) sources of constitutional meaning. Just as with international law, there is no single, authoritative decider of what constitutional law in fact requires. Courts will not touch questions like this; and even if they did, it is far from clear why a president backed by a popular majority and commanding the military would yield to the opinions of judges. When President Obama's chief counter-terrorism advisor made it known that his administration "had never found a case that our legal authorities . . . prevented us from doing something that we thought was in the best interest of the United States to do," he was talking about constitutional law as much as international law.[12]

Perhaps constitutional law is not so different from international law after all. As Hobbes recognized, any attempt to impose law upon Leviathan will have to overcome a common set of challenges. These can be summarized as "law without settlement" and "law without the sword."

Law Without Settlement

The first task of any legal order is to establish what the law is. That is the reason Hobbes's Leviathan first comes into being: for the purpose of resolving otherwise intractable disagreements about the content of the law. In the state of nature, when every person is left to serve as "his own judge,"[13] divergent interests, values, and perspectives make it impossible to coordinate on legal order, resulting in irresolvable conflict. Only by enlisting Leviathan as the singular and decisive source of authoritative norms can coordinated order be made possible.[14]

Applying a similar perspective to the modern state, positivist legal theorists have long assumed that a functional legal system depends on the state's institutionalized ability to provide legal "settlement."[15] As Hart puts the point, legal systems must solve the critical problem of "uncertainty" by providing institutions and procedures capable of resolving what counts as law, "either by reference to an authoritative text or to an official whose declarations on this point are authoritative."[16] Hart famously goes on to describe how mature legal systems accomplish this task through "secondary rules" of recognition, change, and adjudication that determine what the primary legal rules are and when they have been violated.[17] Within the institutional framework of the modern state, these secondary rules serve to identify legislatures, executive agencies, and courts as the authoritative sources of legal norms and the authoritative arbiters of disputes over their meaning.

This is not to say, of course, that all of state-created law is clear. Everyone understands that the meaning and application of statutes, regulations, and common law rules are often ambiguous and contested. But that kind of routine uncertainty is usually amenable to authoritative settlement through the lawmaking and adjudicative institutions of the state. When it is unclear whether Amazon is violating antitrust law or Apple is infringing a patent, some combination of Congress, federal regulatory agencies, and the judiciary will eventually step in to resolve the dispute. The deeper uncertainty that afflicts international and constitutional law arises precisely because the authoritative legal settlement institutions of the state are not available to resolve the meaning of law that is directed toward the state itself.

International Law

The seemingly indispensable role of the state's institutional machinery of legal settlement has been a major reason for skepticism about international law. Lacking a centralized legislative institution and a centralized judiciary, international law is less capable of creating the kind of consensus about operative legal norms that is taken for granted in well-functioning state-run legal systems. A system of law that is uncertain and perpetually contested is not likely to be very effective, and may not even count as a legal system at all.[18]

This critique invites a closer look at how the international legal system actually works. In the absence of a centralized global legislature, international legal rules are created through two decentralized mechanisms: treaties and customary international law (CIL). A treaty results from the consent of two or more states, and binds only those states that ratify it. The vast majority of treaties are bilateral, involving only two states. A small number of treaties, including the U.N. Charter and the global trade agreements that have created and expanded the World Trade Organization (WTO), have been ratified by most states in the world. But even these broad multilateral treaty regimes—the closest the international system comes to the kind of universal legislation that is routine within states—must be laboriously constructed through the same decentralized process of negotiation and consent. CIL also originates through a decentralized process; its content is derived from those customary state practices that states follow out of a sense of legal obligation (*opinio juris*).

These decentralized lawmaking processes give rise to pervasive uncertainty about the content of international legal norms. The problem is most apparent with respect to CIL, which lacks any clear rule of recognition to determine when state practices have generated binding legal norms, or even what counts as a state practice. Official pronouncements, certain types of legislation, diplomatic correspondence, bilateral and multilateral treaties, the writings of jurists, nonbinding statements and resolutions of multilateral bodies, and moral and ethical claims are all invoked as evidence of CIL. These various sources often point in different directions, and there is no formula or agreed-upon set of principles for reconciling them or determining when they count as evidence of *opinio juris*. In the absence of any authoritative institutional mechanism for definitively resolving what counts as CIL—the functional equivalent of a centralized legislature—the "unstructured and heterarchical" process of identifying and applying CIL leads to frequent and persistent contestation over their existence and content.[19]

The secondary rules for treatymaking are relatively well settled, and there is much less disagreement over what counts as a treaty. Nonetheless, the certainty of treaty-based international law is often undermined by the absence of any settled rules for resolving the relationships among different treaties or between treaties and CIL. For example, the U.N. Charter asserts that Charter obligations trump other international law obligations.[20] But when NATO countries bombed Kosovo in violation of the U.N. Charter's prohibition on the use of force, many scholars contended that there was a developing CIL exception for humanitarian intervention.[21] More recently, Russia made a similar claim, invoking the CIL norm of "responsibility to protect" in defense of its Charter-violating invasion of Ukraine—while scholars and officials in Europe and America invoked the same principle as a justification for military intervention on the side of Ukraine.[22] Analogous questions about the validity of important treaty obligations that conflict with the Charter, with obligations imposed by the WTO, and with one another, proliferate unresolved.[23]

In state-run legal systems, courts might step in to resolve these kinds of legal uncertainty through authoritative, case-by-case adjudication. International law does have courts at its disposal—both domestic courts of states and international tribunals. But the ability of these courts to resolve uncertainty about the existence and content of international law is severely limited by their lack of centralization, coordination, and hierarchy. Predictably, the courts (as well as the executive branches) of different states interpret international law differently, in light of their different interests, values, and legal traditions. While the international system does have various courts of its own, formally independent of the direct control of any one or several nations, their jurisdictions are narrow and segmented. The result is a patchwork of adjudicative authority, with gaping holes and areas of uncoordinated overlap. There are many matters—immigration, war, human rights, and so on—over which international courts have little or no authority. At the same time, regional courts (like the European Court of Justice) and international bodies (like the Human Rights Committee) have overlapping claims to partial jurisdiction to resolve or pronounce upon international law, but with no second-order rules or institutional mechanisms to coordinate their decisions.

Unable to rely upon the centralized, hierarchical ordering that domestic legal systems create through their legislative and judicial institutions, the system struggles to coordinate public understandings of the content and application of its norms. Seeking to rectify this deficiency, cosmopolitan internationalists have called for a global legislature and supreme court to centralize and coordinate the governance of world affairs. While that degree of institutional centralization remains a distant hope, the international order has, in fact, succeeded in building lawmaking and adjudicative institutions like the U.N. Security Council and the appellate body of the WTO, which possess centralized jurisdiction over important if circumscribed issue domains. Another special case is the European Union, which has consolidated legal and political authority in its supranational governance institutions and for many purposes has begun to resemble and function as a proto-state.[24] Perhaps the international system will continue to make progress along these lines, achieving legal settlement by replicating the institutional architecture of the state on a global scale. For now, however, much of the international legal order remains without state-like governance.

The unsurprising result is an international legal system that is commonly described as "fragmented"[25] or "pluralistic."[26] Treaty commitments conflict with one another, as well as with CIL, which is itself subject to multiple interpretations. The multiplicity of international adjudicatory institutions with over- and under-lapping jurisdictions is incapable of resolving the resulting uncertainty and in fact often exacerbates it through inconsistent decisionmaking. In sum, lacking legislative and adjudicatory centralization, international law continues to struggle to provide the kind of authoritative legal settlement characteristic of domestic legal systems run by and through states.

Constitutional Law

At least at first glance, constitutional law appears to be more fully embedded in the institutional structure of state-run legal systems.[27] Constitutional norms are created in the first instance through a proto-legislative process (such as a constitutional convention) and codified in an authoritative text, with specified procedures for amendment. And ambiguities in the meaning and application of the constitutional text are authoritatively resolved by a hierarchical judiciary headed by a supreme or constitutional court.

But this formal picture disguises much of the reality of constitutionalism, at least as it is practiced in the United States.[28] To start, the constitutional text does not function like a legislatively enacted statute. Chief Justice John Marshall famously spelled out the contrast in the early years of American constitutionalism. Because the constitution was "intended to endure for ages to come," he explained, it should not be expected "to provide, by immutable rules, for exigencies which, if foreseen at all, must have been seen dimly, and which can be best provided for as they occur." "To have prescribed the means by which government should, in all future time, execute its powers, would have been to change, entirely, the character of the instrument, and give it the properties of a legal code." In other words, the constitutional text is not supposed to provide detailed rules or resolve the content of constitutional law with any specificity. Unlike ordinary legislation, which is continuously updated and can avail itself of "the prolixity of a legal code," the constitutional text leaves most questions of constitutional law open to future decision. A constitution that attempted to provide sufficient detail to give specific content to all the potentially relevant constitutional rules and rights into the future, Marshall says, "could scarcely be embraced by the human mind."[29]

Marshall was right about this. The constitutional text, including its occasional amendments, settles some basic features of the structure of government and its operation. But most of the content of constitutional law depends on how abstract, open-ended, and indeterminate provisions of the text are interpreted and re-interpreted over time. A centrally salient feature of American constitutionalism is the absence of any consensus about how that interpretation is supposed to work, or what constraints, if any, bound the practice. Constitutional interpreters disagree about whether the meaning of the text should be derived from historical understandings of the Founding generation, subsequent historical practices, functional inferences from the basic structure of government, deeply rooted values and moral principles, or some combination of these sources. Even in cases where interpreters are focused on the same sources and purporting to employ the same methodological approaches, they routinely disagree among themselves about what the constitution should be understood to mean.

Constitutional disagreement can be cast as competing interpretations of a singular, authoritative constitutional text. But the exclusive authority of text as a source of constitutional meaning is itself a matter of controversy. Some constitutional systems do not rely on a text at all, or, like the British system, subsume a patchwork of texts into a broader set of unwritten conventions. But even in the American system, centered on a written text, most constitutionalists believe in the existence of constitutional norms stemming from sources other than, and in some cases inconsistent with, the text and formal amendments of the U.S. Constitution. These sources range from patterns of institutional practice, to more elaborate theories of constitutional lawmaking and change through "constitutional moments" or "super-statutes," to the kind of "construction" that even textually grounded originalists believe is necessary to derive much of what counts as constitutional law. Here again, constitutionalists have reached no consensus on which of these sources is legitimate, how they should be prioritized, or the substantive constitutional norms they should be understood to have produced.

Disagreement about interpretive methods and sources leaves many constitutional issues open to continual controversy.[30] Lawyers, judges, government officials, and citizens disagree about whether women have the constitutional right to an abortion; whether individuals have a right to bear arms; whether affirmative action is permitted; whether religious groups and practices must or can be afforded special treatment; whether the death penalty is constitutional; whether the president can fight an undeclared war; whether Congress's legislative power is effectively unlimited or restricted to the kinds of regulations that were contemplated at the Founding; whether independent agencies and other incursions on the "unitary" executive are permitted; whether the modern administrative state is a wholesale constitutional violation; and any number of other fundamental questions. Throughout American history, presidential administrations, political parties, states, groups of judges, and social movements have advanced dramatically different constitutional visions. The Progressive assault on laissez-faire and Roosevelt's New Deal assertion of expansive national and executive powers contended with the *Lochner*-era paradigm of federalism and economic liberty. The abolitionists' antislavery constitution and the NAACP's campaign against segregation challenged Southern states' constitutional defenses of slavery and Jim Crow segregation. The post-9/11 war on terrorism has pitted proponents of unbridled executive power in the domain of national security again civil libertarian opponents of an imperial presidency. Contemporary progressives argue for an "anti-oligarchy" constitution,[31] while libertarians advocate for a "classical liberal" constitution,[32] and anti-liberals counter-propose "common good constitutionalism."[33]

What is supposed to save constitutional law from this cacophonous controversy is a fundamentally important institutional feature of the U.S. and many other constitutional systems: a hierarchical judiciary, headed by a supreme or constitutional court, with final say over constitutional meaning. As in ordinary state-run legal systems, centralized judicial review offers constitutional law a powerful mechanism of legal settlement that international law for the most part lacks. The consolidation of constitutional interpretation into a single, authoritative tribunal has prevented constitutional law from devolving into the kind of legal system—or failure of legal system—that Daniel Webster long ago decried:

> Instead of one tribunal, established by all, responsible to all, with power to decide for all, shall constitutional questions be left to [multiple] bodies,

each at liberty to decide for itself, and none bound to respect the decision of others; and each at liberty, too, to give a new construction on every new election of its own members? Would anything ... with such a destitution of all principle, be fit to be called a government? No sir.... It should be called, rather, a collection of topics, for everlasting controversy; heads of debate for a disputatious people. It would not be a government. It would not be adequate to any practical good, nor fit for any country to live under.[34]

Such a regime of endless legal contestation would be immediately recognizable to skeptical observers of international law.

As Webster emphasizes, what makes constitutional law different is the Supreme Court's ability to create constitutional settlement—to the extent that ability exists.[35] The Supreme Court does, in fact, create significant measure of settlement on the American constitutional system, by resolving specific disputes over constitutional meaning and, in the course of so doing, constructing relatively stable and determinate doctrinal frameworks. But the settlement function of the Court extends only so far. Many of the most consequential constitutional questions are not, in fact, resolved by the Supreme Court or any other court. These include constitutional issues such as war powers, foreign policy, and partisan gerrymandering that the Court explicitly deems "political questions" or otherwise nonjusticiable. But there are any number of other (potentially) constitutional issues—involving economic regulation and redistribution, racial and gender inequality, free speech on social media platforms, mass incarceration, and much else—that the Court avoids simply by curtailing the scope of the constitutional doctrine it constructs.[36] Either way, the result is that much of the (arguable) domain of constitutional law is left to be resolved by political actors in Congress, the executive branch, and state governments.

When these actors and institutions disagree about what the Constitution requires or allows, there is no mechanism for settling the ensuing conflicts other than the ordinary channels of political contestation.[37] Thus, major separation of powers conflicts between Congress and the president—in the context of war powers, foreign policy, appointments, executive privilege, unilateral presidential policymaking, or impeachment—lead to "constitutional showdowns" without any agreed-upon rules for reaching authoritative resolution or lasting settlement.[38] The same is true of conflicts between states, or between states and the federal government, ranging from the legality of voting procedures and outcomes to secession and the Civil War.

Constitutional disputation in these vast extrajudicial domains is no more amenable to consensus settlement than ordinary political disagreements, and often not clearly distinguishable. The reality of the American constitutional system is that "the meaning of most of the Constitution is determined through ordinary politics," as political actors debate and determine constitutional meaning "in the course of ordinary political struggles, without much attention to legal and constitutional values that lawyers and judges think important."[39]

This still leaves the relatively settled realm of legalistic constitutionalism, where the Supreme Court has final say over constitutional meaning. But the boundaries of that realm are themselves contested. Even as the Court has come to insist that it is "supreme in the exposition of the law of the Constitution,"[40] presidents, Congresses, and other political actors throughout American history have disclaimed any obligation to bow to judicial decrees when they had different views of what the constitution required or permitted. Abraham Lincoln announced his refusal to accept the Court's *Dred Scott* decision as binding on the president, Congress, or anyone else beyond the parties to the case,[41] and at the outset of the Civil War he pointedly ignored a direct order from the chief justice.[42] After the war was over, the Republican Congress, anticipating judicial resistance to the project of Reconstruction, stripped the Court of jurisdiction to hear constitutional challenges and manipulated its size and partisan composition.[43] President Roosevelt threatened to pack or otherwise take control of a Court that stood in the way of his New Deal program, seemingly bullying the Court into submission.[44] During the civil rights era, Southern state governments and mobs of their citizens responded to the Court's desegregation decisions by denying their legality and mobilizing massive resistance.[45]

These striking instances of political and popular resistance to the Supreme Court can be viewed as failures of the American constitutional system. But they can also be viewed as manifestations of an indispensable feature of the system, namely its commitment to what is sometimes called "popular constitutionalism."[46] From the Founding through the present, democratically grounded claims of constitutional authority by the political branches and "the people themselves" have challenged and constrained judicial supremacy.[47] Judicial supremacy has prevailed only within "politically constructed bounds," which are continually being renegotiated pursuant to shifting patterns of political power and preferences.[48] "The deference due to judicial opinions and judgments is worked out, issue by issue, over time, with distinct points of equilibria achieved and unsettled in substantive disputes over controverted questions of constitutional government."[49] More simply put, the ability of courts to provide authoritative settlement of constitutional law is itself a perpetually unsettled question of American constitutionalism.

The limited and shifting domain of judicial supremacy leaves broad swathes of the American constitutional system in something like the condition Webster abhorred. Compare Larry Kramer's description of an American constitutional order existing largely outside the bounds of judicial settlement:

> There are no easy rules of recognition to identify how a constitutional issue arises, much less how it gets resolved. There are not even clear rules about how one knows if something *is* a constitutional issue. Instead, such matters are left to the free play of interbranch and intergovernmental politics. Actors in any institution can try to turn something into a constitutional question, and the only measure of their success or failure is how other political actors and the public respond. Nor is the ability to initiate a debate limited to formal institutions of government. Social movements, different parts of civil society, even individuals may equally launch a campaign based on a novel reading of the Constitution, with the test of validity being only whether they can persuade enough others to embrace or adopt their position.[50]

Once again, a description of international law along these lines would hardly raise an eyebrow. If it is startling as a description of constitutional law, that is only because American constitutionalists have created a more convincing facsimile of state-like institutional forms. Kramer urges us to look behind the facade of authoritative text and judicial settlement and recognize that constitutional law is "not like ordinary law at all."[51] We should not expect in constitutional law "to find a rule of recognition that assigns someone the power to resolve controversies with a degree of certainty and finality: so at the end of the day we have something we can point to and say 'yes, *that*, is the law.' "[52] Such expectations of how law must work are based on the kind of "ordinary law" created and run by states. Regimes of law for states—constitutional law, as well as international law—are, in this and other respects, extraordinary.

The State and Stakes of Settlement

To recognize that international and constitutional law work differently from ordinary law is not to say that they do not work. Deprived of the full panoply of institutional supports normally provided by the state, the international and constitutional legal systems have found other ways of achieving at least some measure of settlement: coopting the existing institutional architecture of states, replicating that architecture in their own systems, and building consensus on non-institutionalized rules of recognition, as well as on primary rules of conduct. If international and constitutional law have not yet managed to match the certainty that well-ordered states take for granted in administering their own systems of law, what they have in fact accomplished is no small matter.

What they have accomplished, to start, is the legal construction of the state itself. The fairly well settled core of the international legal system is the recognition of sovereign states, generally possessed of legal control over their territories and the authority to consent to binding legal obligations. Before international law can be unsettled in all the ways described above—uncertainty about what counts as CIL, how to resolve conflicting treaty obligations, or the authorities of different adjudicative and regulatory bodies, and so on—there must be a significant degree of settlement at the foundational level of constituting sovereign states as international actors.

The role of constitutional settlement in constituting the state is all the more transparent. Settlement of the basic structure and authority of the state's core political and legal institutions is a prerequisite for the existence of a functioning or recognizable state. Constitutional uncertainty about presidential powers or the permissible boundaries of political gerrymandering need not undermine the existence and foundational stability of the state. But constitutional disagreement about who is the president or whether elections matter risks collapsing the state entirely. States in which constitutional settlement has broken down at the level of the basic system of government are what we call "failed" states. In states that have not failed, constitutional settlement, to a considerable extent, has prevailed.

Beyond structuring states in their international and domestic forms, regimes of international and constitutional law, as described above, have made further strides toward settlement. In the international system, the basic rules for entering into binding treaties are widely recognized and agreed upon, and decisions by lawmaking and adjudicatory institutions like the U.N.

Security Council and the appellate body of the World Trade Organization are generally recognized as authoritative within their (limited) domains.

In the American constitutional system, setting aside spectacular exceptions like the Civil War, core features of the constitutionally specified structure of government—the existence of a bicameral Congress with the power to make laws, equal representation of states in the Senate, the procedures for presidential elections—have seldom been subject to controversy.[53] Where greater controversy over constitutional meaning exists, the consolidation of interpretive authority in the courts, at least in some areas, has allayed fears that constitutional disputation will routinely "degenerate into naked power struggles, raising the Hobbesian specter of social chaos."[54]

Other constitutional systems have gone further in fostering legal settlement. European constitutional systems formed after World War II, centered on specialized constitutional courts with unquestioned supremacy over constitutional decisionmaking, can rely (even) more heavily on the judiciary to resolve constitutional controversies.[55] These constitutional systems also feature more recently written and ratified constitutional texts that articulate legal rules in more detail and are easier to amend than the U.S. Constitution. It seems likely that the greater legislative and adjudicatory capacity of such constitutional systems has made them at least somewhat more successful at resolving uncertainty about the content of constitutional law than the less settled American system.

The actual extent of legal uncertainty or settlement in different constitutional systems, or in the international system, is an empirical question. For present purposes, the important point is just a conceptual one. The challenge of resolving uncertainty and achieving settlement is different and greater for systems of law for states than for state-run legal systems, simply because the former cannot rely upon the lawmaking and adjudicatory apparatus of the state.

One final note. The discussion thus far has taken the Hobbesian view that legal uncertainty is a problem to be solved. For international law skeptics and for constitutionalists like Webster, as for Hobbes, the inability of international and constitutional law to provide the kind of legal settlement characteristic of state-run systems counts as an obvious failing. Viewed from a different perspective, however, unsettlement may have its own set of virtues. Proponents of international "pluralism" argue that unified, hierarchical legal systems tend to favor powerful over weak interests; suppress legitimate differences among nations, peoples, and groups; and prevent changes in governmental structures that might better reflect contemporary preferences. The prevailing, nonhierarchical system of international law, they argue, allows for ongoing experimentation and contestation in ways that promote optimal change, empower weaker groups, enhance accountability, check powerful interests, and promote individual self-governance.[56] Along similar lines, proponents of an "unsettled constitution" join popular constitutionalists in exalting the multivocality, inclusiveness, and generativity of constitutional uncertainty and contestation.[57]

Perhaps the paradigmatic model of state-run legal systems, and the centralized, authoritative, legal settlement they are often capable of providing, has warped our normative judgment of what a legal system should aspire to be. Or maybe internationalists and constitutionalists are making a virtue of necessity. Either way, the descriptive point remains: for better or for worse, legal settlement comes less easily to regimes of law for states.

Law Without the Sword

If the first concern of a legal order is to say what the law is, an obvious second concern is that legal subjects obey it. Because law often requires its subjects to do things they would not otherwise want to do, a seemingly crucial feature of an effective legal system is the capacity to enforce compliance.[58] In state-run legal systems, that capacity is underwritten by the state's monopoly on the means of coercive force. On the Hobbesian understanding, a prerequisite for law is a sword-wielding Leviathan with the "coercive Power, to compel men equally to the performance of their Covenants, by the terrour of some punishment, greater than the benefit they expect by the breach."[59] Without the coercive power of Leviathan, law becomes pointless: laws "without the sword, are but words, and of no strength to secure a man at all."[60]

International Law

The absence of any sword-wielding super-Leviathan capable of coercing states to comply has long been a source of skepticism about the reality or efficacy of international law. Hobbes and his legal positivist successors, defining law as the command of a sovereign backed by force, disqualified international law on both grounds. Because international legal obligations are enforced only by moral sanctions, Austin concluded, international law was law only in the sense that we might speak of the "laws" of honor and fashion.[61] Again, conceived as a jurisprudential claim about the nature of law, the Hobbesian-positivist perspective has proven too limited. As Hart convincingly demonstrated (while updating Leviathan's weaponry) law cannot be understood simply as the commands of a "gunman writ large."[62] Nonetheless, Hobbesian skepticism about law without the sword has remained a source of serious doubt about the practical efficacy and real-world significance of international law, if not its jurisprudential status. Many continue to agree with Hobbes that the "force of law" comes from its backing by the coercive apparatus of the state.[63]

From this perspective, international law clearly falls short. The international legal system conspicuously lacks a "gunman": there is no centralized international enforcement authority capable of coercing states and their armies. The original plan for the United Nations actually did include a military force, to be requisitioned from member states and put under the command of the Security Council to enforce its dictates. But that system of centralized, coercive enforcement did not come to pass. Instead, international law enforcement against noncomplying states, to the extent it exists at all, operates in a decentralized way, through the actions of other states. Enforcement is not "vertical," coming down from a super-Leviathan, but "horizontal." And enforcement does not always or even typically involve military force; more often the means are nonviolent. The most common method of international law enforcement is for other states to exclude the noncomplying state from the benefits of international cooperation by means of reciprocal noncooperation. A state that is party to a treaty that has been breached by another state is permitted to take proportionate countermeasures, such as withdrawing its own compliance in response; a state that is injured by trade practices in violation of WTO rules is authorized to retaliate by imposing reciprocal tariffs or other protectionist measures. As Scott Shapiro and Oona Hathaway highlight, this kind of horizontal enforcement by "outcasting" is a basic structural difference between international law and the "modern state conception" of centralized law enforcement by a sword-wielding Leviathan.[64]

Scholars of international law and relations have long grappled with the implications of this structural difference. International realists take the Hobbesian view, rejecting the possibility that a legal system without a Leviathan-like enforcer could ever prevent powerful states from simply thumbing their (metaphorical) noses at legal obligations. In the realist view, decentralized enforcement amounts to a system of self-help that leaves weaker states helpless. As leading realist Hans Morgenthau explained, powerful states "can violate the rights of a small nation without having to fear effective sanctions on the latter's part," and they can "proceed against the small nation with measures of enforcement under the pretext of a violation of its rights, regardless of whether the alleged infraction of international law has actually occurred or whether its seriousness justifies the severity of the measures taken."[65] International law enforcement might work better if other, stronger states could be counted on to come to the defense of weaker victims. But realists question why self-interested states would be willing to incur the costs of international law enforcement for the benefit of others. Realists acknowledge that the interests of stronger states may, on occasion, align with the interests of weaker ones, giving them self-interested reasons to intervene. But such cases of aligned interests are likely to be the exception that proves the rule—the rule of powerful states in an international system that has no means of coercing them. Morgenthau thus concludes, "There can be no more primitive and no weaker system of law enforcement than [international law]; for it delivers the enforcement of the law to the vicissitudes of the distribution of power between the violator of the law and the victim of the violation."[66]

Why, then, are even the most powerful states seldom seen flouting international law? As Louis Henkin famously asserted half a century ago, it appears that "almost all nations observe almost all principles of international law and almost all of their obligations almost all of the time."[67] For realists, however, this observation might be true but trivial. For one thing, the uncertainty and unsettlement of international law, discussed above, allows states in a wide range of cases to recast apparent violations as merely re-interpretations. It might seem obvious that Nazi Germany violated any number of international legal obligations, starting with rearmament (which was prohibited by the Treaty of Versailles), and proceeding through the invasions of Austria, Czechoslovakia, Poland, Denmark, Norway, Belgium, Holland, and France, and the atrocities that followed. But Hitler never admitted to violating international law; to the contrary, international lawyers in Germany generated elaborate legal justifications for everything the Third Reich did.[68] Of course, that does not mean that international law, as it was widely understood at the time, was not, in fact, violated. But to the extent states can "observe" principles of international law by offering up more or less colorable legal justifications, it is no wonder—and little matter—that explicit violations remain rare.

Realists emphasize another reason states often act in accordance with international law, which is that the relevant law often coincides with their interests. To the extent international law only commands states to do what they would have done regardless of law, then compliance with international law comes without cost or consequence. And given the voluntary nature of the international legal system, we should generally expect states to avoid incurring legal obligations that run counter to their interests. This is especially true of powerful states, which exercise disproportionate influence over the content of international law through political, military, and economic pressure. That is why we see, for instance, anti-proliferation regimes that allow nuclear nations to maintain nuclear weapons but ban non-nuclear nations from seeking them; intellectual property agreements that significantly advantage rights holders in developed states; the customary international law rule prohibiting expropriation of alien property; and the U.N. Charter, which gives powerful nations a veto in the Security Council. It should come as no surprise when the powerful states that created these rules and regimes happily comply, and encourage or coerce weaker states to do the same. Much of what might appear to be legal compliance can thus be explained as merely "coincidence of interest."[69]

Hobbesian realism paints a pessimistic picture of how well law can work when it must do without the sword. But there are more optimistic perspectives, as well. One follows directly from the logic of horizontal enforcement by outcasting.[70] Where the broader or longer-term benefits of cooperation with other states through legal rules and institutions outweigh the costs, and where noncompliance will lead to reciprocal noncompliance or noncooperation, states will have a self-interested reason to comply with legal rules that cut against their immediate interests. The threat of being shut out of valuable cooperative opportunities may well provide states with the Hobbesian "terror of some punishment greater than the benefit they expect by the breach."

Reasoning along these lines, international relations "institutionalists" deploy the tools of game theory to demonstrate how international law can shape and constrain the behavior of states even in the absence of any higher-level enforcement authority through the decentralized threat of losing—or being outcast from—the benefits of cooperating with other states through law.[71] Institutionalists conceptualize broad swathes of international relations as taking the form of a prisoners' dilemma game, in which two or more states know that restraining the pursuit of short-term or private interests will make them better off in the medium or long term, but each is worried that if it cooperates in the short term the other will defect. States can overcome this dilemma and achieve mutually beneficial outcomes if they agree on what counts as cooperation and engage in repeat play. The role of treaties and customary international law, institutionalists posit, is to establish the terms of cooperation and facilitate iteration, as well as to structure international governance and adjudicatory bodies that can help to monitor compliance and link issues to expand the scope of sustainable bargains. Many regimes of international law—governing diplomatic immunity, extradition, the WTO, investment and arms control treaties, the law of the sea, and the laws of war, among other subjects—can be understood in this light. Institutionalists explain other forms of international cooperation and legal compliance using the alternative logic of coordination games. In circumstances where two or more nations will benefit from behaving symmetrically but cannot initially agree on which of many possible common actions should be chosen (often because the choice has distributional consequences), treaties and CIL can help select and embed the focal point for coordination. Treaties ranging from boundary settlements to communication protocols plausibly reflect the logic of coordination.[72] The common-denominator is that states will choose to comply with law when the benefits of cooperating and coordinating through legal rules and institutions exceed the gains from going it alone.

Institutionalists share with realists the premise that forcing self-interested states to follow the law requires coercive enforcement, whether by threat of sword or solitude. For other theorists of international law and relations, however, this premise fails to capture the full complexity of states or their behavior. International "constructivists" emphasize that states' interests and identities are pervasively shaped by law, generating "intersubjective understandings and norms"[73] of appropriate behavior that lead states to cooperate and comply with law irrespective of material incentives.[74] Most fundamentally, constructivists point out that the very existence of sovereign states and their international relations is in large part a product of legal construction. Rationalist accounts of international law that start from the premise of states and their instrumental interests take these "'givens' of international relations" for granted. But that is to miss how international law operates invisibly in the background to establish the basic rules of the international game, which inevitably "shape the policies of nations and limit national behavior."[75] As states proceed to build and act under international law, moreover, processes of negotiation, mutual education, and principled argumentation continue to shape the self-understanding of state actors as legal compliers. As one prominent constructivist explains, "The international system can change what states *want*. It is constitutive and generative, creating new interests and value for actors. It changes state action, not by constraining states with a given set of preferences from acting, but by changing their preferences."[76]

The constructivist perspective has been especially congenial to international lawyers, who have gravitated toward the view that states follow the law not because of coercive enforcement or self-interested calculations of material benefit but because they see it as the morally right or intrinsically preferable thing to do. International lawyers thus describe the inherent "pull toward compliance" exerted by "legitimate" legal norms;[77] how states "internalize" these norms, "incorporating [them] into [states'] own internal value system";[78] and how states are "socialized" into compliance.[79] In sympathy with constructivists, international lawyers understand compliance to be endogenous to international law. States comply with international legal rules because the they have been acculturated by the international legal system to behave legally.

Summing up, theorists of international law and relations have devoted considerable attention to the puzzle of why or when states might comply with international law in the absence of a super-state enforcement authority. Rationalists—realists and institutionalists—see compliance, to the extent it exists, as turning on the decentralized interactions of states cooperating or competing in pursuit of their narrower or broader self-interest. Constructivists and similarly oriented legal theorists see compliance as a product of the normative force of international law and its ability to shape the interests and values of states in the first place. But all share the premise that enforcement and compliance in international law presents a distinctive problem that does not arise in ordinary legal systems backed by a sword-wielding Leviathan.

Constitutional Law

One might expect constitutionalists to be focused on the same problem. After all, as Hobbes had no trouble recognizing, constitutional law also lacks a super-Leviathan standing above the state, capable of coercing government actors to comply with its dictates.[80] If we wonder why a global superpower like the United States would ever bow to a rule of international law that threatens its vital interests, we might also wonder why a U.S. president, backed by a popular majority and commanding the same military force that makes the country a global superpower, would ever bow to constitutional rules and rights that stand in the way of vital national interests. Recognizing that presidents and popular majorities have, in fact, sometimes broken or rewritten constitutional rules under exigent circumstances of war and economic crises, we might wonder why they do not do so more regularly, whenever constitutional limitations prove politically inconvenient. Americans are not surprised when, in other parts of the world, constitutional rules and rights are disregarded or replaced by authoritarian leaders or parties who have no interest in submitting themselves to the rule of law. To the extent constitutionalism works differently in the United States and other constitutional democracies, we might wonder what accounts for that difference.

In fact, however, constitutional lawyers in the United States seldom pause to ask how, or under what conditions, constitutional law can effectively constrain presidents, popular majorities, or other powerful political actors.[81] Even as constitutional theorists obsess over how to justify imposing constitutional limitations on the power of democratic majorities, they mostly ignore the conceptually prior question of why politically empowered majorities and their elected representatives would ever choose to comply with legal limitations. Constitutional constraints are conventionally conceived as contractarian obligations or commitments against pathological political decisionmaking, but constitutionalists offer no explanation of what prevents the politically powerful from breaching constitutional contracts or commitments. Ordinary contracts are enforced by the state; Ulysses needed ropes and a mast to commit himself against the lure of the Sirens. Is there some equivalent device that binds political actors to the constitution?

For American constitutionalists, the affirmative answer of first resort has been *courts*. In a constitutional system centered on judicial review, it is tempting to imagine courts as effective enforcers, possessed of the authority to force state actors to comply with constitutional rules and rights. And indeed, for constitutional lawyers in the United States, serious doubts about constitutional compliance tend to surface only in settings where courts might not be available to play this role. Worries that presidents might ignore constitutional limitations on their power come to the surface in national security domains where courts are least likely to intervene. Concerns about constitutional noncompliance have also taken root among proponents of popular constitutionalism, who call for "taking the constitution away from the courts." Once judicial enforcement is out of the picture, the difficulty of somehow making constitutional law "self-enforcing" becomes harder to ignore.[82]

But the difficulty does not disappear when courts reenter the picture. The judiciary, after all, is hardly a sword-wielding Leviathan capable of coercing presidents and other powerful political actors. Quite the contrary, as constitutionalists emphasize in other settings, the judiciary is "the least dangerous branch" of government, lacking the powers of purse and sword.[83] We might well wonder, then, why "people with money and guns [would] ever submit to people armed only with gavels?"[84] Judges who attempt to enforce constitutional rules and rights against powerful political leaders in other parts of the world are ignored, imprisoned, or shot. Even in the United States, powerful political actors—presidents, state officials, and mobilized groups of citizens—have not always deferred to courts. To the extent government officials in this country have, in fact, been willing to bend the knee to judges, accepting judicial supremacy and complying with the Court's dictates, that is something that needs to be explained. As one prominent political scientist puts the puzzle, "Given the evident power of elected government officials to intimidate, co-opt, ignore, or dismantle the judiciary, we need to understand why they have generally chosen not to use that power and instead to defer to judicial authority."[85] Without some further explanation of how courts can stand in the way of a determined president or popular majority intent upon violating the constitution, judicial enforcement is merely a deus ex machina.

The puzzle of constitutional compliance goes even deeper than this. The question of how the Supreme Court or constitutional law can constrain the president presupposes that we *have* a Supreme Court and a president, in their constitutionally specified forms. Before constitutional law can aspire to constrain political actors, it must constitute them. Yet the success of the American, and other, constitutional orders in accomplishing this constitutive work is no more self-explanatory than the ability of an up-and-running system of constitutional law to regulate or constrain the constituted government. Why do powerful social groups who are disadvantaged by the basic structural arrangements of the constitutional system of government not simply ignore or reconstitute them, say by getting rid of the Senate or by installing a military dictatorship? Why have large groups of Americans not more frequently followed the lead of the Confederate South in rejecting the U.S. constitutional order altogether?

If contemporary constitutionalists have managed to repress such questions, the original designers of the constitution experienced them as immediately pressing. The constitutional Framers had good reason to fear that constitutional limitations on government would create mere "parchment barriers" that the powerful would override at will.[86] The essential problem, Madison explained, was that "[i]n our Governments the real power lies in the majority of the Community." In the absence of any enforcement authority capable of resisting the power of majorities and the government officials who answer to them, Madison worried, constitutional rules and rights, "however strongly marked on paper will never be regarded when opposed to the decided sense of the public."[87]

But the Framers did not succumb to Hobbesian hopelessness. Even if constitutional law could not be enforced by an external power greater than the national government, the hope was to contrive a system that would be internally self-enforcing, converting parchment barriers into meaningful political constraints. The trick would be to encourage and empower political actors within the constitutional system of government to enforce constitutional limitations against one another. Thus, Madison famously theorized that the constitutional system of separation of powers and federalism would leverage the "personal motives" of "those who administer each department" to induce them to police and prevent one another's transgressions. The "[a]mbition" of political actors within the constitutional system, Madison explained, "must be made to counteract" the ambition of others.[88] Elaborating the same idea at the level of democratic politics, Madison stressed the importance of "guard[ing] one part of society against the injustice of the other part" by means of shifting authority to the national government of an extended republic that represented a "multiplicity of interests."[89] "[T]he society itself will be broken into so many parts, interests and classes of citizens, that the rights of individuals, or of the minority, will be in little danger," Madison hypothesized, because a tyrannical majority would have a hard time becoming hegemonic.

As subsequent chapters will discuss, not all of the structural mechanisms Madison envisioned worked in the ways he and the other Framers anticipated or hoped. Nonetheless, Madison's basic insight was sound: in the absence of any external enforcement power, constitutional law must be internally self-enforcing. That insight should sound familiar. Constitutional enforcement through the decentralized interactions of the different parts of government and the different factions in democratic politics parallels the international system of decentralized enforcement by states against one another. Like international law, constitutional enforcement cannot operate vertically, through a Leviathan standing above its subjects, but must instead operate horizontally, with the subjects of law enforcing it against one another.[90]

This basic structural similarity with international law has seldom been noticed by constitutionalists. Nonetheless, from Madison through the present, constitutionalists who have tried to understand how enforcement and compliance can work in a legal system without Leviathan have, not coincidentally, followed in the footsteps of their international counterparts.

To start, a current of what might be called constitutional "realism" has sustained some measure of Hobbesian and Founding-era skepticism that parchment barriers can constrain the politically powerful. We have already seen the example of presidents breaking free of constitutional bounds under exigent circumstances. America's greatest president, Abraham Lincoln, explicitly rejected any strict imperative of constitutional compliance during the Civil War, defiantly asking, "Are all the laws but one to go unexecuted and the government itself go to pieces lest that one be violated?"[91] In the infamous case of *Korematsu v. United States*, upholding the forced relocation of Japanese Americans from their homes on the West Coast to prison camps, Justice Robert Jackson candidly recognized that the Court would not stand in the way when wartime presidents violated the constitution. "It would be impracticable and dangerous idealism," Jackson said, to expect military commanders to "conform to conventional tests of constitutionality." Rather, "the paramount consideration is that [military] measures be successful, rather than legal."[92]

Few constitutional actors have been so forthright about the necessity or reality of constitutional noncompliance. Presidents seeking to avoid constitutional constraints, like states seeking to avoid international law, are more likely to interpret their way out of legal constraints than explicitly violate them. Lincoln defended most of his dubiously constitutional actions during the Civil War with lawyerly arguments that at least muddied the legal waters enough to allow him to deny outright lawbreaking. Subsequent presidents have followed suit. Close observers of White House decisionmaking in the context of the post-9/11 war on terrorism, for example, have been struck by the willingness of executive branch lawyers to "time and time again . . . fudge, stretch, or retrofit the law to accommodate national security,"[93] even to the point of concluding that legal review is merely "a rubber stamp for the President."[94] More generally, prominent constitutional scholars assert that "the law does little to constrain the modern executive,"[95] and that the president operates in a "culture of lawlessness" in which "short-term presidential imperatives... overwhelm sober legal judgments."[96]

Realist skepticism extends beyond the president. Officials across all the branches and units of government are accused on a daily basis of disregarding particular constitutional prohibitions or interpreting them in bad faith.[97] That includes officials in the judicial branch. Since the beginning of the Republic, Supreme Court Justices have been suspected of doing "politics" rather than "law," opportunistically interpreting the constitution to fit their ideological predilections.[98] Even while denying such charges when they are leveled by outsiders, the Justices regularly accuse one another of issuing opinions that have "no foundation in American constitutional law, and barely pretend to," and they lament in their dissents that "[p]ower, not reason, is the [] currency of this Court's decisionmaking."[99]

Attempts to prove or disprove the realist view are hindered by the difficulties of constitutional settlement. Adjudicating constitutional compliance and noncompliance requires an agreed-upon standard of what constitutional law permits or allows. As we have seen, the closest American constitutionalism comes to such a standard is authoritative specification of constitutional meaning by the Supreme Court. As we have also seen, however, that standard is not always available. It is never available as applied to the Court's own constitutional decisionmaking. And the Court's constitutional decisionmaking is treated as authoritative by others only within the limited, shifting, and contested bounds of judicial supremacy. Outside of those bounds, as in the case of Lincoln, the content of constitutional law is self-determined by the government institutions and officials it purports to constrain. Presidents, members of Congress, and other officials are left free to make their own law—and, one must suspect, often do so in ways that align with their extralegal interests. In the constitutional realist view, just as powerful states will be happy to comply with international law that corresponds to their own interests, powerful domestic political actors will be happy to comply with constitutional law that reflects their own preferences.

Even within the bounds of judicial supremacy, much of what appears to be constitutional compliance can be understood as merely coincidence of interest. The Court's version of constitutional law may just mirror the preferences of the political actors who are supposed to be governed by it. Political scientists have long observed that judicial interpretations of constitutional law generally track the preferences of politically powerful constituencies, particularly dominant national political coalitions. In the words of Robert Dahl, "the policy views dominant on the Court are never for long out of line with the policy views dominant among the lawmaking majorities of the United States."[100] The reasons for this correspondence are hardly mysterious. Supreme Court Justices are selected by ruling coalitions based largely on their political and ideological views. And then, once appointed, the Justices are subject to ongoing control by the political branches and other constituencies, which can credibly threaten to coerce, marginalize, or ignore a judiciary that stands in the way of their agenda. The result is that powerful political actors will seldom find themselves confronted with constitutional rules and rights that contradict their strongly held preferences.[101] In constitutional law, as in international law, it can be said that almost all political actors obey almost all the rules of constitutional law almost all of the time. From a realist perspective, however, that observation might just reflect the fact that political actors are largely empowered to decide for themselves which rules they will be bound to obey.

All of this said, few observers take an entirely realist view of the American constitutional system. There may be room for doubt about how tightly presidents are constrained by constitutional law in particular domains of decisionmaking, but there has been much less doubt that we have a constitutional presidency, elected and empowered according to relatively well accepted constitutional rules. Even the most popular presidents do not run for third terms or routinely grant themselves emergency powers to rule by decree or suspend constitutional rights. Beyond the presidency, basic features of the constitutional structure of government—from the Article I, Section 7 lawmaking process to equal state representation in the Senate—are treated as settled by political actors even when different structural arrangements would better serve their interests. Decisions and doctrine of the Supreme Court are ordinarily accepted as authoritative and binding, commanding reflexive compliance even from government officials and constituencies who seem to suffer serious costs. Some measure of meaningful constitutional constraint appears difficult to deny.

The question then comes back to *why* powerful political actors are apparently willing to abide by constitutional constraints. One approach to answering this question—introduced by political scientists, but increasingly gaining uptake among legal scholars—follows the rationalist path of international institutionalism. Like powerful states at the international level, powerful political actors at the domestic level may be willing to sacrifice their short-term interests in exchange for the broader or longer-term benefits of cooperating through constitutional rules and arrangements.

Theorizing along these lines, political scientists and the occasional legal scholar have explained compliance with various parts of the constitutional structure of government as reflecting a cooperative equilibrium among political actors engaged in an iterated prisoners' dilemma game. Self-consciously drawing upon institutionalist international relations theory, scholars have hypothesized, for example, that constitutional norms governing the presidency and the separation of powers between the president and Congress might be enforced through the threat or application of tit-for-tat countermeasures or reciprocal noncompliance.[102] By the same logic, electoral losers might respect democratic outcomes because the benefits of future victories and political stability outweigh the short-term costs.[103] A system of federalism might be maintained by repeat-play cooperation between states or regional coalitions that implicitly agree to defend one another against overreaching by the national government.[104] Enforcement of the constitution more generally might similarly be understood as an equilibrium resulting from the tacit agreement of two or more social groups to rebel against a government that transgresses the rights of either group.[105]

Other accounts of constitutional compliance track the game-theoretic logic of coordination. Adherence to constitutional rules and institutions might follow from the self-interested calculation of most political actors that even less-than-ideal constitutional rules and institutions are better than none at all. As a general matter, constitutional arrangements that successfully constitute a functioning state—one that can make and enforce laws, maintain order, foster economic prosperity, and provide public goods—are enormously beneficial. Even if some (or all) groups would prefer a different arrangement, the expected benefits of improvement must be weighed against the costs of unsettling a functional constitutional order and risking civil war or anarchy, lending a considerable degree of stability to the constitutional status quo.[106] Constitutional scholars have speculated that the U.S. Constitution might be especially well suited to sustaining coordination inasmuch as it combines specificity on low-stakes issues (where agreement is more important than any particular outcome) and generality on high-stakes issues (where the value of agreement may not be sufficient to settle outcomes).[107] Constitutional scholars have also appreciated the possibility of non-textual coordination, suggesting for instance that ambiguous separation of powers questions can be resolved by focal regularities of practice that are not worth the political costs of controversy to unsettle.[108]

Political scientists and legal scholars have further drawn upon institutionalist ideas to explain the authority of courts and the willingness of political actors to defer to their constitutional judgments.[109] Where the constitutional text is indeterminate or substantively unacceptable, judicial specification of constitutional rules and rights can serve as an alternative locus of constitutional coordination.[110] Courts might also play the valuable role of coordinating collective responses to constitutional violations. As Madison recognized, constitutional rights might serve "as a standard for trying the validity of public acts, and a signal for rousing & uniting the superior force of the community."[111] By authoritatively identifying when constitutional rights have been violated, courts might provide a kind of "fire alarm" that facilitates coordinated political retribution against misbehaving government officials.[112]

Further reasons for supporting judicial authority follow from the logic of repeat play and reciprocity. For example, competing political coalitions might tacitly agree to support an independent judiciary in order to hedge against the risk of all-or-nothing reversals of political fortune.[113] On this "insurance" model, the coalition in power may prefer to cede some authority to the courts in order to deprive its rivals of unchecked power once they take over the government.[114] One implication of this model, corroborated by historical experience, is that support for judicial independence depends upon a competitive political marketplace and the foreseeable possibility of the party or coalition in power losing elections. In the early years of American constitutionalism, when competitive political parties were a new and possibly fleeting phenomenon, Federalists and Republicans alike engaged in blatantly partisan manipulation of the judiciary.[115] Likewise, political attacks on the Court by the relatively secure Republican majority in Congress during Reconstruction, and by the relatively secure Democratic coalition during the New Deal, may have reflected the calculation that any benefits of judicial independence were beyond prevailing political time horizons. In contrast, close political competition between the two parties and frequent rotation of control of the federal government in recent decades may have contributed to the consolidation of judicial supremacy.

Institutionalist explanations of judicial independence and constitutional compliance more generally follow from the Madisonian premise that effective enforcement of constitutional rules and rights must stem from the self-interested incentives of political actors within the constitutional system of government. But that is not the only way of thinking about constitutional compliance. Rejecting the rationalist assumptions of realism and institutionalism, a constructivist strain of constitutional thought runs parallel to the international version. It is widely believed that constitutional law, like international law, affects the behavior of officials and citizens by shaping—not just constraining—their interests and values. The starting point for constitutional constructivism is recognition of constitutional law's constitutive role in creating the government that it will then attempt to constrain. Again, the question of how constitutional law can constrain the president arises only after constitutional law has created the presidency, along with the rest of the institutions and structure of government. These "givens" of the constitutional system are presupposed by the rationalist accounts of constitutional realists and institutionalists, much as the givens of sovereign statehood are presupposed by their international counterparts.

If constitutional law is capable of constituting the state and its system of government without regard to the rationalist calculations of political actors, constructivists reason, then it must also be capable of shaping how these actors behave within the system without recourse to material incentives. Even Madison, skeptical as he was of parchment barriers, was willing to acknowledge the possibility that an unenforced Constitution might influence political behavior by inculcating constitutional values in the citizenry: "The political truths declared in that solemn manner acquire by degrees the character of fundamental maxims of free Government, and as they become incorporated with the national sentiment, counteract the impulses of interest and passion."[116] Many constitutional lawyers and judges continue to hold such a view, believing that political actors can come to possess an intrinsic interest in constitutional compliance, "obeying the law not just because they fear the consequences but because they think they ought to obey."[117]

Constitutional lawyers often speak of this disposition to obey the law in Weberian terms of "legitimacy."[118] One thing that might make constitutional law legitimate, and exert a pull toward compliance, is simply its status as *law*. The Supreme Court often expresses a view like this of its own authority, proclaiming that public support for the institution of judicial review rests on the public's belief that the Justices are following the law rather than their own moral or political preferences. During oral arguments in the case in which the Court would overrule *Roe v. Wade* and the constitutional right to abortion,[119] Justice Sotomayor asked rhetorically, "Will this Court survive the stench that [overruling *Roe* would] create[] in the public perception that the Constitution and its reading are just political acts?"[120] That same view of judicial legitimacy is echoed by commentators on both the political left and right, who agree that avoiding the perception of politicization is crucial to sustaining public support and differ only in their assessments of how best to avoid that perception—by adhering to stare decisis and upholding *Roe*, or by following the originalist dictates of legally correct interpretation to overrule it. Scholars in the social sciences have begun to develop more nuanced accounts of legal legitimation, suggesting that officials and citizens may be more inclined to comply with constitutional rules and decisions that appear to be "neutral," "principled," or "impartial" regardless of the public's agreement or disagreement with the outcomes on the merits.[121] Constitutional constructivist theories remain less well developed than their international counterparts, but the basic idea is the same: that constitutional law, like international law, can build legal compliance into the identities and interests of its subjects.

These lines of constructivist, institutionalist, and realist constitutional thought have lagged their international counterparts. But it is no coincidence that they have run in parallel. Constitutional law shares with international law the distinctive challenge of understanding how enforcement and compliance work in legal systems that cannot rely on sword-wielding Leviathans.

Legal Order Within and Without the State

The point of this chapter has been to develop a set of seemingly fundamental differences between legal regimes run by and through states and legal regimes for states. What distinguishes ordinary legal systems run by states from constitutional and international law is the ability of the state to authoritatively and effectively promulgate, settle, and enforce law. As this chapter has also emphasized, however, that ability cannot be treated as a deus ex machina. The legal, legislative, and law enforcement institutions that empower the state as lawmaker and law enforcer are themselves the products of constitutional and international law. Without legal settlement of and compliance with the institutions through which states make and enforce law—legislatures, courts, bureaucracies, police forces, and armies—there would be nothing like ordinary, state-run legal systems as we have come to know them. This is just to restate the familiar insight of Hartian jurisprudence that state-imposed law cannot simply be understood as the "gunman writ large," or the gavel-wielding judge writ large, without some further understanding of why the people who have the guns and gavels will use them to settle and enforce the law.

The existence of state-run legal systems thus depends upon the existence of a constituted state, which is itself a kind of legal order that needs to be explained. The most plausible explanations for why officials and citizens might be willing to support and comply with the international and constitutional legal rules that constitute the state and its legal institutions are the ones this chapter has surveyed. Simplifying slightly, these explanations come in two basic flavors. Law compliers may be intrinsically motivated to follow the law, whether because it is the morally right thing to do or because they are psychologically or sociologically pulled by legitimate legality. Or law compliers may be acting instrumentally, in order to capture the broader or longer-term self-interested benefits of coordination or cooperation (if not the immediate benefits of acting consistently with legal rules that conveniently coincide with their interests).

Some combination of these motivations must be foundational to all legal order. That includes legal order within the state. In the crudely Hobbesian picture of state-run legal systems, the intrinsic and instrumental motivations of officials and citizens are only *indirectly* foundational. These motivations lead officials and citizens to establish and support the governmental structure of the state, making it self-enforcing. Then the state, acting through that structure, becomes an enforcer, authoritatively coercing compliance with its laws. The same people who were intrinsically or instrumentally motivated to create legal order for the state now have a different reason to get in line with legal order under the state. Instead of internalizing law or making moral or game-theoretic calculations about compliance, people obey state-imposed law because of state coercion backed by state-monopolized violence.

Less crudely, people no doubt comply with the laws of their states for a variety of reasons, in many cases acting on the same intrinsic and instrumental motivations that underwrite the constitutive legal order of the state itself. The rules of ordinary domestic legal systems may create focal points for coordination or otherwise facilitate game-theoretical, interest-based compliance.[122] Compliance with these rules may also turn on perceptions of substantive justice or procedural legitimacy, or on the internalization of the values they embody.[123] And of course, people, like states and governments, may find themselves acting consistently with legal rules simply because these rules track how people would choose to behave in any case.

Still, standard accounts of legal order assume that these motivations will not be sufficient to render legal order within the state self-enforcing. To the contrary, it is typically assumed that coercive enforcement by the state will be needed to supplement people's independent inclinations toward legal compliance—even as those independent inclinations remain sufficient to keep the constitutive legal order of the state self-enforcing. This asymmetry explains both why state enforcement matters and how it is possible. State enforcement matters because people need an additional incentive to comply with the law, making up for the motivational shortfall. State enforcement is possible because officials and citizens remain fully motivated to support legal order at the constitutive level of the state.

Yet it is far from obvious why legal order would work differently at these two levels. If people are not adequately motivated to support legal order in the absence of coercion, then how will legal order at the constitutional level become and remain self-enforcing? If the answer is that people do not, in fact, (adequately) support constitutional order, that lack of support would also undermine state-imposed legal order, as the institutional apparatus of coercive enforcement would crumble. If we are imagining a stable and effective system of state-imposed law, we are presupposing the success of self-enforcing, constitutional-level legal order. But that success must be the product of intrinsic and instrumental motivations for legal compliance that could just as well support legal order internal to the state even in the absence of state coercion. The willingness of officials and citizens to support legal order at the level of the state and its legal institutions might extend to supporting legal order within—or without—the state.

This, then, is the deep puzzle of state-imposed legal order: if people are willing and able to create a state, why would they need a state? Hobbes himself had no good answer to that question.[124] If people in the state of nature are engaged in a war of all against all, then what would make them suddenly lay down arms and socially contract, or cooperate, to create Leviathan? Or if Leviathan were already up and running, what would lead the people who retained their arms—officials, if not also citizens—to cooperate in keeping it going? Alternatively, if, as Hobbes imagined, people in the state of nature might be driven by rational self-interest or some other motive to cooperate, why would that cooperation need to be channeled into the creation of Leviathan? Why not just cooperate by getting along, respecting rights, and the like, without bothering to create a Leviathan state? These questions remain unanswered. We lack any good theory that would explain why self-enforcing legal order is easier to consolidate or more effective at the constitutive level of the state than within the state.

That explanatory gap extends to the more and less successful instances of self-enforcing order that seem to exist *within* regimes of law. For instance, constitutional lawyers and theorists take for granted that some parts of the constitutional order are more stable and constraining than others. Once again, the question of whether or how the Supreme Court can constrain a popular and powerful president seems worth worrying about; but the premise that we *have* a Supreme Court and a president, with their constitutionally specified institutional forms and powers, is typically taken for granted. Another pervasive premise of constitutional thought is that the institutional structure of government and democratic politics will be more durable and constraining than rights. Recall that, even while denigrating rights as merely "parchment barriers," Madison had faith that structural safeguards would somehow possesses greater constraining force. Contemporary constitutional theorists continue to view the constitutional structure of government, in contrast to parchment rights, as "substantially self-executing" and "inspir[ing] reflexive conformity."[125] Assumptions along these lines are not exceptionally American. As Chapter 4 will describe in greater detail, scholars focused on a number of different countries around the world share the assumption that the structure of electoral democracy will be a more reliable mechanism for securing the interests of vulnerable groups than constitutional rights.

Prominent lines of work in the social sciences similarly focus on "self-enforcing" structures and institutions as anchors of legal and political order. Influential theories of economic growth, for example, rely upon the relative stability of separation of powers and federalism as structural commitment mechanisms that make it possible for governments to reliably respect property rights and preserve markets.[126] Political scientists of the "structure and process" school describe how a temporarily dominant political coalition can entrench its preferred policies by delegating to an administrative agency that is insulated by structure and process from political redirection.[127] International relations theorists hypothesize that global governance institutions such as the WTO and the International Criminal Court (ICC) operate as relatively secure devices for locking in free trade or human rights rules that would otherwise be susceptible to violation or change.[128] In these and other settings, social scientists join constitutional theorists in casting self-enforcing structural arrangements as the unmoved movers of legal and political order.

What is missing from all of these accounts is any explanation of why legal order is easier to achieve or more stable at the level of institutional structure—separation of powers, federalism, electoral democracy, or the state as a whole—than at the level of particular rights or rules. Just as Hobbes never explained why the creation of Leviathan was more viable than the creation of legal order in its absence, Madison never explained why constitutional structures that stand in the way of powerful political actors will be any more durable than parchment rights. Contemporary constitutional theorists and political scientists have done little better.[129] If powerful political actors want to exploit vulnerable groups or violate their rights, why will they not be willing to change the rules of constitutional structure or electoral democracy? If governments cannot credibly commit to respecting property rights, what makes their commitments to separation of powers or federalism any more credible? Why would a powerful state inclined to reject rules of free trade or human rights nonetheless respect the binding authority of the WTO or the ICC?

The standard toolbox for explaining legal and political order seems ill-equipped to answer these questions. Constructivist accounts of legitimation and internalization do not explain why these processes would be more effective at the level of states or structures than at the level of particular rights or rules. The same is true of rationalist, institutionalist accounts of self-interested coordination and cooperation. Political scientists and constitutional theorists have offered game-theoretic explanations of compliance at all levels of the system, from discrete rights and rules, like free speech and the Senate filibuster; to broader arrangements like electoral democracy and separation of powers; all the way up to the constitutional system of government as a whole. Likewise, in the domain of international law and relations, the very same game-theoretic models are variously used to explain compliance with isolated rules and norms, the authority of international tribunals, broader global governance regimes, and the international legal order as a whole. Theorizing legal and political order as equilibrium behavior in some sort of game-theoretic frame is an easy sport. So long as playing by a set of rules can generate some cooperative surplus—which will always be the case if the alternative is war, anarchy, or the Hobbesian state of nature—then legal and political order can always be modeled as a potential equilibrium. The real challenge of understanding legal order is to explain why the particular equilibria we actually observe are the ones that emerged, instead of others of different location or scope (or none at all).

In particular, for present purposes, the challenge lies in explaining the centrality and stability of legal order in the shape of the state. For centuries the state has played a distinctive role in coordinating shared understandings of law and mobilizing the collective will to enforce it. But legal order is entirely possible without the state—not just in theory, but to a considerable extent in practice, as existing regimes of constitutional and international law demonstrate. The state remains the indispensable fulcrum for understanding legal order as we have come to know it in the modern world. But it is important to recognize that the state is a contingent product of history, not a conceptual or social scientific necessity. There are other worlds—including the world that existed before the rise of the modern state, and the world that might someday move beyond it—in which legal order no longer turns on the distinction between law by and for Leviathan. And even in our present world, the distinction, important as it is, only goes so deep.

2
Law Versus Sovereignty

Sovereignty is an old idea that perpetually defies extinction. Following a long period of perceived decline, during the first decades of the twenty-first century sovereignty has come roaring back to life. Celebrating his nation's decision to exit the EU, British Prime Minister Boris Johnson declared that the British people had "recaptured sovereignty" and "taken back the tools of self-government."[1] Shortly after entering office, U.S. President Donald Trump went before the U.N. General Assembly to announce that America's victimization by "mammoth, multinational trade deals, unaccountable international tribunals, and powerful global bureaucracies" would come to an end. Trump vowed to renew the "founding principle of sovereignty," which is that "the [American] people govern, the people are sovereign."[2] At the same time, "populist" political movements sweeping through Europe and North America have posed an existential threat not only to the international legal order but also to constitutional democracy. Echoing the Brexiteers' call to "take back control" over their countries, authoritarian political leaders—Erdogan, Orban, Maduro, et al.—have asserted an extreme version of popular sovereignty. Claiming to act on behalf of a unified national People possessed of omnipotent political and moral authority, these rulers reject all impediments to the realization of popular will, including threats to national sovereignty stemming from globalization, immigration, or international cooperation; constitutional structures of limited government; judicial independence; and liberal rights. Political opponents and dissenters are dismissed as enemies of the People, corrupt elites, or outsiders to the political community. Only the ruler speaks in the People's authentic voice.[3]

Populist autocrats might have looked to Hobbes for inspiration. The populist political imaginary is a modern-day reenactment of *Leviathan*, calling for absolutist rule in the name of a unified people, whose will, personality, and authority have been absorbed into the person of the sovereign.[4] Possessed of illimitable power, the ruler stands above the law, unbound by any contract or constitution. Leviathan would never have bowed to Brussels, kowtowed to constitutional courts, or brooked internal dissent.

As current events remind us, sovereignty has never just been a philosopher's conceit. In its origin, the concept served as an ideological crutch for the rise of the state in early modern Europe. Sovereignty expressed in shorthand the core feature of the modern state's distinctive identity and self-image: its possession of supreme authority within a territory, superior to any internal or external power. Domestically, sovereignty was supposed to explain and legitimate the political authority of the nascent state's government over its subject population. At the same time, sovereignty was supposed to establish the autonomy of states vis-à-vis one another in the international realm. Supreme authority within the state and international independence without are "the inward and outward expressions, the obverse and reverse sides, of the same idea."[5]

It is no coincidence that the international system of sovereign states, formally recognized by the Peace of Westphalia in 1648, took shape at the same time Hobbes was describing the internally directed concept of sovereignty in *Leviathan*.[6] State sovereignty was invented to solve the then-pressing problem of political and religious conflict, both within and between European states. For more than a century after the Reformation fractured Christian unity, Europe had been destabilized and decimated by bloody wars of religion. Sovereignty was supposed to be the solution, the best hope for restoring international peace and domestic social order. The premise of the Westphalian order was that each state would be empowered to decide for itself matters of religion and other divisive issues without foreign intervention, putting an end to international war and conflict. The premise of Hobbes's *Leviathan*, written during a period of civil war in England, was that the sovereign ruler within each state would have the sole and uncontested authority to make and enforce those decisions over its subjects, putting an end to internal dissent and rebellion.

For present purposes, an important implication of both the external and internal forms of state sovereignty is that the sovereign, possessing the sole power to make and enforce law in its territory, must itself stand above the law. Conceiving of sovereignty as "Power Unlimited,"[7] Hobbes categorically rejected the possibility of legal limitations. As Hobbes's nineteenth-century successor, John Austin, put it plainly: "Supreme power limited by positive law[] is a flat contradiction in terms."[8] The Hobbesian view of unlimited state sovereignty was in part premised on perceived practical realities. As discussed in the previous chapter, the absence of any centralized enforcement authority standing above states created doubts about whether there was any reliable way of coercing their compliance. But illimitable sovereignty was also a matter of moral principle. For Hobbes and other early theorists of the state, the unshackled autonomy of the sovereign followed from its origins in the social contract. Sovereign authority was created and legitimated by the mutual consent of persons in the state of nature, who agreed to sacrifice their individual autonomy and subject themselves to Leviathan. In the absence of a contract among sovereign Leviathans, however, there was no legitimate super-authority authorized to bind them.

The illimitable sovereignty of Leviathan would seem to bode poorly for any kind of law for states. And, indeed, both international law and constitutional law have been forced to contend with sovereignty-based objections to their very existence. As the actual and ongoing existence of these regimes of law demonstrates, however, sovereignty has proven less of an obstacle to law for Leviathan than Hobbes imagined. This chapter describes how international law and constitutional law have managed to evade or accommodate themselves to the demands of sovereignty—so successfully, in fact, that we might wonder what is left, or worth preserving, of the Hobbesian concept.

Sovereignty Versus International Law

From its inception, international law has struggled with the apparently self-contradictory project of attempting to impose law upon states it simultaneously conceives as sovereign. "One of the most persistent sources of perplexity about the obligatory character of international law," recounts H.L.A. Hart, "has been the difficulty felt in accepting or explaining the fact that a state which is sovereign may be 'bound' by, or have an obligation under, international law."[9] If states are sovereign, one might suppose, then they cannot be subject to the legal obligations that international law purports to impose; and if states are subject to genuine legal constraints under international law, then they cannot really be sovereign.

International law has attempted to escape from this dilemma by returning to the kind of consent theory pioneered by Hobbes. States may not have consented to the creation of a super-Leviathan possessed of the kind of super-sovereignty that could supersede their own. But consistent with the sovereignty they have retained, states might be able to legally bind themselves by consenting to specific legal obligations. This is the basic premise of the international legal system: states can be made subject to legal constraints where, but only where, they have made the sovereign decision to bind themselves.[10] The key principle is "voluntarism": voluntary consent is supposed to transform legal obligations from illegitimate constraints on state sovereignty to legitimate exercises of that sovereignty. The analogy is to contract law for ordinary persons. By allowing individuals to consent to binding obligations, contract law makes it possible for them to accomplish things that would otherwise be impossible. Constraints that are more enabling than limiting arguably increase autonomy on net, and for that reason might be seen as consistent with personal liberty—or with state sovereignty.

Hobbes himself rejected the analogy to ordinary contracts. Deeming sovereignty essentially inalienable, he explicitly rejected the possibility of self-binding law for Leviathan:

> The Soveraign of a Common-wealth ... is not subject to the Civill Lawes. For having power to make, and repeale Lawes, he may when he pleaseth, free himselfe from that subjection, by repealing those Lawes that trouble him, and making of new.... Nor is it possible for any person to be bound to himselfe; because he that can bind, can release; and therefore he that is bound to himselfe onely, is not bound.[11]

Hobbes's successors have taken the same view, dismissing the possibility of even fully consensual limitations on sovereign power. While recognizing that "sovereign bodies have attempted to oblige themselves," Austin proclaimed the futility of subjecting sovereign power even to self-limitation, because "[t]he immediate author of a law of [this] kind ... may abrogate the law at pleasure."[12]

International law has taken a different view—the contractual one. The principle of *pacta sunt servanda*, reflected in both customary international law (CIL) and treaties, holds that consensual agreements by states become irreversibly binding; states cannot escape these agreements simply by withdrawing consent. Once a rule of CIL has been established, states cannot unilaterally decide to unbind themselves from the rule.[13] This is also the default rule for treaties: states may not unilaterally withdraw unless the treaty makes exit allowable.[14] While many treaties do provide for exit, withdrawal is often restricted at least by procedural hurdles, and a number of major treaties (including the U.N. Charter) are irrevocable. Prior consent can be binding in perpetuity. Contemporary theorists of international law with Hobbesian sympathies continue to speak of the "sovereignty costs" suffered by states any time international law interferes with their present autonomy, regardless of prior consent.[15] But most internationalists have embraced the contractual conception of sovereignty, which allows ex ante consent to justify ex post constraint.

Still, the sovereignty-based demand of consent stands as a major obstacle to what the international legal system can aspire to accomplish. As the first chapter emphasized, an effective legal system is supposed to be capable of making its subjects do things they otherwise would not want to do, or preventing them from doing things they would otherwise want to do. A strictly voluntarist, consent-based system of international law—making states do only what they want to do—would seem to fall short of that ambition. Aspiring to accomplish more, international law has increasingly breached the boundaries of voluntarism.[16]

The decline of the sovereign consent requirement has been most evident in the application of CIL. In theory, states are supposed to give at least tacit consent to norms of CIL by following and recognizing these norms in practice. In reality, however, CIL is often used to bind states to norms they have never chosen to embrace.[17] When courts, diplomats, and scholars identify CIL, they do not require evidence of actual or even tacit consent by every state; instead, CIL can be grounded in "general and consistent" state practice that need not be unanimous.[18] To the extent the decisions of individual states are considered, moreover, the standard for identifying consent is ill-defined and often rather dubious. Consent is routinely constructed from an ambiguous amalgamation of national policy statements, legislation, and diplomatic papers that do not express any clear intent to be legally bound. Consent can also be inferred from a state's failure to object to an emerging customary norm—from silence.[19] Dispensing with the pretense of consent altogether, international law holds new states immediately subject to the CIL created by old states, regardless of their agreement.[20] Louis Henkin's awkward attempt to rationalize this rule pretty well captures the status of CIL and, increasingly, consent more generally in international law: "[The rule] can be explained (and even justified) in that . . . customary law is not *created* but *results*; that it is therefore not a product of the will of states but a 'systemic creation,' reflecting the 'consent' of the international system, not the consent of individual states."[21]

Treaty law, too, has in many respects drifted away from any meaningful basis in state consent. A growing number of treaties now purport to bind nonconsenting parties. Provisions of the U.N. Charter, for example, commit the U.N. to ensuring that nonmember states act in accordance with the Charter and empower a supermajority of Security Council members to order enforcement actions (as long as one of the big five does not veto) over the objection of a minority voting member.[22] The movement toward universal treaty obligations has also spurred a rejection of treaty reservations, explicit statements of nonconsent by states to certain terms.[23] The International Criminal Court is now authorized to prosecute nationals of nonparties who commit crimes in the territories of party states,[24] including heads of state.[25] And the ever-expanding array of "global governance" institutions created by treaty—the WTO, International Monetary Fund (IMF), International Court of Justice (ICJ), and many others—routinely bind states with nonconsensual regulatory requirements which are voluntary only at the level of states' initial agreement to join the treaties that created and empowered these organizations.[26]

Other strategies for expanding the scope of international legal obligations dismiss the necessity of sovereign consent altogether. The modern doctrine of jus cogens, or peremptory norms, has made an array of human rights prohibitions binding on states without regard to consent.[27] Many internationalists would push further in this direction. Proponents of humanitarian intervention have made the case that state sovereignty entails the responsibility to protect the population within the state's territory from genocide, war crimes, ethnic cleansing, and crimes against humanity. If a state fails to meet that obligation, or itself becomes the perpetrator of human rights abuses, then the international community has an obligation to intervene.[28] In this view, humanitarian interventions are not a threat to state sovereignty but a response to the failure of states to exercise their sovereignty, rightly understood. Generalizing the same approach, other theorists call for a more thoroughgoing reconceptualization of sovereignty to make it more suitable for a world of global interdependence, requiring sovereign states to take account of the effects of their policies not just on their own citizens but on "humanity at large."[29] At the most ambitious end of the spectrum, cosmopolitan internationalists are content to dispense with sovereignty altogether, arguing that states (to the extent they still exist) should be obligated to advance human rights and global welfare, regardless of their own self-interested preferences.[30]

Still, for all its discontents, sovereignty continues to stand as a foundational principle of international law. The voluntarist requirement of state consent has been eroded, but it is a long way from extinction. And sovereignty remains the shorthand explanation for a number of other basic principles of the international legal order, starting with the primary role of sovereign states as legal actors. Sovereignty is also supposed to be the font of states' territorial jurisdiction, political independence, and formal equality. Even as international law chafes against the limits sovereignty imposes on what it can accomplish, state sovereignty continues to be understood as central to the legal construction of the international order.

In fact, the value of sovereignty has been reinvigorated, if not reinvented, in the twentieth century by a shift in thinking about who should count as the sovereign. As will be described below, the birth of constitutionalism gave rise to the concept of popular sovereignty, putting ultimate political authority in the hands of the people rather than their rulers. Feeling the pull of popular sovereignty, internationalists have come around to the view that the sovereignty of states should be exercised in the service of their citizens.[31] Consistent with the basic goals of the Westphalian order, sovereignty is supposed to serve as a proxy for the self-government and self-determination of the people, or "peoples," that states represent.[32] In situations where state sovereignty clearly disserves those values, internationalists have increasingly prioritized the "people's sovereignty" over the "sovereign's sovereignty." Calls for the enforcement of international human rights against states that are failing to protect or affirmatively oppressing their people are one manifestation of this view.[33]

But linking state sovereignty to the collective will and welfare of citizens has also provided a renewed, democratic justification for the old-fashioned, Hobbesian conception of sovereignty as the possession of Leviathan. The resonance of this democratic conception of sovereignty is evident in real-world politics, where nationalist assertions of state sovereignty against international law and global governance are now seamlessly coupled with claims to democratic self-government. Recall the Brexiteers' equation of restoring British independence and making it possible for the British people to "take back control" of their own country. In the United States, international law and global governance institutions are routinely portrayed as substituting rule by unaccountable foreigners "far removed . . . from those they seek to govern" for democratic self-rule at home.[34] Objections along these lines have accompanied America's resistance to international cooperation dating back to its refusal to join the League of Nations and continuing through the Trump administration's "America First" foreign policy. As Trump's U.N. Ambassador and National Security Advisor John Bolton had earlier hammered home the point, "For Americans . . . sovereignty is our control over government";

whereas international law "is unquestionably a formula for reducing U.S. autonomy and reducing our control over government."[35]

Sovereignty Versus Constitutionalism

For at least some who take this view, the opposite of sovereignty-threatening international law is U.S. constitutional law. Constitutional law is conceived not a constraint on American sovereignty or self-government but as the ultimate expression of these values. John Bolton's resistance to internationalist incursions is thus coupled with declarations that the Trump administration "will fight back to protect American constitutionalism" and "popular sovereignty," as if these were one and the same.[36] Political theorist Jeremy Rabkin likewise sees the growing reach of international law as a threat not just to American sovereignty but also, and seemingly synonymously, to "constitutional government."[37] Taking a similar view, Justice Scalia famously fulminated when international law was invoked as a source of constitutional interpretation: "The notion that a law of nations, redefined to mean the consensus of states on *any* subject, can be used . . . to control a sovereign's treatment of *its own citizens* within *its own territory*, is a 20th-century invention of internationalist law professors and human-rights advocates."[38] Constitutional scholar Jed Rubenfeld sees it the same way: "To support international law is to support fundamental constraints on democracy" and popular sovereignty, whereas constitutional law, "our nation's self-given law," represents the fundamentally democratic exercise of sovereignty and self-government by the American people.[39]

At the same time, however, as Rubenfeld cannot help but recognize, constitutional law seems to threaten sovereignty and self-government in much the same way as international law. Both systems of law "stand against majority rule at any given moment," are "made outside the ordinary, democratic lawmaking process [and] impose obligations on a country that the nation's legislature cannot . . . amend or undo," and operate as "bod[ies] of higher law that check[] the power of ordinary national" governance.[40] This set of parallels would have come as no surprise to Hobbes, who viewed constitutional law, no less than international law, as a misguided and futile effort to impose legal limitations on the illimitable sovereignty of the state.

No less than international law, however, constitutional law has largely triumphed over Hobbesian sovereignty. Since American constitutionalism took hold in the late eighteenth century, constitutional systems of government, constrained by legal rules and rights, have become the standard operating procedure in the United States and most other countries around the world. But constitutional development has been forced to contend with sovereignty every step of the way. Like their internationalist counterparts, constitutionalists have always had to bear the burden of justifying legal constraints on the sovereign state.

That said, the challenge of sovereignty for constitutionalists has been at least somewhat different. The external version of sovereignty that internationalists have long had to negotiate was attributed to states as unitary actors, or personified Leviathans in possession of their own claims to autonomy and self-determination. For purposes of constitutional law, however, sovereignty must be located more precisely *within* the state. Who, exactly, is empowered to assert sovereignty against the prospect of legal constraint?

The most obvious answer to that question is, the state's government. That was Hobbes's understanding of internal sovereignty: upon the creation of Leviathan, sovereignty became vested in its governing head (preferably a monarch, but conceivably a parliament or some other structure of government). But if sovereignty is attributed to a government with absolute authority to rule the state, then constitutional rules and rights that impose limits on what the government can do—the core of constitutional law as we now understand it—becomes a Hobbesian impossibility.

The Hobbesian view of internal sovereignty has indeed been a hindrance to the development of constitutionalism. British constitutionalism, in particular, has long struggled against an absolutist understanding of Parliamentary sovereignty that resists constitutional limitations. Channeling Hobbes, Sir William Blackstone saw Parliament as "the place where that absolute despotic power, which must in all governments reside somewhere, is intrusted," with the consequence that constitutional constraints on Parliament were impossible: "What the Parliament doth, no authority upon earth can undo."[41] Residues of this view were carried over to American constitutionalism in the form of sovereign immunity doctrines, which in some cases continue to insulate government from constitutional accountability in court. Upholding President Trump's ban on travelers from a number of majority-Muslim countries, the Supreme Court explained, "For more than a century, this Court has recognized that the admission and exclusion of foreign nationals is a 'fundamental sovereign attribute exercised by the Government's political departments largely immune from judicial control.'"[42] In fact, the theoretical basis for sovereign immunity dates back much further than a single century. As Justice Oliver Wendell Holmes traced back its foundation, "A sovereign is exempt from suit, not because of any formal conception or obsolete theory, but on the logical and practical ground that there can be no legal right as against the authority that makes the law on which the right depends"—citing Hobbes's *Leviathan*.[43]

Holmes and Hobbes notwithstanding, sovereign immunity has become something of an "obsolete theory" in American constitutionalism, an isolated and atavistic exception to the general rule that government can, in fact, be subject to constitutional constraints.[44] Establishing the general permissibility and desirability of holding government to constitutional constraints entailed the rejection of Hobbesian sovereignty—or, at least, its relocation. In the American constitutional tradition, legal constraints on government need pose no threat to sovereignty at all, because sovereignty, for constitutional purposes, has been definitively divested from government and reassigned to ... the people. This, of course, is the now-familiar idea of popular sovereignty.[45]

The conceptual shift to popular sovereignty opened the door to the modern theory of constitutionalism. Lodging sovereignty in the people allows constitutional limitations on the power of government to be recast not as limitations of sovereignty but as exercises of it. The sovereign people are empowered to exercise control over their subservient agents. Such is the understanding of sovereignty and constitutionalism that was elaborated in the context of the American Founding. Making clear that ultimate political authority was the possession of the people, the Declaration of Independence explained that governments "deriv[e] their just powers from the consent of the governed" and proclaimed "the Right of the People to alter or abolish" any government that did not uphold their "unalienable Rights" or conduce to their "Safety and Happiness."[46] The authority of "We the People" would then be deployed to enact a constitution, creating a complex system of government with legally specified and limited powers that were at all times amendable or revocable by the sovereign People.[47]

The move to popular sovereignty was an ingenious way of sidestepping the apparent conflict between the imposition of legal limitations on government and illimitable sovereignty.[48] But popular sovereignty collides with another core feature of constitutionalism, which is that constitutional law constrains not just government agents, but the people themselves. As Madison presented these dual constitutional imperatives, "It is of great importance in a republic not only to guard the society against the oppression of its rulers, but to guard one part of the society against the injustice of the other part."[49] In fact, guarding one part of society against the injustice of the other part has become the central focus of modern constitutionalism—as when constitutional rules and rights guard individuals and minorities against the tyranny of the majority. But to serve this function, constitutional constraints most be imposed on the people who are supposed to be sovereign, and the apparent conflict between constitutionalism and (popular) sovereignty reappears. Abraham Lincoln captures the perplexing tension between constitutionalism and popular self-rule in his First Inaugural: "A majority held in restraint by constitutional checks and limitations . . . is the only true sovereign of a free people."[50]

That tension is magnified in a democratic system of government, which blurs Madison's distinction between rulers and "parts of society." Democratically elected rulers are supposed to represent and be politically responsive to majorities and other parts of society. All decisions made by representative government are supposed to in some sense reflect popular will. But then all constitutional constraints on government can be viewed as assaults on popular sovereignty, preventing the people from acting on their democratically decisive preferences. Thus, Noah Webster's Founding-era objection: "A Bill of Rights against the encroachments of Kings and Barons, or against any power independent of the people, is perfectly intelligible; but a Bill of Rights against the encroachments of an elective Legislature, that is, against our *own* encroachments on ourselves, is a curiosity in government."[51] The paradox of democratic constitutional sovereignty is that the authority of the constitution is premised on its speaking for the sovereign self-rule of the people, but the constitution functions pervasively to prevent the people from exercising self-rule by restricting their democratic choices.[52]

Constitutional theorists have tried to resolve this paradox in many different ways, but the most influential solutions take a common form. Decisions made by the people in their sovereign capacity are distinguished from decisions made by the people and their government representatives through the ordinary democratic political process. Constitutional law, representing higher-order decisions made by the sovereign, capital-P People, trumps quotidian democratic decisionmaking by the small-p people. Sovereignty remains sacrosanct, as the sovereign People make constitutional law, but only the sub-sovereign people are bound by it.

The simplest form of this theory is originalism, which grounds the legitimacy of constitutional law in decisions made by We the People, acting in our sovereign capacity at the moment of the Founding, memorialized in the text and original understanding of the Constitution.[53] We the People remain free to amend the Constitution at any time through the requisite process of sovereign decisionmaking detailed in Article V. But unless and until we exercise that power, we are presumed to continue to consent to our prior decisions, and our constitutional commands remain authoritative over the ordinary workings of democratic governance. This is the prevailing account of constitutional obligation and how it is supposed to square with popular sovereignty.[54] Present-day Americans are bound by the U.S. Constitution because it represents the sovereign will of We the People, expressed more than 200 years ago and amended only infrequently since then.

As it happens, such a vision of a sovereign rousing itself only occasionally to issues orders that remain in place for long periods of time was anticipated by Hobbes. In *Leviathan*, Hobbes presented sovereignty as the complete and irrevocable transfer of authority from the people to their rulers. In his earlier work, *On the Citizen*, however, Hobbes was attracted to the analogy of a "sleeping sovereign," a king who remains sovereign even during his lengthy slumber, leaving his ministers to make decisions governed by the king's last waking orders.[55] Popular sovereignty might work in the same way. The sovereign People might be conceived as "sleeping" for most of the time, leaving day-to-day government bound by their last waking orders in the form of constitutional law. The People might at any time rouse themselves to reconsider and revise their previous decisions by means of constitutional amendment. So long as the People choose to leave constitutional law alone, however, the inference should be that they remain satisfied; silence should be taken as the tacit consent of a contentedly napping sovereign.[56]

Operationalizing this view requires some way of determining when the People are sleeping and when they are awake. Constitutional originalists maintain that waking sovereignty should be established formalistically, by reference to the procedures prescribed by Articles VII and V for accomplishing constitutional ratification and amendment. Exalting those procedural pathways distinguishes expressions of popular sovereignty from the more routine expressions of popular will that happen through elections, legislation, and the other institutional channels of ordinary democracy. Democratic decisionmaking is merely sub-sovereign sleepwalking. Nonoriginalists, in contrast, see no reason to limit the expression of popular sovereignty to the arbitrary pathways laid out in the constitution. To the contrary, they argue that the difficulty of formal amendment makes it practically impossible for the people to express their current will, leaving them bound by constitutional decisions they disagree with but cannot change. In the Hobbesian metaphor, the people are not sleeping; they are wide-awake but rendered mute. Unable to voice their constitutional opinions, the present-day people are saddled with the constitutional decisions of prior generations, ruled not by themselves but by the dead hand of the past.[57]

Equating constitutionalism to dead-hand rule, some have rejected the enterprise of constitutionalism altogether, seeing it as fundamentally incompatible with ongoing popular sovereignty. Carrying over the Hobbesian view of inalienable sovereignty to popular sovereignty, critics of constitutionalism have rejected the international law acceptance of irrevocable commitments and insisted that the People maintain meaningful control over constitutional decisionmaking at all times. Constitutional decisions inherited from the past that cannot practically be changed in the present lose any presumption of ongoing consent and become externally imposed, illegitimate constraints on sovereignty. This was the anti-constitutionalist position of prominent members of the Founding generation. Noah Webster argued that "the very attempt to make *perpetual* constitutions, is the assumption of a right to control the opinions of future generations; and to legislate for those over whom we have as little authority as we have over a nation in Asia."[58] Thomas Jefferson agreed that "no society can make a perpetual constitution" because "[t]he earth belongs always to the living generation." At the very least, Jefferson believed, the constitution would have to be rewritten by every generation because "one generation is to another as one independent nation is to another."[59]

Contemporary critics of originalism concur: if constitutional law means subjecting people in the present to rule by the foreign country of the past, or rule from the grave, then it cannot be squared with popular sovereignty.[60] Constitutional law must be self-imposed, by living and breathing Americans. But constitutionalism cannot be *too* living, lest it lapse into ordinary democracy. If popular sovereignty means that the people are always awake, and that their day-to-day democratic decisionmaking reflects sovereign will, then there is no longer any possibility of justifiable constitutional constraint. Some constitutional skeptics take precisely this view.[61] But nonoriginalist constitutionalists—who reject originalism but continue to embrace constitutional law—need a conception of popular sovereignty that allows for present-day expression of popular will but in forms that are distinguishable from the subconstitutional routines of democratic government.

Constitutional theorists have attempted many different ways of threading this needle. Theorists of "dualist" democracy join with originalists in holding that popular sovereignty is something that happens only on special occasions, distinct from ordinary democratic decisionmaking, but they apply different criteria to determine when the people are speaking in their sovereign voice. Looking past the formalities of the constitutional ratification and amendment processes, dualists point to historical periods during which the American people have been more broadly and deeply engaged in democratic decisionmaking as occasions of genuine sovereignty. Decisions made during these "constitutional moments," dualists maintain, should be privileged over the sub-sovereign vicissitudes of ordinary politics.[62] As with originalism, the resulting model is one of punctuated equilibrium, with long stretches of sleepy politics governed by the decisions made during occasional awakenings of constitutional lawmaking by the popular sovereign. Other nonoriginalists attempt to make waking constitutionalism a more regular occurrence. Proponents of "popular constitutionalism" portray the sovereign people as exercising "active and ongoing control over the interpretation and enforcement of constitutional law" by mobilizing through social movements and political campaigns to advance new understandings of constitutional rights and principles.[63] Popular sovereignty, in this view, comes to life when democratic politics focuses on constitutional values and presses for constitutional change through courts or other government actors.

Further blurring the boundary between popular sovereignty and ordinary democracy, political process theorists accept that popular will can be expressed through the ordinary institutions and processes of democratic government—but only under the right conditions. When the democratic expression of popular will is distorted by the political disempowerment of disadvantaged groups or other democratic failings, it loses its sovereign authority. Constitutional law is then authorized to substitute the hypothetical results of a "perfected" democratic process, standing for an idealized expression of popular will.[64] Theorists of constitutional "precommitments" similarly demote the results of ordinary democratic decisionmaking when it is subject to distortion on account of myopia, panic, or other short-term pathologies. Priority is instead granted to the clear-headed, far-sighted judgments that are supposedly reflected in constitutional rules and rights. Invoking the fable of Ulysses and the Sirens, precommitment theorists contend that binding us to our constitutional commitments is a way of giving effect to our authentic, sovereign preferences even when we lose sight of them during moments of weakened or corrupted popular will.[65]

All of these approaches to constitutional theory, originalist and living constitutionalist alike, seek to explain how the people can constitutionally bind themselves while still remaining sovereign. All attempt to do so by distinguishing the authentic acts of sovereignty that create constitutional law from the remainder of democratic decisions that are subject to constitutional control. But this is where the agreement ends. The multifarious lines that theorists have attempted to draw between sovereign and sub-sovereign expressions of popular will are highly divergent and deeply contested (not to mention in many cases dubiously discernable). Does popular sovereignty manifest through procedurally marked pathways of creation and amendment? Through historically identifiable moments of qualitatively superior democratic deliberation or special channels of constitutional politics? Through counterfactual constructions of perfected democracy, or idealized democratic decisionmaking contexts?

Constitutionalists agree that the People should decide for themselves; but they cannot come close to agreeing about who the People are, or how or what they have decided. Like democracy (and not clearly distinct from it), popular sovereignty is a highly malleable concept. Indeed, without its remarkable shape-shifting ability, it is hard to see how sovereignty could have survived the development of constitutionalism; or the other way around.

Dispensing with Sovereignty

We have seen internationalists and constitutionalists forced to grapple with the same basic problem of reconciling legal constraints with the presumptive sovereignty of self-governing political communities. Notwithstanding the views of America-first skeptics of internationalism, the threat to state sovereignty posed by the WTO or the European Union is no different in kind from the threat posed by U.S. constitutional law to democratic self-government in America. The defenses of international and constitutional law against sovereignty-based skepticism have also run in parallel. The shared strategy has been to attribute legal constraints to prior acts of sovereign consent—taking advantage of the slipperiness of what it means to give consent, and the moving target of who possesses or benefits from sovereignty.

Internationalists and constitutionalists have used these strategies with such success that the ongoing significance of sovereignty might be called into question. Contemporary theorists of international law are increasingly inclined to view sovereignty as a defeasible presumption that can be outweighed by more pressing concerns, such as preventing human rights violations or dealing with climate change. And international law doctrines have continued to develop in the direction of expanding the legal constraints that can be imposed upon states regardless of their (actual) consent, to such an extent that leading scholars have come to view international sovereignty as little more than "organized hypocrisy."[66] Moving in the same direction, constitutional theory has rendered popular sovereignty such an ephemeral and contested concept that it can now be reconciled, on one theory or another, with pretty much any constraint on democratic government.

Contemporary political theorists have mounted a more direct attack on sovereignty. If the Hobbesian, absolutist conception of the sovereign state was at one time a sensible political strategy for avoiding religious war and conflict, there is a strong case to be made that it has now outlived its usefulness.[67] In the modern world, Hobbesian absolutism is associated not with peace and prosperity but with Hitler and Stalin. Hannah Arendt credited the American revolutionaries with the practical "abolition of sovereignty" based on "the insight that in the realm of human affairs sovereignty and tyranny are the same."[68] Constitutional law and international law, in contrast, are now seen as among our best hopes of preventing tyranny and war. So why not just come out in favor of law over sovereignty? Rather than exalting the idea of illimitable sovereignty while frantically inventing ingenious theoretical contortions to limit it, we could just accept the reality and priority of international and constitutional law over an outdated view of the sovereign state that purports to make such enterprises impossible.[69]

In fact, that is the view that has largely triumphed at the level of jurisprudence, owing primarily to the work of H.L.A. Hart. For Hart, the difficulty of squaring the theory of absolute sovereignty with the well-established practices of constitutional and international law was reason enough to dismiss sovereignty altogether from a theory of law.[70] Rejecting the Hobbesian view of law as sovereign command, Hart pointed out that international and constitutional law do not represent the commands of any super-sovereign. Nor do these regimes merely impose constraints on pre-existing sovereigns. Instead, international and constitutional legal rules are constitutive of statehood and sovereignty, indispensable to the institutional forms and legal status of the state and its exercises of sovereign authority. This includes popular sovereignty, which can only be expressed through institutional forms—constitutional conventions, constitutional moments, or the like—prescribed by legal rules of recognition. Law cannot be reduced to the command of a sovereign, because law precedes, and shapes, sovereignty. Hart's critique, and the flourishing fact of international and constitutional law that underwrites it, reverses the Hobbesian priority of sovereignty over law. Law can exist without sovereignty; and the extent to which sovereignty exists is left up to law.

International and constitutional law might feel free, then, just to dispense with sovereignty altogether. Certainly, neither regime should feel bound by the kind of exogenous, inflexible conception of sovereignty that Hobbes treated as a necessary feature of the state. Nonetheless, as we have seen, Hobbesian sovereignty remains central to the self-understanding of these legal regimes. Even as constitutionalists and internationalists devise Houdini-like escapes from its bonds, they accept the straightjacket of sovereignty as a necessary premise of law for states. There is something about sovereignty that is hard to shake.

Part of that something, undoubtedly, is the Leviathan imagery of the state as a person and the deeply ingrained analogy between the liberty and autonomy of real-life persons and the sovereign self-determination of the state. For Hobbes and a long line of thinkers who came after, the idea of state sovereignty emerged from the same social contractarian perspective that was invented to justify how free and autonomous individuals could be subject to state authority and bound by the law of the state.[71] From the perspective of the individual person, the legal and political authority of the state demands justification in just the same way that the authority of international and constitutional law demands justification from the perspective of the state. And the justification provided by Hobbes and other social contract theorists for the authority of the state over the individual is the same as the standard justification for the authority of international and constitutional law: namely, sovereign will or consent.[72] Thus, the story Hobbes tells starts in the state of nature, where there is no legitimate source of political or legal authority above the individual. The sovereign state comes into existence only when individual persons agree collectively to transfer their natural rights and autonomous decisionmaking authority to the state in exchange for the benefits of state-provided order and protection. Before this transfer occurs, there is no legitimate source of political or legal authority above the individual. In the state of nature, persons are left free and autonomous—or, it might be said, sovereign.[73] And that is the position in which Leviathan itself remains.

This picture of states as autonomous beings, possessed of sovereignty that can only be surrendered with consent, continues to exert considerable pull on the political and legal imagination. Yet there is every reason to question the foundational analogy between sovereign states and autonomous persons. The reasons we value personal autonomy simply do not apply to the very different creature we call the state. As political theorist Charles Beitz puts the point, "States are not sources of ends in the same sense as are persons. Instead, states are systems of shared practices and institutions within which communities of persons establish and advance their ends."[74] We have reason to value the autonomy and self-determination of the actual persons who make up these communities, but that is not the same as valuing the autonomy of the state as such.

This is the crucial distinction that is missed when the force of state sovereignty is tied to the value of self-determination and democratic self-government. Those values can only be realized at the level of people, not at the level of states. To be sure, respecting state sovereignty can sometimes serve to advance the project of popular self-government. But it can also do the opposite. In the international system, sovereignty facilitates the pursuit of collective goods on a national scale by protecting the prerogatives of political communities to govern themselves. But empowering independent polities to act in their own self-interest also makes it despairingly difficult for these communities to deal effectively with global collective problems like war, poverty, climate change, and pandemic disease. Protecting the territorial integrity and political sovereignty of states against foreign intervention can facilitate the collective self-determination of their autonomous peoples. But the shield of sovereignty can also prevent humanitarian interventions that would protect the people of these states against genocide, war crimes, and other human rights violations perpetrated or not prevented by their own governments.[75] From the perspective of democratic self-government and its human participants, state sovereignty is a double-edged sword.

In constitutional law, it is all the more transparent that sovereignty and self-government do not go hand-in-hand. Quite the contrary, exalting the constitutional sovereignty of an abstract People comes at the expense of the freedom of actual, present-day people to engage in democratic self-government. This is not to fall into the facile view that constitutionalism is inherently at odds with democracy. Constitutional sovereignty can further the project of self-government by creating stable structures of democratic politics and representative government, and perhaps also by preventing political pathologies from distorting democratic outcomes. But constitutional rules and rights can also impede democratic responsiveness and block decisions that a self-determining polity would prefer. Americans had to fight the Civil War to get rid of the constitutionally entrenched institution of slavery; and they continue to live with institutional impediments to democracy like the Electoral College and the Senate that would never be adopted in the same form if contemporary Americans were writing on a blank slate.[76]

The simple point is that sovereignty is not always in the service of popular will or collective self-government. If those are the values we ultimately care about, it might be better to put sovereignty aside and simply pursue them directly. The same is true of other values that might be advanced by legal limitations on sovereign self-determination, such as rights and social welfare. If there are ways of constructing international and constitutional law that would do more to improve the lives of people who live under them, why should sovereignty be any barrier?

Of course, this view takes the selfish perspective of the people who build and benefit from law, ignoring the perspective and interests of the sovereign itself. And for good reason. Sovereign abstractions like states and People do not have interests, moral rights, or welfare of their own. In the words of Jeremy Waldron, "states are not the bearers of ultimate value" but "exist for the sake of human individuals."[77] It is the autonomy, rights, and well-being of these humans rather than the prerogatives of sovereigns that the systems of law we create should seek to serve. As Waldron further emphasizes, states themselves do not possess any "morally reputable interest in being unconstrained by law, in the way that the individual does":

> For the citizen, absence of regulation represents an opportunity for individual freedom. But absence of regulation represents a very different case for the state. If official discretion is left unregulated, if power exists without a process to channel and discipline its exercise... then this is not an opportunity, but rather a defect, a danger, and a matter of regret.[78]

Oddly, legal culture seems to have drifted toward the opposite view. Whatever the philosophical difficulties of justifying political and legal authority over individuals within the state, in practice the restrictions on individual freedom and autonomy that come with state-run legal systems are now accepted without a second thought.[79] The restrictions imposed by international law and constitutional law on the freedom and autonomy—or sovereignty—of the state, in contrast, continue to provoke push-back, hand-wringing, and genuine doubt.

Perhaps it is time to get beyond these doubts. We might conclude that "artificial man" of Leviathan has created an artificial problem for regimes of law governing the state. The project of imposing law on the state raises a whole host of genuine difficulties, which are the subject of this book. But the difficulty of overcoming the supposedly illimitable sovereignty of Leviathan seems entirely dispensable. We could continue to care about the benefits of democracy and collective self-determination, as well as the sometimes-conflicting benefits of upholding rights and pursuing social welfare on both a national and global scale. And we could continue to debate how best to realize those benefits through an international system of law that gives greater or lesser autonomy to individual states, and through systems of constitutional law that structure and constrain governmental and democratic decisionmaking in different ways. These debates would only have to proceed without jingoistic assertions of national sovereignty, constitutional appeals to the mystical authority of a popular sovereign whose commands we must continue to obey, and demagogic claims by authoritarian populists to speak for an authentic people who can tolerate no dissent. If that seems like a large price not to have to pay, so much the worse for sovereignty.

PART II
MANAGING STATE POWER

3
State Building and Unbuilding

During the Trump presidency it became shockingly commonplace to hear the United States described as a "failed state." If a failed state is one that "ceases to be able to function, giving up on all its responsibilities, including its ability to enforce law and order . . . and is unable to provide public services,"[1] it is no wonder that description has hit home. While other rich countries implemented comprehensive public health strategies to combat the COVID pandemic,[2] the United States "reacted like Pakistan or Belarus—like a country with shoddy infrastructure and a dysfunctional government whose leaders were too corrupt or stupid to head off mass suffering."[3] China's massive clamp down and containment efforts, by comparison, seemed, at least for a time, to demonstrate the power of effective governance that America lacked. Then, while hundreds of thousands of Americans were dying of COVID, demonstrators filled the streets of American cities to protest police brutality and racial injustice, leading to clashes with militarized police units and national guard troops, rioting, and images of apparent anarchy. The sight of the president of the United States emerging from a bunker underneath a fortified White House and marching through clouds of tear gas to conduct a photo-op against the background of a burned and graffitied church did little to reassure Americans that legal order and effective government would prevail. Even less reassuring was the final act of Trump's presidency, when a Trumpist mob stormed the U.S. Capitol looking to hang the vice president and overthrow the results of the election Trump had lost.

The failures of the country go beyond Trump. Notwithstanding America's wealth and world power, it has become increasingly difficult to imagine government and society pulling together to solve major problems or advance the public good. The impediments to effective governance are painfully familiar: fragmented, disorganized, and conflicting governmental authority; politicized, denuded, and crippled bureaucracy; entrenched racial and economic inequality; political polarization, gridlock, and elite capture; and widespread distrust of scientific expertise, media objectivity, and political leadership. These are all common afflictions of failing states.

Law for Leviathan. Daryl J. Levinson, Oxford University Press. © Oxford University Press 2024.
DOI: 10.1093/9780190061616.003.0004

In the case of the United States, at least some of these failures are by design. Our constitutional system of government was built to prevent "tyranny" by making it unusually difficult for government to accomplish anything at all, dividing and dispersing power among different branches and levels in ways that frustrate concerted action. It is this feature of the constitutional design that makes it so difficult for the country to implement a coherent public health strategy or even to figure out whether the president or state governors are responsible for setting pandemic policies, securing medical supplies, or policing American cities. Effective governance is further hamstrung by the dubious constitutional legitimacy of the administrative state and the continuous demands for political accountability it provokes, eroding the professional competence and credibility of agencies like the Centers for Disease Control and the Department of Justice. Constitutional rights to freedom of speech, association, and gun ownership make it impossible for the government to suppress protests (whether against public health lockdowns or police racism) and require a militarized police force to manage an armed population. Libertarian objections to, and limitations on, "big government" have prevented the development of a more robust welfare state or public health infrastructure and perpetuated deep social and economic inequalities along lines of race and class. Distrust of authority, and severe constraints on state power, are hard-wired into the American model of democracy and constitutionalism.

Hobbes, to put it mildly, would not have approved. Portraying centralized state power as an unambiguous good, Hobbes presented omnipotent Leviathan as a clearly preferable alternative not just to the miseries of the state of nature, but also to the failings of an ineffective state. Hobbes's attraction to absolutist government was based on the belief that dividing or limiting the power of the state would inevitably reduce its efficacy. His preference for an absolute monarchy over democracy was likewise premised on the efficacy of concentrated power in contrast to the inefficiencies of government by committee. For Hobbes, the enemies of effective government were disputation, doubt, paralysis, and weakness. A state that did not possess absolute sovereignty and effective power was destined to devolve into disagreement, conflict, and ultimately civil war—doomed to fail.[4]

When it comes to the failure of *other* states, the Hobbesian view has largely prevailed among American policymakers, who have come to view weak and failing states as a major global problem. Beyond the immiseration of their own populations, failed states breed global terrorist organizations and drug-trafficking networks, unwanted migration flows, and pandemic diseases. America's costly post-9/11 state-building projects in Iraq and Afghanistan are a testament to the perceived and pressing value of developing stronger states.

On the home front, however, Americans have resolutely ignored Hobbes's advice, intentionally designing for ourselves a state built, if not to fail, at least not to fully succeed. And perhaps for good reason. In the centuries since Hobbes, we have learned the hard way—from the tyranny of absolute monarchs to Hitler and Stalin—that state success is not always preferable to state failure. If the American government today is less capable than its Chinese counterpart of taking control during a pandemic or riot, it is also less capable of totalitarian control over day-to-day life or repression of all forms of dissent. The very same capabilities that make the Chinese state apparatus so effective in implementing lockdowns for purposes of pandemic control also make it effective in administering a regime of comprehensive surveillance and pervasive social control. A state that is capable of locking down 26 million people for months is also capable of constructing the Great Firewall, "keeping order" in Tiananmen Square and Hong Kong, and eliminating the Uighurs. If the alternative to state failure is authoritarian tyranny, then a weaker state may well be preferable to a stronger one. This is why Americans since the Founding have embraced the disabilities of their system of government as crucial safeguards of liberty against the threat of tyranny.

But there is a fine line between limiting the power of the state and crippling it. In their embrace of limited government and dread of tyranny, American constitutionalists have too often ignored the costs of constraining state power. Those costs are hard to miss during times of crisis. But even under more ordinary circumstances, the political fragmentation and fecklessness of the United States and other Western democracies threaten to push frustrated citizens seeking effective governance toward authoritarian alternatives.[5] The rise of China as a global superpower, as well as the rise of Trump and autocrats abroad, have provoked increasing doubts about the viability of constitutional democracy and its approach to fragmenting and limiting state power. States that cannot effectively govern are destined to fail.

This chapter reconsiders the risks and rewards of state power, from the perspective of both international relations and constitutional design. It starts by recasting the Hobbesian image of the state from "artificial man" to artificial, man-made technology. Like other powerful technologies—think, for example, of artificial intelligence or nuclear fusion—the state comes with enormous potential benefits for human welfare, but also grave risks. The first-best approach for dealing with such technologies is to develop them fully, but then carefully control how they are used. But when perfect control of a dangerous technology is impossible and the downside risks sufficiently severe, we might fall back on the second-best strategy of blocking the development of the technology altogether, or rolling it back. In the case of state power, this nuclear (or *no*-nuclear) option might be understood as the opposite of state building: state *un*building. As the chapter will go on to describe, similar dynamics and trade-offs among building, controlling, and unbuilding state power run through foreign policy and domestic constitutionalism alike.

The Risks and Rewards of State-Building

The state is plausibly the single most powerful technology ever invented, one that has revolutionized life for many on the planet. By consolidating control over the means of violence, the state has secured social order and protected its citizens against both internal and external threats.[6] By securing property rights, enforcing contracts, organizing markets, and establishing financial systems, the state has facilitated economic growth and prosperity. And by providing collective goods like education, scientific knowledge, public health, and social welfare programs, the state has improved the life prospects of its citizens and created new opportunities for human flourishing. Hobbes was right: the state has made life for many in the world much less "solitary, poore, nasty, brutish, and short."[7]

But the state is also a threat. As world history since the time of Hobbes tragically demonstrates, the same monopoly over the means of violence that can be used to keep the peace and build prosperity can also be used to prosecute mass warfare, brutal repression, and totalitarian misery. Viewed as a technological innovation, the state is a decidedly mixed blessing.

That has been true from the time of its invention. The modern state came into being for the purpose of organizing violence. In Charles Tilly's memorable summation, "states make war and war makes states."[8] Engaged in perpetual warfare and desperate for resources to bolster their military might, European kings came to see that they could support large armies by extracting wealth from populations under their control and protection. This led them to build bureaucratic infrastructures for the purposes of taxation and conscription of military manpower. Eventually, rulers figured out that by creating a legal system and supporting trade, they could increase their tax base and thus grow their resources for fighting wars and accumulating territory. Over time, administrative capabilities built up for fiscal and military purposes found new uses, and the state provided additional public goods to meet the demands of its citizens and to ensure their ongoing cooperation. At the end of this developmental road stands the modern state as we know it: capable of delivering the quality of life of contemporary Denmark; but also of contemporary North Korea.[9]

The fundamental dilemma of state power is that a state powerful enough to deliver valuable goods is also powerful enough to inflict grave harms.[10] That dilemma is confronted both by those who live within the boundaries of the state and those on the outside. From the outside, foreign states can be enemies or allies, and often some of both at the same time. The realist view of international relations emphasizes the enemy relationship, portraying sovereign states as above all else rivals, competing for relative gains in economic and military power. But, of course, states also pursue mutual benefits through various forms of cooperation, ranging from security alliances and cross-border trade to multilateral efforts to prevent global warming and the spread of pandemic disease. Foreign policy must balance the benefits of cooperation against realist concerns about relative power and vulnerability. From the domestic perspective, the dual examples of Denmark and North Korea should suffice to illustrate the dilemma of investing states with substantial control over the life prospects of their citizens. Our own states, too, can be allies or enemies.

Not surprisingly, then, we are often of two minds about state power. Sometimes we take the Hobbesian view of state power as an obvious good. That is the view that has motivated America's costly state-building projects in Iraq and Afghanistan, as well as many other state-building projects elsewhere in the world that have been supported by the international community. Development policy leaders like the World Bank and the International Monetary Fund now place a premium on building strong governance institutions capable of enforcing property rights and the rule of law, delivering education and healthcare, and effectively exercising other core state capacities.[11] Working with weak or failed states, the goal is "getting to Denmark."[12]

But there is always the risk of getting to North Korea, instead. If, as some have feared, Iraq eventually grows into a "Frankenstein's monster" of the Gulf, the United States might look back on its post-9/11 state-building efforts there with some measure of regret.[13] That is the view that American foreign policy strategists have taken of China in recent years. For a half-century, America pursued a self-conscious strategy of engagement in the hope of integrating China into the global economy and turning it in the direction of liberal democracy. American cooperation has been instrumental to China's astronomical growth in economic and geopolitical power. But this strategy has conspicuously failed to align China's values and interests with America's. Reflecting back on what his pivotal turn to China had wrought, Richard Nixon wistfully concluded, "We may have created a Frankenstein."[14] As the case of China also illustrates, state-building as an instrument of economic development also carries risks to the target state's own citizens. The recent emphasis on strengthening governance institutions represents a reversal from the prior "Washington Consensus" that followed Milton Friedman's mantra of "privatize, privatize, privatize."[15] Fearing that strong states would suppress free markets, expropriate wealth, and oppress their populations in other ways, the perceived direction of progress was the opposite of Scandinavian socialism.

The general risk of state-building, then, is that the states that are built may not serve the interests of their builders, internal or external.[16] When that risk becomes too great, state-*un*building might be the more prudent course.

Morgenthau Versus Marshall

As it happens, the most celebrated state-building project of the twentieth century could well have gone in the opposite direction. The post–World War II Marshall Plan is now credited for the successful reconstruction of Europe, the lasting peace and prosperity of the Pax Europaea, and the emergence of an economically and politically integrated European Union with Germany at its center.[17] At the close of the war, however, the desirability of rebuilding a German state that had instigated two world wars in a generation was far from a foregone conclusion.

Two competing positions emerged among President Roosevelt's advisors. State Department officials made the case for the economic reconstruction of a devastated Germany, along with the rest of Western Europe. They argued that rebuilding European economies was crucial, not just for the well-being of the European people, but also for U.S. trade. They also pointed out that an impoverished Europe would be fertile grounds for the growth of communism. Treasury Secretary Henry Morgenthau Jr. took a different view. His single-minded objective was to permanently dismantle Germany's war-making capabilities. Morgenthau's "Program to Prevent Germany from Starting a World War III" included not just complete demilitarization, but also the destruction of the nation's industrial capacity and dismemberment of its territory.[18] Rather than rebuilding Germany, the Morgenthau Plan called for demolishing its factories, flooding its mines, clear-cutting its forests, reallocating its territories to France and Poland, and dividing what was left of the country into two independent states, south and north. The goal was to transform the remnants of Germany into small, pastoral states populated by peaceful farmers.[19]

This is the program that President Roosevelt was initially persuaded to embrace.[20] (Roosevelt apparently had fond memories of a bucolic Germany from his rambles around the German countryside as a child.[21]) But the U.S. government was ultimately persuaded to switch course. In view of a slowly starving population reliant on U.S. aid to survive, and dim prospects for economic recovery in Europe without the engine of German industry, Morgenthau's approach came to seem not just imprudent but unconscionable. And, of course, there was the increasingly urgent goal of preventing the spread of Soviet communism. As Occupation General Lucius Clay put it, "There is no choice between becoming a Communist on 1500 calories and a believer in democracy on 1000 calories."[22] By the time President Truman appointed retired general George Marshall as Secretary of State in January of 1947, a consensus was forming in favor of state-building rather than unbuilding.[23]

So the Morgenthau Plan was out and the Marshall Plan was in. From 1948 to 1951, the United States poured billions of dollars of financial aid into Europe. By the time Marshall Plan support ended, the economic output of every European state had grown to surpass pre-War levels, and political stability had been restored.[24] Europeans were not the only beneficiaries. As expected, European economic growth was a boon to the U.S. economy, making Europeans wealthy enough to buy U.S. exports and facilitating international trade.[25] Marshall Plan funding was also channeled into rebuilding the militaries of Western Europe, allied with the United States in defending against Soviet expansion.[26]

In subsequent decades, as Germany has regrown into a formidable economic and political power, doubts about the wisdom of the Marshall Plan have from time to time resurfaced. Echoing Morgenthau, opponents of

Germany's 1990 reunification saw a renewed threat of militarism and Nazism. British Prime Minister Margaret Thatcher, who carried in her purse a map of Germany's bloated wartime borders, warned European leaders at a summit in 1989, "We have beaten the Germans twice. Now they're back."[27] Similar grumblings were heard during the European financial crisis of the 2010s, as newspapers in Southern Europe ran cartoons depicting Chancellor Angela Merkel wearing a Hitler moustache.[28]

Nonetheless, after generations of normalization, democracy, and integration into an increasingly unified Europe, Germany is now widely, if warily, accepted by its European confederates and the United States as a peaceful ally and a partner in economic prosperity. The Marshall Plan has gone down in history as a great triumph of state-building.

Anti-Federalists Versus Federalists

Another famously ambitious and successful American project of state-building, self-directed rather than externally imposed, is the U.S. Constitution. The American constitutional Framers aspired to create a strong, centralized state capable of standing toe-to-toe with established European nations in the international arena. That would require building a state capable of borrowing and taxing, regulating commerce and promoting trade, and, if push came to shove, fighting wars. These were the definitive powers of the European "fiscal-military" state of the eighteenth century, focused on the core functions of revenue raising and war making.[29]

Held up to that standard, the early version of the American state, under the Articles of Confederation, was pathetically weak. Dependent for revenues upon unenforceable requisitions from the state governments, the U.S. government was unable to repay its debts. Deprived of a permanent military presence, the country was vulnerable to foreign aggression and domestic insurrection. Unable to bind the states to a common trade policy or treaty commitments, the nation had no coherent foreign policy and no ability to negotiate access to markets for international trade.

The ambition of the Constitutional Framers was to create a national government powerful enough to fulfill these military and economic requirements of respectable statehood.[30] But the constitutional state-building project immediately ran up against deep suspicions of centralized state power. After all, the United States had not long ago fought a revolution against the oppressive power of a fiscal-military behemoth. The prospect of recreating "[s]tanding armies, centralized taxing authorities, the denial of local prerogatives, [and] burgeoning castes of administrators" on American soil did not strike many Americans as an obviously great idea[31]—much as resurrecting Germany had not seemed like a great idea to Morgenthau.

Constitutional ratification debates thus pitted the state-building ambitions of Federalists against Anti-Federalist fears that a national government with expansive fiscal and military capacities would become a Frankenstein's monster. Anti-Federalists were quick to remind their fellow citizens of "the uniform testimony of history, and experience of society . . . that all governments that have ever been instituted among men, have degenerated and abused their power."[32] And they prophesied that the fearsome powers of a fiscal-military state here at home would inevitably be turned against its own citizens. An expansive federal tax bureaucracy would invade "every corner of the city, and country—It will wait upon the ladies at their toilet[], and will not leave them in any of their domestic concerns."[33] The prospect of a standing army raised further alarms. A prominent feature of "all the monarchies of Europe," standing armies had proven themselves a "bane to freedom," propping up "tyrants, and their pampered minions."[34] Anti-Federalists feared that the United States would be no exception. Armed with a professional military, a dictatorial president or an oligarchical cabal of senators would be able to rule "at the point of the bayonet," like "Turkish janizaries enforcing despotic laws."[35]

Federalist defenders of the Constitution had to grant that "in every political institution, a power to advance the public happiness involves a discretion which may be misapplied and abused."[36] But they urged their fellow Americans to focus on the benefits of state power. Without a large measure of centralized coercive authority, there could be no national defense, domestic security, or effective governance of any kind. As threatening as the fiscal and military capabilities of the state might seem, these were also the "powers by which good rulers protect the people."[37] "If we mean to have our natural rights and properties protected," Federalists argued, "we must first create a power which is able to do it."[38]

Standing armies were one source of such power. Publius asked incredulously whether

> [w]e must expose our property and liberty to the mercy of foreign invaders and invite them by our weakness to seize the naked and defenseless prey,

because we are afraid that rulers, created by our choice, dependent on our will, might endanger that liberty by an abuse of the means necessary to its preservation.[39]

A state that was not permitted to maintain an established defense would "exhibit the most extraordinary spectacle, which the world has yet seen—that of a nation incapacitated by its Constitution to prepare for defense before it was actually invaded."[40] Federalists argued that the Anti-Federalists' precautionary opposition to state-building was tantamount to "cut[ting] a man in two in the middle to prevent his hurting himself."[41]

For the Federalists, it was not American citizens but America's rivals in Europe who "must naturally be inclined to exert every means to prevent our becoming formidable."[42] In fact, however, the posture of England and France toward American state-building ambitions was as much Marshall as Morgenthau. England and France had long been frustrated by the weakness of an American proto-state that lacked the centralized power to uphold treaty obligations and repay debts.[43] From their perspective, consistent with the Federalist view that ultimately prevailed, building a more powerful American state might be a risk worth taking. As we shall see, however, a fair measure of Anti-Federalist risk-aversion was ultimately built into the constitutional bargain.

Managing State Power

Returning to the analogy between state and nuclear power, the basic challenge of managing a potentially beneficial but also potentially dangerous technology is to harness the benefits while mitigating the risks. The first-best strategy for so doing is to exercise control over how the technology will be deployed—encouraging beneficial applications but banning harmful ones. Such control can be exercised through rules and prohibitions that directly govern *uses*, specifying which are permissible and which are impermissible. We might permit nuclear fusion to be used to generate electricity but not to generate weapons of mass destruction. Control can also be exercised indirectly, by selecting for trustworthy or well-motivated *users* of the technology and creating channels of accountability and influence over their decisionmaking. We might decide that the United States can safely possess nuclear capabilities but North Korea and terrorist organizations cannot; and we might elect presidents who will make wise decisions about when (not) to launch nuclear attacks, and hope that other elected and unelected officials will help prevent any unwise decisions from being executed.

When it comes to controlling the power of the state, these two approaches—selecting and influencing users and regulating uses—take familiar forms. From inside the state, users of power are selected and controlled by democratic politics, and uses of power by constitutional rules and rights. Representative democracy is supposed to select government decisionmakers who will use the power of the state to benefit citizens and make those decisionmakers accountable to their constituents for success and failure. At the same time, constitutional rules and rights regulate the exercise of state power directly, legally forbidding some uses and mandating others.

Controlling states from the outside works somewhat differently. Lacking votes and representation, outsiders cannot play a direct role in selecting the leaders of other states (although they can sometimes resort to under-the-table methods of exerting influence over foreign elections). And outsiders are not ordinarily protected by constitutional rights. But outsiders do have available a parallel pair of approaches to controlling state power, political and legal. Political forms of influence, broadly construed, are the domain of international relations. Nations, and interested groups within them, can influence the behavior of foreign states through bilateral and multilateral diplomacy, military threats or the actual deployment of force, trade relationships and economic incentives, and various forms of soft power. States also attempt to control one another's behavior by means of legal rules and requirements established through treaties, custom, and the decisionmaking authority of international tribunals, as well as through regional and global governance institutions such as the European Union, the World Trade Organization, and the United Nations. This is the domain of international law.

Democracy and constitutionalism, representation and rights, international relations and international law: these political and legal methods of controlling power from the inside and the outside are the subject of the next chapter. The remainder of this chapter focuses on a different, and more drastic, approach. Rather than attempting to control the uses or users of a powerful technology, we might simply decide to get rid of it, foregoing the benefits, but also eliminating the downside risks. Nuclear power might be banned altogether, or its development prevented in the first place. This was the approach to state power pressed by Morgenthau and the Anti-Federalists.

Incapacitation

That approach might be described as state *un*building, or as *incapacitating the state*. The terminology of incapacitation invokes the penal strategy of preventing crime by physically disabling potential criminals, whether by means of incarceration, or, (even) more brutally, execution, or cutting off the hands of thieves. The metaphorical body of Leviathan can be similarly disabled. Like locking up criminals, incapacitating the state is a potentially effective, albeit costly, method of preventing the state from inflicting future harms.

More literally, incapacitation is simply a reduction in state "capacity"—a term of art in development economics and political science, meaning the ability to accomplish the kinds of things states are supposed to be good for: providing domestic order and protection from violence, raising revenue, adjudicating disputes, enforcing property rights and contracts, building transportation and communications networks, providing healthcare and education, and so on.[44] State capacity is what state-building is supposed to build. Doing so requires marshalling the resources and assembling the infrastructure that states use to generate and project power: a strong military and police force, a competent and efficient bureaucracy, a coherent and decisive system of lawmaking and dispute resolution, and so on.

State capacity can also be augmented by making the populations and territories that states aspire to govern more easily manageable. To this end, as political scientist James C. Scott describes, states have "worked to homogenize their populations and break down their segmentation by imposing common languages, religions, currencies, and legal systems, as well as promoting the construction of connected systems of trade, transportation, and communication."[45] Modern states have developed ever more effective tools for monitoring and managing their populations, ranging from conventions of permanent surnames,[46] to elaborate systems of information collection and management,[47] to the extensive data mining, video surveillance, and DNA databasing operations of the contemporary "national surveillance state."[48] Even the mundane urban grid turns out to be a powerful and multifaceted tool of governance, one that facilitates "[d]elivering mail, collecting taxes, conducting a census, moving supplies and people in and out of the city, putting down a riot or insurrection, digging for pipes and sewer lines, finding a felon or conscript . . . and planning public transportation, water supply, and trash removal."[49]

Here again, it is important to keep in mind that all of these tools can be used for good or for ill. The Rwandan genocide of 1994 could not have been perpetrated in most African states, which lacked Rwanda's high level of bureaucratic capacity. To effect an extermination campaign of such scope and swiftness, the Rwandan government enlisted administrative officials to collect and distribute information about targets, mobilize citizens for attacks, maintain records of who had been killed, and dispose of the corpses.[50] As another example, Scott points to an exquisitely detailed map produced by the City Office of Statistics of Amsterdam in 1941 entitled "The Distribution of Jews in the Municipality."[51] Tragically, the map was put to use by the Nazis to round up and deport the city's Jewish population. Scott reminds us, however, that the same cartographical capacity "could as easily have been deployed to feed the Jews as to deport them." The other way around, "[a]n illegible society ... is a hindrance to any effective intervention by the state, whether the purpose of that intervention is plunder or public welfare."[52] In the present-day United States, a contact-tracing app might be used to control the COVID pandemic; but the same technology might also be used to track and threaten Black Lives Matter protestors or to prevent pregnant women from getting abortions.

Incapacitating a state means, simply, eliminating or withholding some of the tools or resources that contribute to state capacity (for better or for worse). Destroying the Amsterdam map or refusing to download contract tracing apps would be small-scale examples. The Morgenthau Plan for post–World War II Germany and the Articles of Confederation's limitations on the power of the national government of the United States offer some larger-scale examples.

Intentional incapacitation is a familiar strategy of both international and domestic statecraft. On the international stage, states routinely take steps to reduce the military, economic, or internal governance capacity of their rivals. Trade, investment, and foreign aid are withheld from competitor states to reduce their wealth and hinder economic growth. Strategic air strikes, arms embargos, cyberattacks, and outright wars are designed to reduce the military power of adversaries. Support for rebel groups or military proxies, economic sanctions, and propaganda campaigns can serve the purpose of destabilizing or weakening foreign states. In all of these ways, states seek not just to influence and control one another's behavior, but to reduce the capacity of actual or potential enemies to inflict harm.

Incapacitation is also a prevalent strategy of domestic politics. Bureaucratic structures, staffing, and administrative capacity can be dismantled and drained. Surveillance and intelligence capabilities can be legally or technologically curtailed. Access to tax and other revenues can be impeded or denied, effectively "starving the beast." Governmental responsibilities and powers can be fragmented and dispersed among different institutions and actors, making coordinated action more difficult. Divisions along lines of race, class, or partisanship can be aggravated and amplified, dialing up the difficulty of social cooperation and effective governance. This chapter's opening example of the American government's failure to manage the COVID pandemic illustrates the "success" of a number of these measures in reducing state capacity.

Incapacitation is a significantly different strategy of statecraft than controlling states through legal rules and rights, though the distinction can become blurry. There is a sense in which any constitutional rule or right could be looked upon as a selective incapacitating measure. We might say, for instance, that the government is "incapacitated" from locking up enemies of the state without trial by rights to due process. An incapacitating constitutional design that impedes the development of the intelligence, administrative, and coercive capabilities necessary to identify and apprehend enemies of the state in the first place, or that denies the government a standing army, may differ only as a matter of degree.

Nonetheless, the difference between narrowly targeted restrictions in the form of rights and rules and broadly structural strategies of incapacitation is well worth marking. Similar distinctions have proven their worth in many other legal contexts. Antitrust law, for example, distinguishes between "conduct" remedies, which mandate or forbid discrete behaviors (such as an order not to raise prices or discriminate against a rival), and "structural" remedies, which change the shape of the relevant firms (such as breaking up AT&T or Amazon into a number of separate companies). Financial regulators concerned about the systemic risks created by banks that are "too big to fail" differentiate between the regulatory strategies of imposing rules and requirements for how these banks must operate and the "structural" solution of eliminating systemic risk by breaking up the banks into entities small enough to safely fail. Along the same lines, gun violence can be prevented by the enforcement of criminal laws against murder or by broad regulatory regimes of gun control; and police violence can be prevented through more stringent legal and political regulation of the use of force, or by wholesale reform or "defunding" of the police force.

The paired regulatory strategies in each of these contexts can be distinguished along two related dimensions. One is between regulation targeting behavior that is immediately harmful and regulation targeting behavior or arrangements that are not intrinsically harmful but that have the potential to cause downstream harms. The latter kind of regulation is sometimes described as "preventative" or "prophylactic." Unlike regulation that is directly targeted at harm, preventative and prophylactic regulation necessarily prohibits some measure of harmless and even beneficial conduct. Amazon, the big banks, and their customers are deprived of economies of scale and coordination; gun owners are deprived of a legitimate tool of self-defense or recreational hunting.

Legal incapacitation of the state is similarly prophylactic and preventative. Like breaking up banks or outlawing guns, incapacitating measures deprive states of capacities that could be beneficial in order to preempt potential downstream harms. Depriving a state of a standing army, as the Federalists were at pains to point out, is an overinclusive and highly costly way of preventing potential harms.[53]

What might justify those costs is the second characteristic shared by incapacitation and prophylactic regulation, namely its greater reliability, compared to more surgical alternatives, in ensuring that harms do not come to pass. If we can be confident that antitrust conduct remedies, banking regulatory rules, or criminal prohibitions on homicide will work perfectly, then there will be no need to suffer the spillover costs of the prophylactic alternatives. Given that enforcement and compliance are often imperfect, however, structural forms of incapacitation pay their way by creating more reliable impediments to harm than bare legal prohibitions. The structural barriers created by breaking up banks or monopolies, or by banning assault rifles, are supposed to be more secure than unreliably or inadequately enforced legal rules.

The same is true of structural barriers to state misbehavior. Anti-Federalists wanted to forbid a standing military altogether because they did not trust constitutional rules and rights to limit how the military would be used. Once a tyrannical president had an army at his disposal, Anti-Federalists feared, such rules and rights would be reduced to merely parchment barriers. Of course, a tyrannical president might also ignore a constitutional prohibition on raising a peacetime army in the first place. In fact, the first derogatory reference to "parchment barriers" in The Federalist Papers comes from Alexander Hamilton, precisely in reference to constitutional prohibitions on standing armies. Hamilton cites the example of Pennsylvania, which, despite a constitutional declaration that standing armies are "dangerous to liberty, and ought not to be kept up in time of peace," apparently could not resist the temptation to raise an army "in a time of profound peace" when confronted with "partial disorders in one or two of her counties." The moral, for Hamilton, is that constitutional "rules and maxims calculated in their very nature to run counter to the necessities of society" will not be effective.[54] That includes structural, incapacitating rules.

Hamilton was right to observe that any legal obstacle can be overcome if there is sufficient political or social will. Still, some obstacles are harder to overcome than others. Raising an army from scratch is politically and logistically more difficult than violating a rule against using an existing army in some abusive way. Building an army requires time and resources. People will see it happening and have opportunities to sound the alarm and mobilize resistance. It seems likely, then, that a structural prohibition on standing armies would serve as a stiffer barrier than regulatory rules governing the army's use.

So, two features distinguish incapacitation from ordinary legal regulation, at least as a matter of degree: a broadly prophylactic approach to limiting state power, and the imposition of structural barriers that are more difficult to override or reverse than typical rules and rights. The relative costs and benefits of incapacitation follow straightforwardly from these distinctive features. The main advantage of incapacitation is that it promises greater efficacy and reliability in limiting the downside costs of state power. The main disadvantage of incapacitation is the opportunity cost of sacrificing the beneficial uses state power. In a first-best world we would exercise perfect control over unlimited state power—enjoying its full benefits while avoiding any costs. It is only when control becomes imperfect, and state power comes with real downside risks, that the possibility of incapacitating the state emerges as a plausible, second-best alternative.

Capacity and Control

Put the other way around, the more confidence we have in our ability to control the state, the more state capacity we will be willing to countenance. This intuitive relationship between the extent of state power and its control has been central to the development of the modern state. Rulers of nascent states who wanted to build capacity by raising tax revenues and recruiting soldiers often met with resistance from unenthusiastic populations. Forced to strike a bargain, these rulers found that the purchase price of cooperation was greater popular control, institutionalized through some combination of legal rights and political accountability.[55] For example, in thirteenth-century England, bargaining between the Crown and local elites resulted in the Magna Carta, as well as the council of barons that evolved into the first Parliament. In the late fifteenth and sixteenth centuries, redoubled efforts by the Tudors and Stuarts to expand the power and wealth of the monarchy provoked Parliamentary pushback and eventually civil war and the Glorious Revolution of 1688. With royal absolutism defeated, England moved forward with what is now described as a system of "limited government," featuring a Bill of Rights, a politically independent judiciary, and an invigorated role for Parliament—here again, legal rights and political representation.[56]

But limited government did not mean limited state capacity. Quite the opposite, once legal and political controls over state power were more securely in place, popular and Parliamentary resistance to centralized state-building diminished.[57] Tax revenues and state expenditures soared, and unprecedented military might was mobilized for war against France.[58] An elaborate, professionalized bureaucracy was assembled, "[with] such a multitude of new officers, created by and removable at the royal pleasure, that they have extended the influence of government to every corner of the nation."[59] In sum, post-revolution England became a "consensually strong state." British citizens consented to make their state stronger; and they were willing to give this consent "precisely because they knew that they could rein in the power of the state if it deviated significantly from the course of action that they wanted to see implemented.[60]

As we have seen, the Marshall versus Morgenthau debate turned in large part on the same relationship between capacity and control. The willingness of the United States to rebuild the power of the German state depended on the prospects of controlling Germany's political direction and allegiances. The gamble of the Marshall Plan was that Germany could be brought into the fold of an economically interconnected Western Europe allied with the United States against Communism. That bet has paid off. The economic, political, legal, and cultural integration of an enduringly powerful German state—from the Marshall Plan through the creation of NATO in 1949, the European Coal and Steel Community in 1951, and eventually the European Union—has led to lasting peace in Europe. Like England after the Glorious Revolution, Germany is now, from the perspective of the United States and its European allies, a "consensually strong" state.

Much of the debate over the U.S. Constitution likewise turned on predictive judgments about how effectively a powerful, central state could be politically and legally controlled by its citizenry. Madison famously recognized that "[i]n framing a government which is to be administered by men over men, the great difficulty lies in this: you must first enable the government to control the governed; and in the next place oblige it to control itself."[61] Madison and his fellow Federalists believed that the constitutional design could accomplish both ends. A newly empowered national government would have the capacity to control the governed. And that government would itself be controlled through a combination of democratic accountability and institutional checks and balances. Or so the Federalists argued.

Doubting that a distant and dangerous national government could be securely controlled, Anti-Federalists resisted building its power. The Anti-Federalists were not inherently opposed to powerful government. Far from libertarians, they had no objection to capable government at the state level. State governments were trustworthy recipients of power, in the Anti-Federalist view, precisely because these governments were closer to the people and more reliably responsive to the interests of their citizens.[62] State governments could be made "consensually strong"—or, as one prominent Anti-Federalist writer put it, "strong and well guarded."[63] But the Anti-Federalists feared that the national government would not be nearly so well-guarded. In the Anti-Federalist imagination, that government would be run by a group of distant and despotic aristocrats who were disconnected from "the body of the people."[64] It was this presumptive failure of political control that led the Anti-Federalists to resist Federalist state-building. When that resistance failed, the Anti-Federalists fell back on the demand for more stringent control over the national government—if not political control through democratic accountability, then legal control through a constitutional bill of rights.[65]

Constitutional State-(Un)Building

The same set of arguments has served as a template for constitutional debates through the present. The American state-building project has come a long way since the Founding, when the national government was "a midget institution in a giant land."[66] At the start of the Jefferson administration, the total federal workforce in Washington numbered 153.[67] As of 1840, the national government employed approximately 20,000 people, 14,000 of whom worked for the Post Office.[68] Fast forward to today, when the federal government employs over 2.5 million civilians and nearly 1.5 million active duty military personnel. American government is not just visibly larger but vastly more capable along countless dimensions in the military, economic, and social spheres.

Even as the American state has grown to become a "global Leviathan,"[69] however, its capacity has remained limited. Some of those limitations, such as the basic structural arrangements of separation of powers and federalism, are built into the original constitutional design. Efforts to overcome those structural limitations through the development of the administrative state and the imperial presidency have provoked counter-reactions, calling for greater political and legal control, if not outright rejection of more expansive centralized power. Contemporary constitutional debates continue to pit neo-Federalists, pressing for a more effective national government, against neo-Anti-Federalist resistance to "big government" and "runaway bureaucracy." As the remainder of this chapter will describe, the dilemma of state power, and the dialectic of building, controlling, and unbuilding that power, remain at the center of constitutional and political contestation over the American version of Leviathan.

Separation of Powers, the Administrative State, and the Imperial Presidency

Widely embraced by Americans as a work of political genius, the U.S. constitutional design of separated powers and checks and balances has long been credited with at least three major virtues. First, by assigning qualitatively different governance tasks to specialized institutions, the system of separated powers is supposed to leverage the efficiency benefits of specialization and division of labor.[70] Separation of powers is supposed to increase the capacity of the national state in much the same way as Henry Ford's assembly line increased the capacity of automobile production. Second, and complementary to increasing capacity, dividing powers is simultaneously supposed to increase control over the national government. By creating more sites of political representation for different interests, and by empowering the branches to check and balance one another, the system is meant to prevent a single, dominant faction or a cabal of corrupt officials from turning the power of the state against the public good.[71]

At the same time, however, it has been common wisdom since the Founding that dividing the national government into separate branches and Congress into separate chambers serves to "preserve liberty by disabling government."[72] By multiplying veto points and increasing transaction costs, the separation of powers makes it more difficult for the national government to threaten liberty—by making it more difficult for the government to do anything at all. For skeptics of centralized state power, from the Anti-Federalists to contemporary conservatives, the incapacitating effect of separation of powers is a centrally valuable feature of the constitutional design, reflecting the view of many in the Founding generation that the "[t]he injury which may possibly be done by defeating a few good laws will be amply compensated by the advantage of preventing a number of bad ones"[73] Those who doubt that the national government will usually be acting in the public interest (or in the interest of their preferred segment of the public) continue to see incapacitation as a positive good. As Ronald Reagan famously captured this outlook two centuries later, "The nine most terrifying words in the English language are: 'I'm from the government, and I'm here to help.'"

For those who hold out hope that national state power might serve the public interest (or their own interests), however, separation of powers is the enemy of effective governance. The stranglehold of separation of powers on state action is why progressives and other proponents of powerful government have long lamented a constitutional design that created a government "divided against itself" and "deliberately and effectively weakened."[74] In recent decades, the combination of polarized political parties and divided party control of government has exacerbated these structural tendencies. The incapacitating gridlock of government in Washington is now more than ever a source of frustration for those seeking activist government solutions to pressing social problems.

Frustration with the limited capacity of the national government has been a driving force in American constitutional and political development. The separation-of-powers-induced difficulties of lawmaking have deflected demands for centralized state power to the executive branch, giving rise, over the course of the twentieth century and into the twenty-first, to what we now know as the "administrative state" and the "imperial presidency." Both of these structural developments have been accompanied by the same set of arguments about building, controlling, and unbuilding state power.

Starting with the administrative state, the constitutional state-building project did not end with the enactment of the Constitution. As soon as government under the constitution was up and running, it became clear that effective governance required administrative institutions that had been left out of the original design. Recognizing that "[e]nergy and effectiveness in administration were critical to the very survival of a union that could easily have disintegrated before it became operational,"[75] governing officials immediately set to work building administrative capacity. That project was spurred along by "America's stunning growth in territory, population, industry, transportation, and communications over the course of its first hundred years under the Constitution," which created governance challenges requiring continual innovation. Starting in the late nineteenth century, that innovation took the modern form of administrative agencies, invested with the kind of independent regulatory authority and expertise necessary to respond rapidly and effectively to governance demands that the cumbersome and politically convoluted legislative process could not meet. Gaining momentum during the New Deal and proceeding through the Great Society, administrative state-building has generated a "fourth branch" of government where much of the effective governance capacity of the national state now resides.

Not surprisingly, the accumulation of power in the administrative state has been closely accompanied by concerns about control. Surveying the historical development of the American administrative state, Jerry Mashaw describes a recurring "three-step process of building and binding administrative capacity":

> First, something happens in the world. Second, public policymakers identify that happening as a problem ... and initiate new forms of governmental action [to address it]. Third, these new forms of action generate anxieties about the direction and control of public power. Means are thus sought to make the new initiative ... accountable.[76]

Thus, the New Deal administrative agencies that were brought into being to transform the national economy, acting independently of Congress, provoked fears that the government was out of control. The result was the Administrative Procedure Act, creating the basic legal framework for administrative accountability, which has been developed into an elaborate set of requirements for public participation in agency rulemaking and judicial review of agency action. Starting in the 1960s and '70s, growing distrust of neutral agency expertise, and the suspicion that agencies were being "captured" by interest groups rather than pursuing the public good, motivated more stringent legal and political controls, including expansive standing to challenge agency actions in court and enhanced oversight by both Congress and the president. Focusing on these and other efforts to make administrative power accountable, "[t]he history of the American administrative state is the history of competition among different entities for control over its policies."[77]

A more extreme reaction to the "rise and rise of the administrative state"[78] has been to resist this form of state-building altogether, or to roll it back. The first response of business interests and their conservative allies to the New Deal regulatory state was to assail the whole enterprise as unconstitutional and try to dismantle it in the courts. During the Reagan years, constitutional originalists joined forces with conservative and libertarian critics of "big government" to launch another sustained attack on the administrative and regulatory state. The Republican political platform since then has evolved from deregulation to outright "deconstruction of the administrative state."[79] That agenda has been at the center of the contemporary conservative legal movement, which has fought for more aggressive judicial review of agency action and a reinvigorated nondelegation doctrine that would render "most of government unconstitutional."[80]

It is not just the political right that has made inroads in debilitating the administrative state. The left has had a role to play as well. Concerned about industry capture and abuse of state power, progressive reformers have pushed for requirements of public participation, transparency, and legal rights as means of holding government accountable. Whatever the benefits for accountability, however, the proliferation of procedural obstacles and veto points has made regulation increasingly difficult to achieve. Progressive efforts to control the administrative state have contributed to its incapacitation, unwittingly furthering the cause of conservative anti-statism.[81]

Another way around separation of powers gridlock is the assertion of unilateral presidential power, a phenomenon that has given rise to the post–World War II "imperial" presidency.[82] The "imperial" epithet actually blurs two different observations about the modern presidency, one speaking to control and the other to capacity. The point about control is that presidents since the New Deal have come to direct or influence more and more of the actions of the federal government, replacing Congress as the primary decisionmaker in government and "unifying" the executive branch so that agencies and bureaucrats increasingly march under White House orders. The point about capacity is that the federal administrative and national security state over which the president presides has grown vastly more massive and capable. Putting these two pieces together gets us the imperial presidency, possessed of unrivaled control over unprecedented state power.

For many Americans, the imperial presidency is cause for alarm. Long-standing fears that the presidency would grow from a "foetus of [m]onarchy"[83] into a full-blown dictatorship seem to be coming closer to fruition. Worse, the vast bureaucratic and military capabilities of the modern executive now threaten to make a presidential dictatorship not just tinpot but totalitarian. From this perspective, Donald Trump's presidency was a vivid demonstration of how imperial power in the wrong hands could become catastrophic. Indifferent to law and norms, and seemingly intent on discrediting the independent press, using the media as a propaganda machine, politicizing the judiciary, sidelining Congress, filling the administration with cronies and loyalists, and stoking fears of security threats and hostility toward immigrants and minorities, Trump seemed to be following the "dictator's handbook" for undermining democracy and seizing authoritarian control.[84] The events of January 6 punctuated the point: authoritarian rule by an autocratic president had become a real possibility in this country.

But presidential power has not always been perceived as threatening. The Progressives and New Dealers who put the presidency on its imperial path shared Alexander Hamilton's Founding-era view that an empowered presidency was a crucial source of energy and efficacy in government and a prerequisite for America's leadership on the world stage. Contemporary proponents of concentrating power in the presidency continue to see "the dominating, energetic leadership of a commanding President" as the only hope for turning what would otherwise be a fragmented and enervated government into "an instrument of effective power."[85] Acting on the same view, contemporary presidents have attempted to unshackle themselves from constitutional rights, congressional limitations, and other constraints on executive power in order to take control over an otherwise ungovernable national state. The rise of presidential imperialism has been an arguably necessary adaptation to demands for effective governance.[86]

As for the downside risks, proponents of presidential power dismiss presidential "tyrannophobia" as underestimating the efficacy of democratic control.[87] The modern presidency may be "the most dangerous branch," but it is also "the most accountable branch,"[88] characterized by "plebiscitary" responsiveness to public opinion and popular demands.[89] Control over the presidency comes not just from democratic elections but from a broader set of legal and political accountability mechanisms. Jack Goldsmith describes how the menacing power of the post-9/11 presidency has given rise to a "synopticon" of "watcher[s]"—Congress, journalists, human rights advocates, lawyers, and judges—who monitor, publicize, and check the president's every move.[90] In Goldsmith's view, expansive executive power begets intensive accountability, which in turn legitimates presidential power and even strengthens it. Capacity and control—or in Goldsmith's synonymous title, *Power and Constraint*—go hand in hand in the modern presidency.[91]

Others place much less faith in political and legal control. Even in the pre-Trump era, presidential alarmists had begun to diagnose the democratic breakdowns that threatened, in the assessment of Bruce Ackerman, a "runaway presidency."[92] Responding to that risk assessment, Ackerman has proposed a set of reforms designed to bring the president back under democratic and legal control by "enlightening politics" and "restoring the rule of law."[93] But Ackerman does not stop there. Fearful that control will be not be sufficient, he also recommends steps to incapacitate the presidency. These range from limiting presidential authority to engage in sustained military actions and fragmenting the unitary and hierarchical structure of the executive branch to eliminating the presidency altogether.[94] Ackerman is clear-eyed about the costs of doing without presidential power, which would require sacrificing some measure "activist government—dedicated to the on-going pursuit of economic welfare, social justice, and environmental integrity." Nonetheless, in light of the grave downside risks, Ackerman, among others, is prepared to make the "tragic choice[]" of dismantling the imperial presidency.[95]

Federalism

Like the separation of powers, the American system of constitutional federalism has long been celebrated as a safeguard against the dangers of centralized state power. It has been common wisdom since the Founding that "the principal benefit of the federalist system is a check on abuses of government power," one that "ensure[s] the protection of 'our fundamental liberties.'"[96] Federalism is supposed to play this role in several different ways.

One, discussed in the next chapter, is that federalism allows groups to effectively exit the domain of national power and govern themselves independently. By turning over policymaking authority in some areas to the states, the federal system allows groups that would be outvoted at the national level to become self-governing majorities at the state level. But federalism is also supposed to give minority interests that do not exit greater *voice*. This is the idea famously elaborated by Madison in a series of Federalist Papers, arguing that the system of constitutional federalism would allow "[t]he different governments...[to] control each other, at the same time that each will be controlled by itself."[97] In particular, states would be empowered to exercise some measure of control over the national government through "the political safeguards of federalism," which included state representation in the Senate and Electoral College as well as the credible threat of armed resistance through state militias. Contemporary American constitutionalists continue to view federalism as a means of empowering state-level interests in the national political process, pointing to additional pathways of influence, such as the role of state governments and officials in administering federal elections, supporting national political parties, and (as will be discussed further, below) implementing national policies through cooperative federalism arrangements.[98]

The exit and voice perspectives on federalism are familiar. But there is another, less appreciated way that constitutional federalism might protect against national power—one that returns focus to state unbuilding and incapacitation. At the time of the Founding, federalism was understood not just as a means of escaping or controlling the power of the national state but also as a strategy for preventing that power from being developed in the first place. By encouraging the national government to make use of the already well-developed governance capacity of states and local governments, federalism was supposed to obviate the need for more extensive national statebuilding. If states and localities could be relied upon for the heavy lifting of governance, the national government could remain safely small and weak.

We might call this strategy *incapacitation by substitution*: substituting governance capacity from the outside for independent state-building. This dynamic has been recognized in the context of contemporary state-building efforts as a problem. Reliance on extensive international resources and hands-on assistance risks "sucking out" the capacity of the developing state to govern itself.[99] When the goal is state *un*building, however, a substitutionary strategy can be advantageous.

Incapacitation by substitution has also been a standard feature of historical state-building processes. A state that lacks adequate capacity to control its territory and population must choose between two options. One is to build its own capacity, which requires substantial investments of time and resources, as well as the ability to overcome entrenched resistance. An easier path, it often turns out, is to cede governance authority to some other entity that already possesses greater capacity and that can be induced to cooperate with the principal state. This is the strategy of "indirect rule."[100] For early states that lacked the means to govern directly, indirect rule was a matter of necessity. Nascent monarchs could assert rule over their territories, but none actually had the ability to build a bureaucratic apparatus capable of governing a population larger than that of a small city. Kings had no choice but to collaborate with local magnates who were capable of exercising direct control over distant populations and territories. These collaborations amounted to a bargain through which the monarch secured a certain measure of political control over, and revenues from, local powerholders in exchange for protection and other forms of assistance from the center. But the local powerholders under these arrangements maintained substantial autonomy over how they governed and retained leverage to resist demands from the center that did not serve their interests. Outsourcing governance capacity placed limits on what the central state was able to accomplish and extract.[101]

Indirect rule would later be replicated as a strategy of colonial governance.[102] Colonial powers that did not want, or could not afford, to invest the resources required to build an elaborate governance infrastructure in their territories chose to devolve authority to preexisting local powerholders vested with "traditional" or "customary" authority. Well-known examples from the British Empire include the Princely States of India and Lord Lugard's Nigeria. Even where British colonial governance was nominally direct, with a British official formally at the helm, the challenges of governing at long distance typically left lots of room for de facto local autonomy. This was conspicuously the case in the American colonies, where the British government lacked the resources and administrative capacity to exercise direct, day-to-day control, leaving the colonists to a considerable extent self-governing.[103] The growing capacity of colonial self-governance and the limited reach of the British state ultimately led to independence. Contemplating the imposition of greater direct rule by the Crown over the American colonies in the late seventeenth century, the Earl of Sandwich cautioned that "they are already too strong to be compelled."[104]

The same pattern of political development has been the progenitor of federalism in many contemporary states. Federal systems tend to emerge when an expanding state either lacks the power to fully subsume smaller, self-governing units,[105] or else lacks the motivation, because these smaller governments come with capabilities that the central state can put to good use.[106] Preexisting political units that possess the "infrastructural capacity" to "tax, maintain order, regulate society, and generally govern their societies" are often maintained as subsidiary governments even as they are absorbed into a larger state with a centralized government at its core.[107]

From the perspective of the center, then, indirect rule serves as a means of leveraging third-party governance capacity for the purpose of extending state power. From the perspective of the governed, however, indirect rule can also be a means of limiting central state power. Rather than building its own capacity, the central state comes to rely upon the resources and capabilities of decentralized units, which retain much of the infrastructural power of governance. Expansion out from the center is resisted by peripheral powerholders, who are loath to give up their own power and have accumulated enough of it often to get their way. Indirect rule initiated as a consequence of central state incapacity can become an ongoing cause.

By the time of the constitutional Founding, many Americans had come to appreciate the virtues of indirect rule and local autonomy as means of guarding against the predations of a central state, Anti-Federalists most of all. The lesson they took from the Revolution was that keeping governance and military capacity decentralized in the states was the surest safeguard against tyranny by a distant despot. Accordingly, the Anti-Federalist vision of constitutional federalism was centered on preventing the national government from "consolidating" the capacity of the states.[108] The national government would be denied a standing army of its own, making it dependent on state militias. Rather than allowing the national government to send hordes of its own tax collectors trampling through the country, it would be forced to rely on easily collectible customs duties at ports and, beyond that, state and local tax authorities.[109] State governments and courts would also do most of the work of implementing and enforcing federal law, eliminating the need to develop a federal administrative state or judiciary.[110]

This is, in fact, to a considerable extent, how federalism in the early Republic developed. States and localities retained primary regulatory authority over economic and family life and carried most of the weight of governance. Only in the late nineteenth century, when industrialization and an increasingly integrated national economy created demands for more centralized state power, did the national government begin to grow into primacy. The Progressive-Era creation of the first federal regulatory agencies, a central bank, and a national police force were the beginning of a sharp upward trajectory in the size and capability of the national government, accelerating through the New Deal and World War II, and continuing through the remainder of the twentieth century. A century of centralized state-building has come close to turning the original constitutional design of federalism on its head.

Still, the role of federalism in limiting the capacity of the national government is far from obsolete. States continue to command capabilities and resources—schools, police forces, and legal systems—that might otherwise be consolidated into the national state. And even as the federal government has taken on primary regulatory responsibility in more and more areas of policy, state and local governments continue to play a pervasive role in implementing federal regulatory programs. Such "cooperative federalism" arrangements remain a structurally necessary feature of American government because the national government, notwithstanding its nearly unlimited de jure power, still has limited de facto governance capacity and remains reliant on the resources of states and localities. As with other forms of indirect rule, cooperative federalism can be viewed as a "tool of national power."[111] But it can also be viewed as a structural arrangement that promotes both control and ongoing incapacitation of the national state. Theorists of contemporary federalism highlight how the modern system of cooperative federalism empowers states and localities to become "uncooperative," leveraging "the power of the servant" to exercise control over national policymaking.[112] At the same time, by substituting the outsourced service of states for in-house national capacity, cooperative federalism removes an incentive for yet greater national state-building.[113] Decentralization as a mechanism of central state incapacitation remains a living feature of the American political and constitutional tradition.

* * *

The same is true of incapacitation more generally. If the United States is at least a partially failed state, that is by ongoing constitutional and political design. Whether by deconstructing the administrative state or defunding the police, Americans continue to unbuild and incapacitate their state. As this chapter has tried to show, such strategies carry high costs. Still, where legal and political controls over the uses and users of state power are unavailing, and the downside risks sufficiently severe, the fail-safe of incapacitation might make second-best sense. Understood in this way, state incapacitation deserves a place alongside legal rights and political representation as one of the basic, time-honored tools of statecraft and constitutional design.

4
Rights and Votes

This chapter takes a closer look at the two basic methods of controlling state power available to those who are subject to it. As the previous chapter introduced, one approach is to lay down legal rules or rights limiting the permissible *uses* of state power. Call that the method of "rights." A second approach is to exercise political sway over the *users* of state power, by selecting who they are or by influencing what they do. Call that the method of "votes." These two methods of state control can be understood as alternative means for accomplishing the same ends. If the goal is to protect subjects, or particularly vulnerable groups of them, against abuses of state power, that can be accomplished in two ways. One is by legally disallowing state power to be used in ways that threaten their fundamental interests, using rights. Another is by politically empowering groups of subjects to protect their own interests by influencing what the state will or will not do, using votes.

This simple way of assimilating rights and votes will be jarring to constitutionalists, who have been acculturated to see the two as opposites. Constitutional rights are conventionally cast as extrapolitical limitations on the exercise of democratic political power. This understanding leads constitutionalists to see an inherent conflict between constitutional rights and democracy (or, when rights are enforced by courts, between "countermajoritarian" judicial review and majority rule). Even where rights and votes are not pitted against one another in constitutional thought, they are treated as categorically different phenomena. Disciplinary boundaries divide political and constitutional theorists, who tend to "think in terms of rights and equality," from political scientists and law of democracy scholars, who are more interested in "the organization of power."[1] The division between rights and votes also cuts through the middle of constitutional architecture. For purposes of doctrine, scholarship, and curriculum, the "structural" provisions of the constitution, which create the institutional framework for the organization and exercise of democratic political power, are separated from the rights provisions, which place limits on what can be done with that power.

Internationalists, for their own part, have been more prone to see political power and legal protections as working in parallel. As the previous chapter described, the legal prohibitions and obligations imposed upon states by and through international law can be understood as the global equivalents of "rights," legally regulating the uses of state power. And techniques of international relations—military, economic, and diplomatic—deployed to influence the political decisionmaking of states can be viewed as the analogue of "votes" in domestic democracy. Unlike their constitutional counterparts, however, internationalists do not see international law and international politics as deeply divided or opposed.

Quite the contrary, international law and politics are commonly understood to be combined and intertwined in statecraft, joint and substitutable strategies for protecting the interests of states and peoples against the threatening power of other states. States protect themselves and their populations against foreign conquest by means of international law prohibitions on aggressive war and also by means of military self-defense. Victims of human rights abuses appeal both to international human rights law and to powerful states capable of humanitarian military interventions. International trade regimes that were once the product of gunboat diplomacy have been increasingly legalized through treaties and treaty-based governance arrangements like the WTO, even while extralegal bargaining and power politics remain a conspicuous feature of economic dealings among states. Geopolitical conflict between the United States and China is channeled through legal disputes over trade and human rights as well as through the strategic use of foreign aid and the formation of military and economic alliances. The terminology of "lawfare"—meaning the use of international law to gain an advantage in armed conflict—nicely captures the more general continuity between international law and the military, diplomatic, and economic tools of international relations.[2]

Recognizing that international law can be a continuation of international politics by other means, legal scholars and political scientists have increasingly collaborated to better understand how the two kinds of regimes work together as both complementary and substitutable modes of interstate cooperation and constraint.[3] This research agenda seeks to explain why and under what circumstances international relations will become "legalized" or "judicialized," exploring the costs and benefits of managing state power through legal or political pathways.[4]

This chapter explores what might be learned about constitutional law and design by thinking of constitutional rights and democratic politics in this same way: as comparable tools for performing the same basic task of controlling state power. Recognizing that rights and votes can be functional substitutes raises the question of why political and constitutional actors in different circumstances might prefer one to the other, or particular combinations of both. This perspective also points to additional tools that might serve the same functional purpose as rights and votes in protecting against state power. The possibility of *exiting* state power, by means of decentralized government or outright secession, is considered at the end of this chapter; and the strategy of *balancing* power is the topic of the next one. But to start, there are rights and votes.

Rights or Representation

Rights and votes appear as functional alternatives in a broad range of settings in which state and governmental power threatens the interests of vulnerable groups of subjects. The collection of examples that follows serves to illustrate the ubiquity of the choice between the two mechanisms of protective control, as well as the array of institutional forms each can take. Beyond casting ballots in elections, the category of "votes" encompasses any form of representation or direct participation in processes of collective decisionmaking over how state power will be exercised, or any institutional or structural arrangement of those processes that better enables groups to influence outcomes. The category of "rights" incudes a wide range of substantive legal limitations on the permissible outcomes of collective decisionmaking processes and the uses of state power, including, in some contexts, affirmative entitlements to certain outcomes (i.e., positive, as well as negative, rights). Again, the key conceptual distinction is between the power to influence political outcomes and legal determinations of what those outcomes must (not) be. The key non-distinction, in each of the contexts that follows, is that both kinds of tools can be put to use for the same basic purpose of protecting against state power.

Constitutional Structure and Rights

The original designers of the U.S. Constitution were well aware of the functional similarity and substitutability of rights and votes. As they sought to build a more powerful centralized state, the Framers were concerned with securing the rights and liberties of citizens against oppression by and through government. As Chapter 1 previewed, however, many of the Framers were also convinced that direct protection by means of enumerated constitutional rights would be futile. So the original constitutional design was contrived to protect rights indirectly, by creating a system of democratic politics and structure of government that would safeguard the interests of vulnerable groups. The now-conventional distinction in constitutional law between rights and the structure of representative government obscures the fact that the original design of the Constitution relied primarily on structural arrangements to protect rights.[5]

To elaborate, Americans at the time of the Founding were concerned about two different types of potentially vulnerable groups. The first was the citizenry at large, who might be tyrannized or plundered by despotic federal officials. This would be the worst-case version of the agency problem created by representative government, and it was the primary focus of Anti-Federalist concern. The primary concern of the constitutional Framers, in contrast, was that the principal-agent relationship between constituents and their representatives would become *too* tight, allowing majorities to use state power to tyrannize minorities. As Madison explained, "In our Governments . . . the invasion of private rights is *chiefly* to be apprehended, not from acts of Government contrary to the sense of its constituents, but from acts in which the Government is the mere instrument of the major number of the constituents."[6]

In the view of Madison and other Framers, majority tyranny was not a problem that could be solved by constitutional rights. The essential problem was that countermajoritarian rights could not be backed by the "dread of an appeal to any other force within the community" more powerful than the very majorities who posed the threat. Possessing "the physical and political power" in society, majorities would always be free to disregard or override any rights standing in their way.[7] This is why Madison initially opposed adding a Bill of Rights to the Constitution. As he explained in a letter to Thomas Jefferson, "[E]xperience proves the inefficacy of a bill of rights on those occasions when its control is most needed. Repeated violations of these parchment barriers have been committed by overbearing majorities in every State."[8]

Convinced of the futility of parchment rights, the Framers took a different tack. If minority rights could not be protected directly, the structure of government might be designed in such a way as to protect them indirectly.

That design, as Madison conceived it, had several components. Insulating national officials from direct electoral accountability would select for the kinds of independent-minded leaders who would "possess most wisdom to discern, and most virtue to pursue, the common good of the society,"[9] and who would be "least likely to sacrifice [justice] to temporary or partial considerations" of the kind that might be pressed by self-serving majorities.[10] Shifting power to the national government of the extended republic would bring more political factions into competition with one another, making it more difficult for a stable majority coalition to capture the government and threaten minority rights.[11] As Madison put it, "[T]he society itself will be broken into so many parts, interests, and classes of citizens, that the rights of individuals, or of the minority, will be in little danger from interested combinations of the majority."[12] And then, as Madison went on to theorize, just as competition among a multiplicity of factions would prevent monopoly power in democratic politics, competition among the branches and levels of government would invite "ambition . . . to counteract ambition," checking and balancing despotic accumulations and assertions of power.[13]

In all of these ways, the structural design of government was supposed to create politically self-sustaining protections for the rights and liberties of citizens: votes would do the work of rights. In the words of Alexander Hamilton, "[T]he [structural] Constitution is itself, in every rational sense, and to every useful purpose, A BILL OF RIGHTS."[14] Even after acceding to demands for the actual Bill of Rights, Madison continued to believe that "[t]he only effectual safeguard to the rights of the minority, must be laid in such a basis and structure of the Government itself, as may afford, in a certain degree, directly or indirectly, a defensive authority in behalf of a minority having right on its side."[15]

Constitutional Protections for Slavery

Madison's belief would be tested by the political and constitutional controversy over slavery. From the Founding through the Civil War, Southern slaveholders looked to constitutional structure for protection of their right to own people as property. That was not a right that was explicitly included in the constitution. Madison, for one, believed that it would be "wrong to admit in the Constitution the idea that there could be property in men."[16] But another reason for excluding a right to own slaves followed from Madison's more general approach to constitutional design. Southern Federalists were convinced that "parchment guarantees for human bondage would not restrain a Northern majority committed to abolishing slavery."[17] The slaveholding South preferred to stake its fortune on the structural design of the federal government. Southerners expected that proportional representation in the lower house of Congress and the Electoral College, bolstered by the Three-Fifths Clause, would ensure Southern control of the House of Representatives and the presidency, empowering them to block any national movement toward abolitionism.

As history played out, however, the Founding bargain over slavery reflected a major miscalculation about the demographic future of the Republic. Northerners and Southerners alike had expected faster population growth in the South than the North, but in fact the opposite happened. The relative population and political representation of the North increased dramatically through the early decades of the nineteenth century, and by the late 1850s, the Northern white population was more than double the Southern white population, and Northern representatives had come to control the House.[18] Although a Southerner occupied the presidency for all but twenty-three of the seventy years of the antebellum Republic, the longer-term prospects of Northern dominance loomed there too.[19]

As Northern population and representation grew, the Senate became the last bulwark protecting slavery. To preserve their veto power in the Senate, Southerners relied upon a sectional balance rule, instituted as an unwritten understanding accompanying the Missouri Compromise, dictating that the North and South would maintain equal representation in the Senate even as new states were admitted into the union. During the several decades the norm was in effect, a relatively stable equilibrium was maintained, as states entered the Union in pairs and the security of sectional stalemate was preserved. Sectional balance thus became a quasi-constitutional substitute for the original constitutional bargain over slavery.[20] Only in the 1850s, when economically and politically viable opportunities for the expansion of slavery ran out and it became impossible to rebalance the Senate after the admission of California as a free state, did this political settlement unravel.[21]

Left politically vulnerable to a now-Northern-controlled national government, white Southerners sought additional constitutional protections for slavery. The possibility of a constitutional right to own slaves was once again considered, but then dismissed as inadequate on the familiar ground that parchment rights would be no match for a determined Northern majority.[22]

As white Southerners had long believed, "no paper guarantee was ever yet worth any thing, unless the whole, or at least a majority of the community, were interested in maintaining it."[23] In place of ineffective rights, Southern political strategists focused on structural defenses against abolitionist majorities.

Chief among these were the "concurrent voice" or "concurrent majority" arrangements advocated by John C. Calhoun. Inspired by the model of sectional balance in the Senate, Calhoun argued that

> [T]he adoption of some restriction or limitation which shall so effectually prevent any one interest or combination of interests from obtaining the exclusive control of the government . . . can be accomplished only in one way, . . . by dividing and distributing the powers of government [to] give to each division or interest, through its appropriate organ, either a concurrent voice in making and executing laws or a veto on their execution.[24]

Pursuant to this principle, Calhoun and his fellow Southern politicians advocated for a constitutional amendment creating a dual executive, comprising a Northern and a Southern president, each with veto power over national legislation, as well as likeminded reforms for balancing the Supreme Court between Justices from slaveholding and non-slaveholding states.[25]

The Madisonian premise of these proposals, and of Southern political thought more generally during the antebellum period, was that bolstering the representation and political power of white Southerners was a replacement for rights—a more effective means of protecting the fundamental interests of slaveholders.

Voting Rights and Civil Rights

The constitutional history of race after the Civil War substitutes a more sympathetic minority seeking protection for their rights by means of political representation. Martin Luther King memorably proclaimed, "Give us the ballot, and we will no longer have to worry the federal government about our basic rights."[26] As Dr. King well understood, political empowerment can serve as an effective shield against discrimination—and thus as an effective substitute for, as well as a means of securing, constitutional rights.

King's position on the sufficiency of the ballot was anticipated in congressional debates surrounding the Reconstruction Amendments and early civil rights laws. There the argument was made that a federal guarantee of political rights for Black people would empower them to secure civil rights through state and local political processes, without any need for further federal intervention.[27] While that prediction proved overly optimistic, the enfranchisement of Southern Black people, by means of the Reconstruction Act of 1867 and the Fifteenth Amendment, did lead to significant improvements in their civil and social status. The three Southern states with Black voting majorities at the time each enacted bans on racial segregation in public schools and places of public accommodation. Other Southern states equalized funding for black and white schools and eliminated bans on interracial marriage. As Black people also began to serve on juries and as police officers, Black citizens came to enjoy greater protection against violence and discrimination than they would experience in the South for another hundred years. All of these benefits disappeared with Redemption and the subsequent disenfranchisement of most Black people in the South in the 1880s and '90s.[28]

The Great Migration of Southern Black people to the North, where they were once again free to cast ballots, led to a surge in Black political power at the national level in the 1930s and '40s. The result was enactment of the first major civil rights policies by the federal government since Reconstruction, including President Truman's creation of a presidential Civil Rights Commission and a Civil Rights Division within the Department of Justice, and his 1948 executive orders forbidding segregation and discrimination in the Army and the federal civil service. Had Black people in the South been voting during this period, the results could have been even more dramatic. It is entirely possible, for instance, that fully enfranchised Black voters could have achieved school desegregation without *Brown v. Board of Education*.[29]

In reality, Black people in the Deep South only began voting in large numbers after the enactment of the 1965 Voting Rights Act. As Dr. King predicted, the results subsumed and exceeded what rights could have accomplished. Black voting power led to the enactment of antidiscrimination legislation and declines in discriminatory law enforcement, as well as improvements in municipal services and employment opportunities.[30] The instrumental relationship between Black political power and protection against discrimination became a central theme in judicial implementation of the Voting Rights Act. Courts have viewed voting rights as special because they are "preservative of other basic civil and political rights."[31] Acting on this understanding, the Supreme Court's foundational vote dilution cases focused on the (non)responsiveness of elected bodies to the interests of minority communities.[32] The Court would go on to justify its aggressive expansion of voting rights on the theory that enfranchising minority voters was a means of securing "nondiscriminatory treatment" with respect to "governmental services, such as public schools, public housing and law enforcement."[33] Even as the Court in recent decades has retreated to a narrower and non-instrumental focus on descriptive representation—electing Black representatives rather than protecting and advancing the interests of Black citizens—scholars and advocates have continued to emphasize the "protective" power of voting rights for minorities,[34] preserving King's vision of political representation as instrumental to equal rights.[35]

Rights as Representation Reinforcement

Madison's and Martin Luther King's idea of turning to democratic representation in place of rights finds its mirror image in constitutional law's *Carolene Products* (or "political process") theory, which calls for the judicial enforcement of rights to protect "politically powerless" groups.[36] Political process theory is premised on the idea that judicially enforced rights can compensate for deficits in political representation. In the first instance, *Carolene Products* calls for courts to repair the democratic process by fully empowering disenfranchised or politically disadvantaged groups, allowing them to exercise their fair share of political power. Failing that, courts are charged with protecting the interests of groups that remain democratically disadvantaged by applying rights. Rights protections are supposed to substitute for fair political representation.

Political process theory has served as a straightforward justification for protecting the rights of disenfranchised groups, such as Black people in the Jim Crow South. It has also been used to justify rights protections for groups that are formally enfranchised but arguably lack adequate political power for other reasons—racial minorities, women, and other classes that might suffer from political disadvantage owing to "prejudice against discrete and insular minorities"[37] or other structural barriers. In recent decades, constitutional gay rights litigation has featured political scientists offering expert testimony on the political power of gays and lesbians and debates among judges and

Justices about whether these groups are "politically powerless"[38] or, quite the opposite, "possess political power much greater than their numbers."[39]

In addition to protecting politically disadvantaged groups, political process theory is supposed to protect courts against the charge that rights-protecting judicial review is inherently antidemocratic, standing in the way of majoritarian political preferences. Political process theorists argue that rights enforcement on the *Carolene Products* model is actually in the service of democratic values. By breaking down barriers to political participation and protecting those groups who have been unfairly denied sufficient political power to protect themselves, judicial rights enforcement arguably contributes to both "the protection of popular government . . . and the protection of minorities."[40]

Comparative Constitutional Law

Looking beyond the United States, the choice between protecting minorities through political empowerment or through rights has been central to constitutional design in societies divided by enduring sociopolitical conflicts between ethnic or religious groups. In these "divided societies," the prospect of unfettered control over the state by a dominant group creates unacceptable risks of oppression. One solution has been the adoption of bills of rights and judicial review as checks on state power. Another solution has been to ensure that vulnerable groups possess enough political power to protect themselves through the processes of democratic decisionmaking and governance.[41] The latter approach is exemplified by the theory and practice of "consociational democracy."[42] The consociational model of democracy features institutionalized power-sharing among the major groups in society through structural arrangements like grand coalition cabinets, legislative proportional representation, and mutual veto power over important decisions.[43] In its emphasis on empowering minorities to block government actions that threaten their fundamental interests, consociationalism follows the logic of John C. Calhoun's concurrent voice proposals.[44]

The making of South Africa's post-apartheid constitution offers one vivid example of the choice between representation-based strategies like consociationalism and judicially enforced rights as mechanisms of minority protection. Under domestic and international pressure in the late 1980s and early 1990s, South Africa's dominant white elite began the process of sharing power with the previously excluded Black African majority. But South African whites had no intention of creating a system of unfettered Black majority rule. Intent on protecting white privilege against impending democracy, Prime Minister F.W. de Klerk and the ruling National Party (NP) pursued two strategies.

The first was to advocate for a power-sharing political structure on the consociational model.[45] Among other institutional measures proposed by De Klerk was a presidency that would rotate between white and Black leaders and a requirement of consensus among the major political parties for all important decisions, effectively creating a white minority veto. The 1993 Interim Constitution did, in fact, incorporate some measure of consociationalism, providing for executive power-sharing between the NP and Nelson Mandela's African National Congress (ANC) in a "government of national unity."[46] Ultimately, however, an essentially majoritarian democratic system prevailed.

Confronted with the inevitability of Black majority rule, the NP turned to a second strategy to protect their interests: rights and judicial review. Judicially enforced rights had been anathema to white elites during the apartheid era. But now, facing the prospect of becoming a permanent minority, the NP seized upon the position that constitutional rights and an independent judiciary to enforce them were necessary checks on the "dictatorship of a democratic majority."[47] Of particular importance to a group that was 15% of the population but owned nearly 90% of land and more than 95% of productive capital in the country was constitutional and judicial protection of property rights.[48] The ANC was understandably skeptical of a judicially enforceable bill of rights, viewing it as a likely means of entrenching the "property, privileges, power and positions of the white minority"—a veritable "Bill of Whites."[49] But ANC opposition eventually softened and rights prevailed.[50] The 1996 Constitution establishes a Constitutional Court with the power of judicial review and contains an extensive Bill of Rights. (The Bill begins, incongruously, by declaring itself a "cornerstone of democracy in South Africa."[51])

Other divided societies have wrestled with similar choices in designing their constitutions, considering both rights and votes as alternative means of protecting minorities and securing their consent to a new constitutional order. The 1950 Constitution of India, for instance, protects religious minorities through a robust array of rights. As in South Africa, the Indian Constituent Assembly also considered but ultimately rejected a set of consociational measures, including reserved legislative seats and representation in the cabinet. The Indian constitutional framers regarded rights protections as sufficient substitutes for these representational guarantees. As one representative in the Assembly explained: "'[W]hen we have passed the different fundamental rights which guarantee religious, cultural, and educational safeguards which are justiciable, . . . I feel that the presence of people belonging to certain groups [in the legislature] is not necessary.'"[52] But it is also possible to include both. The Dayton Peace Accords, which serve as the effective constitution for Bosnia and Herzegovina, incorporate the European Convention on Human Rights into domestic law while also creating consociational power-sharing arrangements among the major ethnic groups (including a three-person presidency consisting of a Serb, a Croat, and a Bosniak representative).[53]

Generalizing from a number of specific settings, scholars of comparative politics and constitutionalism have developed broader theories of democratization and rights premised on functional substitution. Daron Acemoglu's and James Robinson's influential account of the origins of modern democracies portrays the process of democratization as following a standard pattern. In a number of different countries, ranging from nineteenth-century Britain to modern South Africa, a small socioeconomic elite has been forced to cede political control over the state to an impoverished and oppressed majority that threatens revolution. Democratization, in the Acemoglu and Robinson view, comes only as a last resort. Elites respond to majoritarian demands for redistribution of wealth and opportunity first by repression, and then, if that fails, by offering concessions coupled with promises to enact and sustain progressive policies in the future. But these conciliatory guarantees of lasting redistribution and reform are not credible, because everyone understands that as soon as revolutionary unrest among the masses subsides the elites will have every incentive to renege. This is where democracy comes in. Broad-based enfranchisement means that the median voter, possessing decisive political power, will share the interests of the masses rather than the elites. Democratization thus creates a long-term commitment to policymaking in the interest of the majority. Consistent with Madisonian constitutional theory, votes serve as a more reliable replacement for guarantees of specific political outcomes.[54]

One of Acemoglu's and Robinson's illustrative cases is South Africa's transition to democracy. When Black Africans began to mobilize against the apartheid regime after World War II, the NP initially responded with violent suppression of demonstrations and the imprisonment of ANC leaders. Despite these measures, demonstrations, riots, and strikes became more widespread through the 1970s and '80s, resulting in large numbers of deaths, industrial shutdowns, and capital flight. The NP then attempted to buy peace through economic concessions such as legalizing African trade unions and removing restrictions on the occupations available to Black Africans. When the ANC refused to settle for these predictably temporary measures, the NP was finally forced to negotiate a transition to democracy.[55]

The South African case also features prominently in political scientist Ran Hirschl's provocative account of the proliferation of constitutional judicial review.[56] Like Acemoglu and Robinson, Hirschl sees a pattern of elites turning over political power to the masses through broad-based democratization. But in contrast to Acemoglu and Robinson's view of democratization as a commitment to redistribution, Hirschl highlights a "hegemonic preservation" strategy that elites have used to *resist* redistribution, even after ceding political power.[57] That strategy is to constitutionalize rights—particularly property and other free-market-friendly forms of rights—and to turn over enforcement to a politically independent judiciary disposed to share and protect elite interests. Thus, in Hirschl's telling, the South African constitutional settlement was a democratically veiled victory for white elites. Forced to hand over democratic control to the Black majority, they were able to preserve their economic dominance by securing judicial protection of their constitutional rights.[58]

Without attempting to reconcile these conflicting theories, it is enough to appreciate what they have in common: a view of political power and substantive rights or entitlements as substitutes. In Acemoglu and Robinson's account, democratic political power serves as a more reliable substitute for the egalitarian redistribution demanded by majorities. In Hirschl's account, judicially enforced rights substitute for the political power that elites have turned over to democratic majorities by blocking the same kinds of egalitarian redistribution.

How to Choose?

These examples illustrate how rights and votes can serve as substitutes for one another. But the examples also illustrate that political and legal actors do not view rights and votes as *perfect* substitutes. Notwithstanding their broad functional similarities, rights and votes come with somewhat different advantages, disadvantages, and domains of feasible implementation. Drawing on the cases surveyed above, the discussion that follows seeks to distill some of the generalizable differences between rights and votes that might bear on the choice between them.

Certainty Versus Flexibility

One fairly obvious conceptual distinction is that votes offer only probabilistic opportunities to prevail in influencing the outcomes of democratic decisionmaking, Rights, in contrast, can function as absolute "trumps" over democratic decisionmaking, dispositively determining, or preventing, particular outcomes.[59] Some things simply must, or must not, be done. Of course, not all rights are so absolute. Rights may be balanced against competing interests, subject to legislative override, aimed only at particular reasons or purposes for decisions, or underenforced.[60] Still, the potential of rights to guarantee their holders victories that would otherwise be up for grabs in the ordinary give and take of political contestation is a distinctive feature. Simply put, as compared to votes, rights create more *certainty* over outcomes.

For the same reasons, however, rights are also more rigid than votes. Votes offer a general currency that can be used by its holders to pursue a broad range of interests and can be redirected toward different interests over time. Rights, in contrast, function by prejudging political outcomes, taking some options off the table. Because rights must be specified in advance of collective decisionmaking processes, rights-based protections tend to be vulnerable to novel forms of evasion or oppression and subject to obsolescence when circumstances change. As compared to rights, votes offer greater *flexibility*.

Trade-offs between the certainty of rights and the flexibility of votes have been salient in a number of the constitutional decisionmaking contexts described above. Starting with the American constitutional Founding, one reason the Framers gave for preferring structural empowerment over rights was the practical impossibility of enumerating every right worthy of protection, now or in the future.[61] "[A]n enumeration which is not complete is not safe," Madison argued to the Virginia Ratification Convention, in opposition to a bill of rights.[62] Hamilton added the thought that even those rights that made the enumerated list might be impossible to express clearly or completely enough to guard against government wrongdoing: "Who can give [a right] any definition which would not leave the utmost latitude for evasion?"[63] Similar observations about the inflexibility of rights relative to votes recur throughout American constitutional history. For example, the priority placed by political process theorists on protecting vulnerable groups through votes rather than rights is partly explained by the worry that "[n]o finite list of entitlements can possibly cover all the ways majorities can tyrannize minorities."[64]

The inflexibility of rights is exacerbated when their permissible forms are constrained by conceptual conventions and administrative imperatives placing limits on the types of interests that can be protected. In some settings, rights are understood to attach only to individuals or particular types of groups; to protect "negative" liberties as opposed to guaranteeing "positive" entitlements; or to stem only from certain justifications or sources of authority. On account of these and other kinds of limitations, rights claims are typically restricted to a subset of the potential political outcomes that might be pursued using votes. For example, a further reason the U.S. Framers had so little use for rights was that government misbehavior, as they comprehended it, was not reducible to individual rights and liberties. The Framers' constitutional aspiration was that "government pursue the common good, not that government pursue the common good by means that did not interfere with individual autonomy."[65] For another example, voting rights for Black Americans yielded a broader range of instrumental benefits than could be encapsulated, or replaced, by conventional forms of rights—higher welfare benefits, improvements in municipal services, increases in government employment, and the like.

Rights can be made more flexible. In American constitutional law, courts routinely adjust the scope and content of textually fixed rights to new circumstances. Conceptual limitations on the kinds of interests or entitlements that can be provided through the vehicle of rights also vary in their restrictiveness. Many constitutions around the world extend rights to affirmative entitlements. The South African Constitution, for example, includes positive rights to adequate housing, food and water, healthcare, education, and social security.[66] The South African Constitution, among others, also includes social and cultural rights, aimed at ensuring the ability of minority communities to preserve their languages and ways of life.[67]

Still, there remains an inherent difference between the flexibility of political power and the relative rigidity of rights. Democratic decisionmaking institutions operate perpetually because members of the political community cannot anticipate or adequately inform themselves about all of the decisions that will arise in the future and decide up front how those decisions should (not) be made. For the same reason, there is a limit to the number and specificity of decision-outcomes, or rights-based prohibitions on acceptable outcomes, that can be enumerated in advance. The informational barriers to ex ante specification of issues and outcomes inevitably creates a flexibility gap between rights and votes. That gap will tend to make votes the preferred tool for protecting against ongoing, unpredictable, shape-shifting threats stemming from state power.

But the relative flexibility of votes must be weighed against the relative certainty of rights. Groups that have numerous or shifting interests across a broad range of issues, or interests that cannot be reduced to the form of rights, will be drawn to votes. But groups that care intensely about protecting fundamental, enduring, and non-negotiable interests may do better with rights. If Martin Luther King were outvoted, he would still have *Brown v. Board of Education* to fall back on. Critics of political process theory worry that even fair political representation may not be enough to protect against racial or religious discrimination; and they argue that such prohibitions should not be viewed as commensurable or exchangeable with other values and interests in the pluralist marketplace of ordinary politics.[68] If the inflexibility of rights makes them less useful for some purposes, the certainty and fundamentality of their protections brings a security that votes cannot match.

Strength

Another dimension of difference between rights and votes was previewed in Chapter 1: democratic decisionmaking structures are commonly believed to be stronger—more durable, deeply entrenched, and reliably constraining—than rights. This is why constitutional Framers like Madison dismissed rights as merely "parchment barriers," in contrast to presumably more efficacious structural guarantees of democratic empowerment. Recall the similar belief of Southern whites that the structural safeguard of representation would provide greater security for slavery than any kind of rights-based protection. Contemporary constitutional theorists tend to agree, describing the constitutional structure of government as "substantially self-executing" and "inspir[ing] reflexive conformity,"[69] in contrast to constitutional attempts "to freeze substantive values by designating them for special protection in the document," which are perceived to have been "ill-fated, normally resulting in repeal, either officially or by interpretative pretense."[70]

Scholars of comparative constitutional design take a similar view, warning against heavy reliance on judicially enforced rights to protect minorities on the Madisonian grounds that determined majorities will undermine rights-based protections by politicizing or overriding purportedly independent courts.[71] Political scientist Donald Horowitz advises constitutional designers in divided societies like South Africa to invest in electoral structures that will encourage political appeals across ethnic groups rather than relying upon "fragile" judiciaries susceptible to political manipulation or override.[72] Acemoglu and Robinson's theory of democratization as a credible commitment to redistribution is likewise premised on the assumption that votes will be more difficult to take away than substantive entitlements—that elites will have a harder time undoing broad-based enfranchisement than retracting redistributive commitments.

As Chapter 1 noted, the greater strength and stability of democratic structure has been more widely assumed than well-explained.[73] Madison and his fellow Framers dismissed rights as parchment barriers but offered no good reason why we should expect constitutional structure to be any stronger than parchment. If powerful majorities could override rights, why could they not also subvert the separation of powers or ignore the Electoral College? Why would the antebellum slaveholders who worried that their property rights would be ignored by abolitionists not be equally worried that an abolitionist majority would evade or overwhelm their Senate bulwark? Acemoglu's and Robinson's theory of democratization likewise offers no explanation for why elites who have the power to cut off redistribution to the demobilized masses do not also have the power to dispense with democracy.

But even without really knowing why—or, in fact, whether—votes are stronger and more durable than rights, many legal and political actors apparently *believe* this to be true. In settings where vulnerable groups are convinced that decisionmaking structures and processes will prove more resilient and protective than rights, that will be a reason for them to prefer votes.

Democracy

Commitments to democracy create normative and functional imperatives that will place different limitations on votes and rights. Voting is off the table for groups viewed as outsiders to the political community. While these groups are often denied rights as well, there may be more room for negotiation on that front. Within the political community, voting arrangements that make minorities politically powerful enough to protect their core interests are often rejected for violating principles of political equality or undermining the workability of democratic governance. Rights, for their own part, may run up against democratic demands for majority rule. The discussion that follows critically elaborates these commonly invoked democratic determinants of the suitability of rights and votes.

A threshold barrier to using votes to protect vulnerable groups is the perceived eligibility of these groups for inclusion in the political community. Regardless of how vulnerable they might be to American state power, foreigners are not permitted to vote in U.S. elections. As a matter of democratic theory, there is a case to be made that everyone in the world whose interests might be affected by a democratic decisionmaking process should have a voice in that process.[74] Political scientist Robert Dahl once questioned why people in Latin America were not permitted to vote in U.S. elections, given the enormous consequences of American politics for their lives.[75] But for practical purposes, the prospect of "giving virtually everyone everywhere a vote on virtually everything decided anywhere" has remained a nonstarter.[76] Perhaps someday there will be a world government that really does allow people all over the planet to participate in all of the governmental decisions that affect their interests.[77] But until that day, political influence over the power of foreign states will likely remain limited to the channels of international relations.

One predictable response to the restricted scope of direct political participation in international politics is to substitute legal rights. Political theorist Robert Goodin has proposed that people whose interests have been adversely affected by the action of states in which they have no vote should be entitled to rights-like claims for redress.[78] Along the same lines, the perceived impossibility of extending meaningful democracy to the EU or to global governance organizations has led legal theorists to call for "compensatory" rights-based protections.[79] Closer to home, constitutional lawyers have invoked political process theory to argue that nonresident aliens who have been subject to indefinite detention by the U.S. government as enemy combatants in the war on terrorism should receive rights protection to compensate for their lack of political representation.[80]

Even where there is no bar on democratic participation, an obvious limitation of votes as a means of protecting minorities is that, in systems of majoritarian democracy, minorities will seldom have enough votes to prevail. Rights, on the other hand, can be used to protect small groups and even isolated individuals against majoritarian decisionmaking. As John Stuart Mill said of free speech rights, "If all mankind minus one, were of one opinion, ... mankind would be no more justified in silencing that one person, than he, if he had the power, would be justified in silencing mankind."[81] Democratic decisionmaking processes are not designed to empower a lone individual against the rest of mankind.

Larger minorities may have somewhat better prospects democratic politics, though how much better depends on the design and dynamics of the political process. Madison's model of pluralist politics in a large republic—featuring shifting coalitions of multiple, diverse factions, none of which dominates as a stable majority—offers one optimistic scenario.[82] Minorities capable of forming coalitions with other groups through pluralist bargaining may be able to exercise considerable power. But interest group pluralism does not always live up to the Madisonian ideal. John C. Calhoun believed that Madisonian pluralism in American democracy had been destroyed by the emergence of political parties, which had pulled the various factions into hardened coalitions. Calhoun's response to Madison was that majoritarian democracy would inevitably evolve along these lines: "If no one interest be strong enough, of itself, to obtain [a majority], a combination will be formed between those whose interests are most alike."[83] And once a majority coalition becomes dominant, Calhoun warned, they will have no reason to temper their tyranny of vulnerable minorities.[84]

The prognosis for Madisonian pluralism becomes even less promising when competing groups are constituted along relatively stable lines of race, religion, or class, and permanent minorities risk perpetual exclusion from power and lasting oppression. Calhoun viewed the economic and ideological division between North and South over slavery in this light. De Klerk's NP in South Africa took a similar view of their prospects under democratic rule by a Black African majority. Writing about the contemporary United States, law professor and democratic theorist Lani Guinier contrasts the ideal of "Madisonian majorities"—shifting coalitions that take turns in power—with the reality of deep racial divisions and racial-bloc voting patterns that render whites in many jurisdictions a "self-interested majority [that] does not need to worry about defectors."[85]

Calhoun, de Klerk, and Guinier all propose the same solution: a democratic decisionmaking structure that selectively boosts the political power of the vulnerable minority group. As we have seen, Calhoun and de Klerk advocated for systems of consociational democracy that would empower minorities to exercise an effective veto over government action. To the same end, Guinier suggested cumulative voting systems and legislative supermajority voting requirements that would enable racial minority groups to elect some of their candidates of choice and block actions that affected their most important interests.[86] As these proposals demonstrate, democratic decisionmaking processes can be designed in such a way as to empower even small minorities to protect themselves. Even a lone dissenter can be protected by a collective decisionmaking rule requiring unanimity. Indeed, Calhoun and Guinier both held up the example of criminal juries as a prototype of consensus-based democracy and a caution against pure majoritarianism when critical interests are at stake.

In practice, however, the kinds of special representation or decisionmaking power that are necessary to protect minorities' fundamental rights and interests will be viewed in many democratic contexts as normatively objectionable or functionally unworkable. Calhoun struggled to defend his concurrent majority model against the charge that it would produce some combination of deadlock or minority rule.[87] In the South African constitutional debates, as well, objections to consociationalism were lodged both on principled grounds of the right of the Black majority to rule and on the prudential ground that a minority veto would lead to gridlock.[88] The jury unanimity requirement, idealized by Calhoun and Guinier among others as a paradigm case of consensus decisionmaking and minority inclusion, has long been criticized for generating high decision costs, hung juries, and dubious acquittals. In some settings, the costs of providing minorities with sufficient democratic power will be deemed too high for votes to be a viable option. In these settings we should expect rights to play a greater role.

In other settings, however, it is rights that will be ruled out by democratic demands. As Chapter 2 described, commitments to popular sovereignty and self-government often cast doubt upon the legitimacy of constitutional limitations on democratic decisionmaking. Democratic concerns are exacerbated where unelected judges are authorized to interpret and enforce rights, giving rise to the "countermajoritarian difficulty" of justifying judicial review. It is not hard to see the basis for such concerns in Hirschl's portrayal of courts in South Africa and other countries enforcing constitutional rights to protect the wealth and privilege of entrenched elites against democratic majorities. Of course, structures of voting and representation that give minorities more than their proportionate share of decisionmaking power might also be seen as presenting countermajoritarian difficulties. Countermajoritarianism as a democratic problem arises on both sides of the line between rights and votes. Nonetheless, concerns about the threat to democracy posed by judicially enforced rights have been an especially salient feature of constitutionalism.[89] All else equal, democracy is on the side of votes.

Recognition and Acculturation

Beyond their instrumental consequences for securing political outcomes and power, rights and votes are thought to send different messages about membership in the political community and to have different effects on the development of moral personality and political culture. The two devices are also thought to contribute to the essentialization or integration of minority groups in different ways.

Enfranchisement and political participation are associated with a distinctive set of social and moral benefits. One is the expressive value of inclusion in the political community. Voting is understood to be emblematic of "social standing" and "civic dignity."[90] Dating back to Aristotle, exclusion from political life has been viewed as a form of dishonor or denigration,[91] and inclusion is a large part of what has distinguished full-fledged members of the polity from slaves and second-class citizens.[92] Securing the ballot thus represents an important victory in the "politics of recognition."[93] In addition to the expressive benefits of voting, political participation has long been viewed through a civic republican lens as a crucial ingredient of individual character formation and communal solidarity.[94] John Stuart Mill believed that participation in democratic governance fostered self-reliance and public-spiritedness.[95] Other democratic theorists have emphasized the benefits of active political participation in developing additional qualities that are valuable for both the individual and society, including personal autonomy and responsibility, reflective moral agency, and deliberative capacity.[96]

Rights in the liberal tradition have sometimes been understood to reflect and further some of the same values as votes—autonomy, free will, rational agency, and equality.[97] But liberal rights have also been subject to a long-standing line of criticism focused on their expressive meaning and constitutive effects. Karl Marx famously argued that "none of the so-called rights of man goes beyond egoistic man, . . . withdrawn behind his private interests and whims and separated from the community."[98] In the Marxist view, liberal rights reflect and perpetuate a culture of selfishness, present a false picture of isolated human nature, and paper over inequalities of economic and political power with empty guarantees of formal equality.[99] Critical and communitarian theorists on both the left and right have continued to echo these themes.[100] In addition to promoting selfishness and hindering solidarity, rights are blamed for heightening social conflict, inhibiting dialogue, undermining responsibility, and generating a culture of passivity, dependence, and entitlement.[101]

Differences along these lines have been cited as reasons for preferring votes to rights in a number of settings. Election law scholars argue that protecting racial minorities with rights invites the depiction of these groups and their members as "objects of judicial solicitude, rather than as efficacious political actors in their own right."[102] Whereas bolstering the political influence of racial minorities has been viewed as a valuable form of "empowerment," affording minorities "the status of insiders" and the opportunity to enjoy "the sense of efficacy or agency associated with being in charge" that majorities routinely enjoy.[103] Theorists of comparative constitutional design likewise see political power, in contrast to judicially enforced rights, as "an essential vehicle for distributing the expressive resources . . . of recognition."[104]

Another commonly drawn contrast between rights and votes surfaces in contexts involving racial, ethnic, or religious divisions. A recurring warning in such settings is that institutionalizing group differences in democratic politics will undermine social stability by entrenching lines of division, exacerbating inter-group conflict, and impeding the development of a shared national identity. In the debates surrounding the design of the South African Constitution, for example, one reason for rejecting consociational power-sharing arrangements was to avoid reinforcing and exacerbating ethnic divisions and conflicts.[105] Rights, on the other hand, tend to be viewed as more conducive to breaking down group identity and facilitating assimilation. Scholars of comparative constitutional design tell us that in societies where race, religion, ethnicity and language [have] served as the grounds of political identity and political division," bills of rights can encourage citizens "to abstract away from" these divisive categories "and to instead view themselves as citizens who are equal bearers of constitutional rights."[106]

These recognitional and acculturative features of rights and votes capture categorical tendencies, but the particular forms of each tool also make a difference. Votes may be more validating and empowering on average than rights, but Lani Guinier views "tokenistic" approaches to enhancing minority representation in much the same way as Marx viewed rights, substituting a superficial kind of formal equality for meaningful group power.[107] As for rights, the claim that traditional, liberal rights promote atomistic individualism does not extend to second- and third-generation rights to the redistribution of economic and social resources, which might have the opposite effect.[108]

The effects of rights and votes on racial and other group divisions and conflicts also seems highly dependent on the particular forms taken by these instruments in different contexts. A system of consociational power-sharing among racial groups in South Africa may entrench and exacerbate racial divides, but the same might be true of the group-differentiated, or "polyethnic," rights found in the South African Constitution.[109] In the United States, rights-based affirmative action programs have triggered concerns about racial essentialism and balkanization in much the same way as racial gerrymandering of electoral districts for the purpose of increasing political representation. Votes, too, can take different forms. As an alternative to consociationalism, comparative constitutional designers have advocated vote pooling systems as a less divisive and essentializing method of minority empowerment. These systems allow voters to choose their group identifications and encourage parties and politicians to appeal for support across ethnic group lines[110] Guinier's cumulative voting proposal is meant to work in much the same way, empowering minorities while ameliorating racial essentialism and separatism.[111]

Rights And Votes as Complements

The primary thrust of this chapter has been to show how rights and votes function as substitutable tools for controlling the state, inviting more finely grained comparisons of their relative competencies, costs, and benefits. But it is also important to recognize that rights and votes can function as *complements*. Political power can increase the value of rights, and the other way around.

Most obviously, political power may be needed to create, preserve, or enforce rights.[112] In order to secure rights in the first place, the beneficiaries usually must possess some measure of social or political power. But if that power dissipates over time, rights may become vulnerable to repeal or nonenforcement. Groups relying on rights protection might be well-advised, therefore, to retain sufficient political power to protect their rights. In the American system of constitutional law and politics, it is well-understood that contentious rights—whether to economic liberty or to abortion—may be sustainable only so long as a majority of sympathetic Justices can be maintained on the Supreme Court. If the beneficiaries of these rights do not have sufficient political power to prevail in the politics of presidential elections and judicial appointments, their political defeats may become constitutional ones.

This is not to say that rights without votes will always be worthless or nonexistent. As Chapter 1 described, politically dominant groups may choose to respect the rights of the less powerful, if not out of any intrinsic commitments to fair play then owing to instrumental calculations about reciprocal treatment should power relations shift. And even in the absence of literal votes or other forms of de jure political power, minorities may retain enough de facto power to protect, or even expand, their rights. After ceding democratic political power to the Black African majority, white elites in South Africa maintained a credible threat of taking their wealth and leaving the country.[113] In the United States, formally disenfranchised civil rights demonstrators secured the 1964 Civil Rights Act through a sustained campaign of direct action.[114] But the point remains that genuinely powerless groups in many contexts will have a precarious hold on rights.

Switching the causal arrow of complementarity, rights themselves can be a significant source of political power. Some rights increase power by serving as rallying points for collective political action. Recall from Chapter 1 that Madison saw a useful role for rights in serving "as a standard for trying the validity of public acts, and a signal for rousing & uniting the superior force of the community" against misbehaving government officials.[115] And indeed, throughout American history, political movements in support of racial minorities, women, gays and lesbians, and other disadvantaged groups have rallied around claims of constitutional and statutory rights.[116] Rights can be instrumental to the effective exercise of political power in other ways, as well.[117] Meaningful democratic participation may be impossible without a robust right to freedom of political speech.[118] Rights to property, freedom of association, and free exercise of religion may be conducive to political organizing, lobbying, and campaigning. Antidiscrimination rights may be necessary to protect minorities against forms of oppression that sap their political power.[119]

Rights and votes can operate as complements at an ideological or expressive level, as well. Recognition of the agency, capacity, or equality of members of a group may lead to both political enfranchisement and recognition of rights. Legal and political philosopher Jeremy Waldron argues that to grant someone a right is to recognize their capacity for disinterested moral deliberation and autonomous decisionmaking, which should also qualify them for democratic participation.[120] A similar connection between the rights and political capacity of Black citizens was asserted during debates over the 1866 Civil Rights Act. Congressional Republicans made the case that "equality with respect to civil rights was premised on a theory of humanity that entailed equality with respect to political . . . rights."[121] Reversing that relationship, Reva Siegel argues that we should carry over the enlightened understandings of women's autonomy reflected in the Nineteenth Amendment to our thinking about women's equality rights under the Fourteenth Amendment. If women's suffrage signified "equal citizenship" and an end to their subordination in the household, Siegel argues, those same constitutional commitments should lead us to embrace rights protecting the equality of women in other spheres.[122] Where rights and votes rest on the same foundational values, we might expect to see them expand (or contract) in tandem.

A Third Option: Exit

Albert O. Hirschman famously juxtaposed two general strategies available to mistreated members of organizations: "voice" and "exit."[123] As applied to the vulnerable subjects of state power, both rights and votes give effect to Hirschman's concept of voice; both are means of influencing state behavior and improving the treatment of its subjects. Hirschman's alternative of exit points to another option for dealing with oppressive state power: fleeing it.[124] Federalism and other systems of decentralized governance effectively permit groups to escape the authority of a centralized state by claiming autonomy over certain issues. Secession and complete political independence are more extreme versions of the same basic strategy.[125]

In a number of the settings discussed in this chapter, subjects seeking to protect themselves against state power have considered exit as an alternative to voice. The original design of the U.S. Constitution and Bill of Rights relied heavily on protecting state and local institutions of self-government to guard against national tyranny—a self-conscious substitute for substantive rights.[126] Constitutional federalism has also substituted, or served as a backstop, for votes. If antebellum Southerners were unable to control national policymaking over slavery through their stronghold in the Senate, they could escape it by invoking self-determination and states' rights.[127] The South's ultimate attempt at secession took the exit strategy a step further. In other parts of the world, as well, constitutional designers concerned with protecting ethnic and religious minorities look to federalism and partition alongside representation and rights.[128] In the case of South Africa, in addition to power-sharing in the national government and rights protection, white elites pushed hard for federalism as a further constitutional safeguard against democratic dominance by a Black majority.[129]

Viewing exit alongside rights and votes as alternative strategies for protecting vulnerable groups against state power raises the question of why such groups, or constitutional designers, might prefer one approach to the others. An assessment of the relative advantages and disadvantages of exit might begin with the same set of considerations that were induced to differentiate rights and votes.

Exit and autonomous decisionmaking combine the flexibility advantages of votes with the certainty advantages of rights. Like political representation, federalism and secession afford groups ongoing and adaptable control over a broad slate of issues, not limited to pre-specified rights. At the same time, groups who comprise a dominant majority in their own (subsidiary) government possess not just some influence over political outcomes but decisive control. The trade-off is that the resulting political autonomy is limited in domain. In exchange for control in their own jurisdiction, groups give up any voice in the decisionmaking processes of other decentralized jurisdictions, even when their interests will be affected. Antebellum white Southerners who demanded local control over slavery had little recourse when abolitionist majorities in other states used their own autonomy to attack slavery from the outside, by helping enslaved people escape or by suffocating the slave economy by banning expansion into the territories.[130]

With respect to democratic demands, territorial governance creates a threshold hurdle for any attempt at decentralization or division. The potential for constituting self-governing political communities is limited to groups of viably self-sufficient size who are, or can become, geographically concentrated within the boundaries of an available territory. Where it is possible, federalism, like other strategies to bolster the political power of minority groups, tends to increase the transaction costs of governance. The antebellum system of constitutional federalism rendered the national government nearly impotent by empowering the South to block any assertion of national power, even in policy areas with no direct connection to slavery.[131] In the South African constitutional context, the ANC and its allies, "with an agenda for economic and social development that would require a strong and effective central government... were deeply suspicious of federalism."[132] Of course, secession further increases the transaction costs of cooperative governance among separate states by requiring international rather than intrastate agreements.[133]

Along the dimension of strength, the Founding view of federalism as a relatively secure structural safeguard has continued to hold sway. In the context of American constitutionalism, federalism is generally believed to provide a stronger and longer-lasting barrier against threatening political forces than judicially enforced rights—serving not merely as a parchment barrier but as part of the durable structure of government. The same is true in other contexts. For example, in much the same way as Acemoglu and Robinson view democracy as a more reliable commitment to redistribution than rights or entitlements, contemporary theorists of "market-preserving federalism" make the case that government decentralization is a more reliable method of *preventing* excessive redistribution than property rights.[134] Secession might be an even stronger safeguard, assuming state borders are more difficult to transgress than intrastate boundaries.

Finally, federalism can be compared to rights and votes in its recognitional and acculturative effects on minority groups and their relation to the broader polity. Making a minority group a controlling majority in its own jurisdiction would seem to provide a form of recognition and empowerment more meaningful than mere enfranchisement in the broader polity.[135] On the downside, like consociational governance in divided societies, federalism has the potential to entrench racial and ethnic divisions, exacerbate conflict, and undermine national unity.[136] Proponents of nationalism and assimilationist integration view ethnicity-based decentralization as a step in the wrong direction. On the other hand, giving minorities effective control in some districts or policy domains may actually diminish the salience of group identity by replacing intergroup with intragroup contestation.[137] And even if that fails, federalism may be the only means of preventing outright secession.[138]

No doubt there is more to say about the costs and benefits of exit in comparison to rights and votes as strategies for protecting against state power, and about the ways these different strategies might fit together. For now, though, perhaps it is enough to close with a final, unifying observation. While exit is usefully understood at the constitutional level as a strategy for managing state power, the sovereign state itself can be viewed as a kind of exit strategy. Recall from Chapter 2 that the Westphalian framework for the international order of sovereign states was conceived as a solution to religious conflict, permitting different sects to segment and self-govern.[139] To this day, much of the value attributed to state sovereignty is tied to its role in shielding self-governing peoples from external state power. From the international perspective, then, the state itself serves as a substitute for the rights and votes of its citizens.

5
Balancing Power

This chapter focuses on another time-honored political and legal strategy for controlling state power. Starting from the premise that "power can only be controlled by power,"[1] political theorists and practitioners of statecraft have long pursued the strategy of managing state power by multiplying it, pitting multiple Leviathans against one another in a self-limiting competition for power. Controlling state power by marshaling the countervailing power of other states has long been the basis for the "balance of power" approach to international relations. From Thucydides to Hobbes to Henry Kissinger, the premise that the stability and peace of the international order depends on the balance of powers among rival states has been at the center of international thought.[2]

The balance of powers idea has been carried over into constitutional thought. Casting the different branches and units of government as power-seeking entities pitted against one another in a contest of "[a]mbition . . . counteract[ing] ambition," constitutionalists since Madison have converted the international balance of powers into a system of "checks and balances" internal to the state. In much the same way that a hegemonic state will be constrained by rivals in the international arena, constitutionalists have reasoned, tyrannical power-grabs by one branch of government will be countered and contained by rival branches. The result, in the constitutional arena as in the international one, is supposed to be a self-enforcing equilibrium of checked and balanced power kept safely within bounds.

In the real world, however, the dynamics of constitutional politics have never matched these predictions. When a demagogic president wields dangerous power, we are supposed to be able to rely upon Congress to push back. But the recent case of President Trump is entirely typical of what tends to happen instead. As has become the norm in Washington politics, the battle lines during the Trump presidency were not between Congress and the White House, but between Democrats and Republicans. Notwithstanding two well-founded impeachments, most Republican legislators remained loyal to their co-partisan president and defended him against Democratic attacks. Even as Trump tried to overturn the results of a democratic election by rallying his supporters to attack the Capitol, most Republican members prioritized partisan loyalties over the threat to Congressional power, democracy, and even their own lives. Perpetually disappointed by the failure of political reality to conform itself to constitutional theory, observers puzzle over these apparent breakdowns of the Madisonian system. In the words of a frustrated Democrat serving as the lead House Manager in the first Senate impeachment trial of Trump, "If the GOP fails to stand up to Trump's unconstitutional act, we will have moved dangerously from a separation of powers, to a mere separation of parties."[3]

The persistent triumph of partisan over institutional loyalties is not the only blind spot in the constitutional vision of balanced power. Invoking Madison's maxim that "the accumulation of all powers . . . in the same hands . . . may justly be pronounced the very definition of tyranny,"[4] American constitutional law has maintained "a deep and enduring commitment to separating, checking, and balancing state power in whatever form that power happens to take."[5] Even the most minor innovations in the structure of government—bearing on the president's authority to remove the head of an agency or make a recess appointment—are scrutinized for their effects on aggrandizing executive power or upsetting the executive-legislative power balance. Yet other seemingly more significant power imbalances in the American political system fly entirely under the constitutional radar. Consider, for example, the increasing concentration of economic and political power in the hands of wealthy elites and business interests, with the consequence that "the preferences of the vast majority of Americans . . . have essentially no impact on which policies government does or doesn't adopt."[6] In light of the Madisonian imperative to guard against potentially tyrannical accumulations of power, a naïve observer might expect that the usurpation of democratic political power by a "moneyed aristocracy" would be a matter of some constitutional concern.[7] In constitutional law as it currently stands, however, even concentrations of power so extreme as to threaten democracy somehow pass the Madisonian maxim in the night.

What, then, is the point of the constitutional balance of powers? In the international realm, the balance of powers among states is supposed to preserve peace and provide security by preventing a powerful state from attacking and conquering its weaker neighbors. But there is no obvious analogy when it comes to the branches of the national government, which are unlikely to take up arms and go to war against one another.[8] Is there some comparable danger that the constitutional version of balancing powers is supposed to guard against? If so, it has never been clearly identified by constitutionalists.[9] For longer than two centuries, American constitutional law has been obsessed with balancing government power, but to no obvious end.

To understand the source of constitutional law's confusion, we need to return to the international balance of power among states—and before that, to Hobbes.

Controlling Power with Power

Developing the analogy between states in the international arena and persons in the state of nature, Hobbes saw both as possessed of "a perpetual and restless desire of power after power, that ceases only in death."[10] While Hobbes's natural persons manage to escape the power-driven war of all against all by leaving the state of nature and subjecting themselves to Leviathan, states are left in their own state of nature, an anarchic international arena, in which they must continue their life-or-death struggle for power. In Hobbes's resonant description, Leviathans face off "in the [] posture of Gladiators; having their weapons pointing, and their eyes fixed on one another; that is, their Forts, Garrisons, and Guns upon the Frontiers of their Kingdomes; . . . which is a posture of War."[11]

The Hobbesian vision of states as "unitary actors who, at a minimum, seek their own preservation and, at a maximum, drive for universal domination," and of the international order as a lawless forum for competition and conflict among these power-hungry Leviathans, remains the basis for realist theories of international relations.[12] Realists also follow Hobbes in taking a surprisingly optimistic view of the prospects for states in this situation. Recall Hobbes's hope that the "misery, which accompanies the Liberty of particular men [in the state of nature]" need not follow for states and their people.[13] Hobbes's reasons for thinking this might speak to differences between Leviathans and natural persons.[14] Realists have their own theory of why the international state of nature need not be a war of all against all. The possibility of peaceful coexistence among states, in the realist view, is based upon what they see as the systemic tendency of the international order toward a "balance of power." Driven by the imperatives of self-interest and survival, realists maintain, states will defend themselves against the threatening power of rivals by bolstering their own power or by forming coalitions to protect themselves against coercion or conquest. In a well-functioning system of balanced power, no state can become dangerously dominant. Even in the absence of a super-Leviathan to keep order, the uncoordinated, self-serving motivations of states might yield the collectively beneficial result of peace and security for all.

Constitutional thought has proceeded on a parallel track. The domestic-facing state, like the international-facing one, has long been portrayed as a power-hungry Leviathan. Hobbes describes the kings who seek to defend and expand their power by waging war against other states as taking a similar approach to their subjects: "Kings, whose power is greatest, turn their endeavors to the assuring of it at home by laws, [just as they do] abroad by wars."[15] What is to prevent a Hobbesian king, unconstrained by any hierarchical superior, from exercising despotic power over his subjects? One long-standing answer to that question, embraced by constitutionalists from Ancient Greek through the present, is the creation of countervailing powers.[16] For modern constitutionalists, that has meant the separation of powers between and among government bodies. Kingly power might be checked by an independently powerful parliament, which might itself be controlled not just by the power of the Crown but by the internal division of power between separate chambers, as well as by courts and other government institutions. Understanding the British constitutional system in this way, Montesquieu famously theorized that, in designing constitutions that will be effective safeguards against misrule, "power should be a check to power."[17]

Embracing this idea, the designers of the U.S. Constitution took it as an axiomatic "truth confirmed by the unerring experience of ages, that every man, and every body of men, invested with power, are ever disposed to increase it, and acquire a superiority over every thing that stands in their way."[18] Proceeding from this Hobbesian premise, the Framers followed the principle of "power checking power"—and the practice of international relations realism[19]—in attempting to create a constitutional structure that would pit power-seeking governors against one another. In Madison's famous exposition, dividing state power among the legislative, executive, and judicial branches of the federal government, and between the federal government and the states, was supposed to allow "[a]mbition [to] counteract ambition." Once "those who administer each department" are given "the necessary constitutional means and personal motives to resist encroachments of the others," Madison explained, ongoing competition for power among the branches and units of government would serve to keep them safely within constitutional bounds.[20] The result would be an equilibrium of checked and balanced power that would prevent tyranny and preserve liberty.

This Madisonian theory of perpetual power competition generating checks and balances within the constitutional structure of government continues to serve as a foundational premise of American constitutionalism. In the domain of separation of powers, the central concern of courts and theorists continues to be the risk posed by self-aggrandizing branches of government intent upon seizing power for themselves and encroaching upon their rivals—tempered by the optimistic hope that interbranch competition for power will produce a self-sustaining system of checks and balances in which an imperial president will constrain a runaway bureaucracy, and both together will be checked and balanced by a legislative branch jealously guarding its own power. The constitutional law and theory of federalism similarly suppose that an imperialistic national government intent on consolidating all power for itself will be checked and balanced by state government deploying the "political safeguards of federalism" to defend their own domains. In the constitutional system of government as in the realist world of international relations, power-mongering Leviathans perpetually threaten hegemony and tyranny, but also prevent it when a balance of power prevails.

Competition or Cooperation?

Internationalists and constitutionalists have moved this far in the same direction. But internationalists have gone in other directions, as well. From the Melians in Thucydides to Immanuel Kant to Woodrow Wilson, international relations idealists and cosmopolitans have emphasized the possibility of cooperation rather than competition among states. That possibility appears to have been borne out in the post–World War II era, as realist predictions of perpetual conflict among rivalrous states have increasingly run up against the reality of burgeoning international cooperation through treaties and treaty-based governance organizations such as the United Nations, the European Union, and the World Trade Organization.[21] Recognizing that "a Hobbesian 'war of all against all' does not usually ensue" among states in the international arena, contemporary theorists of international relations have been driven to offer alternative explanations of state behavior that can make better sense of the more cooperative political dynamics that often seem to prevail.[22]

One type of explanation, offered by international relations institutionalists, maintains the realist assumption of states as unitary, self-interested, rational actors but emphasizes that shared policy goals and the possibility of mutual gains from trade and other collaborative arrangements will often create cooperative rather than conflictual political dynamics.[23] In the realist world of survival-of-the-strongest, what matters is the relative power and resources of states, and competition among them is necessarily zero-sum. Institutionalists, in contrast, make room for the possibility that states are interested in absolute, not just relative, gains and will pursue mutually beneficial forms of coordination and cooperation (including, as we saw in Chapter 1, through regimes of international law).[24]

Another approach to explaining state behavior poses a more conceptually fundamental challenge to the realist model. Rather than treating states as the interest-bearing units of behavioral analysis, internationalists increasingly have trained attention on the domestic political processes through which state interests are formed. Contemporary "liberal" models of international relations emphasize that states are not personified actors with interests or wills of their own; instead, states "represent some subset of domestic society, on the basis of whose interests state officials define state preferences and act purposively in world politics."[25] Because the interests and influence of domestic constituencies differ among states, liberals argue, it is a mistake to assume that all states will be driven by the same motivations in their international behavior. Instead, we should expect states to pursue different "interpretations and combinations of security, welfare, and sovereignty preferred by powerful domestic groups enfranchised by representative institutions and practices."[26] Where the internal interests of states diverge, we should expect conflict; but where these interests converge, we should expect cooperation.

The basic premise of liberalism seems difficult to dispute: what else would drive state behavior other than the preferences and power of the people who control what the state does? Realists need not disagree. If power and security are widely shared interests among the populations of states, or if other domestic goals can only be achieved through power politics at the international level, then it may be methodologically convenient simply to attribute realist interests to states as such. From this perspective, Leviathan serves as a useful fiction, or shorthand. But the Leviathan model becomes misleading when state interests and behavior deviate from realist assumptions of incessant power-competition among inherently rivalrous states. Observing patterns of peaceful and constructive cooperation among states that realism cannot explain, theorists of international relations have made progress in developing more realistic explanations of state behavior.

Constitutional law, in contrast, has never questioned the veracity or limitations of its own crude version of realism. From Madison through the present, constitutional law and theory has simply taken for granted that the branches and units of government behave like Hobbesian states in a posture of war, perpetually driven to "aggrandize" their own power at the expense of rivals.[27] Seldom have constitutional lawyers and theorists paused to ask *why* we should expect government bodies to behave in these ways. Madison seems to have followed Hobbes and the realist tradition in personifying political institutions, imagining that each department of government would have a "will of its own,"[28] and specifically, a self-interested will to power.

As many internationalists have come to appreciate, however, states and governments do not really have their own wills. Their behavior is a product of the wills of the people who control what they do—government officials and their constituents. Officials and constituents do compete for political power. They do so by organizing themselves in political parties, interest groups, and other coalitions, and competing in democratic elections and politics to advance their positions and policy agendas. What constitutional lawyers and theorists have failed to appreciate, however, is that these lines of competition align only haphazardly and coincidentally with the power of government institutions. Officials and constituencies care about institutional power contingently and instrumentally, seeking to increase the power of institutions that they control or that share their policy goals and to decrease the power of institutions controlled by different interests or possessing different policy goals. But none of the relevant wills are directed toward aggrandizing the power of government institutions as such.

This is why the Madisonian model consistently fails to predict political dynamics on the ground. Consider, for example, the "separation of parties" observation that competition and cooperation between the branches of government are driven primarily by patterns of partisan control.[29] Especially during periods like the present, when the two major parties are ideologically coherent and highly polarized, partisan identification is typically the single best proxy for political interests and agreement or disagreement. As a result, the willingness of Congress to cooperate with the White House in enacting the president's preferred policies, to confirm the president's appointees, to impose oversight and investigations on the executive branch, and much else depends heavily on whether the two branches are controlled by the same party. When Republicans control Congress and a Democratic president sits in the White House, no one should be surprised when Congress rejects the president's legislative agenda, or when Democrats in the House and Senate encourage the president to take unilateral action with respect to environmental regulation, immigration reform, or humanitarian intervention. No one should be surprised when a Republican-controlled Senate votes not to remove a Republican president who has been impeached by a Democratic-controlled House. Yet all of these dynamics fly in the face of the Madisonian model of separation of powers, featuring checks and balances among rivalrous branches.

More realistically, we might recognize (with only slight exaggeration) that the constitutional structure of government has not one separation of powers system but two. When control over the branches of the national government is divided by political party, party lines track branch lines and partisan competition is therefore channeled through the branches, generating a simulacrum of Madisonian rivalry, competitive ambition, and checks and balances. When government is unified by political party, however, intraparty allegiance tends to trump interbranch competition, and separation of powers dynamics become cooperative rather than conflictual. The branches engage with one another not as realist rivals but in the manner of cooperative states pursuing convergent interests.

Similar dynamics prevail in the political and constitutional system of American federalism.[30] States serve as sites of partisan mobilization and political contestation along lines that cut across and bear no consistent relationship to the division of power between the states and the national government. Contra Madison and the "political safeguards" perspective on federal–state relations, there is no political motivation that unifies states to oppose expansions of federal power or to support decentralized government across the board. Political and legal challenges to assertions of federal power by a Democratic president or Congress will predictably come from the governments of Red states, while Blue states will militate for greater assertions of federal power pointed in their preferred policy directions.[31]

The general point is not specific to parties. What matters are the underlying interests that political actors are striving to advance through government institutions. Even where these interests do not divide along party lines, there is no reason to expect them to divide along institutional lines—and therefore no reason to expect institutional conflict or competition. The same is true when relatively undivided interests are advanced by political actors through all of the relevant government institutions at once. In the context of federalism, for example, the secular growth of national power over the course of the twentieth century was largely a product of broad-based political demands for federal regulation stemming from the integration of the national economy and the country's expanding international role. This wholesale transformation of constitutional federalism was not a matter of federal hegemony overwhelming state resistance but of widely shared interests channeled through state and federal political processes alike.

The development of the modern administrative state tells a similar story. The growth of the administrative state since the Progressive Era represents a massive delegation of power from the legislative to the executive branch. This seismic shift in the separation of powers defies all Madisonian logic. Far from jealously guarding its power against rivalrous encroachments, Congress apparently has been happy to turn over much of its legislative power to the executive branch. But this Madisonian mystery turns out to have a straightforward solution. Like international cooperation among states, delegation furthers the shared interests of the branches in getting things done. That has been especially true during times of unified government, including the New Deal and Great Society periods, when it is broadly the *same* things the two branches want done. Even when government is divided, however, the branches have responded to the least-common-denominator democratic demands of their shared constituencies for effective governance—demands that have increasingly outstripped the legislative capability of Congress and can only be met by cooperatively harnessing the efficacy and expertise of the executive branch. At the same time, more cynical incentives to delegate stem from the shared, self-serving political strategies of professional politicians, who have learned to use delegation to take credit for getting things done without needing to agree on precisely how those things will be done, or incurring blame when they are done in ways that turn out to be costly or unpopular.[32] Either way, the simple explanation for delegation and the rise of the administrative state is that members of Congress care more about pleasing their constituents and getting reelected than they do about aggrandizing the power of their branch of government.

The same separation of powers dynamic has contributed to the rise of the imperial presidency. Especially during times of emergency—the 9/11 attacks, the 2008 financial crisis, the COVID pandemic—Americans have come to expect that Congress will largely abdicate power to the president: "Legislative action during emergencies consists predominantly of ratifications of what the executive has done, authorizations of whatever it says needs to be done, and appropriations so that it may continue to do what it thinks is right."[33] The same has been increasingly true in ordinary times. Against the background of Congressional gridlock and passivity, presidents have been driven to act unilaterally, stretching their legal authority to deal with pressing problems like climate change, immigration, and gun violence.[34] If this counts as a presidential power-grab, it is not one that Congress has much contested. To the contrary, legislators are usually more than content to let the president lead, especially if it is in their preferred policy direction. And even if the president's direction is dispreferred, the political-support maximizing strategy for members of Congress is more often to criticize from the sidelines rather than risk taking responsibility themselves. Those who fear presidential dictatorship would be well-advised not to rely on the Madisonian ambitions of Congress to rebalance power.[35]

What the Madisonian vision of the structural constitution has missed is that the political actors who decide how power will be allocated among government institutions have no intrinsic interest in the power of government institutions. Officials and democratic-level constituencies pursue power by furthering their own political interests, not the interests of government bodies. And government bodies lack interests, or wills, of their own. The Hobbesian-Madisonian model of power-seeking Leviathans reflects a fundamental misunderstanding of how states and governments behave—and of what states and governments really are.

Balancing Whose Power?

That misunderstanding calls into question what the constitutional version of balancing power is supposed to accomplish in the first place. Here again, the contrast with the international relations theory is illuminating. The point of balancing power among states in the international realm is, ultimately, to benefit the people who live in those states, providing them with security and protecting them against conquest and hostile rule. The same is true of the Westphalian system of sovereign states more generally. As Chapter 2 described, the sympathetic purpose of state sovereignty is to empower self-determining communities of people to pursue their common interests and conceptions of the good free from external interference and conflict.

As Chapter 2 also highlighted, the Westphalian system is imperfect. Groups of people who are oppressed or disempowered within their states gain nothing from state sovereignty. The Tutsi victims of the Rwandan genocide and black South Africans during the Apartheid regime were only harmed by the sovereignty of their states. An international order based on cooperation among states will work to the benefit of groups whose interests are well-represented at the level of states but leave out groups whose interests are ignored. The rise of populism in recent years has been attributed to a globalized (neo)liberal order that serves the interests of economic elites at the expense of workers.[36] Balance of power competition among states on the realist model protects state populations that share an interest in security against threats posed by other states, but it does nothing to protect groups who are threatened by their own states (like the Uyghurs in China) or who are under the protection of no state (like the Palestinians). The simple point is that the statist system of international law serves the interests of just those groups who are empowered to act through states.

Presumably, the constitutional system of balance of power is supposed to work in a similar way. The point of balancing the power of the legislative and executive branches is not to protect Congress or the White House against conquest but, as Madison suggested, to protect citizens against tyranny. But the relationship between balancing power at the level of government institutions and protecting groups of citizens in the constitutional context is obscure. Madison himself seemed concerned with balancing power at both levels. His admonition against allowing "the accumulation of all powers . . . in the same hands" was meant to apply both to groups of citizens and the metaphorical hands of representative institutions: "The accumulation of all powers, legislative, executive, and judiciary, in the same hands, whether of one, a few, or many, and whether hereditary, self-appointed, or elective, may justly be pronounced the very definition of tyranny."[37] Madison's *Federalist No. 51* account of the balance of powers among the branches and units of government was about balancing power at the institutional level. Madison's *Federalist No. 10* was about balancing power among groups of citizens, hypothesizing that pluralist political competition among the numerous "factions" in democratic politics on a national scale would make it more difficult for any one of them to become dangerously dominant.[38] What Madison left unexplained is how, if at all, these two goals relate to one another. Is there any connection between the distribution of power among government institutions at the level of constitutional structure and the distribution of power among democratic factions or interests?

Some constitutional systems intentionally create such a connection. There is a long history, and in some parts of the world a present reality, of designing constitutional structures of government intentionally for the purpose of balancing power among specific political interests. This is the ancient theory of mixed, or "balanced," government, dating back to Plato, Aristotle, and the Roman Republic. Mixed government is motivated by the idea that "the major interests in society must be allowed to take part jointly in the functions of government, so preventing any one interest from being able to impose its will upon the others."[39] Most commonly this has meant ensuring independent representation for the rich and poor—as in representation of the aristocracy and the plebians in the Roman Senate and assembly; or representation of nobility and commoners in the British House of Lords and House of Commons. A more modern form of mixed government, described in Chapter 4, is consociational democracy. Proceeding on the same, mixed government principle, consociational constitutions institutionalize power-sharing among conflicting groups in society through structural arrangements that guarantee each group a voice in, and typically an effective veto over, government actions that affect their vital interests. As the leading theorist of consociationalism puts it, the overarching goal "is to *share, diffuse, separate, divide, decentralise, and limit* power"[40]—or, more simply, to balance it.

The traditional conception of mixed government was a source of ambivalence for the U.S. constitutional Framers. Many admired the British constitutional model of ensuring independent representation for different social orders.[41] Yet by the time of the Founding, most Americans had rejected formal class divisions. The hope and expectation was that the American republic would replace fixed, hereditary status categories with cross-cutting distinctions too various to be "embodied in the government."[42] In such a society, mixed government would be both impossible and unnecessary.

At the same time, Founding-era political thought had fixated on a very different, more recent, line of thought relating to separation of powers that had grown out of conflicts between the Crown and Parliament in seventeenth-century England. As theorized by the great "oracle" Montesquieu,[43] the idea was that three qualitatively different types of government power—legislative, executive, and judicial—should be assigned to separate government departments, and administered by different personnel. This sense of separation of powers has nothing to do with the mixed government idea of creating concurrent or shared powers among competing groups, or with Montesquieu's corresponding idea that "power should be a check to power." As the British system exemplified, mixed government could be accomplished by representing groups in a single, omnipotent branch; checking the power of conflicting groups and interests in society did not depend on multiplying branches of government.[44]

The U.S. constitutional scheme of separation of powers is a peculiar mash-up of Montesquieu's two ideas.[45] Following the advice of functional separation, the Constitution assigns the three different types of government power to three structurally distinct branches of government. Oddly, however, the Constitution then proceeds to sacrifice the supposed benefits of functional separation by giving these branches a set of "checks and balances" over one another, preventing unilateral action and requiring mutual cooperation to accomplish the tasks of governance. This is the legacy of mixed government, power checking power—except now substituting branches of government for the social and political interests whose power is supposed to be at stake. As Gordon Wood describes, "Americans had retained the forms of the Aristotelian schemes of [mixed] government but had eliminated the substance, thus divesting the various parts of the government of their social constituents."[46] Attempting to combine two different design strategies, the constitutional Framers failed to accomplish either one.

The failure of the constitutional design to give effect to mixed government was immediately evident. Recognizing that the branches of government had been disconnected from any social group or interest-based constituency, many at the Founding were confused about how the power of the national government would be checked and balanced. Alexander Hamilton worried at the Convention:

> If government [is] in the hands of the *few*, they will tyrannize over the many. If (in) the hands of the many, they will tyrannize over the few. It ought to be in the hands of both; and they should be separated. . . . Gentlemen say we need to be rescued from the democracy. But what the means proposed? A democratic assembly is to be checked by a democratic senate, and both these by a democratic chief magistrate. The end will not be answered—the means will not be equal to the object.[47]

Anti-Federalist critics of the Constitution were equally perplexed. As Patrick Henry put it, "To me it appears that there is no check in that government. The President, senators, and representatives, all, immediately or mediately, are the choice of the people."[48] The Federal Farmer aptly dismissed "the partitions" between House and Senate as "merely those of the building in which they sit: there will not be found in them any of those genuine balances and checks, among the real different interests, and efforts of the several classes of men in the community we aim at."[49]

Madison's convoluted attempts to rationalize the constitutional design encapsulate the confusion of American constitutional thought to this day. In Madison's telling, the threat of political oppression by a dominant group or class—the motivation for mixed government—is replaced by the threat of a "legislative department . . . everywhere extending the sphere of its activity and drawing all power into its impetuous vortex."[50] Rivalrous groups whose power might be balanced in a well-designed system of mixed government are replaced by "the interior structure" of the national government, which might be "so contriv[ed] . . . as that its several constituent parts may, by their mutual relations, be the means of keeping each other in their proper places."[51] In the manner of class politics, these branches are to be pitted against one another in a competition for power, creating a stable equilibrium in which "[a]mbition . . . counteract[s] ambition."[52] But no longer to any apparent end: if there is no connection between the power of the branches and the power or protection of groups or interests in society, then it is hard to see why we should care about the institutional balance of power.

Befuddled by what the Madisonian design was supposed to accomplish, contemporaries like John Adams charitably or optimistically concluded that the Framers must have meant to create mixed government in accordance with the traditional model—institutionalizing a class divide between the aristocracy and the masses by providing separate legislative chambers for each, mediated by an independent executive power.[53] And indeed, some of the Framers had hoped to accomplish exactly that. Appalled by the prospect of popular majorities controlling the entirety of government and committed to the belief that the country should be run by "the rich and well born,"[54] a number of Federalists had advocated for a bicameral legislature on the model of the British Parliament, with an upper house representing wealthy property owners.[55] Even after losing on that issue, some continued to hope that Senators not subject to direct election and chosen from among the elites would represent their class interests.[56] But at least formally, the constitutional structure of government that emerged from the Convention called for each of the branches to be homogeneously democratic, representing an undivided American people.

Another failed attempt at mixed government interest-balancing in the constitutional design was directed at the sectional divide over slavery. As Madison reminded his fellow delegates in Philadelphia, "the great division of interests in the United States ... did not lie between the large and small states. It lay between the northern and southern" states, and this division came "principally from the effects of their having, or not having, slaves."[57] Invoking the mixed government principle that "every peculiar interest whether in any class of citizens, or any description of states, ought to be secured as far as possible," Madison proposed at the Convention that the structure of government be designed to provide Northern and Southern states with a mutual "defensive power" to protect their distinctive sectional interests.[58] Madison's initial proposal was that one branch of the national legislature be apportioned according to states' free populations while the other be apportioned according to total population, with slaves and free persons counting equally.[59] Even after that proposal was rejected, the hope remained that proportional representation in the House and the Electoral College, coupled with the three-fifths compromise for counting slaves, would be sufficient to secure Southern control over the House of Representatives and the presidency. On the assumption that the greater number of Northern states would have control over the Senate, each section would hold a mutual veto over the other, locking in a balance of power on the issue of slavery.[60]

As Chapter 4 described, however, this plan broke down when the population and political power of the North grew much faster than expected, threatening Southern control of the House and White House. The failure is revealing of what the constitutional design left out. Missing a hard-wired system of mixed government, the constitutional separation of powers did nothing to protect minorities like Southern slaveholders from a majority that could take control over *all* the branches of the national government and exercise absolute power.[61] Lasting security could be found only in the kinds of consociational arrangements sought by John C. Calhoun, which would have properly implemented mixed government by "dividing and distributing the powers of government [to] give to each division or interest, through its appropriate organ, either a concurrent voice in making and executing the laws or a veto on their execution."[62] But this would require "mak[ing] the several departments the organs of the distinct interests or portions of the community,"[63] which is precisely what the constitutional design did not do. The constitutional separation of powers provides for checks and balances among the branches and requires "concurrent majorities," such as the dual House and Senate majorities needed to enact legislation. But there is no linkage between the branches and any of the underlying social and political interests that might need representation and protection.

Or at least no *necessary* linkage. As the Founding bargain over slavery anticipated, there will be periods of time during which different institutions are predictably controlled by different interests and consequently display divergent policy preferences. Everyone understands today that when Democrats control the White House and Republicans control the House and Senate, policy outcomes on many issues will turn on the relative power of the president and Congress, and proponents of more stringent environmental regulation or permissive immigration policies will prefer that the relevant policy decisions be made in the White House. But absent the kind of hard-wiring between institutions and interests created by consociational structures, institutional preferences will be contingent on shifting patterns of partisan control. As soon as a Republican president occupies the White House, proponents of progressive environmental and immigration policies will prefer that power be reallocated to a more sympathetic decisionmaker.

To be sure, there have been periods as long as decades when, owing to the vagaries of politics, certain interests have had relatively stable control over institutions and for that reason could be reliably empowered or disempowered through shifts in the separation of powers or federalism. For participants in antebellum contests over slavery or the race-related controversies of the civil rights era, the interest-level stakes of federalism were clear. So, too, were the consequences of activist judicial review by the ideologically predictable runs of the Taney or Warren Courts. During the forty-year period when Democrats controlled the House of Representatives or the twenty-year period when Presidents Roosevelt and Truman sat in the White House, the partisan stakes of separation of powers were similarly transparent. Beyond enduring patterns of partisan control, some structural arrangements predictably favor political agendas aligned with the interests of a particular constituency or political party. Multiplying veto points in processes of legislative decisionmaking—whether through the Senate filibuster or activist judicial review—broadly disadvantages groups with more ambitious legislative agendas, including the modern Democratic party.[64]

But still the point remains: pursuant to the American constitutional design, the balance of power among institutions is connected only contingently and coincidentally to the distribution of power among political interests. As a consequence, the political actors who decide how power will be allocated among government institutions have no intrinsic interest in the power of these institutions. Only insofar as the distribution of institutional power has predictable effects on the relative power of competing democratic interests will it make any difference to these actors. Behind a constitutional veil of ignorance as to the constellation of interests that will control the relevant institutions, the structural balance of powers will be mostly a matter of indifference.

That is why institutional loyalty in American politics is so fickle. It is a commonplace observation that positions in political and constitutional debates over institutional power frequently "flip-flop," depending on which political party or coalition controls the relevant institutions.[65] Proponents of expansive presidential power become critics of the imperial presidency when a president of the opposite party moves into the White House. The Senate filibuster is an indispensable safeguard of stability and fairness when our preferred political party is in the minority but becomes an atavistic impediment to democracy when that party becomes the majority. Those who disagree with Supreme Court decisions on the substantive merits (including dissenting Justices) brand these decisions as activist and antidemocratic, while applauding (or authoring) no less activist or antidemocratic opinions when they have the votes. What is commonly cast as hypocrisy is in fact the perfectly rational behavior of political actors who care primarily about advancing their partisan and policy agendas and only derivatively and strategically about the power of government institutions.

Which, finally, brings us back to the question of why the balance of powers among the branches or levels of government should matter so much to American constitutionalism. The entire edifice of structural constitutional law, separation of powers and federalism, is oriented around policing the power of the presidency, Congress, administrative agencies, and the national government as a whole, with the aim of preventing these institutional actors from aggrandizing themselves at the expense of their rivals, or accumulating too much power and upsetting the constitutional balance. But to what end? What, exactly, would be so bad about a system in which one political institution possessed all of the power of the state?

Perhaps it would help to imagine what would happen to the American constitutional system if the presidency and judicial review were eliminated altogether, as well as any limitations of constitutional federalism, concentrating all power in the legislative branch. Would this be "the very definition of tyranny"? Actually, it would be England. This is roughly how the British Westminster model of government works, vesting nearly unconstrained power in Parliament, and therefore in the party that controls Parliament at any given time. Political scientists and comparative constitutionalists have long debated the advantages and disadvantages of the Westminster system as compared to the U.S. presidential system.[66] But no one equates parliamentary governance with tyranny; and it is far from obvious why the concentration of powers in Congress (or the presidency or the national government) would be any more tyrannical.

Why anyone should worry about imbalances of power at the level of government institutions in the American constitutional system remains a mystery. The idea of balancing power as a mechanism for permitting groups with deeply divergent interests to live together peacefully makes perfect sense in the context of mixed government and consociational democracy—just as it makes at least imperfect sense in the context of realist power balancing in international relations and the Westphalian system of sovereign states. What constitutional law hopes to accomplish by way of balancing the power of government institutions that have been hollowed of interest-based constituencies and hence rivalries is much harder to discern.

A more straightforward concern for constitutional law would be the mixed government one of balancing power at the level of groups in society. Madison was right to recognize the constitutional imperative of "guard[ing] one part of society against the injustice of the other part,"[67] preventing the "tyranny of the majority" over an oppressed minority, or the tyranny of a commanding minority over the rest of society. Unfortunately, as we have seen, his constitutional design of balancing power at the level of government institutions was not a solution to this problem (or, really, to any other problem). Balancing power between the president and Congress, or between states and the national government, does nothing to ensure that power will be balanced between religious sects, racial groups, Democrats and Republicans, or the rich and poor.

This has left structural constitutional law with no resources for addressing the most glaring power imbalances in American politics and society. It is why the accumulation of all power in the hands of the rich, for example, does not register in constitutional law as any kind of tyranny at all. It is also why constitutional law is at a loss during periods of party-unified government, when the minority party is shut of power entirely and checks and balances disappear. Belatedly recognizing that the constitutional separation of powers does nothing to prevent economic elites, dominant parties, or other powerful factions from taking control of all the branches of government and tyrannizing their rivals, constitutional scholars have begun to look longingly back on the mixed government tradition.[68] But the kinds of constitutional reforms the mixed government model would recommend—redesigning one chamber of the U.S. Congress to make it reliably represent the interests of the non-wealthy,[69] or "balancing" the Supreme Court by political party[70]— would require radical changes to a constitutional structure that was designed to balance power only at the institutional level. Constitutionalists concerned about the balance of power at the level of social groups and political interests—the balance of *democratic* power—will need to look beyond the structural constitution.

Balancing Democratic Power: Rights and Votes, Redux

And in fact, constitutional law has looked beyond the structural constitution. As Chapter 4 described, the primary tools deployed by constitutional law to protect vulnerable groups against oppression through the state are rights and votes. What is missing from the constitutional jurisprudence of rights-based protection and democratic empowerment, however, is the kind of overarching commitment to balancing power and preventing domination that has been misdirected to the structural constitution. The remainder of this chapter sketches how the American constitutional system might be beneficially reshaped by redirecting the balance of power imperative to the parts of constitutional law—rights and votes—where it could actually do some good.

Starting with votes, one of the primary purposes of democracy has always been precisely that of balancing power among groups in society. To be sure, democracy might serve other purposes, as well—contributing to political legitimacy, the production of knowledge, and the expressive recognition of equal citizenship, among other goods. But the most basic function of democracy is to distribute power more broadly and equally among social groups. Throughout history, groups that are politically powerless in systems of monarchy, oligarchy, and dictatorship, have pressed for democracy as a means of gaining a share of control over state power.[71] Once democracy is established, moreover, the ideal of equalizing political power continues to serve as a guiding principle in the design of electoral rules and institutional structures.[72] Precisely what "equality" of political power should be understood to mean and how it should be operationalized are notoriously difficult and contested issues,[73] but most would agree, at a minimum, that democratic institutions should be designed to prevent one group in society from unfairly dominating another.[74]

The American constitutional and statutory law of democracy has at times emphasized that goal, providing vulnerable groups with the democratic power needed to protect themselves against domination through the state. In particular, the Supreme Court's most ambitious interventions in the electoral realm have been aimed at enfranchising and securing representation for previously excluded Black voters. From ensuring access to the ballot to requiring majority-minority election districts, the Court in the context of race has at least sometimes been self-consciously concerned with the mixed government agenda of "regulating, rationing, and apportioning political power among . . . groups."[75] Many scholars have urged the Court to more fully embrace that agenda, arguing that achieving a fair distribution of "the ability of groups of voters to exercise political influence" should be central to the law of democracy across the board.[76] Lani Guinier, for instance, has advocated for a pluralist model of the law of democracy that would make it possible for racial and other minorities to "share in power" with other groups and secure a fair share of political outcomes reflecting their interests. Guinier calls this approach "Madisonian"—invoking *Federalist No. 10*'s vision of balanced powers among groups in society.

For the most part, however, the Court in election law cases has maintained a narrow focus on individual rights that makes it easy to ignore systemic questions about how electoral rules and institutions affect the power of social groups and political interests.[77] The Court's approach to the regulation of money in politics is more representative of how the law of democracy tends to work in this regard. Political spending is arguably the most flagrant source of inequality in American democracy, permitting business interests and wealthy individuals to leverage their economic power into disproportionate political power. Far from seeking to balance democratic power in this domain, the Court has fixated on protecting the rights of the rich to spend as an exercise of free speech rights, categorically rejecting "the concept that government may restrict the speech of some elements of our society in order to enhance the relative voice of others."[78] Balancing political power in this context has been deemed unconstitutional.

Even where the Court has been most attuned to the distribution of democratic power, in the context of race, the Court's ambitions have been limited. The law of democracy ensures that racial minority voters can cast ballots and elect candidates of their choice, but it stops well short of guaranteeing meaningful political power to secure their substantive interests. Guinier thus describes the legal quest for minority representation as mere "tokenism."[79] What matters, Guinier and others argue, is that minority groups be empowered to influence actual policy outcomes.[80] As Nick Stephanopoulos puts the point:

> If blacks seem not to be satisfied with (mostly) uninhibited access to the polls and (close to) proportional representation, this is because they should *not* be content with these achievements. What really matters in a democracy is getting policies enacted that correspond to people's views. And on this front, blacks still have a long way to go. Their opinions—on vital issues like crime, welfare, and housing—are too often ignored by elected officials when they conflict with whites' preferences.[81]

Glaring gaps between formal representation and functional political power exist not just for Black Americans but for other groups as well. Recall the political science evidence that nearly all influence over government decisionmaking is possessed by economic elites, whereas "mass-based interest groups" and "average citizens" have "little or no" actual influence over policy outcomes,[82] with the result that "America's claims to being a democratic society are seriously threatened."[83] The demise of democracy in American seems like it should be a rather pressing problem for the constitutional law of democracy. But even the most ambitious reformers of that body of law have become resigned to the conclusion that balancing democratic power—in the meaningful sense of control over what government does or does not do—is "too ambitious a goal for election law to achieve."[84]

Groups left lacking in democratic power are remitted to constitutional rights protections. As Chapter 4 described, the idea that rights can make up for an absence of political power is the basis for the *Carolene Products*-political process approach to judicial review, calling on courts to protect "politically powerless" groups. In theory, such an approach might lead courts to use rights to replicate the policy outcomes that would have prevailed in a "perfected" democratic system, one in which power was fairly distributed among all groups and interests. In practice, however, the Court's agenda has not been nearly so ambitious. Rights protections have been granted only to a handful of groups, chosen on grounds that are dubiously related to real-world political powerlessness. And courts have done little more for those groups than eliminate blatantly discriminatory laws and policies, never attempting to recreate the full set of outcomes that balanced democratic power might have produced.

Thus, under constitutional equal protection doctrine, racial minorities, women, and (more recently) gays and lesbians have been the primary beneficiaries of rights protection. But the Court has done little to explain why these, and only these, groups count as "politically powerless" in American democracy.[85] The political process case for protecting disenfranchised Blacks in the Jim Crow South, or women before they were enfranchised by the Nineteenth Amendment, is fairly straightforward. But as the Court has extended the *Carolene Process* rationale to include groups that are formally enfranchised, including racial minorities and women in the present day, the criteria for identifying powerless groups have become obscure. Courts have based assessments of political power or its absence on an inconsistent grab bag of criteria—groups' numerical size, financial resources, access to the ballot, levels of descriptive representation, and ability to secure antidiscrimination legislation, among others—without any explanation of why these are the relevant variables or how they should be weighed against one another.[86]

Lacking any objective metric, courts inconclusively debate whether groups such as gays and lesbians are "politically powerless"[87] or, quite the opposite, "possess political power much greater than their numbers."[88] Other groups plausibly lacking in political power have been ignored by courts entirely: poor and working-class Americans, immigrants, and convicted felons, among others, have received no special rights protections. Indeed, the groups with the very least political power may also be the least likely to gain rights protections. Constitutional theorists have noted a "paradox of power" in judicial assessments of political powerlessness, as only groups that have managed to build a significant measure of political power have succeeded in securing the "powerless" designation, leaving truly powerless groups out in the cold.[89]

Beyond the question of which groups should be protected, the form and substance of rights protection has become increasingly disconnected from the project of redistributing political power or compensating for its absence. The high-water mark of political process theory was the Warren Court's campaign to dismantle the Jim Crow systems of segregation and criminal justice, making policy less hostile to disenfranchised Black Americans in the South. In recent decades, however, even while the Court has continued to talk about political powerlessness, the focus of equal protection has shifted from advancing the interests and welfare of disadvantaged groups to prohibiting any form of differential treatment, even for the purpose of benefiting those groups—from antisubordination to anticlassification.[90] Constitutional concern with racial subordination has been replaced by an anticlassification commitment to "colorblindness" that rules out affirmative action programs and ignores the many not-explicitly-race-based policies that perpetuate inequality. Whatever might be said in favor of an anticlassification approach to equality, it is a non sequitur to political process theory or to an overarching concern with the balance of democratic power among social groups. As Chapter 6 will go on to describe, so are a number of other, more enduring constitutional doctrines that prevent constitutional law from using rights as substitutes for the kinds of social and economic benefits that democratic power can be used to secure.

In sum, while constitutional law has occasionally viewed rights and democratic representation as tools for balancing group power, that has seldom been its primary concern. Only when it comes to the power of government institutions does balancing become centrally important. Yet we might conclude that constitutional law would work better the other way around. Balancing power among the branches of government serves no obviously useful purpose. But applying the balance of power principle to rights and votes might point constitutional law toward a more productive and politically just agenda of redistributing and equalizing political power among groups in society. Preventing one group in society from dominating or subjugating another, as through oligarchy or slavery, is a self-evidently attractive principle of justice; but the principle loses any obvious force when it is applied to government institutions like Congress and the president. The ideal of equalizing political power shines brightly when monarchies and dictatorships are replaced by democracy; but when it comes to equalizing the power of government institutions it is hard to see any spark. Madison's recourse to pluralism and countervailing power in *Federalist No. 10* makes perfect sense; but his translation of those ideas to government institutions in *Federalist No. 51* remains difficult to parse.

Constitutional law's wrong turn in thinking about the balance of powers is another manifestation of its failure to see through the image of Leviathan as a self-interested, self-directed being possessed of a will and welfare of its own. Constitutionalists would do well to follow the lead of their internationalist counterparts in shifting focus to Leviathan's subjects and controllers—the people who possess political power *over* the power *of* the state. As this part of the book has emphasized, it is the interests of these state-controllers, the efficacy of their tools of control, and the balance of power among them that determine how states and governments behave, whether they compete or cooperate, and what good or bad things they will be used to accomplish.

PART III
BAD STATES

6
Personal Morality and Political Justice

A characteristic feature of constitutional law is its categorical indifference to what many see and experience as the deepest injustices of American society. There is systemic racial inequality: Black families own a fraction of the wealth of white families and are disproportionately living in poverty; Black income and high school and college graduation rates are substantially lower; Black men are far more likely to be unemployed, incarcerated, or killed by the police; and so, tragically, on.[1] There is persistent gender inequality: women continue to suffer from a significant gender wage gap, vulnerability to domestic and sexual violence, the disproportionate burdens of childcare and domestic labor, and other long-standing patterns of economic and social subordination.[2] There is increasingly severe economic inequality: income inequality has returned to Gilded Age levels, with American CEOs, who in 1965 earned about twenty times the income of a typical worker, now getting paid close to 300 times as much as their average employee; the top 10% of Americans hold nearly 70% of U.S. wealth, while the bottom 50%, comprising 160 million people, may well be collectively less wealthy than the three richest Americans; measured by Gini coefficient, the economic inequality of the United States now ranks higher than any other developed country, on a par with Haiti and the Democratic Republic of the Congo.[3]

None of this counts as a violation of anyone's constitutional rights. In all of these domains, American constitutional law invites the government to absolve itself from responsibility simply by ignoring existing patterns of inequality and subordination. So long as the state avoids actively and intentionally inflicting additional harms by purposeful discrimination, it is under no constitutional obligation to concern itself with structural inequality or distributive injustice. As constitutional law sees it, the state's obligations to its citizens are no greater than the legal obligations of citizens to one another. The legal subjects of the state are prohibited from inflicting various kinds of harm upon one another; but they are seldom obligated to go out of their way to help one another. Constitutional law treats Leviathan in the same way, applying the same moral and legal frameworks that permit ordinary persons

Law for Leviathan. Daryl J. Levinson, Oxford University Press. © Oxford University Press 2024.
DOI: 10.1093/9780190061616.003.0007

to go about their day-to-day lives with limited regard for their fellow human beings.

States as Moral Persons

Constitutional law is not alone in looking at the state through the lens of personal morality and legality. Captivated by the analogy between persons in the state of nature and states in the international arena, Hobbes was tempted to transpose their moral and legal natures. His vision of autonomous, morally independent persons in the state of nature was a reflection of the sovereign state, as Hobbes saw it, pursuing its self-interest in the anarchical domain of international relations.[4] The other way around, Hobbes also projected the legal and moral standing of persons onto states: "[B]ecause commonwealths once instituted take on the personal qualities of men," he wrote, "what we call a natural *law* in speaking of the duties of individual men [becomes] the *right of Nations*, when applied to whole commonwealths."[5] Thus, according to Hobbes, "every Soveraign hath the same Right, in procuring the safety of his People, that any particular man can have, in procuring the safety of his own Body."[6] To be sure, Hobbes also saw a crucial disanalogy in the circumstances of states and persons. The fact that persons but not states lived under a lawgiving Leviathan meant that they alone were subject to obligations of law and justice.[7] But this disjunction was merely a matter of circumstance. In their natural conditions, Hobbesian states and persons were similar beings.

Hobbesian personification remains highly influential in thinking about the moral rights and duties of states in the international realm. Following Hobbes most literally are realists who dismiss the relevance of law and morality in the international, anarchical state of nature. But pursuing the Hobbesian analogy between states and persons need not lead to nihilism about international legality and morality. As Chapter 2 described, sovereign states have long been conceived as possessing rights comparable to the liberty and autonomy rights of ordinary persons. Political theorist Michael Walzer's account of sovereign states as personified rights-holders captures this line of thought:

> [T]he recognition of sovereignty is the only way we have of establishing an arena within which freedom can be fought for and (sometimes) won. It is this arena and the activities that go on within it that we want to protect, and

we protect them, much as we protect individual integrity, by marking out boundaries that cannot be crossed, rights that cannot be violated. As with individuals, so with sovereign states: there are things that we cannot do to them, even for their own ostensible good.[8]

For Walzer and many other theorists of international relations, as for Hobbes, "states possess rights more or less as individuals do."[9] Walzer's influential theory of just war extends that moral equation. Reasoning from the Hobbesian analogy between states in international society and persons in domestic society, Walzer proceeds to derive principles of permissible war-making behavior on the part of states from the legal and moral rules regarding self-defense and harm to innocents that apply to ordinary people in "the familiar world of individuals and rights."[10]

As important as the states-as-moral-persons analogy has been to the development of international thought, however, sophisticated internationalists have always been attuned to its limitations. That includes Hobbes, who, having cast states in a war of all against all on the model of persons in the state of nature, nonetheless recognized that the "misery, which accompanies the Liberty of particular men" need not follow for states.[11] Developing that disjunction, subsequent theorists have recognized that, because "states are different kinds of agents from natural individuals," they "can more peaceably coexist with other states" even without the kind of Leviathan necessary to maintain order among persons within states.[12] States are also arguably different in their status as rights-holders. As we saw in Chapter 2, critics of the analogy between state sovereignty and personal autonomy have emphasized that "[s]tates are not sources of ends in the same sense as are persons" and cannot claim rights on their own behalf.[13] Notwithstanding the use he makes of the states-as-persons analogy, Walzer himself is well aware that, in many respects, "[s]tates are not in fact like individuals (because they are collections of individuals) and the relations of states are not like the dealings of private men and women."[14] In common with other theorists of international relations, Walzer recognizes that the moral and legal rules that govern the behavior of states will not always match the ones that apply to regular people.

Moral and political philosophers focused on the domestic-facing side of the state have gone further in decoupling the status of states and persons. In particular, they have emphasized that states have special moral duties and obligations that ordinary persons do not. To start, liberal political morality demands that Leviathan treat its citizens impartially, with equal concern and respect. Ronald Dworkin tellingly refers to this principle as the "special and indispensable virtue of sovereigns."[15] The virtue is special because, in the view of Dworkin and other political liberals, it does not apply to ordinary persons, who are morally permitted to display greater concern for their own lives and the lives of people close to them than for the lives of distant strangers. That permission reflects the fact that real-life persons have private lives, personal projects, ambitions, and attachments, which many believe they should have the freedom to pursue without perpetual and equal regard for the welfare of others. Leviathan, in contrast, lacks any similar set of self-centered interests—for the simple reason that it lacks a self.

Leviathan is different in other ways as well. Following Hobbes, the prevailing view among political philosophers is that the special set of moral demands stemming from political justice are applicable only to the state. John Rawls thus begins his landmark *A Theory of Justice* by identifying the domain of justice as the "basic structure" of society, comprising the major political and legal institutions of the state.[16] Because the principles of justice do not apply to "individuals and their actions in particular circumstances,"[17] Rawls draws a "division of [moral] labor." The state alone is subject to the demands of justice, while individuals are subject to a different set of more localized and limited legal and moral obligations in their personal lives.[18] In constructing a theory of justice distinctively suitable to the state, Rawls starts from the premise that "[t]he correct regulative principle for anything depends on the nature of that thing."[19] The nature of Leviathan, in the view of Rawls and others, is simply different from the nature of ordinary persons.

As the discussion that follows will describe, that difference appears to have been lost on constitutional law. Disregarding the special demands of political justice, distinctive moral virtues suitable to sovereigns, and division of moral labor, constitutional law more or less holds the state and its government to the standards of ordinary personal morality and legality. The moral and legal framework that constitutional rights create for Leviathan looks as if it were built for an ordinary person.

Constitutional Justice

Abstracting from specific rights and the complexity of doctrinal rules, the basic architecture of constitutional rights jurisprudence is broadly consistent. Most rights protect citizens only against "state action"—specific, active, interventions by government that result in harm. State *inaction*—the failure or disclination of the state to prevent or repair harms, or to make any attempt to remediate inequality or disadvantage—is normally not held constitutionally culpable.[20] Even within the domain of state action, moreover, the state is typically held responsible only for *intentionally* inflicted harms.[21] Policies and practices that create, exacerbate, or predictably reproduce inequalities or disadvantages usually fall outside of constitutional rights protection so long as the government does not act with the purpose of bringing about these consequences. Layered on top of these limitations is the basic premise of constitutional adjudication that government liability is assessed one action, or transaction, at a time. The standard unit of constitutional analysis is a specific, discrete policy or intervention. Harms resulting from an array of policies and interventions over longer periods of time, or cumulative conditions caused by a mix of factors including but not limited to state actions, seldom come into focus as constitutional cases.

The upshot is that constitutional law focuses on discrete, small-scale harms while blinding itself to big-picture, systemic injustices. Specific acts of discrimination based on race or gender are constitutionally prohibited, but entrenched conditions of racial and gender inequality are invisible to constitutional law. A modest program of racial preferences in public university admissions or economic assistance to women workers will be a clear target for an equal protection challenge, but the broad conditions of inequality that such programs are meant to address remain off the constitutional radar. Constitutional alarm bells sound when government regulation diminishes the value of a particular parcel of property, but broad poverty and economic inequality generate only constitutional shrugs. Restrictions on political spending violate free speech rights, but systematic inequality of political influence and the general degradation of political discourse raise no constitutional issues at all.

Constitutional theorists and political advocates have long lambasted this cramped approach to constitutional responsibility. From the progressives and legal realists of the early twentieth century through the critical race studies and law and political economy movements of the present, critics have questioned why the state should be free to ignore and exacerbate racial, gender, economic, and other constitutionally salient forms of inequality and subordination that are within its power to ameliorate or prevent.[22] When the state decides to do nothing about these constitutional injustices, or blindly takes action that perpetuates them, critics contend, that is no less a choice than the decision to actively inflict harm, and therefore no less a matter of constitutional responsibility.[23] Moreover, critics emphasize, the state is, in fact, actively implicated in all of these injustices. Present-day racial inequality, for instance, is obviously in large part a product of actively implemented state policy, ranging from support for slavery and Jim Crow segregation to directly imposed discrimination in the laws and policies governing housing, criminal justice, work, family, and other domains.[24]

Some of these lines of critique have on occasion gained traction. During the Great Depression, proponents of more expansive economic regulation made the case that government should take broad responsibility for the economy and its social consequences. Against the prevailing constitutional view that government regulation and redistribution were impermissible interferences with economic liberty in a "free market," New Dealers reminded the public that there was, in reality, no such thing as a government-free market in which people were left alone in their liberty to make private choices. Quite the contrary, government was pervasively responsible for creating, structuring, and regulating the economy through law. That responsibility began with the common law rules of property and contract that determine who owns what and create the basic infrastructure of market exchange. Progressives and legal realists had already debunked the notion of "private property" by pointing out that property rights depended on legal recognition and enforcement by the state;[25] they were a delegation of public "sovereignty."[26] The same was true of the "free market" more generally, which relied not just on the common law but on the legal creation of corporations, the banking system, antitrust, securities, labor law, and so on. Removing the state from markets, the New Dealers rightly observed, would not make them free; it would make them collapse.[27]

The moral, for FDR and his allies, was that government must be held responsible for the economic and social outcomes that the market produces. Where markets were failing to provide people with basic needs or a decent life, that failure was the responsibility of the state. President Roosevelt thus instructed Americans that we "must lay hold of the fact that economic laws are not made by nature. They are made by human beings," with the implication that, "when people starve, it is the result of social choices, not anything sacred or inevitable."[28] By "social choices," Roosevelt meant democratic decisions given effect by government laws and policies: when citizens starved, it was ultimately government's responsibility. Embracing that responsibility, Roosevelt, in his 1944 State of the Union Address, promised the country a

"Second Bill of Rights," including rights to "a useful and remunerative job," to "earn enough to provide adequate food and clothing and recreation," to "a decent home," to "adequate medical care and .. good health," to "protection from the economic fears of old age, sickness, accident, and unemployment," and to "a good education." Flipping the constitutional premise of economic liberty, Roosevelt argued that the failure of the state to provide these foundational goods and opportunities would amount to a denial of freedom.[29]

Roosevelt's Second Bill of Rights marks a path not taken by American constitutional law.[30] But constitutions in many other countries around the world do, in fact, provide for these kinds of social welfare rights.[31] The South African Constitution, for instance, guarantees access to adequate housing, food and water, healthcare, education, and social security.[32] And courts in South Africa have taken at least tentative steps toward enforcement of some of these rights, ordering the state to take "reasonable measures within its available resources to achieve [their] progressive realization."[33] Even in the United States, there was a period during the 1960s and early '70s when the Supreme Court flirted with the possibility of creating and enforcing some version of constitutional welfare rights.[34] And American state courts have stepped up to enforce state constitutional guarantees of educational adequacy and equality, ordering increased spending on public education and redistribution of funding to under-resourced school districts.[35]

Holding government responsible for preventing its citizens from starving, or being denied other basic necessities of life, is at least within the bounds of constitutional imagination. But the more revolutionary seeds of the New Deal critique have never bloomed. For constitutional lawyers in the United States and other countries, it remains unimaginable that the state could be held legally responsible for eliminating broad social inequalities or preventing subordination. Beyond minimal welfare rights, the prospect of recognizing a constitutional requirement of thoroughgoing economic justice would stretch constitutional rights jurisprudence beyond recognition. The same would be true of constitutional demands for the kinds of social and economic restructuring and redistribution that would be necessary to alleviate entrenched forms of racial and gender inequality. Such demands would swamp the structure of constitutional doctrine and adjudication, requiring a radical reconceptualization of what rights entail, who possesses them, and how they should be enforced. Even the most far-reaching "justice-seeking" constitutionalists, therefore, must resign themselves to the inevitability of a "durable moral shortfall" between what constitutional rights can hope to accomplish and the full-fledged demands of social and political justice.[36]

What explains constitutional law's moral shortfall? Part of the story, quite obviously, is political. The ideals of racial, gender, and economic equality pressed by progressives, and the kinds of activist government interventions that would be required to realize these ideals, are a hard sell for many Americans, and an impossible one for conservatives and libertarians. Yet political disagreement cannot be the complete explanation for the limited horizons of constitutional rights. Roosevelt and the New Dealers were not lacking in political support, but they did not seriously believe that even the kinds of relatively limited welfare rights represented by the Second Bill could become part of constitutional law. Academic theorists constructing utopian visions of the American constitutional system are entirely unconstrained by political reality, yet they, too, perceive limited prospects for translating egalitarian political ideals into constitutional forms.

One sticking point is the expectation that constitutional rights will be enforced by courts. The complex distributive trade-offs and aggressive restructuring of social and economic arrangements that would be necessary to implement sweeping structural reforms would be widely regarded as beyond the institutional capability and democratic legitimacy of the judiciary. But the scope of constitutional ambition need not be limited by what courts can accomplish on their own. Courts in South Africa and other countries have implemented welfare rights not through "strong-form" judicial review but by guiding and prodding the political branches to do the heavy lifting.[37] Constitutional obligations could apply entirely to the political branches without any judicial involvement at all.

Yet even constitutional theorists who appreciate the possibility of "judicially underenforced rights" may have a hard time conceiving of rights beyond the forms in which they have been created by courts.[38] And it is probably no coincidence in the American system of constitutional adjudication by ordinary courts that the form of constitutional rights has been cast in the common law mold. The traditional, classically liberal model of a common law case features atomistic individuals who interact only at the point of a discontinuous event, tightly bound in space and time. In the case of a tortious injury, for instance, the unit of legal analysis is defined by the self-contained, harm-inflicting interaction that disrupted the otherwise unrelated lives of the two parties. The focus of liability is on the harm to the plaintiff, measured by the marginal, negative deviation from her position just prior to the collision with the defendant. The corresponding remedial goal is to achieve corrective justice by restoring the plaintiff to her pre-harm, status quo ante position.

Constitutional rights violations are conceptualized in much the same way. Constitutional cases, too, focus on whether state action has inflicted a discrete harm on an individual or protected group with respect to some constitutionally protected interest. And that harm is typically measured relative to a status quo ante position that is treated as independent of any prior state action or preexisting responsibility.[39]

As applied to ordinary persons in common law cases, this legal model closely tracks commonsense morality. Familiar intuitions of deontological morality direct blame to specific bad acts that cause harm to others. Leaving others alone—omitting to help them, even when help is possible—is viewed as less blameworthy; as are harms inflicted accidentally or inadvertently, as opposed to intentionally. For purposes of both conventional morality and the common law, killing someone is worse than merely allowing them to die; and intentional killings are more culpable than merely negligent ones.

The structure of constitutional rights seems to reflect similar intuitions extended to the state. When government fails to prohibit discrimination, censorship of speech, or any other harmful conduct that is proximately perpetrated by private actors, or when it chooses to leave structural inequality alone, those apparent omissions might be deemed less blameworthy than actively inflicted harms. And even when government itself is the active and proximate inflictor of harm, perhaps it deserves less blame where its actions were not intentionally discriminatory or purposefully targeted at constitutionally protected conduct or groups.

Here, then, is another explanation for constitutional law's approach to responsibility and rights: constitutional law has followed in the footsteps of the common law, repurposing legal and moral frameworks that were designed to regulate the behavior of ordinary people. Anchoring itself on private legality and personal morality, constitutional law and adjudication have likewise focused on localized, self-contained transactional harms, emphasizing negative responsibility and intentional wrongdoing. Constitutional law regulates the behavior of the state as if it were an ordinary person—or a personified Leviathan.

Yet Leviathan is conspicuously different from an ordinary person in ways that make the standards and expectations of private legality and personal morality a poor fit. To start, Leviathan is a giant, with vastly greater capability and causal efficacy in the world than any ordinary person. This basic fact has correspondingly large implications for how we should think about government's responsibility for harm. To start, the more that government is capable of doing, the more that its failures, or omissions, to do those things should be understood as culpable choices that can and should be made differently. Ordinary people have limited ability to help most others in the world, and their omissions are not usually the cause of anyone's suffering. Holding them legally or morally responsible for harms beyond the ones they actively caused, in most cases, would be unfair and instrumentally pointless. Leviathan is different. States and governments operate on a different scale and are capable of accomplishing things that no ordinary person possibly could. That includes preventing or alleviating all manner of constitutionally salient harms suffered by its citizens. When the state ignores harms that it is fully capable of preventing, its omissions can more fairly be construed as culpable choices, and culpability can realistically motivate different and more beneficial behavior.[40]

Indeed, simply holding the state to the ordinary-person standards of liability for omissions could generate nearly boundless legal and moral responsibility. In cases where a person is distinctively well-situated to prevent harm to someone nearby or is in a special relationship with them, private law will sometimes make an exception to the normally dispositive distinction between acts and omissions, imposing a special duty to rescue. For reasons of instrumental efficacy and fairness, that duty is especially likely to attach in contexts where there is a single, salient rescuer. When a swimmer drowns near a crowded beach, the multitude of beachgoers will not be held legally liable—doing so would seem unfair given the collective action problems and diffusion of responsibility; and the threat of liability for all might only serve to incentivize chaos.[41] Whereas the lifeguard who fails to attempt a rescue might well be subject to liability based on her special duty. Leviathan is the lifeguard. Created as a solution to collective action problems among its subjects and the provider of public goods, and specially equipped to prevent harms to its subjects, the state might well be held generally liable for constitutional harms based on a duty to rescue. The exceptional circumstances that occasionally justify omissions liability for regular people is the ordinary case for Leviathan.

At the same time, Leviathan's massive causal efficacy and impact also dramatically expands the scope of its responsibility for harm-causing *actions*. As the New Deal critique of "free markets" illustrates, the state's (invisible) hand has played a causal role in creating the social, economic, and legal conditions that make possible and affect nearly everything that happens in society. The pervasiveness of state action and its consequences is what drives the standard critique of the public/private distinction: nominally "private" decisions, institutions, and arrangements invariably turn out to be shaped and supported by state action. A business that discriminates on the basis of gender is not operating in some fictional realm of purely private choice and contracting. The business would not exist without the state's creation and enforcement of property and contract rights, security, transportation and trade networks, and the market economy in which all of these are embedded. In the state of nature, there would be no discrimination because there would be no business. The same is true of gender discrimination in nominally private families and households that would also not exist in anything like the same form without the accrued actions and policies of the state. Even the beliefs and preferences of individuals that motivate their "private" behavior are inevitably shaped by law and the state. In short, as generations of constitutional critics have argued, there is *always* state action: any constitutionally salient harm or condition of inequality or subordination can be causally attributed to what the state has actively contributed to making the world turn out that way.[42]

Treating Leviathan as a legal and moral person—but one of exceptional size and power—might lead us to hold it personally responsible for both causing and failing to prevent everything that happens in the world. But there is a further and more fundamental question of whether the standards of personal morality and private legality are suitable for Leviathan at all. Particularly questionable are the familiar principles of deontological morality that make acts more blameworthy than omissions and intentional harms more blameworthy than inadvertent or merely foreseeable ones.[43] In the case of ordinary persons, the most compelling justification for these principles is that they serve to limit responsibility in ways that protect individual autonomy. The strictly consequentialist view that everyone is fully obligated to do, and not do, all they can to avoid harm or create good in the world would seem to require people to spend their entire lives in the service of undifferentiated others,[44] eliminating any room for personal projects, relationships, or free choices about how to live. Deontological limitations on responsibility insulate individual lives against the insatiable demands of serving the collective good, creating morally valuable space for people to put others aside and pursue their own projects. Within the broad bounds of not intentionally inflicting harm on those around us, we give ourselves legal and moral permission to live our own lives.[45]

But Leviathan does not have a life of its own to live. As political philosophers and theorists of international relations have stressed, a fundamental disanalogy between states and persons is that states do not have personal interests, special relationships, or autonomous lives to lead; they are essentially selfless. The state exists only to serve others: to further the collective good of the real persons who are its subjects. Absent any reason for concern about Leviathan's personal autonomy or particularistic attachments, deontological limitations on its responsibility might be simply misplaced.[46]

Leviathan's special relationship with its subjects combined with its giant footprint in the world creates further problems for the common law approach to liability and adjudication. Recall that in the prototypical common law case involving ordinary persons, the focus is on self-contained harms suffered as a result of one-off transactions between otherwise disconnected parties. If I run you over with my car or breach a contract with you, it is easy to identify and isolate the harm I have caused, which can be measured as the diminution in your welfare from the baseline position you occupied before I came crashing or contracting into your life. Difficulties arise only in cases involving more complex or multifaceted interactions. Suppose that you are not a stranger but my longtime neighbor, and this particular interaction is one of a long series of harm-causing and benefit-conferring exchanges between the two of us. Yes, I ran over your toe today; but yesterday, I took care of your child while you were at work, and the day before you lost control of your lawn mower and destroyed my flower garden. Now it becomes possible for the law to "frame" a transaction between the two of us in more than one way. Instead of drawing a tight circle around your toe, the law might widen the frame to include the childcare, the garden, or other harm-causing and benefit-conferring interactions in our past or future.[47] At the extreme, the law could keep a single ledger for the entire course of our relationship, calling for a reckoning only at the relationship's end, at which point the bottom-line debtor might be required to compensate the bottom-line creditor. Some legal regimes governing repeat-play and multidimensional relationships—within marriages and families, workplaces, and corporations—do, in fact, deploy strategies like this. But for present purposes, the important thing to see is that, once we move from isolated interactions to extended relationships, how to frame the relevant legal transaction is no longer intuitively determinate.

That indeterminacy is endemic to constitutional cases. Because Leviathan is engaged in a continuous, multifaceted relationship with its subjects, there is no objective or clearly intuitive way of framing constitutional transactions. The state's enormous causal footprint and the multiple ways it affects the lives of its citizens creates no obvious joints for slicing-off discrete, self-contained transactions as legally cognizable events. Conceptualizing a constitutional harm or rights violation as a set-back from some status quo ante position of independence becomes impossible because there is no position of prior independence from the state.[48] Focusing on one specific state action seems arbitrary, given the many and multifarious other state actions that will have always already affected the constitutionally protected interest and its holder and the many more that will continue to do.

Moreover, because the raison d'être of the state is to benefit its subjects, even those subjects who are harmed in some specific way by the state are also likely to have been benefited by the state in multifarious ways. Indeed, almost all citizens are likely to be better off by virtue of their relationship with the state than they would have been in the state's absence. Certainly if the comparison is to their welfare in the state of nature, even those citizens who have been subject to significant harm by Leviathan will be better off on net. The very idea of a state-inflicted "harm," or rights violation, dissolves in a sea of offsetting benefits.[49]

Consider a constitutional claim brought by an owner of beachfront property arguing that her property rights have been violated (or "taken") by state environmental regulations that prevent her from building a house on the parcel. Narrowly framed, the relevant regulation inflicts an economic harm on the owner by diminishing the value of her property. Yet the same environmental regulatory regime might have prevented beach erosion or flooding that would have rendered the property worthless. The state might also be credited for providing the roads and electricity that made the property accessible and habitable, not to mention the property and contract law without which there would be no property or market value in the first place. Any or all of these government benefits could conceivably be bundled together and offset against the localized harm inflicted by the environmental regulation. And, of course, the same is true of the benefits and harms flowing in the opposite direction, from the citizen to the state, including the payment of taxes. At the logical limit, we might be driven to ask whether, taking account of the entirety of their relationship, the claimant has been harmed by the state on net. Again, if the benchmark is the Hobbesian state of nature, Leviathan should almost always prevail.

Not all constitutional rights are aimed at protecting individuals against harm relative to some baseline position. Other rights are keyed to equality, measuring harm relative to how the state has treated some other individual or group. But equality cases are no less dependent on arbitrary framing choices. Race-conscious benefit programs can be challenged as violating equal protection by framing the benefit in isolation, focusing on that single dimension of unequal treatment on the basis of race. But race-conscious benefits can also be more broadly framed as remedial, compensating for disadvantageous, racially discriminatory treatment in the past. Widening the frame still further to encompass the entire history of slavery, segregation, and discrimination would turn the equality claim on its head, entitling Black Americans to massive, additional remedial measures. For another example, the state can be portrayed as violating the principle of religious neutrality when it provides funding to religious schools; alternatively, widening the frame, the state can be portrayed as violating neutrality by *refusing* to fund religious schools, given its support of secular education. In equality cases and individual rights cases alike, transactional frames can be freely adjusted to portray the state as harming, benefiting, or acting neutrally.

So: the common law model of liability and adjudication—designed around the occasional, harm-inflicting interactions of non-altruistic strangers—loses its conceptual grip when transposed to the very different situation of the state's dealings with its citizens. The model also loses a large part of its normative appeal. The common law concern with transactional harm is intuitively grounded in corrective justice, giving victims a claim to the preservation or rectification of their status quo position against wrongful alterations by injurers. When that model is applied to ordinary individuals, the question immediately arises why corrective justice should be prioritized over other values—particularly distributive justice.[50] After all, there will be many cases in which the status quo ante positions of the parties are distributively unjust, and in which the relevant transaction brings them closer to justice. (Imagine: an impoverished parent steals a loaf of bread from the backyard table of a wealthy homeowner to feed the parent's starving child.) The standard explanation for why the law should prevent or rectify such transactions is that there is independent value in protecting even unjust status quo distributions. Certain kinds of nonconsensual transfers may be intrinsically wrong; or forcing compensation may create instrumentally efficient incentives to avoid harm in the future. But what about the trade-off with distributive justice? Legal theorists propose a best-of-both-worlds solution, based on an institutional division of labor. While legal rules operate on one track to prevent localized harms and preserve status quo distributions, the state operates on a parallel track to pursue distributive justice through taxation and spending.[51] It is this bifurcated model that legal theorists have in mind when they describe corrective justice as "personal or individual justice," and distinguish it from the kind of distributive, or "social justice," that applies not to individuals but to the state.[52]

When corrective justice is imposed upon the state, however, the problem is obvious. If the state is subject to the same constraints on upsetting status quo distributions as private actors, then it cannot play its assigned role in bringing about distributive justice. Conceptualizing constitutional rights on the model of common law ones carries precisely this consequence. When government takes property from a rich developer to build low-income housing, levels down the political influence of wealthy individuals and corporations by regulating campaign expenditures, or provides race-conscious remedial measures, constitutional law is quick to perceive a problematic departure from the status quo baseline of entitlements or equality. That perception is conceptually problematic, for the transactional framing reasons just discussed. But it is also normatively problematic in the priority it places on corrective over distributive justice—protecting an unjust baseline distribution against redistributions that would make it more just. That priority is justified in the case of private actors only because distributive justice is being handled by the state. But if the state is required to adopt the same hands-off posture toward existing distributions as private actors, then distributive justice along constitutionalized dimensions is sacrificed altogether. In constitutional law's personified perspective, the state's special role in redistribution is disappeared, along with much else that makes the state distinctive.

Political Justice

Up to now, the point has been that legal and moral frameworks designed around ordinary persons do not translate easily to the state. The reverse is also true. Frameworks of political justice that have been developed for the state are meant to apply only to the state, and not to ordinary persons.

Recall Rawls's "division of moral labor" between the state and private persons, holding the state solely responsible for maintaining the background conditions of systemic social justice and remitting ordinary persons to the different and less demanding standards of personal morality.

Rawls's sharp contrast between political justice and personal morality has provoked a meta-ethical debate about how deep the distinction can cut. Philosophers disagree about whether the normative principles governing the personal and political spheres must evolve from a common set of fundamental first-principles, or whether the two spheres should be understood as morally distinctive all the way down.[53] For Rawls, the distinctive moral character of the state entailed that the standards of political justice could not be derived from the same moral principles that govern ordinary persons. Opposed to this deep moral "dualism" is the "monistic" view that "any plausible overall political/moral view must, at the fundamental level, evaluate the justice of [political] institutions with normative principles that apply also to people's choices."[54]

We will come back around to this debate, but for now, it is enough to appreciate what monists and dualists can agree upon. Even if the moral obligations of states and persons are ultimately reducible to a single set of standards, the special role and capabilities of the state in making it possible for people to live up to those standards can generate very different, state-specific responsibilities.[55] Utilitarians, for example, take a fundamentally monist view of morality, applying the single moral metric of maximizing utility to everyone and everything. Nonetheless, an influential strain of utilitarian thought—so-called government house utilitarianism,[56] as articulated by Bentham and Austin, among others—takes the position that maximizing utility for society as a whole requires holding the state and ordinary persons to very different moral standards. Government is to be directly guided by the utilitarian calculus in setting public policy, while ordinary people in their quotidian lives are permitted to forego utilitarian calculations and live according to commonsense moral principles.[57] For all practical purposes, monist utilitarians agree with dualist Rawlsians that the operative principles of political justice can be entirely different from those of personal morality.

Rawlsians and utilitarians, as well as political philosophers of other stripes, also agree on *how* political justice differs from personal morality. One distinguishing feature of political justice is that it is *systemic* in orientation. The unit of analysis for purposes of moral assessment is not discrete decisions or actions but the basic institutional structure of government and society as a whole.[58] This macro-level focus contrasts with personal morality's micro-level concern with discrete interactions among ordinary persons and narrowly drawn transactional harms.[59] Neither Rawlsian principles of justice nor the optimal set of rule-utilitarian social arrangements is meant to directly govern micro-level interactions. As Rawls puts it, justice applies to a different domain than "the rules applying directly to individuals and associations and to be followed by them in particular transactions."[60]

This least common denominator difference between political justice and personal morality is cogently captured by philosopher Samuel Scheffler, who describes personal morality as:

> encourag[ing] us to be, as it were, good citizens of our moral neighbourhood: to be mindful of how we conduct ourselves toward those people who, because of their physical or social or emotional proximity, or because of the directness or immediacy of our causal interactions with them, are taken to fall within the proper sphere of our moral concern. These "limiting" values and norms, as we may call them, are most at home in the context of small-scale personal relations and interactions.

In contrast, Scheffler continues, "[i]deas of justice, fairness, equality, human rights, and the equal worth of persons have implications that transcend the arena of small-scale interpersonal relations." These ideals reflect "an expansive understanding of the proper scope of moral concern" that is directed toward political morality and the institutional structure of society and state.[61]

The separation of systemic political justice from localized personal morality is supposed to serve the interests of everyone in society. Allowing ordinary persons to ignore systemic justice in their everyday economic and social interactions leaves them, as Rawls puts it, "free to advance their ends more effectively within the framework of the basic structure, secure in the knowledge that elsewhere in the social system the necessary corrections to preserve background justice are being made."[62] Joining Rawls in embracing this kind of "moral division of labor," Thomas Nagel emphasizes the advantages of permitting ordinary persons to channel their concerns about the welfare of others into support for just background institutions, freeing them from the kinds of oppressive demands that would otherwise threaten to suffocate their personal and private lives.[63] Many utilitarians take a similar view, maintaining that it is unrealistically and undesirably demanding to direct people to treat strangers the same as relatives, give away all their money to the poor, or follow other dictates of the utilitarian calculus as applied to their individual, day-to-day decisions.[64] From this perspective, limiting justice to the systemic level of government policymaking serves essentially the same purpose as deontological limitations on personal morality, creating space for the kind of personal lives and attachments that have value for individual human beings.

But not for Leviathan. Accordingly, a second feature that tends to differentiate political justice from personal morality is that theories of justice tend to jettison deontology and take on a broadly consequentialist cast. Nagel distinguishes the personal standpoint of ordinary morality, which takes account of individual rights and autonomy, from "the impersonal consequentialist standpoint that surveys the best overall state of affairs."[65] The latter standpoint is distinctly suitable for the state. Government house utilitarians obviously take the same view, holding the state to a consequentialist, utilitarian standard that is deemed unsuitable for ordinary persons. But even staunch critics of utilitarianism gravitate toward its consequentialist perspective in the domain of political justice. Rawls, for one, focuses his principles of justice on the outcomes likely to be generated under different institutional arrangements. Pursuant to the Rawlsian division of moral labor, this broadly consequentialist posture of political justice oriented toward systemic outcomes is limited to the basic structure of the state, leaving deontological morality to ordinary people living within that structure.[66]

Constitutional law is on the wrong side of this division of moral labor. Rather than embracing the impersonal and systematic posture of political justice that philosophers have identified as distinctively suited to the state, constitutional law has taken the deontological and transactional stance of personal morality. By now it will be clear that many of constitutional law's most troubling difficulties and discontents stem from precisely that mismatch. Conceptually futile and morally arbitrary efforts to draw and justify categorical distinctions between government acts and omissions, and between intentional and merely foreseeable government-inflicted harms, would have no place in a system of constitutional law that adopted the impersonal, consequentialist outlook of political justice. Nor would the myopic focus on small-scale transactional harms and corrective justice, which are swamped by political justice's systemic focus. Political justice fits the state along precisely the dimensions that constitutional law's borrowed wardrobe of personal morality and private legality do not.

That misfit has not escaped the attention of political philosophers, who recognize that constitutional law, as it is currently conceived, can play only a limited role in achieving political justice. In Rawls's theory of justice, constitutional law is charged with delivering a set of "constitutional essentials" that includes the "equal basic rights and liberties of citizenship that legislative majorities are to respect," such as voting rights, freedom of political speech, and liberties of thought, association, and conscience.[67] These are the familiar kinds of small-scale negative rights that constitutional law specializes in. But Rawls does not look to constitutional law for achieving the more ambitious goals of political justice, including fair equality of opportunity and egalitarian distributive justice pursuant to the difference principle. Nagel, too, sees a restricted role for constitutional law in enforcing the traditional kinds of constitutional rights, like "[f]reedom of speech and religion, due process . . . and protection against racial, religious, and sex discrimination," which "can be hard-wired into a democratic society and enforced by an independent judiciary." But like Rawls, he believes the "the bases of broader economic and social equality" lie beyond the reach of constitutional command.[68] In this regard, political philosophers join constitutional critics in recognizing that constitutional law is not built to achieve justice.[69]

Are Rights Left?

Or at least constitutional law is not built to achieve one kind of justice: the kind focused on broad equality and fair distributive outcomes. For many political philosophers, however, the kinds of localized, transactional rights violations that constitutional law adjudicates are also matters of justice. Rawls famously offers not one but two principles of justice. Rawls's second principle is distributive, requiring fair equality of opportunity to attain positions of status and power in society and the distribution of economic resources to achieve the greatest benefit for the least well-off. Rawls's first principle, in contrast, which takes priority over the second, calls for the protection of basic liberties, including voting and political participation, freedom of speech and assembly, and religious liberty.[70] Most of these liberties are cast as strictly negative rights, not affirmative claims on the social and economic resources that might be necessary to realize their "equal worth" or "fair value."[71] Fittingly, these are the liberties that make up the core of Rawls's "constitutional essentials."[72] Constitutional rights cast in the traditional form of transactional, negative liberties leave out the distributive dimension of justice. But these rights are supposed to serve justice along a different, and no less important, dimension.

For other political philosophers, the rights dimension of justice is the *only* dimension. Libertarians believe that justice consists of nothing more than some version of Rawls's first principle. Like constitutional lawyers, their exclusive focus is on protecting negative rights against discrete, transactional violations by the state, rejecting any broader concern with distributive justice or structural inequality. In fact, any attempt by the state to engage in egalitarian redistribution or restructuring is likely to threaten libertarian rights. Constitutional law's prohibitions on uncompensated takings of property (even in the service of egalitarian redistribution), specific restrictions of political spending and speech (even in the service of equalizing political influence or improving political discourse overall), and instances of race- or gender-discrimination (even in the service of broader equality) fit neatly with the libertarian view of justice.

It should come as no surprise, then, that libertarianism is vulnerable to the same kinds of criticism as constitutional rights conceived on the model of negative liberty and transactional harm. Critics of libertarianism point out that the status quo positions protected by libertarian rights are not pre-political possessions but products of the state. Libertarian claims to rights-protected ownership of property and wealth are met with precisely the counterpoints raised by FDR and the New Dealers to constitutional economic liberty rights: individuals can claim no "natural" right to what they are able to take away from the "free market," because the market and its outcomes are, in fact, pervasively determined by actions and decisions of the state. Libertarian assertions of rights to private property are thus lambasted for missing the truth that "property and law are born together, and die together. Before laws were made, there was no property; take away laws and property ceases."[73] Libertarian complaints of state-inflicted harm from taxation or regulation are also met with reminders of the many, more-than-offsetting benefits conferred by the state and the system of social cooperation it supports. In response to libertarian invocations of natural rights to ownership, critics respond that libertarians in the state of nature would securely own nothing, not even their lives.

What libertarianism misapprehends, in the view of its critics, is the state's pervasive impact on, and responsibility for, the lives and fortunes of the people who live within it. In common with constitutional lawyers, libertarians myopically focus on a select subset of state–citizen interactions while ignoring the vastly broader, and grossly beneficial, relationship in the background. And libertarians join constitutional lawyers in misapplying a personalized moral framework to the state, focused on bad acts and discrete, transactional harms rather than systemic consequences. In short, libertarians treat the state as if it were an ordinary person.[74] As Scheffler observes, "The libertarian gives priority to the values and principles that regulate small-scale interactions among individuals, and treats the larger-scale values of social justice and equality as valid only insofar as they can be construed as applications of values and norms that are at home in the context of one-on-one personal interactions."[75]

Recall, though, that libertarians are not the only political philosophers who take this view of rights. Rawls and other egalitarian theorists of political justice reject libertarianism when it comes to economic rights, substituting systemic distributive justice for protection of individual entitlements. But they continue to embrace the libertarian—and constitutional—architecture of rights when it comes to non-economic liberties, such as speech, religion, and anti-discrimination. The basis for this distinction is not self-evident. If claims of economic liberty can be denuded and dissolved into distributive justice, so too can other liberty claims, including the liberal rights that egalitarians want to preserve. Rights-based concerns about transactional instances of race- or gender-discrimination can be subsumed into distributive concerns about the systemic subjugation of racial minorities and women.[76] A rights-based focus on discrete acts of censoring speech or restricting religion can be replaced by a broader perspective on the quality and diversity of public discourse or the flourishing of religious pluralism. Rights that protect individual liberty against broadly beneficial criminal justice or national security measures can be bypassed in pursuit of the best overall strategy of providing liberty and security for all.[77]

Of course, it could be the case that some individual rights and liberties have independent moral value that is worth protecting regardless of any systemic outcomes—and that others do not. Perhaps free speech, religious liberty, and antidiscrimination have a kind of intrinsic value that economic liberty lacks.[78] Even if so, however, the difficulties described in this chapter of making constitutional rights fit the state, coupled with the appreciation of seemingly better-fitting models of political justice, raise some difficult questions about how rights against the state, regardless of substantive content, can be justified and made to work.

First, there is the question of priority. As we have seen in constitutional law, there are many cases in which individual rights can conflict with systemic, distributive goals, in the same way that libertarian property rights conflict with economic redistribution. A right against race discrimination can be invoked to block the kinds of affirmative action and desegregation policies that progressives see as contributing to racial justice. Constitutional prohibitions on gender discrimination similarly have been invoked (by men) to block gender-specific policies designed to materially benefit women in ways that would plausibly promote gender equality. Constitutional free speech rights stand in the way of campaign spending reforms aimed at equalizing political influence and prevent prohibitions on hate speech that might prevent the silencing of disadvantaged groups. Constitutional rights to guns for self-defense are not obviously consistent with a system of gun control that provides the most overall security against crime and violence. In cases like these, a choice must be made between prioritizing the protection of these individual rights and pursuing systemic forms of justice. Yet it is not at all clear how these two forms of justice should be weighed against one another or combined in an optimal scheme of overall justice.[79]

Even where individual rights do not conflict with systemic justice, or where they take priority over it, we need some way of determining when these rights have, in fact, been violated. As we have seen, however, the continuous and multidimensional relationship between the state and its citizens renders the transactional frames that we ordinarily rely upon to identify violations conceptually indeterminate. Government "takings" of property can be reconceived as broader transactions between the individual and the state that are on net advantageous with respect to the very interest in holding property that the right is supposed to protect. In just the same way, violations of rights to free speech, antidiscrimination, and religious liberty can be reframed by widening the focus to consider the broader and beneficial course of dealings between the individual right-holder and the state. As transactional frames expand, discrete rights violations dissolve.

Finally, the most fundamental question about individual rights is what independent moral value they are supposed to serve.[80] The answer is not obvious, even to those who hold the strong intuition that such a value must exist. Nagel, for one, recognizes that "it has proven extremely difficult to account for such a basic, individualized value in a way that makes it morally intelligible."[81] Any plausible account must go beyond pointing out the special value of the interests that rights protect. A right to free speech may be of great and distinctive value to the right-holder, and the right to life even more so. But that does not explain why individual rights should be inviolable in contexts where the value of the very same interests that the right protects could be increased through violation. Even if suppressing one person's speech creates greater freedom of speech overall (as could be true of political spending regulation), or if sacrificing one person's life saves more lives overall (as is arguably true of the deterrent effect of the death penalty), individual rights are supposed to be sacrosanct. The justification for such a view, Nagel surmises, must be "agent-relative," providing reasons why it would be wrong for an agent, from that agent's own perspective, to violate a right, even in the service of a greater good.[82] These reasons are not consequentialist but deontological, prohibiting an agent from intentionally aiming to inflict the harm of violating a right, regardless of the comparable harms that might be prevented as a result.

The intuitive pull of deontological reasoning along these lines is evident in the case of ordinary persons. Intentionally aiming at harm, or violating a right, often seems like the wrong thing for a person to do, even when it accomplishes greater overall good.[83] Here again, however, the moral agent we are talking about is not an ordinary person; it is the state. And as we have seen, there are good reasons to think that agent-relative, deontological morality applies less strongly to the state, if it applies at all. This is a point Nagel himself emphasizes outside the context of rights, arguing that public morality should lean consequentialist, with "a heightened concern for [overall] results, "a stricter requirement of impartiality," and correspondingly weaker deontological restrictions on means.[84]

Now, the reasons for treating the state differently in this regard are not exactly the same as the reasons for relaxing deontological constraints on the state's moral obligations, as was the focus of the discussion above. The issue here is not whether the state should be able to assert its own autonomy and self-interest against demands that it act in the service of others. The issue instead is whether the state must limit its efforts to act in the service of others by respecting and upholding deontological rights. But the two issues are closely connected. Rights and other deontological constraints on the means that can be used to pursue good ends reflect the subjective perspective of personal morality. We are supposed to care about the harm we directly inflict, and the intentionality of that harm, more than the harm we fail to prevent. But it is far from clear that this subjective, morally myopic outlook makes the same kind of sense as applied to the state. The state can and should see and care about the big-picture, valuing the harms that it can prevent just as much as the harms it causes, if there is even a coherent difference. The standard deontological moral distinctions between acts and omissions, doing and allowing, and intending and foreseeing speak to aspects of personal autonomy, special relationships, and human psychology that do not apply in the same way to Leviathan.[85]

Perhaps there is some better way of understanding the nature of individual, inviolable rights that explains why at least some such rights should apply against the state. It is hard to escape the intuition that it would be morally wrong for government to torture or execute an innocent person, even if doing so would save a number of other lives. Nagel argues that the same moral intuition should cause us to recoil at violations of individual rights to free speech.[86] As Nagel recognizes, however, the justification for these intuitions remains far from clear. We should at least consider the possibility that our intuitions are based on deeply ingrained principles of personal morality that are too easily transposed to a personified vision of the state.

Even if so, there is another approach to justifying and shaping rights that is perfectly well suited to the impersonal state, and consistent with the consequentialist perspective of political justice. Rights can be understood not as morally fundamental, but simply as instrumental tools for achieving systemic goals, such as "protect[ing] against the abuse of governmental and collective power."[87] As it happens, that is the understanding of rights that was developed in earlier chapters of this book. Chapters 3 and 4 presented rights not as intrinsic components of justice but as instrumental tools for achieving it. By ruling out, or requiring, certain uses of state power, rights work alongside votes to empower citizens to control the state, maximizing the benefits it provides while protecting themselves against the dangers it presents. This conception of rights is entirely consequentialist, geared toward achieving the best outcomes for the stakeholders of state power. It is also systemic in orientation, seeking the best consequences overall. That set of consequences might be described in terms of justice.

Constitutional rights do, in fact, sometimes work in this way. Chapter 5 described the *Carolene Products* approach to deploying rights for the purpose of redistributing and fairly balancing democratic power and political outcomes overall. Progressive critics of constitutional rights jurisprudence have pushed for similar strategies for putting rights in the service of systemic justice. Equal protection rights might be designed around the systemic goal of anti-subjugation, prohibiting only the kinds of discrimination that are likely to increase racial inequality while permitting or even requiring government to engage in race-conscious forms of redistribution for purposes of promoting equality. Free speech rights might be designed around the systemic goal of best promoting democratic self-government, permitting or even requiring government to restrict or selectively subsidize some types of speech in order to equalize influence or improve the quality of public debate. In place of protecting property rights, constitutional law might incorporate Roosevelt's Second Bill of Rights, and beyond that hold government to the more ambitious aspirations of distributive justice.

A thoroughgoing effort to make constitutional rights work as instruments of systemic justice would require rethinking not only the substantive content of rights but also the structure of adjudication and the role of courts. In some cases, the relevant constitutional obligations might be directed to the political branches, casting courts as occasional monitors of progress or leaving them out altogether. Courts aside, there may be some imperatives of systemic justice that cannot usefully be served through any kind of rights-based requirements. Reconceptualizing and redesigning constitutional rights and liberties as instrumental tools of systemic justice is no simple matter, morally, empirically, or institutionally. But it promises a better return on investment than continuing on the present path. The prevailing conception of constitutional rights, modeled on personal morality and private legality, has floated too far free from political justice, and from its subject, the state.

Is the State Left?

One direction, then, is to focus constitutional law and political justice on the distinctive, impersonal nature of the state as a legal and moral actor. But there is another way of depersonifying the state. Rather than looking at the state as the relevant actor in its own right, we might switch focus to the actual persons who act through the state. As the next chapter considers in greater detail, Leviathan itself can be disaggregated out of moral existence.

Already in this chapter we have encountered skepticism about treating the state, or political justice within the state, as a separate moral subject. Rejecting the Rawlsian view that the state and its basic institutional structure should be subject to special principles of political justice inapplicable to ordinary persons, moral monists insist that the same normative principles must ultimately govern both. Again, that does not necessarily mean that the same moral and legal standards should be applied in all cases; monists accept that political justice could turn out to be very different in practice from personal morality. But monists do believe that political justice must be derived from, and reduceable to, moral principles about how people ought to behave in general. If political justice requires egalitarian redistribution of wealth, for example, that is because people themselves have a moral duty to pursue that end. To the extent the state is the best vehicle for achieving distributive justice, then ordinary people may fulfill their moral duties simply by supporting and appropriately directing the state and its institutions. But if there are other or better ways of bringing about distributive justice, then people may be morally obligated to act outside of the state, for example by engaging in private altruism to make up the state's shortfalls.[88] In the monist view, then, the state loses its status a moral being or subject in its own right. Consistent with the portrayal in Part II, it is merely a technology for accomplishing the collective moral goals of actual persons, who remain the sole moral agents and bearers of moral responsibility even when they are acting through the state.

A similar line of anti-statist moral thought has gained ground in philosophical and legal debates about justice in war. The traditional approach to thinking about just war conceives of war, like other matters of international relations and international law, primarily as something that happens between states. As we saw at the beginning of this chapter, that approach lends itself to casting states as personified moral actors. Moral and legal principles of *jus ad bellum*, protecting state sovereignty and territorial integrity against outside aggression and permitting states to fight in self-defense, are bolstered by the view that "[s]tates possess rights more or less as individuals do."[89] Legal and moral rules of *jus in bello*, seeking to minimize harm to innocents during war, are likewise derived by analogy from "the familiar world of individuals and rights."[90]

Even where traditionalists are inclined to disaggregate the state—considering the morality and legality of fighting and killing from the perspectives of soldiers, political leaders, and democratic citizens—there is something distinctively statist about their approach. The moral and legal rights and duties of the relevant persons are understood to be fundamentally transformed by their relationship to the state.[91] When Michael Walzer turns his attention to the moral responsibility of political leaders for the bad acts of their states, for instance, he embraces the Machiavellian view that special reasons of state permit or demand that leaders and officials sometimes take actions that would otherwise be morally prohibited. By virtue of their relationship to the state, officials become subject to a consequentialist code of political morality that can justify "dirty hands"—meaning, hands that would be morally dirty by the standards of ordinary, deontologically inflected personal morality.[92] Something similar is true of soldiers, in the traditionalist view, who become subject to special, statist standards of morality and legality when they are engaged in war. Soldiers are not held responsible for killing their enemies on the battlefield, for example, even when they do so in pursuance of an unjust war. Responsibility for injustice is effectively transferred from persons serving as soldiers to their state.[93]

In recent years, however, the traditionally statist view of just war has been subject to sustained challenge.[94] Just war revisionists reject the statist premise that "the moral principles that govern the activity of war apply primarily to the acts of states and only derivatively and thus indirectly to the acts of persons." Instead, revisionists focus on the actions, rights, and welfare of the persons engaged in and affected by war without regard to the intermediation of states.[95] That means looking past traditional doctrines of state sovereignty and nonintervention to prioritize the rights and welfare of the people who might benefit from humanitarian interventions.[96] It also means applying "familiar principles of liability as they apply in relations among persons" to conclude, for instance, that combatants fighting an unjust war can be held guilty of murder when they kill enemy soldiers.[97] If traditionalists vacillate between treating states as persons and persons as states, revisionists simply treat persons as persons, dropping out the state.

A similar anti-statist revisionism has emerged in debates over the boundaries of distributive justice. Rawls's original theory of justice was explicitly limited to justice *within* states. When Rawls came to consider justice *among* states, he turned to a version of the domestic analogy. Substituting an idealized version of morally virtuous states for persons in the original position, he imagined these "peoples" coming together to agree on principles to govern their relationships.[98] The principles Rawls imagined being chosen by states were much less demanding than the principles chosen by persons within a state. In particular, Rawls's peoples reject an egalitarian principle of distributive justice, disclaiming any duty on the part of the global rich to redistribute to the global poor. For Rawls and his followers, then, the full-fledged obligations of justice arise only within the special context of the state and do not apply to relations between states or among people in different states.[99]

Critics have rejected such a starkly statist divide. Pressing the monist view that moral obligations are indifferent to state boundaries, cosmopolitan proponents of global justice contend that the mutual demands of justice apply to all people in the world.[100] From this perspective, sovereign states are at best vehicles for, and at worst barriers to, achieving justice among global citizens. Located between cosmopolitan monists and Rawlsian statists are those who accept that the obligations of justice must be limited to groups of people with special relationships, but who see the potential for such relationships outside of the sovereign state. In this view, the institutional and relational features of the state that Rawls saw as singularly significant—thick forms of interdependence among people, a common economic system, an overarching political and legal governance structure—can be, and have in fact been, replicated to a considerable extent by the international order beyond the state.[101] Even in the absence of an actual world-state, the argument goes, the international order has become sufficiently state-like in the relevant respects to give rise to the demands of political justice.[102] The Hobbesian boundary between order and justice within the state and anarchy outside it has been blurred.

Still, that boundary may continue to matter. For Thomas Nagel, as for Hobbes:

> [S]overeign states are not merely instruments for realizing the preinstitutional value of justice among human beings . . . [but] precisely what gives the value of justice its application, by putting the fellow citizens of a sovereign state into a relation that they do not have with the rest of humanity, an institutional relation which must then be evaluated by the special standards of fairness and equality that fill out the content of justice.

What remains special about the state is its characteristically Hobbesian combination of legitimate coercive authority exercised over, but also by or on behalf of, its subjects: the state "exercises sovereign power over its citizens and in their names." For Nagel and other traditional statists, that is the fundamental reason why the citizens of sovereign states "have a duty of justice toward one another through the legal, social, and economic institutions that sovereign power makes possible." This duty, like Leviathan itself, is "*sui generis*."[103]

The aim of this chapter is not to take a definitive side in this, or the many other, debates that have arisen about justice and the state. The point is just to show how these debates trace back to a common source. Recall Rawls's methodological first principle: "The correct regulative principle for anything depends on the nature of that thing." How we think about the morality and legality of what the state does and does not do will depend on what kind of thing we understand the state to be. Should we understand the state as a personified moral agent and moral subject in its own right? As a distinctively impersonal one, with special responsibilities and permissions? Or, alternatively, should we look inside the state to focus on the actual people who act and relate through and within it? Are their actions and relationships meaningfully different from other kinds of organized and institutionalized collective actions and interactions? Or is there in fact nothing special about the state at all? As we have now seen, the answers to these questions have varied dramatically across moral and legal contexts and among theorists and practitioners of different outlooks. The moral nature of Leviathan remains unresolved.

7
No Body and Everybody

Following on the previous chapter's question of how the legal and moral wrongdoing of states should be assessed is the further question of who, exactly, should be blamed, or punished when states are deemed to have misbehaved. The default answer provided by international and constitutional law is, Leviathan itself. But even if it makes moral or practical sense to hold the abstraction of the state responsible for wrongdoing, there is no meaningful sense in which the state itself can be punished or penalized. Sanctions will pass through the immaterial body of Leviathan and land upon the real people who are Leviathan's subjects. That is invariably true even in cases where most or all of these people bear no personal responsibility for the wrongdoing of their states or political leaders, and where they have no ability to prevent that wrongdoing from occurring. Consider, for example, the economic sanctions against Iraq authorized by the United Nations Security Council during the 1990s in response to Iraq's invasion of Kuwait and Saddam Hussein's suspected development of weapons of mass destruction. The effect of those sanctions was to immiserate the Iraqi people, quite possibly causing the deaths of hundreds of thousands of children from disease and malnutrition.[1] The further decision of the United States to bomb, invade, and occupy the country cost the lives of hundreds of thousands more Iraqis.[2] Few if any of these victims were in any personal way responsible for the actions of Saddam Hussein or the Iraqi state; to the contrary, they were terrorized by a repressive regime that had little regard for their lives. It is not hard to see why many viewed the sanctioning and slaughtering of innocent Iraqis as a morally dubious and functionally fruitless form of group punishment. Surely, one might think, America would never treat its own citizens the same way. Yet constitutional liability at home can create results that are comparably cruel and pointless. According to one report, the city of Chicago in recent years has been spending more than $50 million annually on liability and settlements stemming from lawsuits against the police. The city has financed a large percentage of these payments through what critics have called "police brutality bonds," at the cost of many more millions of taxpayer dollars, paid to Goldman Sachs and J.P. Morgan. This is money that could have been used instead to fund schools, housing, healthcare, or economic development programs in the communities of the victims. What has all this money bought the people of Chicago instead? Not, as far as anyone can tell, a reduction in police violence; and not a reduction in other forms of criminal violence in a city with one of the highest homicide rates in the country. For communities suffering from crime, poverty, and abusive policing, the constitutional version of sanctioning the state may also amount to gratuitous group punishment.[3] The image of an embodied Leviathan that can be blamed and punished has too often masked the moral and functional consequences of what are, in fact, collective sanctions imposed on innocent groups of people. As this chapter will go on to describe, that image has distorted political and legal thought in other ways, as well. The impetus to make Leviathan pay for its wrongdoing follows from the fiction that Leviathan itself possesses and values money and other resources, and would prefer to have more. That fiction feeds perpetual fears of a creature called Big Government, voraciously engorging its girth or purse by swallowing up the wealth and resources of its subjects. In fact, however, Big Government is as mythical as embodied Leviathan. States and governments have no intrinsic interest in growing richer or bigger, just as they have no intrinsic interest in avoiding the kinds of losses that sanctions impose. What matters to states, and what matters *about* states, is not their corporeal size, but the consequences they create for the lives of their citizens.

Sanctioning the State

Collective Responsibility

The stakes of blaming and punishing the state are made transparent by the imagery of *Leviathan*'s frontispiece. Leviathan's body is made up of the bodies of its subjects—all the human beings who will suffer any sanction imposed upon their sovereign. Do they deserve it? As the animating force of Leviathan's being, the citizens of a state might be deemed collectively responsible for its actions and held remedially accountable for its wrongdoing. At least some of what Hobbes says suggests such a view. Because the citizens of a state are the collective "authors [] of every thing [Leviathan] saith, or doth, in their name," Hobbes reasons, they should be the ones "owning all [these] actions."[4] In other passages, however, Hobbes is at pains to separate actions of the sovereign from any decision or "approbation" by the subject, and he concludes that anything a subject "is compelled to do in obedience to his sovereign, and doth it not in order to his own mind, but in order to the laws of his country, that action is not his, but his sovereign's."[5] Hobbes seems to have been of two minds about the relationship between Leviathan's two kinds of bodies.[6]

Theorists of international law and relations have likewise found the question of the collective responsibility of citizens for the actions of their state a vexing one. As a formal matter, states are the primary subjects of international law, the entities to which rights and duties attach—and, for most purposes, stay attached, even as the populations of states change over time. When a state violates these rights and duties, it is the state that has an obligation to pay reparations for harm and becomes subject to an array of countermeasures imposed by other states, ranging from economic and trade sanctions to military force. Moral and political responsibility is also assigned to states as such. Many believe, for example, that wealthy, industrialized nations like the United States should take remedial responsibility for climate change by reducing emissions or paying reparations to compensate for its disproportionate contributions to the stock of greenhouse gasses.[7]

When a state is held legally or morally liable, however, it is hard to miss the fact that any material consequences fall not upon the state itself (whatever that could mean), but on the real-life people who live within its borders. The costs of reparations, economic sanctions, and climate change mitigation measures are paid out of the pockets of taxpayers and participants in the economy; missile strikes pass straight through the state to kill human beings, soldiers and civilians. Making matters morally worse, many of those people seem personally blameless for the wrongs of their state. As the Iraqi example renders vivid, many of the people who bear the costs of international sanctions may have opposed the wrongdoing of their leaders or suffered from it themselves, while being powerless to prevent it. In other contexts, those who bear the costs were not even alive at the time of the relevant wrongdoing. Present and future generations of Americans inherited the dangerously large stock of greenhouse gases from their industrializing ancestors.

Looking past the statist abstractions of international law and relations, when states are punished or sanctioned in the real world, it is the people of the state who suffer.[8] That inescapable fact has been a long-standing source of consternation for moral individualists. Hans Kelsen, reflecting on who should be held accountable for the Nazi atrocities of World War II, described international law as a "primitive" legal system premised on collective responsibility and indiscriminate punishment of the innocent and guilty alike.[9] In comparison, Kelsen viewed the Nuremberg Tribunal's individualization of moral blame and punishment as a civilizing step forward.[10]

Kelsen's descriptive of international law as "primitive" carries a specific meaning. Collective responsibility for wrongdoing and collective punishment have long been associated with systems of social order preexisting law and the state. In societies without states or centralized governments, social groups—kinship clans, tribes, or villages—were notoriously held collectively responsible for the wrongdoing of their members. When a member of one group wrongfully harmed a member of another group, violent retaliation would be visited indiscriminately upon members of the wrongdoing group without regard to individual responsibility or blame.[11] In societies with surplus wealth, blood vengeance eventually gave way to non-sanguinary compensation—"blood money"—paid to the victim or his kin.[12] But the principle of collective responsibility followed blood to money, holding the wrongdoer's group collectively responsible for making payments, and collectively vulnerable to violent retaliation in the event of default.[13]

Such "primitive" systems of collective responsibility have been thought to reflect a pre-liberal conception of groups rather than individuals as the atomic moral unit.[14] Legal historian Henry Sumner Maine famously theorized the "progressive" growth of societies from the primitive stage, where the basic legal unit is the family, clan, or village, to the modern stage, where the basic legal unit is the individual.[15] Maine saw collective responsibility, moral and legal, as a logical corollary of primitive law's communalism: groups are sanctioned because it is groups that misbehave.[16] Once society has progressed to point of assigning responsibility and blame at the level of individuals, we should expect to see sanctions redirected toward individuals as well. In the view of Maine and many others who now take liberal individualism for granted, group punishment is a "barbarous" atavism of the primitive past.[17]

It is no wonder, then, that enlightened liberals have shared Kelsen's discomfort with a system of international law that continues to impose collective responsibility and extract compensation in blood or money from groups of mostly innocent people. As one recent commentator puts it, "The international community is so primitive that the archaic concept of collective responsibility still prevails."[18]

One response to that skepticism has been a philosophically prodigious effort to rehabilitate the concept of collective responsibility in modern terms. Following in the footsteps of Hobbes, contemporary philosophers have attempted to conceptualize the state as a collective subject, capable of acting, intending, and wrongdoing in its own right—a modernized version of Leviathan. This approach is premised on the theory that certain kinds of organized, or "incorporated," groups, including the state, can be appropriately treated as moral agents and held responsible for their own misbehavior.[19] Even if states can be personified as wrongdoers, however, it remains a separate question why the individual members of the state should be responsible for the consequences, or how that responsibility should be distributed among them. Maybe there is some sense in saying that the state of Germany, personified as a moral actor, is responsible for the Holocaust. But that alone does not provide any obvious justification for holding each and every German citizen responsible, including present-day Germans who were not alive during the Nazi regime.[20]

The real challenge for the kind of collective responsibility imposed by international law lies in explaining why people who have personally done no wrong should nonetheless be held responsible just on the basis of shared citizenship with those who did. Meeting that challenge remains a work in progress.[21] One approach, following from the Hobbesian premise that "states speak and act in the name of their subjects," links collective responsibility to legitimate political obligation.[22] If it can be said of a state that each citizen plays the "dual role as one of society's subjects and as one of those in whose name its authority is exercised," that could provide a Hobbesian justification for both state coercion and collective responsibility. Subjects might be obligated to submit to law because law is in some meaningful sense collectively self-imposed.[23] And for the same reason, they might be held collectively responsible for the state's wrongdoing. As we saw in the previous chapter, a condition for understanding law to be self-imposed might be that the political community govern itself according to principles of justice.[24] A further condition might be that citizens exercise some degree of democratic voice.[25] But assuming the necessary conditions are met and a state can claim to act in the name of its citizens, then perhaps the legitimacy of coercion and collective responsibility can go hand-in-hand.

Hard-core moral individualists are unlikely to be persuaded by this, or any other, justification for collective responsibility. Even if there is some sense in which a state's citizens can be assigned responsibility for what their state has done, surely they are not all *equally* responsible. Some participated directly, others did nothing; some enthusiastically supported, others protested and resisted; some benefited, others were harmed. Even granting that every individual citizen bears *some* responsibility, the lack of individualized calibration leaves international sanctions irreconcilably at odds with the kind of liberal individualism that objects to the "primitivism" of collective responsibility.

On the other hand, insisting on full individualization of international responsibility presents problems of its own. For one thing, it seems hard to reconcile with the statist premises of the international legal system as a whole. Collective responsibility at the level of the state is not just a feature of liability and sanctions, but also of international legal *compliance*. Individual citizens of every state are bound and burdened by international legal obligations entered into by their state, regardless of whether these people approved or were even alive at the time. The individualist complaint of a current business owner who is disadvantaged by a tax treaty signed on to by her state, or of current taxpayers forced to repay sovereign debt taken on long ago by a different government, seems indistinguishable from the individualist complaints of citizens saddled with sanctions in response to the illegal actions of their states. An insistence on fully individualized moral accounting would threaten to take down the entire international legal system, which is fundamentally based on the principle of state, and therefore collective, responsibility.[26]

Even focusing solely on the remedial context, fully disaggregating responsibility for state wrongdoing and reassigning it to individuals would be no simple task. Following the lead of the Nuremberg Trials, a starting point might be to attribute state wrongdoing to a relatively small number of political and military leaders. But as the Nuremberg Trials also demonstrated, parsing responsibility among government officials is seldom straightforward. To start, there is the problem of "many hands": "Because many different officials contribute in many different ways to decisions and policies of government, it is difficult even in principle to identify who is morally responsible for political outcomes."[27] The difficulties multiply when we consider the many more hands of ordinary citizens who, in multifarious ways and differing degrees, may have contributed to, benefited from, or failed to prevent the wrongdoing of their government.[28] Precisely parceling out the individual responsibilities of citizens and their representatives for the actions of the state seems empirically, if not conceptually, impossible. If collective responsibility in international law lacks a clear or convincing moral justification, it is perhaps bolstered by the difficulty of imagining a realistic alternative.

Collective Sanctions

An affirmative case for collective responsibility can more easily be made on consequentialist grounds. That is true of state responsibility in the international legal system writ large, which is at least arguably justified by the instrumental benefits of enabling groups of people to enter into collective, intergenerational contracts and commitments.[29] Even if citizens cannot be blamed for state misbehavior, forcing them collectively to bear the costs might motivate them to do more to control their states and prevent wrongdoing.

Sanctioning or punishing collectives is a time-honored (if morally dishonored) means of motivating groups to monitor and control their wrongdoing members. The instrumental value of collective sanctions was probably not lost on the "primitive" societies that put the practice to such conspicuous use. In stateless societies lacking centralized law enforcement capabilities, punishment for wrongdoing might sensibly have been directed at groups not because groups were deemed collectively responsible for wrongdoing but simply because the members of tightly knit social groups were in an advantageous position to identify, monitor, and control individual wrongdoers—and could be motivated by the threat of sanctions to do so. On this understanding, the imposition of collective sanctions might not have reflected morally primitive communalism. Instead, it might have served as a sophisticated strategy for indirectly policing the behavior of individual wrongdoers by leveraging the enforcement capacity of social groups.

In medieval Iceland, for example, social order was maintained through the institutionalized practice of blood feud, a self-help system of vengeance premised on collective liability and punishment. The object of a vengeance killing was typically a kinsman of the wrongdoer, just as the expiator was typically a kinsman of the victim. But the group orientation of blood feuding was entirely consistent with the assignment of individual responsibility. As a leading study makes clear, "Avengers were able to distinguish individuals in their opposition. They did not see the opposing group as an undifferentiated Them."[30] Groups on the receiving end of vengeance, too, were highly conscious of the individual responsibility of their own members. Individual troublemakers who invited vengeance against their kinsmen were targeted for suspension or expulsion from the group or offered up to outsiders for personalized retaliation. Icelanders appear to have viewed kinship groups not as personified moral agents but merely as useful intermediaries for controlling individual behavior. To be sure, blood feuding may have reinforced the communal social structure. A good way to bring family members closer together is to threaten them with slaughter when their relatives misbehave. But sociological communalism is entirely consistent with systems of social control focused on individual wrongdoing.

Medieval England took the instrumental approach to collective sanctions a step further, creating groups just for the purpose of punishment when one of their members committed a crime. In common with Iceland and other stateless societies, medieval England faced severe problems of social disorder with limited state resources for solving them. Violent crime was rampant: homicide rates may have been double those of contemporary America (quite a feat in the absence of firearms).[31] Lacking a state-run police force or centralized law enforcement bureaucracy, the Crown created a system of collective punishment known as frankpledge. Most adult men in England were required to organize themselves into groups of ten that were held collectively liable for the crimes or misdeeds of any member who escaped prosecution. No one would have thought of frankpledge groups as communal wrongdoers in themselves; these groups were entirely artificial creations, lacking any independent social identity to which wrongdoing could be ascribed. The point of the frankpledge system was simply to mobilize groups as instruments of social control, creating incentives for members to identify and apprehend individual wrongdoers and offer them up for punishment.[32]

International law might lean heavily on collective sanctions for essentially the same reasons. In common with stateless societies, the international order lacks a centralized law enforcement apparatus and is therefore left to rely upon decentralized, self-help enforcement by organized groups (i.e., sovereign states). Like Icelandic kinship groups, moreover, states in the international system have limited ability to identify individual wrongdoers in other states or target them with effective sanctions.[33] The regime of collective sanctions solves these problems by effectively delegating responsibility for monitoring and controlling wrongdoers to the most capable enforcer: their own group. The wrongdoers primarily responsible for state misbehavior in most cases will be the political leadership—government officials and influential constituencies. Sanctioning states imposes collective responsibility and costs on the state's population in the hope of motivating them to change the behavior of their political leaders and hence the behavior of the state. As one theorist of international collective responsibility explains:

> "[A]llowing liability to be distributed to citizens gives them an incentive to exercise their political participation rights to control the state, minimizing harms to outsiders. If citizens can be held task-responsible to repair the damage when the state [behaves] incorrectly, then citizens have an incentive to ensure the state gets it right, through voting, public dissent, and civil disobedience.... [They] can contest and object to [liability-incurring policies] and sanction the government that imposes them.[34]

Laying bare the logic of this strategy reveals its potential utility, but also its limitations. The efficacy of collective sanctions will obviously depend on the ability of the sanctioned population to control the behavior of their state, using votes or other forms of political influence. In democratic systems of government, there is at least some prospect that imposing broad-based costs on state populations will motivate electoral majorities to redirect their government. But in an autocratic state like Saddam Hussein's Iraq, the leader and ruling coalition will often be able to insulate themselves not only from the economic costs of sanctions but also from any political costs stemming from the suffering of their populations, by ignoring or repressing dissent. It is no wonder, then, that the economic sanctions leveled against Saddam Hussein's Iraq, for all the suffering they imposed on the Iraqi people, did nothing to change Hussein's policies, threaten his hold on power, or cut into his multi-billion-dollar personal fortune.[35]

The Iraq debacle, and the longer track record of ineffective sanction regimes, has finally led to a reassessment. Seeing through the image of Leviathan, scholars and policymakers have looked inside the state to identify the constituencies bearing the costs of sanctions and the likely internal political consequences. One predictable conclusion has been that broad-based economic sanctions are unlikely to have much of an effect on the behavior of authoritarian leaders and states.[36] Instead, the U.S. foreign policy community and the U.N. have come around to the use of targeted, or "smart," sanctions, aimed specifically at politically efficacious constituencies such as military generals and economic elites. The sanctions imposed on Iran during the Obama administration successfully created pressure on the Iranian political leadership to abandon its nuclear program by freezing the assets held by members of the ruling regime and restricting the oil imports that fed their coffers.[37] America got a taste of its own medicine when, in retaliation for import duties on steel and aluminum imposed by the Trump Administration, the EU and China targeted tariffs at Harley Davidson motorcycles, bourbon, and orange juice, among other products manufactured in the districts of leading Republican Senators or in swing states Trump needed for reelection.[38] In response to the Russian invasion of Ukraine in 2022, the United States, EU, and other countries imposed a sanctions regime that, among other measures, targeted Russian oligarchs and members of Vladimir Putin's inner circle, seizing their yachts, freezing their assets, and banning international travel and the importation of luxury goods.[39]

The turn to strategic targeting highlights the failings of unstrategic international sanctions directed against states. There is no meaningful sense in which states can be punished; and it makes no sense to indiscriminately sanction the population of a state if the people bearing the costs can do nothing to prevent wrongdoing. Where collective sanctions fail, instrumentally or morally, the Nuremberg approach of individualizing responsibility and punishment may be preferable after all. Following the failure of sanctions and the carnage of two wars, Saddam Hussein was finally captured and put to death.

The Corporate Analogy

Before turning to state responsibility in the context of constitutional law, there is another common application of collective responsibility that is helpful to have in hand. Like states, corporations and other business firms are routinely held legally and morally responsible for their wrongdoing.[40] Also like states, corporations are often personified in law and the public imagination, conceived as autonomous, self-directed agents, possessed of their own motivations, moral characters, and legal rights and obligations.[41] Yet personifying or otherwise reifying corporations risks losing sight of the real people whose interests are at stake in legal regulation of the firm.[42] Particularly subject to doubt on this score is the practice of sanctioning or criminally punishing corporations for wrongdoing. The obvious problem is that, in the words of a long ago Lord Chancellor of England, corporations have "no soul to be damned, no body to be kicked."[43] Like states, corporations cannot be sent to prison or physically punished;[44] and monetary penalties "flow through the corporate shell and fall on the relatively blameless" shareholders, who own but do not directly control the decisions of the firm.[45] Meanwhile, the people who do directly control the decisions of the firm, managers and employees, are left untouched by sanctions aimed at the abstraction of the corporate entity.

It is not hard to understand why some contemporary commentators view corporate liability as continuous with the "primitive" practice (so-called, here again) of personifying and punishing a collective entity without regard to the individual responsibility of its members. Believers in corporate responsibility "truly personify and hate the corporation": "[They] hate the mahogany paneling, the Lear jet, the smokestack, the glass tower, and all of the people inside. They—the mahogany and all of them—are responsible for the medical fraud, the oil spill, the price-fixing, and the illegal campaign contributions. To superstitious people, villains need not breathe."[46]

Improving on superstition, philosophical justifications for the moral responsibility of corporate entities or the collectively responsibility of shareholders for corporate wrongdoing have been developed along the same lines as justifications for the responsibility of states or their citizens. One approach is to attribute moral agency and responsibility to the corporation itself, not reducible to the acts or intentions of any of the individuals involved, much as responsibility is sometimes assigned to the state as an "incorporated group."[47] But as with the state and its citizens, forcing individual shareholders to pay the costs of the corporation's wrongdoing requires further justification. Some moral philosophers would hold these individuals responsible on the basis of their voluntary decisions to associate with the firm[48]—a rationale that is not readily available in the context of most citizens' involuntary relationship with the state.[49] Not available in the corporate context is the kind of justification based on the special relationship of citizens to a state that speaks and acts in their name.

Whatever its moral status, corporate liability is commonly understood, from a functional perspective, as an instrumentally useful application of collective sanctions. The alternative to corporate liability is individual liability for the corporate managers who are most directly responsible for the corporation's wrongful acts. Similar to wrongdoing in "primitive" and international society, however, the relevant individual corporate wrongdoers often are difficult for outsiders to identify, and also difficult to sanction adequately, given that the magnitude of corporate liability is typically far in excess of the assets of individual employees. Imposing collective sanctions on shareholders offers a potential solution to these problems, effectively delegating enforcement to a group that may be better positioned than outside enforcers to monitor and control managerial wrongdoing. The success of this strategy will depend on the enforcement capabilities of shareholders as a group (in combination with other market forces). As with state citizens and their political leaders, the diffuse and diversified shareholders of large, publicly traded corporations may not have much inclination or ability to play a major role in policing managers.[50] But the optimistic view is that motivating shareholders to make use of corporate governance structures to control internal misconduct will be more effective in most cases than attempting to impose direct liability on individual agents from the outside.[51] Viewed in this functional light, corporate liability has been aptly compared to medieval frankpledge: not as punishment of an artificial person, but as a means of conscripting group members to police wrongdoers in their midst.[52]

Constitutional Responsibility and Remedies

We have learned thus far—from theorists and practitioners of international and corporate law, as well as medieval kings and Icelanders, among others—that the practice of holding personified entities responsible for wrongdoing is more complicated, morally and instrumentally, than it might appear. Even if states, corporations, and other groups can sensibly be understood and held responsible as legal or moral agents, any penalties or punishments that follow will be passed through to actual persons, becoming de facto collective sanctions. Sanctioning innocent people for the wrongdoing of others raises rather obvious moral concerns that are difficult to put to rest. Morality aside, holding groups responsible can function as an effective strategy for policing and preventing wrongdoing under particular circumstances. But understanding just what those circumstances are requires close attention to the instrumental logic and limitations of collective sanctions.

Constitutional law appears to have learned none of this.[53] When constitutional rules and rights are violated, liability and remedial responsibility are attributed to government entities, such as local governments, federal agencies, and the United States. But these entities are no more capable than states or corporations of bearing the moral or material costs on their own; instead, the costs of constitutional violations are passed through to individual citizens. Most of the individuals who bear these costs are not themselves wrongdoers, and in many cases, they are powerless to change the behavior of their political leadership. In short, constitutional law relies upon collective responsibility and collective sanctions in much the same way as international and corporate law. The difference is that constitutional lawyers and judges have proceeded with no apparent recognition that this is what they are doing, much less any effort to understand the moral or instrumental consequences.

Consider a constitutional case in which a city is held liable and ordered to pay millions of dollars in damages for implementing a racially discriminatory policing practice of stopping and frisking young men in high-crime neighborhoods. Such a judgment would be understood by courts and the public as a penalty or punishment for constitutional wrongdoing imposed on the city government and its police department. But these government entities are, for all practical purposes, institutional abstractions. The real costs of constitutional sanctions will pass through government and fall upon its constituents. More specifically, compensation payments for constitutional violations will be paid for by raising taxes or cutting spending or other government services. The costs will therefore be borne by some combination of taxpayers and the beneficiaries of the spending or services that are sacrificed. All else equal, we should probably expect politically weaker constituencies to bear a greater share of the costs—dispersed groups of taxpayers perhaps, or disempowered groups of beneficiaries, such as students in underfunded public schools or workers relying on public transportation.

To state the obvious, it is hard to see why any of these people should bear special responsibility for police misconduct. Plausible wrongdoers in a case like this might include police officers, city officials, or the voters and interest groups who supported the unconstitutional practices. But if the goal is to target the actual wrongdoers, constitutional sanctions that impose costs on a morally random (if predictably politically disadvantaged) subset of citizens will almost always miss their mark.

Courts and constitutional scholars have devoted little sustained attention to the question of who, specifically, should be held responsible for constitutional wrongdoing.[54] And they often seem unaware of who, in fact, is paying the costs. That is certainly true in cases brought against government entities, as described above. But it is also true in the constitutional cases brought against individual government officials. For reasons of historical path dependence, most civil rights actions against the police name individual officers as defendants.[55] The working assumption in these cases has been that, following the formality of the pleading, any damages will be paid personally by the defendants. The prospect of saddling individual cops trying to do their job in good faith with millions of dollars in liability has provoked fairness concerns, as well as functional concerns that officers will respond by prioritizing "personal risk minimization" over public service.[56] Courts have responded to these worries by fashioning special immunity doctrines to shield officers from liability for violating constitutional rights, including the "qualified immunity" defense that has become a particular flash-point in legal and political debates about police violence and racism.

But all of this is premised on the formalistic falsehood that individual officers are paying the costs of constitutional violations out of their own pockets. In fact, officers are nearly always indemnified by their government employers;[57] and even if they were not, the costs would still fall upon government through the vastly higher salaries that would be necessary to hire officers subject to personal liability. We know that costs paid by "the government" are ultimately paid by ordinary citizens. In reality, therefore, constitutional liability imposed upon an individual police officer amounts to the same thing as liability imposed upon the police department or the city. Both end up imposing costs on some morally arbitrary subset of ordinary citizens.

In other contexts, courts and scholars have taken entirely different views of who does or should bear the costs of constitutional violations. The constitutional law of "just compensation" for takings, for example, toggles between two different perspectives. One is that the costs of takings are paid by a personified or reified government entity that is fairly charged for the loss "it" has imposed. A second perspective on takings is that the purpose of compensation is "to bar Government from forcing some people alone to bear public burdens, which in all fairness and justice, should be borne by the public as a whole."[58] Here the focus shifts from government to citizens, with the goal of holding "the public as a whole" collectively responsible for the costs of takings. Broad-based taxation to cover the costs of compensation might accomplish something like that. It is at least as likely, however, that "some people alone" will be forced to pay through targeted revenue measures or selective reductions in expenditures.

There is at least one context in which courts and theorists have been more closely attuned to the connection, or lack thereof, between constitutional responsibility and cost-bearing. Race-based preferences in employment or university admissions that are designed to compensate for past discrimination against racial minorities, are understood by conservatives as "reverse discrimination" against white applicants who are placed at a disadvantage. Even if they are open to compensating the victims of discrimination, conservatives question why in-kind compensation should be paid by a subset of arbitrarily chosen individuals who are not personally responsible for the racist wrongs being remedied. Liberals, on the other hand, have been willing to countenance race-based remedies for "societal" discrimination, holding all present-day Americans (or white Americans) collectively responsible for historical race discrimination. That view extends to broad-based reparations for slavery and racial injustice, which proponents justify as owed collectively by all white Americans to all Black Americans, without regard to individual responsibility—in the same way that all Germans might be thought responsible for the Holocaust.[59]

Constitutional law's erratic approach to the attribution and apprehension of responsibility has been coupled with consistent confusion about the instrumental consequences of constitutional remedies. Courts and scholars commonly assume that making government pay for rights violations by the police, takings of property, or other constitutional misdeeds will force it to internalize costs and deter misconduct in just the same way as damages imposed upon an ordinary person. This assumption replicates the naïve view that personified states in the international arena can be hurt by sanctions. States and governments are not hurt by losing money (or, really, by anything). The only cost- and pain-bearers are ordinary citizens, who are subject to de facto collective sanctions. The consequences of making government pay on the welfare of various groups of citizens, and the consequences in turn for how those citizens exercise control over government decisionmaking, cannot be predicted on the simple model of personification.

Another model comes closer, though it is still too simple: that is the model of corporations. Like persons, corporations predictably behave as if they were "hurt" by having to pay money. But the mechanism that produces the behavioral resemblance is more complicated, running through collective sanctions against corporate shareholders and their resulting incentives to monitor and control managers in such a way as to maximize firm profits. A similar mechanism, one might think, could cause government to behave in the same way. Citizens of a political jurisdiction might be viewed as the comparable owners and residual claimants of their government, exercising democratic control over the behavior of the government officials who serve as their managerial agents. The crucial disanalogy, however, is that citizens are not seeking monetary profit from government but pursuing their welfare along a number of different dimensions. Groups of citizens with divergent interests and varying amounts of political control over government officials will not create the homogeneous force of corporate shareholders pushing for profit-maximization. In many cases, the resultant of political vectors will be a government preference for *losing* money—and for violating constitutional rights.

Consider a constitutional takings case challenging state environmental regulations that would restrict the development of beachfront property, imposing significant costs on the owners. Suppose a court will require the state to pay just compensation. Would the prospect of paying that cost create a disincentive for government to regulate, in the same way that forcing a private firm to pay compensation for polluting or eroding the beachfront would create a disincentive? The answer is no. In fact, compensation might actually make the government *more* likely to regulate. In the absence of compensation, government regulators will face strong political opposition from beachfront property owners, a wealthy, well-coordinated, intensely interested, and politically efficacious group. If these property owners can be bought off with compensation, the political costs to government officials of regulating will plummet. To be sure, paying compensation will create a different group of regulatory opponents: the diffuse taxpayers or defunded beneficiaries of government programs who will end up bearing the costs. But switching the regulatory losers from powerful property owners to weaker political constituencies might well lower the political costs to government officials on net. In that case, a constitutional requirement of compensation would facilitate regulatory takings rather than discourage or deter them.[60] That is, after all, why governments often *voluntarily* pay compensation in cases like this: to buy off concentrated opposition to socially beneficial regulatory programs. (Given the possibility of voluntary compensation, a compensation *requirement* might predictably increase political costs for government, if it were applied only in those cases in which government had calculated that *not* compensating was the political-cost-minimizing strategy. A constitutional *prohibition* on compensation would have the same effect.[61])

Counterintuitively, then, making government pay for constitutional violations does not reliably push in the direction of constitutional compliance. Instead, the behavioral consequences of making government pay constitutional compensation will depend on whether that payment increases or decreases the political cost to government officials. That, in turn, will depend on which constituencies bear the monetary costs and on how much political power these constituencies possess. Generally speaking, if the groups that end up funding compensation are more politically powerful than constitutional victims and their supporters, making government pay will tend to increase political costs. If the groups that fund compensation are less powerful, however, as in the regulatory takings case, the result will be the opposite: constitutional liability will actually *lower* the political costs of rights violations for government officials and *encourage* government to violate rights.

The possibility of compensation leading to constitutionally perverse consequences seems never to have occurred to courts or constitutional lawyers, who mostly take for granted that government will respond to costs in the same way as an ordinary person or profit-maximizing firm. That assumption is sometimes made explicit. The textbook analysis of the economic consequences of compensation for constitutional takings starts from the premise that government "operate[s] with an incentive structure similar to that of a similarly situated private enterprise."[62] The standard instrumental justification for compensation follows straightforwardly: "If the government were free to take resources without paying for them, it would not feel incentives, created by the price system, to use those resources efficiently."[63]

One way of appreciating what is fundamentally misguided about modeling the government in this way—as a cost-internalizing, profit-maximizing private firm—is to consider how the *benefits* of government action factor into the equation. Returning to the regulatory takings case, if the goal is to induce the state to weigh the costs of environmental regulation against the benefits, then presumably the state needs to take account of both. We are told that government will take account of the costs of regulations only if forced to pay money in compensation. But how, then, will government be made to take account of regulatory benefits? After all, those benefits are not usually converted into monetary inflows. Government *could* seek restitution from the beneficiaries of its policies or programs, for example by imposing a special tax on everyone who benefited from its environmental regulations. But in reality that hardly ever happens, and it certainly is not constitutionally required. Nonetheless, the conventional constitutional analysis assumes, oddly and asymmetrically, that government will always, automatically internalize the regulatory benefits it confers. On the cost side, government is supposed to behave like a profit-maximizing person or firm, internalizing only those costs that it pays out in dollars. On the benefit side, however, government is supposed to behave like a public-spirited altruist, internalizing social benefits as if they were enjoyed by the government itself, even though the government is not typically getting paid.

The confusion here is at multiple levels. If we are to imagine that government behavior is driven by the government's own welfare function, then it would be helpful to start by understanding what the government is supposed to want. If what it wants is to maximize *social* welfare, then the government will presumably take account of both the social costs and social benefits of regulation, without regard for the money flowing into or out of the treasury. Compensation for takings or other constitutional violations, in that view, would make no difference whatsoever. If, on the other hand, what government wants is to maximize dollars in the treasury, then compensation for regulatory costs without any form of restitution for regulatory benefits would incentivize the government to do absolutely nothing, because it would have nothing to gain (but regulatory costs to lose).

The deeper level of confusion comes from thinking of "the government" as wanting anything. By now we should know better. The behavior of states and governments is not a product of their own wills or welfare (whatever that could mean); it is driven by the decisions of officials, which are influenced in turn by democratic interests. Making government pay compensation for takings or constitutional violations has no direct impact on officials, who care about government dollars only because collecting and spending them in different ways generates political support and opposition among constituents.[64] The effect of constitutional compensation depends on how the payment of government money affects these interests; on how moving dollars changes votes. And, as the takings case illustrated, the relationship between dollars and votes is entirely contingent on political circumstances.

Violations of other constitutional rights are no different. Let us return to the case of unconstitutional policing. For courts and constitutional scholars, the purpose and effect of constitutional liability is straightforward. "Imagine a city police force that conducts racially discriminatory searches, employs excessive force against suspects, or engages in other forms of unconstitutional conduct. Though a damages award does not require discontinuation of such practices, it exerts significant pressure on government and its officials to respect constitutional bounds."[65] Does it really? Suppose that aggressive and even unconstitutional police tactics in high-crime neighborhoods are politically supported by a majority of voters who are afraid of crime and not themselves likely to be stopped by the police. Some measure of political opposition to unconstitutional policing will come from the high-crime communities that bear the costs. But since these communities are also the ones that suffer most of the costs of crime, their members are often ambivalent or divided about policing.[66] In this (not unrealistic) political scenario, it is easy to understand why government officials would tend to come out in favor of aggressive, and even unconstitutionally aggressive, policing.

Will the imposition of constitutional liability change the political calculus? The effect of damages liability would be to shift some of the costs of unconstitutional policing from the immediate victims and their allies to other groups—the now-familiar alternatives of taxpayers and defunded beneficiaries.[67] Raising the costs of unconstitutional policing to suburban taxpayers might dampen their enthusiasm, creating a larger and more influential base of political opposition. Alternatively, and perhaps more likely, recalling the introductory example of Chicago, redirecting the costs of compensation to politically weaker constituencies—through reductions in spending on social services or public education, or through bond financing that shifts costs onto future taxpayers who are not present voters—might have the opposite effect.[68] The precise political dynamics are hard to predict, but it seems at least as likely that constitutional liability would result in an *increase* in political support for unconstitutional policing than a decrease. As a general matter, there is no reason to expect that making government pay will create fewer constitutional violations and not more.

Following the trajectory of international sanctions, constitutionalists might get "smarter" about constitutional remedies. Responding to patterns of police brutality, courts and federal regulators could rely more heavily on injunctions and structural reform of police departments. Another obvious alternative is aiming sanctions at individual wrongdoers. Bad cops can be made to pay personally, if not through damages liability than by means of criminal prosecution and punishment. Recalling Kelsen's view of Nuremberg and the ultimate disposition of Saddam Hussein, individual sanctions in some cases can be both more effective and more just than collective ones. But the first step is for constitutionalists to understand who is actually paying the price when government is held responsible for constitutional violations. Government is not a creature with its own wealth and welfare that can be punished for wrongdoing. In constitutional law as in international law, attempts to achieve justice or deterrence by directing sanctions at Leviathan invariably miss their target—because the version of Leviathan imagined by these regimes of law does not actually exist.

Big, Bad Leviathan

Imagining government as a personified Leviathan with its own wealth and welfare has afflicted constitutional law in other ways, as well. We saw in Chapter 5 the pernicious consequences of viewing the government and its sub-parts as self-aggrandizing maximizers of their own power. A parallel view is that government is not just imperialistic but avaricious, voraciously intent upon maximizing its own wealth. As the remainder of this chapter describes, the image of a self-serving, self-engorging Leviathan gobbling up society's resources has been a pernicious influence on constitutional law, and on American political thought more generally.

Empire-Building

Constitutional law and politics in America have long been obsessed with the dangers and diabolical strategies of a version of Leviathan known to Americans as Big Government. This insatiable creature feeds its ever-expanding girth by ingesting more and more of the nation's wealth and resources, preying on citizens who desperately try to protect themselves by "starving the beast."

This is not just Fox News rhetoric. Ostensibly sophisticated political scientists and economists working in the public choice tradition deploy what is aptly termed a "Leviathan model" of the state.[69] As it was initially developed by Nobel-laureate James Buchanan, that model starts from the Hobbesian premise that an all-powerful Leviathan is needed to protect its subjects against the war of all against all that would otherwise arise in the state of nature. The Leviathan imagined by Buchanan and his followers, however, is not a benevolent protector of its subjects but a self-interested maximizer of its own wealth that will use its monopoly on coercive force to prey upon them. In an alternative backstory, organized societies emerge from anarchy when a warlord offers protection to a group of people who are being preyed upon by "roving bandits." But the warlord himself is a "stationary bandit" who has made the calculation that he can collect more wealth from a bounded group of subjects under his control. By stealing—or, as it is euphemistically called, taxing—only part of his subjects' incomes, and by providing public goods that increase their productivity, the ruler increases the amount of social wealth over time. But only for the purpose of maximizing his longer-term personal take.[70]

This Leviathan, or "antisocial contract,"[71] model of the state contains at least a grain of historical truth.[72] In the Hobbesian environment of early state formation, with kings in a perpetual "posture of war," the survival of the state and its king really did depend on building military strength by raising manpower and money. States that were successful in battle acquired more territory, and with it more human and capital resources, while the losing states became smaller and weaker and eventually disappeared. Through the eighteenth century, that Darwinian situation drove monarchs to conquer and colonize territories, going to war in pursuit of resources. The rise of global trade channeled interstate rivalry into economic warfare, conducted through the strategy of mercantilism. States competed with one another to amass currency and capital, expand export markets, and extract natural resources and manpower through colonialism. Classical realist theorists of international relations carry elements of this picture into the modern world, emphasizing the linkage between economic and military power, and insisting that state survival depends on competing for relative superiority in resources and strength.

Yet there are limits to what can be understood about the modern state by picturing warring kings competing for wealth and territory. By the end of the eighteenth century, the world had absorbed Adam Smith's lesson that the "wealth of nations" was not the wealth of a king or Leviathan but the wealth of the state's citizens; and was more productively pursued through a strategy of peaceful free trade and mutual advantage than through competitive mercantilism, colonialism, or warfare.[73] The rise of international trade and other forms of interstate cooperation combined with the declining threat of war and conquest "allow[ed] states to reap many of the benefits of being big, even if they themselves are quite small."[74] States no longer needed to amass resources and population to support self-sufficient markets and military might; imperial powers no longer needed to incur the high costs of colonial governance; and colonies could survive and prosper as independent states.[75] Since the end of World War II, the number of independent countries in the world has more than doubled, and more than half of them are smaller in population than Massachusetts.[76] Empire-building has been replaced by empire-*un*building.

The model of empire-building Leviathan has lost descriptive traction on the domestic front, as well. Modern states are not ruled by kings seeking to pile up bullion or warlords seeking to extract as much wealth as possible from their captive populations. Or at least most modern states are not. The

Leviathan model might remain a good fit for the unfortunate states that are still run by kleptocratic dictators and oligarchs who treat the treasury as their personal bank accounts and care only about maximizing their personal wealth at their countrymen's expense. But in the vast majority of countries, even allowing for some measure of corruption, political leaders do not profit from their offices in the manner of kings.[77] Government officials have no intrinsic interest in increasing the number of dollars flowing through the treasury, because the money is not theirs; all the money taxed or borrowed by the state is spent on the citizenry.[78] And citizens, who are both the payers and recipients of all the money passing through the state, also have nothing to gain by increasing the state's fiscal size. That leaves only the state itself, Leviathan, with a self-interested incentive to amass wealth and resources for its own benefit. Fortunately, however, there is no such thing.

Here again, the corporate analogy is illuminating. From the Gilded Age trusts to contemporary Big Tech, corporate Leviathans have also been accused of seeking to maximize their economic power and wealth at the public's expense, joining their state and governmental counterparts in inflicting the "curse of bigness."[79] There may be good reasons for focusing on corporate size when it bears on monopoly and market competition. But the vision of inherently threatening, self-aggrandizing Big Business is as mythical as that of Big Government. As sophisticated analysts now take for granted, corporations are not driven to maximize their size (measured by assets, sales, or market cap), but simply to maximize the profits of their owners. Managerial agents pursuing the interests of their shareholding principles follow the dictates of efficiency, not empire-building, in setting the size of their firm. Efficient firm size will depend on factors such as the costs of internal governance relative to the costs of outside contracting.[80] Just as the optimal size of states shrinks as the costs of international cooperation decrease, the optimal size of firms shrinks as the costs of outside contracting decrease. But neither states nor firms have empire-building incentives to expand beyond the size that serves the interests of their citizens and shareholders.

Now, here is a footnote. Empirical evidence suggests that corporate managers do, in fact, sometimes take advantage of agency slack to expand the size of their firms some distance beyond the profit-making scale in an effort to raise their own salaries or reduce the risk of takeovers. That is the technical definition of corporate "empire-building."[81] But this form of managerial misbehavior is the marginal exception that proves the rule. The predominant motivations of managers is serve the empire-indifferent interests of shareholders. That is why, in the corporate context, the entirety of the theoretical and empirical evidence points to profit maximization, not growth maximization, as the best approximation of corporate behavior.

Government, as we have seen, does not maximize profit. But government officials are similarly bound to the interests of their constituents through democratic politics and other forms of political control, leaving limited space for them to pursue their purely selfish ends. And even within that limited space, it is hard to see what self-serving officials would have to gain for themselves by increasing the size of government. In a democracy, the self-interest of elected officials is served by gaining and keeping hold on political power and advancing their preferred policy agendas. Those goals are typically best served by responding to the interests of constituents, or at least politically efficacious subsets. Constituents may care about their own wealth, and more broadly about their own welfare, but they have no reason to care about the wealth of the state as such. Some policies favored by constituents and officials will result in increasing taxes, spending, and government resources: for example, fighting a war or expanding social welfare programs. But other policy agendas will call for lower taxes, less spending, and smaller government. The size of the state will grow or shrink depending on the contingencies of political and policy demands. But there is no hard-wired tendency toward expansion, much less a self-directed agenda of empire-building on the state's own behalf.

Yet American political thought cannot free itself from the image of the government as an empire-building Leviathan. That image has been made especially vivid in political and constitutional attacks on the administrative state.[82] Outrage about the "rise and rise of the administrative state,"[83] a constitutional abomination conceived as a lawless "Leviathan," with a "voracious appetite . . . for consuming an ever-growing share of our incomes and wealth,"[84] has become a staple of conservative constitutional discourse. This outlook has contributed to the sustained legal and political assault on the post–New Deal administrative state, generating constitutional challenges to legislative delegations, independent agencies, and judicial deference to administrative decisionmaking. Conservative critics have detailed many different grounds for objecting to the administrative and regulatory state, from its arguable absence of originalist and historical warrant to its variously plausible democratic deficits. But looming over these specific objections is the specter of despotic rule by an avaricious and rapacious Leviathan.[85]

This kind of Leviathan has so long been a fixture of constitutional and political mythology that courts and scholars take its existence for granted. In reality, however, there is even less reason to believe in a pervasively empire-building administrative state than to believe in pervasively empire-building corporations. As it happens, the primary theoretical basis for predictions of an empire-building administrative state closely follows the logic of empire-building by corporate managers. This is the "imperial model" of the bureaucratic behavior, yet another public choice model of the Leviathan state, advanced by economist William Niskanen and his followers. The model purports to show that the administrative state has a predictable tendency toward over-spending and over-regulating at the public's expense. Niskanen hypothesizes that self-interested agency officials, like corporate managers, will want to expand their budget as a means of increasing their compensation and perquisites, future employment prospects, or capability to effectuate regulatory goals to which they are personally committed. Taking advantage of their greater information about the costs of regulating, Niskanen argues, these officials will dupe their legislative overseers into approving a larger agency budget and greater regulatory output than would be socially optimal.[86]

Few political scientists have been persuaded that Niskanen has identified even a reliable tendency in bureaucratic behavior, let alone a reason to suspect the entire administrative state of Leviathan-like empire-building. Starting with the motivations of agency officials, in the words of a leading scholar of American bureaucracy, "One wonders why Niskanen thinks bureaucrats are so desirous of maximizing their budgets if they can enjoy so few of the fruits."[87] Agency officials would seem to have much less to gain from larger budgets than their corporate managerial counterparts. Pointing to a larger agency budget is unlikely to get officials a big raise, in the way it actually might for corporate managers. And getting a raise is unlikely to be the primary motivation of the kinds of people who choose careers in government as opposed to in corporations where the pay is much better. More plausibly, bureaucrats might be interested in increasing their power and discretion, or in decreasing their workload and living the "quiet life." But neither of these self-serving agendas would be furthered in any obvious way by budgetary or regulatory maximization.[88] Nor would the more public-regarding agenda of advancing the regulatory mission of the agency. Bureaucrats may well be personally committed to the core missions of the agencies in which they work—protecting the environment, enforcing civil rights, educating children, and the like.[89] And they might have some motivation to expand output and budget in order to advance these missions. On the other hand, a commitment to a *particular* mission, or to a particular vision how that mission ought to be accomplished, would give bureaucrats a reason to resist any expansion of agency activity outside of those boundaries.[90] Empire-building with respect to regulatory intensity is therefore likely to be offset by empire-abnegating with respect to regulatory scope.

All of this assume that bureaucrats have free rein to run their agencies for their own benefit. But, of course, that is not how the administrative state works. Just as corporate managers are agents of shareholders, and elected representatives are agents of voters and citizens, bureaucrats are agents of elected officials—the president and Congress. Agencies are also subject to more direct control by the democratic constituencies and affected interests who have a voice in administrative decisionmaking. Indeed, Niskanen aside, the public choice perspective on the administrative decisionmaking has been dominated by the view that agencies are controlled or captured by interest groups—a view that would leave little room for the possibility of capture by their employees. In any event, democratic demands and constraints will leave bureaucrats limited autonomy to pursue self-interested goals. And again, of the various self-interested goals that individual bureaucrats might pursue, budget-maximization seems among the least plausible. Bureaucratic empire-building, like corporate empire-building, may be a real phenomenon. But it is no more than a rounding error in any plausible account of how government or corporations generally behave.

Impervious to reality, Leviathan mythology has crept into other areas of constitutional law, as well. Theories and doctrines of constitutional federalism are built around the assumption that states and localities—cast as mini-Leviathans, or profit-maximizing firms—will compete to enlarge their tax bases by attracting residents and businesses. Such competition is supposed to create a virtuous, market-driven impetus toward better government, substituting an efficient market of interjurisdictional competition for the national government as monopolist: "By harnessing competition among jurisdictions," we are told, "federalism secures in the political arena the advantages of economic markets—consumer choice and satisfaction, innovation, superior products at lower prices."[91] In this view, competition among governments will deliver higher quality public schools, lower taxes, and a check on overregulation and excessive redistribution.[92]

But interjurisdictional competition is also understood to have a dark side. Competition among governments in some settings is said to spur a socially destructive "race to the bottom," as jurisdictions forego beneficial forms of regulation for fear of driving away businesses. Thus, a commonly cited reason for nationalizing environmental regulation is that effective state-level regulation will be undermined by competition for industry. This race to the bottom story is duplicated in debates about globalization. A widely assumed consequence of economic globalization is that competition among countries to attract mobile business and capital to expand their tax base will drive them to lower environmental and labor standards. For labor unions and environmentalists, this has been an important reason for resisting free trade and other international economic agreements. For multinational corporations and investors it has been the opposite, an opportunity to use the credible threat of mobility to resist costly regulation. But both sides agree that profit-maximizing firms will benefit from a regime in which revenue-maximizing states compete globally for investments.[93]

The least common denominator of all these arguments is that states (both kinds: states in the United States and states in the international arena) will be driven to pursue commercial and population growth in order to maximize tax revenues. To be clear, this is a prediction about the behavior of polities, not the behavior of the individuals and firms who respond to policies. It is one thing to recognize that if people, businesses, and capital are freely mobile, all else equal they will choose the jurisdiction that offers their most-preferred policy package combining public goods, regulations, and tax rates.[94] But these demand-side dynamics—constituent sorting and "foot voting"[95]—tell us nothing about how government will behave on the supply side.[96] On that side of the equation, what is motivating governments to compete is supposed to be their inherently expansionist "desire to attract taxpayers and jobs [and] promote policies of economic growth and expansion."[97]

Here again, however, that kind of empire-building Leviathan is a figment of the imagination. The reality, as ever, is political decisionmaking by government officials and their constituents. Government officials gain nothing for themselves by increasing tax revenues unless they will be rewarded by politically efficacious constituencies for doing so. But growth is often the opposite of what these constituencies want. NIMBY coalitions campaign against building more housing for new residents. Opportunities for industrial development and economic growth are routinely rejected on account of environmental, congestion, or other quality of life concerns. A new Amazon headquarters that promises thousands of jobs and a big boost in tax revenues may prove highly unpopular among current residents who fear being pushed out of their neighborhoods by gentrification. Redistributive policies like living wage ordinances attract broad political support, even if they encourage some businesses to relocate.[98]

In taking these positions, democratic constituencies are acting straightforwardly to maximize their own welfare. But their welfare has no straightforward relationship to the size of the population or the tax base of the jurisdictions in which they live. Attracting new residents who consume more in public services than they pay in taxes will increase the tax base but decrease the aggregate welfare of the current population. The same is true of new businesses that impose environmental or other costs in excess of any spillover economic benefits. Driving away these people and industries to "competing" states is exactly the outcome that constituents in these states want and that they will reward government officials for delivering. Of course, political support and opposition does not always track social welfare. Politically powerful constituencies acting in their self-interest may oppose policies that would be better for everyone but costly for themselves. But that includes pro-growth policies, as the political success of NIMBYism exemplifies. To be sure, there will be other settings in which pro-growth interests prevail, whether because growth is broadly beneficial or because it benefits other powerful groups.[99] But there is nothing about democratic politics or promoting the public welfare that points to a general predilection for growth.[100]

Looking past Leviathan to the political incentives of officials and constituents casts doubt on much of the conventional wisdom about jurisdictional competition as a feature of constitutional federalism, and of international globalization as well. Devolving power to state and local governments is not a reliable recipe for increasing economic growth or improving the quality of public goods and services. Nations, states, and localities will not be driven to compete for businesses and residents just for the sake of maximizing growth and tax base. Nor will state regulation and redistribution invariably trigger races to the bottom. States and countries where majorities or powerful constituencies place a high value on environmental protection or other regulatory benefits will not hesitate to enact stringent regulations, even at the cost of losing business and industry.[101] States and governments will not race one another to the bottom or the top, but will move as the patterns of political demand dictate.

In short, there is no such thing as empire-building Leviathan. And there is no such thing as Big Government, at least not in the form of a hungry giant that lives to feast on the resources of society for its own pleasure and perpetual growth. To be sure, "big government" is sometimes meant not as an actual figure, but merely a figure of speech—an epithet meant to indicate aversion to socialism as opposed to free market capitalism, or disapproval of higher tax rates or stricter environmental standards. There is nothing mythological about that set of political and policy positions. But the issues at stakes are not much illuminated by talking in terms of government "bigness." Government is not clearly bigger in any meaningful sense when it regulates or redistributes as compared to when it leaves market outcomes alone. Nor is the neoliberal, deregulated and privatized "shrinking state" any smaller. As we were reminded in the previous chapter, the "free market" is itself a product of government, and implementing its outcomes is as big a government thing as changing them. In any event, what matters about government for most political purposes is not its metaphorical size but the material substance of what it does. Criticisms of Obamacare or calls to defund the police could continue on the substantive merits, unencumbered by the rhetoric of bigness or the fiction of empire-building. Little would be lost if we put the figure of Big Government to rest.

Corporeality Versus Capacity and Causality

What does it actually mean for government to be "big"? The most common metrics for measuring the size of states and governments look to the resources they have in their possession: primarily, money and manpower. Assessments of how big government is, or is becoming, typically take count of the amount of money that a government spends (measured in total or as a percentage of GDP or some other way) or the number of employees on the government's payroll. Yet an overarching lesson of this chapter is that what matters about states and governments is not the size of the treasury or payroll but what those resources are used to accomplish. Sizing up the piles of dollars deployed or number of people employed by states and governments measures the size of Leviathan's metaphorical body. But we may just as well be counting the number of public buildings or square feet in the capitol. These measures do not speak to what Leviathan actually does with its body: how much control over the world it possesses or exercises; how much of an impact it ultimately has. A more perspicacious measure of size would focus not on Leviathan's *corporeality* but instead on its *capacity* and *causality*—on how much power it can and does exercise over its subjects' lives.

Corporeality will sometimes correlate with the state's capacity to affect the lives of its subjects. Recalling the discussion of state capacity in Chapter 3, a state with a large army or bureaucracy at its disposal may be better able to win wars and regulate its economy than a state lacking those resources. But money and manpower can also be deceptive metrics of actual state capacity, and even more so of what or how much states use that capacity to accomplish. A state that raises lots of money in taxes or employs hordes of bureaucrats will be seen as big by the conventional measures, but if the money merely passes through the treasury or the bureaucrats do little more than shuffle paper, then the state's actual impact will be small. A state that sucked up 100% of GDP in taxes and then returned each dollar to its original owner through spending programs would register on conventional metrics as a maximally massive Leviathan, but it would have no meaningful impact on the world.[102]

The other way around, states and governments can have a great deal of impact without making use of their own money or manpower at all. They can do so simply by *regulating*—ordering private actors to do things, or not to do things. A basic fact of public administration is that nearly anything government could accomplish by taxing and spending or by deploying its own workers could also be accomplished by means of regulatory mandates (and the other way around).[103] Government can provide healthcare for its citizens by taxing and spending to create a national health service or, alternatively, it can require employers to provide health insurance to their employees or mandate that every individual or family purchase health insurance in the private market. Government can educate its citizens by taxing and spending and hiring to create public schools, or it can require that all children get a certain level of education and leave it to parents and the market to provide private schools. Government can handle trash collection by hiring and paying civil servants or by mandating that residents and businesses take their own trash to the dump. In each of these examples, only the first approach—involving taxing, spending, and public employment—would register on the standard metrics as an increase in the size of government. When government regulates instead, there be no change in its visible size. Yet a visibly tiny government that relied entirely on regulation could in theory accomplish just as much as a visibly gigantic one that relied on taxing, spending, and public provision.

Regulation might be understood as a form of government expansion by "outsourcing," conscripting other agents to do its bidding. States and government outsource in other ways, as well, increasing their capacity and causality but not their corporeal size. A characteristic feature of the American national state since the Founding, for example, has been its heavy reliance on states and localities and private individuals and organizations to administer and advance federal programs and policy initiatives. That has allowed the national government to remain unusually small in appearance. But it would be a mistake to equate the American state's small stature with a lack of strength. The commonly drawn comparison between the "weak" American state, evidenced by its modest visible footprint, and the "strong," centralized states of Europe, mistakenly conflates strength with conventional measures of size.[104] Many Americans have made the same mistake, failing to perceive exercises of national government power in the form of cooperative federalism, government contracting, and tax cuts.[105] The state is no less active and powerful when it is "out of sight" or "submerged."[106] If what we care about is the state's power and impact, as opposed to the size of its metaphorical body, then money and manpower will not be adequate metrics.

What is the alternative? Like the personified figure of Leviathan, the state's corporeality at least has the advantage of being easy to see: money, manpower, and buildings are all things we can lay eyes on. Seeing the state's power, and beyond that, what the state has actually used its power to accomplish, is a much greater challenge. The challenge is as much conceptual as empirical. Measuring the state's impact on the world requires knowing what the world would look like in the state's absence. That is a point that many opponents of Big Government have missed. Relying on a naïve "everyday libertarianism," they imagine that a stateless world would look "roughly as it is now, with jobs, banks, houses, and cars, and lacking only the most obvious government services such as Social Security, the National Endowment for the Arts, and the police," or the most obvious disruptions of market ordering such as environmental regulation and taxation.[107] But we know this is far from the truth: markets, money, security, social order, and much else would disappear along with the state.

As Hobbes reminds us, a world without states or governments is something very different: the state of nature. Even if life in the state of nature might be somewhat less solitary, poor, nasty, brutish, and short than Hobbes himself envisioned, it would be dramatically different from the world as we know it. Precisely how different—the true measure of the state's effect on the world and on our lives—is hard to know. But asking the question at least focuses attention on a more meaningful measure of state size. For Hobbes, as for us, what matters most about Leviathan is not its corporeal girth, but what it has done to and for the lives of its subjects.

CONCLUSION

8
New Leviathans

A book about law for states might seem perfectly timed for obsolescence. After a triumphant run of half a millennium since Hobbes, Leviathan appears to be weakening, if not withering away. Hyper-globalization—the borderless flow of goods, capital, people, and information—has swamped the autonomy and capability of sovereign states. The inability of states to cooperate in responding to climate change, terrorism, pandemic disease and other global threats has cast further doubt on the efficacy of government on the state-level scale. Increasingly usurping the state's functions are a proliferation of international, regional, and nongovernmental organizations engaged in "global governance." At the same time, the power of states to control their economies and societies has been challenged and rivaled by multinational corporations, which have increasingly come to resemble privatized, nonterritorial Leviathans. As power flows to entities above and independent of the state, the historical processes of state formation appear to be running in reverse, eroding the Westphalian order.

The impending demise of the state has been a staple of punditry for at least a generation. In reality, however, reports of the death of the state have continued to prove greatly exaggerated. Recent resurgences of nationalism, reassertions of borders against migration and trade, backlashes against Big Tech, and resorts to nuclear diplomacy remind us that contemporary states retain formidable power and popularity. Disruptive innovations have not spelled the state's doom. At the turn of the twenty-first century, for instance, many believed that the borderless, "sovereign Internet" would make the territorial state obsolete.[1] In reality, the supposedly self-governing communities that were supposed to flourish in cyberspace have found themselves dependent for their survival on the coercive capacity of the state and its legal system. Instead of ushering in a new era of statelessness, the Internet revolution has proven "the enduring relevance of territory and physical coercion, and ancient principles governing law and politics within nations, and cooperation and conflict between them."[2] Perhaps the same will be true of

Law for Leviathan. Daryl J. Levinson, Oxford University Press. © Oxford University Press 2024.
DOI: 10.1093/9780190061616.003.0009

globalization and other forces that seem to threaten, but may end up further empowering, Leviathan.[3]

Nonetheless, this final chapter proceeds to explore what might be different—or not so different—in a world in which states have ceded their position of centrality and power to other actors. The hope is to show that a better understanding of law for Leviathan can be usefully applied to these non-state powerholders and the legal regimes that could grow up to govern them in a world of state decline.

Corporate Leviathans

Leviathan is not the only "artificial man." As Chapter 7 described, corporations have long been viewed as personified Leviathans in their own right.[4] Hobbes himself saw the similarity, describing corporations as "lesser commonwealths in the bowels of a greater, like worms in the entrails of a natural man."[5] More exalted images of corporate Leviathans portray them, like Hobbes's greater commonwealth, as independent beings that absorb and are animated by a collection of natural persons. Here is British jurist A. V. Dicey, paying homage to Hobbes: "When a body of twenty or . . . two hundred thousand men bind themselves together to act in a particular way for some common purpose, they create a body which by no fiction of law but by the very nature of things, differs from the individuals of whom it is constituted."[6] Assimilating the corporation to a "live person," legal theorists have proceeded to "assign to them a will, i.e., the faculty of taking resolves in the midst of conflicting motives; a governing brain and nerves, in the shape of institutions and agents; a capacity for the promotion and the defence of interests."[7] At times, legal thought has even gone so far as to elevate the metaphysical status of corporate persons from "artificial" to "real" or "natural."[8] But even when personhood has been understood as a legal formalism or fiction, the metaphorical pull of corporate personification has rivaled that of Leviathan for the state. In law, politics, and popular culture, corporations are commonly conceived as autonomous, self-directed beings, with wills, motivations, characters, and rights of their own.

The linkage between corporations and the state is not just anthropomorphical. For much of Anglo-American legal history, corporations were for many purposes indistinguishable from the state.[9] In England, cities and towns were incorporated by royal charter in the same way as economic corporations. Other chartered corporations defied any distinction between economic and governmental purposes, serving the Crown's mercantile and colonial state-building efforts. The East India Company conquered and ruled large parts of India, collecting taxes, making laws, and commanding a private army twice the size of Britain's. Most of the American colonies were founded by British trading corporations, which served as the colonies' first governments; following American independence, corporate charters became state constitutions.[10] American governance in the early Republic continued to rely heavily on corporations: from the City of Baltimore to the Pennsylvania Railroad to the Bank of the United States, "[c]orporations were the nation's original administrative agencies, its original provincial legislatures, its original public-private partnerships—its original governmental institutions."[11] Only in the nineteenth century did private corporations split definitively from the public realm of government. Private, business corporations became subject to state power in the same way as ordinary persons, while public, municipal corporations became part of the "Hobbesian sphere of command" possessed solely by the state.[12]

But the private corporation has not lost its resemblance to a state or government. Legal theorists continue to view corporations as "institutions whose rules govern how shareholders, workers, directors, executives, creditors, consumers, and other groups can represent and exert power over one another. Outside the corporate context, we call these sorts of representative, power-balancing institutions *governments*."[13] For present purposes, the comparison between governments and corporations has already proven illuminating. Chapter 7 laid out the parallels between corporate and governmental responsibility, collective sanctions, and empire-building, stemming from the similar structures of corporate governance and political democracy.

Those are not the only parallels. Debates over state sovereignty and the rights of corporations have also proceeded along similar lines. As Chapter 2 described, the best defense of state sovereignty is grounded not in the rights of personified states but in the rights and welfare of the actual people who live in those states. That has long been the view that American courts have taken of the constitutional rights of corporations. Where corporations have been granted rights—to free speech and political spending, religious liberty, criminal procedure protections, and the like—it has not been because courts have viewed corporations as people who are entitled to rights of their own. Critics and comedians who wonder whether the First Amendment rights of corporations to spend money on political speech might be defeated by proving to courts "their inability to love," among other nonhuman characteristics, have missed the point of recognizing corporate rights.[14] The argument for assigning legal rights to corporations has always been an instrumental one, aimed at protecting the rights of the real-life people who act collectively through the corporate form.[15] This is not to say that all or any corporate rights are necessarily beneficial on net; much less state sovereignty. But debates on both fronts might benefit from a clearer understanding of how the rights of personified entities relate to the interests of their human stakeholders.

Extending the comparison, corporate and constitutional law have taken parallel approaches to managing the power of their subject entities and protecting vulnerable groups who might be harmed by its use. To start, corporate and constitutional law are both concerned with dual problems of democratic failure. One is the agency problem that comes with the separation of ownership and control: the danger that corporate managers and democratic representatives will deviate too far from the preferences of shareholders and citizens. The second problem is majority or factional tyranny: noncontrolling shareholders are vulnerable to opportunistic behavior by controlling groups in much the same way that racial, religious, and other minorities are vulnerable to discriminatory treatment by democratic majorities. In addressing these risks, corporate law has deployed a number of the same strategies as constitutional law, including the ones described in Chapter 4 as votes, rights, and exit.[16] Corporate law gives shareholders direct or representative voice in corporate decisionmaking, empowering majorities by allowing them to select directors, while also protecting minorities by requiring supermajority votes for the most consequential corporate decisions. Corporate law further relies on rights, such as judicially enforced duties of loyalty and limitations on anti-takeover tactics, to guard shareholders as a class against self-dealing by their managerial agents. And then different forms of rights, such as those to appraisal and pro rata investment, are used to protect minority shareholders against majoritarian exploitation. Finally, shareholders are empowered to protect themselves against managerial and majoritarian misfeasance by taking the "Wall Street walk"—selling their shares and exiting. Comparing the use of these tools in the constitutional and corporate contexts might be informative to scholars and practitioners in both areas.

This is not to lose sight of the ways in which states and corporations are essentially different. Most fundamentally, as Hobbes was at pains to emphasize, corporations are the subjects of states. Like ordinary persons, their lives and societies—from their charters and internal governance structures to their market habitats—are created and regulated by the state and its legal system. No matter how powerful they might be, private corporations have not challenged the state's monopoly on coercive force. Together with ordinary persons, they remain at the pointed end of Leviathan's sword.

But even that difference may be less consequential than Hobbes imagined. The "corporate state"[17] has sometimes been viewed as a Leviathan in its own right, wielding its own kind of coercive force. Reacting to the corporate monopolies that emerged from the industrial revolution, Progressive Era intellectuals and reformers made the case that corporate power was no less threatening than state power. Equating the economic power of "property" with the political power of "sovereignty,"[18] Progressives argued that large concentrations of capital could coerce and control the lives of workers and consumers in much the same way as the state's monopoly on legal control and coercion backed by violence. "There is government," pronounced Progressive lawyer-economist Robert Hale, "whenever one person or group can tell others what they must do and when those others have to obey or suffer a penalty."[19] "Private government" by corporations was no less a threat to liberty than government by the state.[20]

In fact, in the view of Progressives, government by corporations was *more* threatening. While the power of states and governments was constrained and controlled by constitutional rights, checks and balances, and democracy, the power of privatized corporations could only be controlled by the state. Alarmingly, however, Progressives argued, the state had become overmatched. Industrial firms had grown so big and powerful that they were no longer subservient to state power or subject to the effective control of democratic majorities. To the contrary, as Progressive reformer turned Supreme Court Justice Louis Brandeis warned, the "concentration of economic power" had enabled "so-called private corporations" to "dominate the state."[21] Now it was corporate Leviathans that wielded sovereign power, unconstrained by any superior.[22]

What, then, was to be done to protect society against these "quasi-sovereigns that possess[ed] arbitrary, dominating power"? Reformers sought solutions in the legal and political models that had been developed for managing the power of actual states.[23] Those models should by now look familiar. To start, there was constitutional law. Turning their critique of the public/private distinction on constitutional law's state action requirement, Progressive Era legal theorists argued that constitutional rights should protect against coercion by firms and employers, not just the state. To equivalent effect, Progressives maintained that the state's general responsibility for the system of private property and market capitalism also made the state responsible for nominally private economic coercion. Recalling the historical role of corporations as arms of the state, reformers portrayed corporate power as delegated state power, and hence subject to constitutional limits.[24]

In addition to rights, there was the possibility of votes. For Progressive reformers, one of the main problems with corporate power was who controlled it: industrialists, financiers, and management, who ruthlessly pursued their own interests at the expense of unrepresented workers, consumers, and citizens more broadly. Brandeis and other Progressives advocated for replacing corporate "oligarchy" or "absolutism" with "industrial democracy."[25] The labor movement had already begun to give workers a democratic voice in how corporations were run, and Progressives applauded the union-driven shift from "industrial despotism" to "a constitutional monarchy, with well-defined limitations placed about the employer's formerly autocratic power." Brandeis's hope of achieving still greater democratic control for workers by replacing the hierarchical corporation with worker cooperatives did not come pass.[26] But the New Deal consolidated a regime of labor law that cast workers as citizens engaged in democratic self-determination and "effectively established a 'constitution' of the private-sector workplace."[27]

If corporate power could not be adequately controlled by constitutional rights and industrial democracy, reformers hoped that it could be balanced. The primary tool for accomplishing that task was antitrust law.[28] From its inception, antitrust had been guided by the analogy between economic and political power, attuned to the dangers of excessive concentration in either realm. "If we will not endure a king as a political power," declared Senator Sherman, chief sponsor of the eponymous antitrust act, "we should not endure a king over the production, transportation, and sale of any of the necessaries of life."[29] For Progressives like Brandeis, the "curse of bigness" applied to government and corporations alike, as did the Madisonian hope that liberty could be protected by dividing and fragmenting power.[30] Much as a multiplicity of democratic factions would prevent any one of them from becoming tyrannically dominant, breaking up industrial monopolies and trusts would diminish their hegemonic power. Switching constitutional analogies from *Federalist No. 10 to No. 51*, market competition among these no-longer-monopolists would create the equivalent of checks and balances, preventing exploitation by dominant actors and channeling the pursuit of self-interest into the broader public good.

Reformers also saw antitrust as a means of balancing *democratic* power. In their view, concentrated industries were converting their outsized economic power into political power, strong-arming government to secure their preferred policies and fend off regulation and redistribution that would benefit the public. Rallying his New Deal supporters, FDR railed against the "economic royalists" who had captured government and created an industrial and political "dictatorship" in which the conditions of economic life were "beyond the control of the people."[31] Cutting financial and industrial firms down to size and then marshaling the countervailing forces of labor unions, immigrants, farmers, and other New Deal coalitionists, was the New Deal plan for rebalancing democratic power.

That plan went hand-in-hand with the New Deal state-building project. If broad-based democratic control over the state could be restored, then the state itself could be empowered to take on big business. As wary of big government as he was of big business, Brandeis had hoped that diminishing the size and power of corporations would reduce the need for countervailing state power. FDR sided instead with the view of his predecessor and cousin. A generation earlier, Theodore Roosevelt had responded to the threat of "big business" becoming "the ruler of the people" by calling forth the full power of the national government, the only entity capable of "controlling and directing it."[32] By the time of the New Deal, FDR was confronting even bigger business: corporations that had amassed "concentrations of power on a scale that beggars the ambitions of the Stuarts."[33] To balance the power of these corporate Leviathans asserting their own form of sovereign "governance,"[34] the New Dealers invested in building state capacity, constructing an administrative and regulatory Leviathan capable of standing up to the financial and industrial might of modern capitalism.[35]

A century later, the threat of corporate Leviathans once again looms large: Big Banks, Big Pharma, and maybe most threatening of all, Big Tech.[36] Facebook, Amazon, and Google are now commonly described as "artificial sovereigns" exercising "state-like powers that increasingly govern our economic, social, and political life."[37] Amazon has taken charge of the market economy. Google surveils like the Chinese state (as well as for it). Controlling discourse in the digital public sphere, Facebook, in the words of its founder, behaves "more like a government than a traditional company."[38]

Big Tech has taken on the appearance of Leviathan in other ways, as well. It's big! Facebook has 1.5 billion active users, exceeding the population of China; Apple's annual revenues beat Switzerland's and Saudi Arabia's.[39] The scope and magnitude of Big Tech's impact on the world—on the lives of workers, the economy, the distribution of wealth, national security, free speech, and democratic politics—has also, arguably, reached state-like scale, as "empire-building" "net states" imperialistically expand their domains.[40] And their power: like their Gilded Age predecessors, critics warn, tech giants are becoming too powerful to be bossed by actual states. Wielding bottomless bank accounts, influence over information flows, legions of lobbyists, and their own foreign policy teams, as well as critical infrastructure and tax revenues that no country can afford to lose, these firms present as formidable powers in both domestic and international politics. Having "determined that tech behemoths now have as much power as many governments[,] if not more," and approaching Big Tech as "a global superpower," Denmark recently appointed an ambassador to Silicon Valley—who proceeded to get the cold shoulder from Big Tech executives who saw themselves as his betters.[41] When it runs up against Big Tech, Leviathan's sword may be blunted.

Thinking of Big Tech firms as "functional sovereigns"[42] has pointed present-day reformers toward a predictable set of solutions. One approach is to treat Big Tech firms as if they really were states, subjecting them to the rules and rights of constitutional and international law. As a matter of American constitutional law, Google and Facebook might be deemed de facto state actors subject to First Amendment limitations on their power to censor speech on their platforms (or, as Donald Trump's lawyers argued—flipping the usual understanding of who the state is and whom it is acting upon—on their power to deplatform the president of the United States).[43] Turning to international law, some have contended that multinational corporations, including Big Tech, should be held accountable for human rights violations.[44] Facebook was accused of complicity in the mass killings of Rohingya Muslims in Myanmar after it became clear that much of the hate speech and propaganda that had incited the violence had spread on its platform.[45]

Quasi-constitutional rights protections can also be self-imposed. Consistent with the view of Facebook as "a global body of citizens that should be united and protected under a popularly ratified constitution," Facebook has, with much pomp and circumstance, proceeded to create an Oversight Board, or "Supreme Court," for the purpose of protecting users' freedom of expression. Quasi-judicial review of Facebook's content moderation was conceived by a constitutional law professor as the first step in the creation of a "quasi-legal system" for the quasi-governmental firm. (It was reported that the Facebook team tasked with drawing up the "constitution" of the Oversight Board affixed feathers to their pens—using quasi-quills to make themselves feel like quasi-Founding Fathers.[46]) A full-fledged constitutional system for Big Tech might add democratic representation to judicially enforced rights. Critics have called for the modern equivalent of industrial democracy for Big Tech, urging firms to "create systems to facilitate voice, participation, and accountability of power . . . analogizing to the role of elections and participatory mechanisms in public law."[47] Heeding such calls, Facebook has experimented with democratic "site-governance," at one point inviting users to vote by referendum on its policies.[48] The new Oversight Board was initially conceived not just as a court but as a representative body whose members would be drawn from all over the world and, balancing democratic power, from "as many segments of society as possible."[49]

Self-imposed schemes of rights and representation along these lines have elicited predictable skepticism. Why would we trust a self-interested firm like Facebook to self-regulate in the public interest? How can Mark Zuckerberg be effectively constrained by a Supreme Court that he funds and appoints and whose policy decisions he is free to ignore? But before dismissing the Facebook Supreme Court as a public relations gimmick, or "a moot court in a state without real courts,"[50] critics might pause to reflect on what is so different about the "real courts" that are supposed to adjudicate and enforce real constitutional law against the real state. Recall that for Hobbes the answer was, nothing: "The Sovereign of a Common-wealth . . . is not subject to the Civill Lawes. For having power to make, and repeale Lawes, he may when he pleaseth, free himselfe from that subjection, by repealing those Lawes that trouble him, and making of new."[51] If we doubt that Mark Zuckerberg would defer to an Oversight Board decision overturning Facebook's ban of then-President Donald Trump, we might also question whether then-President Trump would have deferred to a Supreme Court decision rejecting his attempt to overturn the 2020 election results. A self-created constitutional regime for Facebook is not so different from a self-created system of constitutional law by and for states and their people. The absence of a higher power standing above the sovereign is common to both.

Seeking more secure solutions than rights and representation, reformers have also called for cutting Big Tech down to size. Reinvigorating the Progressive view of bigness as a curse, reformers have targeted tech firms with a "neo-Brandeisian" approach to antitrust regulation. Rejecting a limited focus on prices and consumer welfare, neo-Brandeisians envision a more ambitious antitrust agenda of deconcentrating economic power in the service of "economic freedom" for workers, competitors, and other market participants.[52] In this vision, breaking up firms like Facebook and Amazon would balance the "unchecked power" of Big Tech by "foster[ing] a larger system of market competition that checks the power of any one firm."[53] The neo-Brandeisian attack on Big Tech is also aimed at reducing and balancing its oversized political power, which threatens to replace democracy with an "oligarchy or a plutocracy."[54] Reformers echo the hopes of their New Dealer predecessors that weakening Big Tech would shift the balance of power back to the state, allowing a democratically responsive Leviathan to reassert dominance over Big Tech usurpers.[55]

Reformers recognize that breaking up Big Tech would likely come at a cost, sacrificing some of the technological benefits of the Internet Age. But that is a cost they are willing to pay: "To the extent we think technology and the power it creates and concentrates is not contestable or controllable, we ought not to permit its continuation."[56] Whether we are talking about Google or the state, powerful technologies are a double-edged sword. When these technologies cannot be securely controlled, unbuilding may be the better course.

Of course, this is just one perspective on Big Tech (or several). But even for those who scoff at the more grandiose claims of Big Tech's critics, the comparison of corporations to states can be illuminating. States and firms resemble one another more than either resembles a real-life person. Focusing on the similarities, as well as the residual differences, sheds useful light on how we should expect both kinds of entities to behave and how best to shape and regulate their behavior through law. That includes the conventional forms of state-imposed law that regulate private firms. As Progressive and neo-Brandeisian critics confronting corporate Leviathans have discovered, however, the model of law *for* states may have more to offer.

Global Leviathans

The power of states is being threatened not just from below but also from above. As self-interested states struggle to solve global collective action problems—war, pandemic disease, poverty, and climate change—the solution to many seems obvious. States might follow the Hobbesian path of self-interested people in the state of nature, overcoming their collective miseries by contracting to create a global Leviathan. Hobbes himself did not recommend that step, but others have followed Hobbes's logic to reach the conclusion that the only solution to international conflict and failures of cooperation is a "social contract among states" resulting in a global super-state.[57]

For all its utopian promise, the project of global state-building has also provoked predictable fears. From Kant's *Perpetual Peace* through the present, skeptics have argued that centralizing power in a world state possessing a "global monopoly on the legitimate use of organized violence"[58] would be not just impractical but far too dangerous. Recalling the double-edged sword of state power, Kant and his successors have worried that the "soulless despotism" imposed by a tyrannical super-state could turn the entire world into "the graveyard of freedom."[59] Less dramatically, skeptics of world government have also cast doubt on the possibility and desirability of imposing a single political order on the heterogeneous and pluralistic peoples of the world, as well as on the viability of democratic self-government on a global scale. Such concerns have led most proponents of world government to back away from a global Leviathan,[60] advocating instead for somewhat less centralized or absolutist arrangements on the model of Kant's "pacific federation" of relatively independent republican states.[61] Even in its less-than-fully-Hobbesian form, however, a federalized system of world government might take on much of the architecture and capacity of the state as we have come to know it, including the legislative authority to issue globally binding rules and even "central coercive mechanisms of law enforcement."[62] In fact, such a state might not be so different from the federalized government of the current United States.

Or the European Union. Like the United States that emerged from the Articles of Confederation, the European Union began merely as a set of treaties among sovereign states but since then has followed a path of economic and political integration toward independent, if federalized, statehood. Whether the EU in its current form should be regarded as a full-fledged state, or what it would take for it to become one, are matters of ongoing controversy.[63] Those who portray the EU as a proto-state regard its constitutive treaties as a "constitutional charter" and speak of the EU as exercising the "pooled sovereignty" of its member states. And they can point to a number of more concrete state-like features. The EU operates with a centralized government apparatus, including a legislative Council and Parliament, an executive Commission, and a supreme Court of Justice. Within the constitutionally defined scope of its competencies, the government of the EU can enact laws over the objections of member states and that are supreme over state laws. EU laws can also be made directly binding on citizens. Further contributing to the EU's state-like character is its common currency, single market, and free mobility of citizens across national borders. In other respects, however, the EU still resembles the United Nations more than the United States. Member states formally remain the "masters" of its constitutive treaties and functionally retain possession of most administrative and financial resources and capacity for direct governance. The EU's member states have also held onto their Weberian monopolies over the use of coercive force, leaving the government of the EU without military or policing capability of its own. Additionally lacking, or at least lagging, at the EU level is a functional system of democratic politics animated by the sense of shared political and sociological identity—a *demos*, of the kind that exists within France or Germany.

Once all of these characteristics have been laid bare, it is hard to see the point of trying to definitively resolve whether the EU is "really" a treaty regime among sovereign states or a state in its own right. That distinction becomes both harder to draw and less profoundly consequential once we recognize, as this book has tried to show, that international and constitutional law are not so structurally different from one another. For many purposes, the law imposed through the EU on France and Germany could be described in either way, as international or constitutional, without any change in consequences. We might just accept that the line between thick, institutionalized treaty arrangements among sovereign states and the emergence of a conglomerated, constitutionalized state is a blurry one.

Further blurring that line is the post–World War II proliferation of transnational institutions engaged in what has come to be called "global governance." The UN, WTO, IMF, ICC, and many such institutions have increasingly exercised state-like regulatory power over individuals, firms, and countries across nearly every sphere of activity.[64] Created through multilateral treaty arrangements, global governance institutions are formally the servants of states. And member states, or at least the most powerful ones, do maintain a considerable measure of control over their decisionmaking, through funding, formal voting procedures, or threats of withdrawal.

Much like the EU, however, as states have delegated more and more authority, global governance institutions have gained significant power to govern independently. Many global governance institutions can effectively bind states and their citizens to rules and judgments even when they disagree. As in the international order generally, these rules and judgments can be coercively enforced by other states, whether through WTO-authorized trade sanctions or state-provided military forces acting to uphold UN Security Council resolutions. And while states whose interests are being disserved typically have the right to exit (or not to sign on in the first place), that can mean effectively dropping out of the global economy or comparably costly self-isolation from cooperative benefits that many states cannot do without. The upshot is that global governance institutions have to a considerable extent taken on lives of their own, exercising autonomous power beyond the control of their creators—much in the manner of Leviathan.[65]

Reflecting the perception that global governance institutions are exercising state-like power, "global constitutionalism" has become a fashionable term for describing their development.[66] Following the constitutional reconceptualization of the EU treaties, theorists have extended the "constitutional" label to the founding treaties of the WTO and the UN Charter.[67] More ambitiously, other theorists describe the multiplicity of global governance institutions, together with other international legal regimes, as comprising a single system of governance ordered by an unwritten global constitution. The idea is to identify or build an overarching set of rules and norms that would bring structure, organization, and coherence to the proliferation of global governance bodies with fragmented, ambiguous, and overlapping jurisdictions. If the goal is not to create the kind of state-like unification, centralization, and hierarchy that would exist in a world government, it is at least to facilitate some measure of legal settlement, in the sense described in Chapter 1. "[I]n a constitutional global order," as one theorist summarizes the constitutional ambition, "it is clear who can issue what norms and standards, and what the effect of such standards will be."[68] As Chapter 1 also described, however, the challenges of resolving legal uncertainty and achieving authoritative settlement outside of the institutional architecture of the state do not disappear when constitutional law is substituted for international law. We should not expect global constitutionalism to be any less susceptible to pluralism and fragmentation than domestic constitutionalism.[69]

Whatever its constitutional organization, global governance comes with the promise and peril of super-state power. Global governance may be the only solution for collective action problems confronting states and their populations, the only realistic means of achieving the benefits of free trade and economic growth or preventing the catastrophes of war and climate change. But the power of global governance institutions has also proved threatening to states and their citizens. Weaker states worry that international institutions will serve the interests of powerful states at their expense, exacerbating and entrenching the global imbalance of power. Powerful states hesitate to subject themselves to international human rights regimes and international criminal courts that threaten their self-interested independence in matters of national security and other high-stakes domains.

State-centric objections to global governance predictably sound in sovereignty. Recall from Chapter 2 the triumphant declaration of Boris Johnson that the British people by exiting the EU had "recaptured sovereignty" and "taken back the tools of self-government." And recall U.S. President Donald Trump's similar assertion, to the UN General Assembly, that America's "founding principle of sovereignty," mandating that "the [American] people govern," would no longer be sacrificed to "mammoth, multinational trade deals, unaccountable international tribunals, and powerful global bureaucracies." The swaggering political rhetoric of sovereignty reflects a current of anti-internationalism that has been especially influential among scholars and policymakers in the United States. So-called new sovereigntists see the international legal order as replacing American constitutional democracy and self-government with external rule by unaccountable foreigners.[70]

One lesson of Chapter 2 is that such assertions of sovereignty do little to illuminate the stakes of international law or global governance. The sovereigntist premise that the international legal order is a threat to, or somehow the opposite of, constitutional self-government misses the basic point that constitutional law, too, imposes constraints on democratic self-government and the ability of citizens to act upon their self-determined interests. Constitutionalists deem the sacrifice of present political autonomy worthwhile because a constitutional system of government enables citizens to realize collective goods that would otherwise be out of reach. Global governance is, in principle, no different. The reason states and their citizens have been willing to cede autonomy to global governors is that global government enables them to accomplish things that would otherwise be impossible owing to global collective action problems. The formal sovereignty that is sacrificed (or "delegated" or "pooled") is traded for "effective sovereignty." This is precisely the trade-off that the American states chose to make in the late eighteenth century when they ratified the U.S. Constitution, giving up some measure of autonomous self-government in exchange for the collective benefits of trade, security, and prosperity that could only be delivered through a more powerful national government.[71]

Moreover, if sovereignty is reconceived as serving not the autonomy of personified states but the welfare and self-determination of citizens, global governance clearly has the potential to improve both. International institutions empower and benefit groups of people seeking free trade, security, and other collective goods. The victims of war and human rights violations turn to international institutions for protection against the sovereign states that threaten their lives. Global governance may also strengthen domestic democracy, by limiting the power of concentrated interests to block trade and other policies that are beneficial to the majority, or by fostering better and more informed deliberation about issues such as climate change.[72]

At the same time, however, global governance has also proven itself a threat to constituencies within and across states. Citizens of developing countries whose governments have minimal influence over international institutions; diffuse publics in more powerful countries whose disadvantages in domestic politics are exacerbated by international delegations that benefit economic elites; exploited workers in global supply chain factories; people without access to life-saving medications because of international intellectual property protections; populations suffering from climate change; refugees and victims of domestic despots propped up by international funding—these and other vulnerable groups have grounds to protest that their interests are being disregarded and disserved by distant, unaccountable global governors. And protest they have. Coalitions on the left have railed against a neoliberal regime of global economic government imposed by the WTO and the EU for the benefit of international capitalists and multinational corporations at the expense of workers, the global poor, and the social welfare state. On the right, populist movements against immigration and in favor of economic nationalization have pushed back against global authority, resulting in the exit of Britain from the EU and the rise of illiberal and anti-democratic politics in Poland, Hungary, Turkey, and other countries.

An alternative to resisting the power of global governors is to assert greater control over them. That is another ambition of the global constitutionalist project. In conjunction with building and organizing supranational power, global constitutionalism calls for the development of legal and political tools for controlling its users and uses, and particularly for the purpose of protecting vulnerable constituencies. The starting point is the formative and ongoing control over international institutions exercised by states;

and, in turn, the control over states ideally exercised by their citizens.[73] But recognizing the limited ability of weaker states to exercise meaningful control over global governance bodies, as well as the limited influence of politically weaker constituencies within states, attention has been turned to other mechanisms for more directly representing and protecting vulnerable groups. These mechanisms have taken the familiar constitutional forms, described in Chapter 4, of democratic political power and legal rights.

Starting with democratic political power, the obvious challenge is that nothing like global democracy currently exists. Proponents of "cosmopolitan democracy" hope to someday replicate state-level democratic institutions on a global scale, for instance by creating a popularly elected global parliamentary assembly.[74] Under current conditions, however, representative democracy seems like a bad fit for global governance. The shifting groups of people, firms, and governments whose interests are affected in different ways by the various decisions and overlapping jurisdictions of global governance bodies are not organized into the kinds of stable, clearly bounded political communities defined by states.[75] And the constituencies whose interests are most affected typically have no direct influence, through representation or voting, over these decisions. It is no wonder that discussions of global governance seldom fail to highlight its seemingly inherent "democracy deficits" and "accountability gaps."[76]

One predictable response to the democratic deficiencies of global governance has been to call for greater rights protections.[77] The European Court of Justice's (ECJ) much-remarked decision in the *Kadi* case is a good illustration.[78] *Kadi* involved a challenge to UN Security Council resolutions requiring states to freeze the assets of individuals and entities suspected of supporting terrorism. The counterterrorism resolutions at issue were products of the expanding role of the Security Council as a global governance body, exercising regulatory powers well beyond what was contemplated in the drafting of the UN Charter. Kadi, who claimed never to have been involved with any terrorist organization, argued that the resolutions violated his rights to property and due process under the European Convention on Human Rights and other sources of EU law. Notwithstanding the UN Charter's self-proclaimed and widely recognized priority in international law, the ECJ held that the Security Council regulations were trumped by fundamental rights protected under the EU legal order. The ECJ's extraordinary reach for rights protection in *Kadi* appears to have been at least partly motivated by the troubling lack of accountability of UN decisionmakers to the individuals and groups whose rights and interests they were threatening.[79]

There is some irony in seeing victims of unaccountable global governors turn to the EU, which suffers from a serious democracy deficit of its own.[80] The absence of direct voting by European citizens for Council representatives or the Commission president, the limited role of the Parliament, the nonexistence of European-level political parties, and the underdevelopment of a pan-European public sphere have contributed to a widely perceived lack of democratic legitimacy in EU governance. Responding to the dubious democratic credentials of the EU in much the same way that the ECJ responded to the Security Council in *Kadi*, member state courts have asserted national constitutional rights as a shield. In a case now known as *Solange I*, the Federal Constitutional Court of Germany declared that although European Community law was generally supreme, it would continue to enforce fundamental rights guaranteed under the German Basic Law. Or at least it would do so until the Community improved along one of two dimensions: either by doing a better job of protecting fundamental rights on its own, or by improving its democratic accountability.[81] Twelve years later, after the creation of the directly elected European Parliament and the adoption of the European Convention on Human Rights, the Constitutional Court revisited its earlier decision and decided that it was no longer necessary to review Community legislation for compliance with German fundamental rights.[82] Constitutional courts in a number of other European states have followed the same approach, expressing their intention to hold national constitutional rights in reserve as a safeguard against the inability of EU governance institutions to maintain sufficient democratic accountability or rights protections on their own.[83]

As these cases demonstrate, stepping up rights protections is one response to supranational democracy deficits. A more direct response, also suggested in the *Solange* cases, is to look for ways of improving the accountability and responsiveness of global governance institutions to the publics who are subject to their power. Proposals for improving democracy in the EU include specific institutional reforms, such as adding a directly elected president of the Commission and empowering national parliaments in the EU legislative process. As applied to other global governance bodies, the inevitable absence of electoral democracy might be replaced by accountability-enhancing norms of transparency and public participation in regulatory decisionmaking,[84] as well as by enhanced oversight by national officials.[85] The further development of transnational political movements and forums for public deliberation is another front on which effective political control over the EU and global governance more generally might advance.[86]

Political accountability and legal rights could be supplemented by other constitutionally inspired tools for controlling and constraining global governors. Some theorists, for instance, have focused on the potential for fostering "checks and balances" among global governance institutions, empowering them "to monitor and even pass judgment over decisions of other institutions."[87] Balancing power at the level of constituencies is another possible direction for reform. One explanation for recent populist backlashes against globalization is that "[e]conomic elites [have] designed international institutions to serve their own interests and to create firmer links between themselves and government" at the expense of middle- and working-class citizens.[88] That diagnosis points to the prescription of rebalancing class power over global governance, directly or through the mediation of states.

The more effective these tools of control turn out to be, the more we should expect states and their citizens to be willing to delegate power upward. Conversely, the greater the risks that global governors will subject states and populations to undesirable or oppressive regulation, the less power they will be willing to surrender. It is sometimes cast as a puzzle that most global governance institutions remain "weak relative to states," while at the same time "critics of globalization view such organizations as relatively uncontrolled, criticizing them as 'unaccountable' while celebrating the democratic accountability of states. Thus, multinational organizations are characterized as both weak and unchecked at the same time."[89] But recalling the standard dynamics of state-building surveyed in Chapter 5, there is nothing surprising about the correlation between capacity and control. As one commentator aptly describes the situation, states intentionally limit the power of global governance institutions that they cannot fully control for fear that these institutions will turn on their creators in the manner of Frankenstein's monster.[90] Or, as we have seen, in the manner of Leviathan.

Whether global governance will continue to grow above the state, and how its institutional shapes will evolve, remain to be seen. But whatever version of global governance might emerge, the hope is that this book will continue to provide relevant resources for understanding how legal regimes can come to grips with state-like power. If international institutions—or multinational corporations, or other kinds of "artificial men"—someday succeed in supplanting the state, the legal systems that grow up around them will in important respects resemble law for Leviathan.

Notes

Introduction

1. See Eric A. Posner, The Perils of Global Legalism xiii (2009) ("law without government"); Kenneth Walz, Theory of International Politics (1979) (developing the foundational distinction between the "anarchy" of international politics and the "hierarchy" of domestic politics).
2. Quentin Skinner, From the State of Princes to the Person of the State, in Quentin Skinner, 2 Visions of Politics 413 (2002).
3. Thomas Hobbes, Leviathan 9 (Richard Tuck ed., 1991) (1651).
4. See Leviathan at lxxiv. In words, Hobbes describes Leviathan using the traditional imagery of the body politic:

> For by Art is created that great LEVIATHAN called a COMMON-WEALTH, or STATE, (in latine CIVITAS) which is but an Artificiall Man; though of greater stature and strength than the Naturall, for whose protection and defence it was intended; and in which, the *Soveraignty* is an Artificiall *Soul*, as giving life and motion to the whole body; The *Magistrates* and other *Officers* of Judicature and Execution, artificiall *joynts*; *Reward* and *Punishment* (by which fastened to the seate of the Soveraignty, every joynt and member is moved to performed his duty) are the *Nerves*, that do the same in the Body Naturall; The *Wealth* and *Riches* of all the particular members, are the *Strength*; *Salus Populi* (the *peoples safety*) is *Businesse*; *Counsellors*, by whom all things needfull for it to know, are suggested unto it, are the *Memory*; *Equity* and *Lawes*, an artificiall *Reason* and *Will*; *Concord*, *Health*; *Sedition*, *Sicknesse*; and *Civill war*, *Death*. Lastly, the *Pacts* and *Covenants*, by which the parts of this Body Politique were at first made, set together, and united, resemble that *Fiat*, or the *Let us make man*, pronounced by God in the Creation.

> Leviathan at 9.

> On the body politic metaphor generally, see David George Hale, The Body Politic: A Political Metaphor in Renaissance English Literature (1971); Judith N. Shklar, Men and Citizens 198–99 (1969). The metaphors for the state offered by prominent political theorists since Hobbes are even more mysterious. Hegel described the state as the "Divine Idea on Earth." Nietzsche referred to the state as the "coldest of all cold monsters"—perhaps recalling the original Leviathan from the Book of Job, a sea monster so powerful that no human could hope to control it.

5. See Alexander Wendt, The State as Person in International Theory, 30 Rev. Int'l Stud. 289, 289 (2004).
6. See Charles R. Beitz, Political Theory and International Relations 69 (1979) ("Perceptions of international relations have been more thoroughly influenced by the analogy of states and persons than by any other device."); see also Edwin Dewitt

Dickinson, The Analogy Between Natural Persons and International Persons in the Law of Nations, 26 Yale L.J. 564 (1917).
7. For a similarly Hobbesian perspective on constitutional law's personification of the state, see Alice Ristroph, Covenants for the Sword, 61 U. Toronto J.J. 657, 660 (2011).
8. In one version of the frontispiece, accompanying a special copy of the manuscript Hobbes presented to King Charles II, Leviathan's face is rendered with an uncanny resemblance to Charles himself.
9. See also Ernst H. Kantorowicz, The King's Two Bodies (1957).
10. Quentin Skinner, The State, in Political Innovation and Conceptual Change 90, 112 (T. Ball et al. eds., 1989); see also Harvey C. Mansfield, Jr., On the Impersonality of the Modern State: Machiavelli's Use of *Stato*, 77 Am. Pol. Sci. Rev. 849, 851 (1983); Quentin Skinner, A Genealogy of the Modern State, 162 Proc. Brit. Acad. 325 (2009). For an exploration of the meaning of the "personality" of the state in Hobbes's and subsequent political thought, see David Runciman, Pluralism and the Personality of the State (1997).
11. This is not to deny that the state can be usefully understood for some purposes through the metaphor of personification, or even that the state *really is* a person, or at least possesses some attributes of personhood. See Wendt. Such claims depend on philosophically contestable accounts of personal and group identity, agency, and intentionality that are referenced throughout the book as they bear upon international and constitutional law but need not be definitively resolved. The philosophically unambitious, pragmatic posture of the book is simply to point out what a personified view of the state might lead us to miss about the distinctive moral and behavioral attributes of the state, and about the consequences of law for the human beings who live in them.
12. Max Weber, Politics as a Vocation, in From Max Weber: Articles in Sociology 77, 78 (H.H. Gerth & C. Wright Mills eds., 1946). See generally Walter Scheidel, Studying the State, in The Oxford Handbook of the State in the Ancient Near East and Mediterranean 5, 9 (Peter F. Bang & Walter Scheidel eds., 2013) (surveying the standard definitions of the state).
13. On the historical origins and rise of the state, see, e.g., Martin van Creveld, The Rise and Decline of the State (1999); Thomas Ertman, Birth of the Leviathan (1997); Joseph R. Strayer, On the Medieval Origins of the Modern State (2005); Charles Tilly, Coercion, Capital, and European States, AD 990–1992 (1992).
14. See Charles Tilly, War Making and State Making as Organized Crime, in Bringing the State Back In 169 (Peter B. Evans et al. eds., 1985).
15. Though traces of personal rule continue to exist, for example, in the American presidency. See Daphna Renan, The President's Two Bodies, 120 Colum. L. Rev. 1119 (2020).
16. Walter Bagehot, The English Constitution 61 (2d ed. 1873).
17. Cf. Michael Walzer, On the Role of Symbolism in Political Thought, 82 Pol. Sci. Q. 191, 194 (1967) ("The state is invisible; it must be personified before it can be seen, symbolized before it can be loved, imagined before it can be conceived.").
18. See generally Quentin Skinner, From Humanism to Hobbes ch. 12; F.H. Hinsley, Sovereignty (2d ed. 1986). In Hobbes's specific version, the state arises when a

"multitude" of ungoverned people become "one person" by agreeing to be governed by a "sovereign" who represents them.
19. The mistake is metaphorical, not metaphysical. Although few people, when pressed, would admit to believing the state *really is* a person, there is nothing necessarily wrong with that point of view. Depending on one's definition of personhood, states (or corporations, algorithms, etc.) might have at least as much of a claim to that status as flesh-and-blood homo sapiens. On some philosophical views, states (among other entities) can act intentionally, rationally, morally, and even consciously. See Wendt. What matters for purposes of this project is not whether the state possesses attributes of personhood, but whether its behavior is descriptively and normatively similar to, or different from, the behavior of flesh-and-blood persons. As the book will show in a number of specific contexts, the answer is often that the state is different. As the book will also emphasize, whatever we might think of the state, we cannot ignore the flesh-and-blood persons who continue to exist independently; their interests, rights, and welfare should not be subsumed into the metaphorical body of Leviathan.
20. Leviathan at 88.
21. Leviathan at 90.
22. Hedley Bull, The Anarchical Society: A Study of Order in World Politics 46–51 (1977).
23. See generally Chiara Bottici, Men and States: Rethinking the Domestic Analogy in a Global Age (2009); Michael C. Williams, Hobbes and International Relations: A Reconsideration, 50 Int'l Org. 213 (1996); Martin Wight, An Anatomy of International Thought, 13 Rev. Int'l Stud. 221 (1987).
24. Leviathan at 90.
25. See Bull at 44–49.
26. David Singh Grewal, The Domestic Analogy Revisited: Hobbes on International Order, 124 Yale L.J. 618, 651.
27. Charles R. Beitz, Political Theory and International Relations 180 (1979).
28. Michael Walzer, Just and Unjust Wars 61 (1977).
29. Id. at 72.
30. Eric A. Posner & Jack L. Goldsmith, The Limits of International Law 193 (2005).
31. Hinsley at 126–213.
32. For a parallel project of recovering the understanding of constitutional, or more broadly "public law," as a special form of law for states, see Martin Loughlin, Foundations of Public Law (2010); see also Questioning the Foundations of Public Law (Michael A. Wilkinson & Michael W. Dowdle eds., 2018).
33. H.L.A. Hart, Positivism and the Separation of Law and Morals, 71 Harv. L. Rev. 593, 603 (1958); see generally Frederick Schauer, The Force of Law (2015).
34. Stephen Holmes, Lineages of the Rule of Law, in Democracy and the Rule of Law, 19, 24 (Jose Maria Marvall & Adam Przeworski eds., 2003); accord Niccolò Machiavelli, The Prince 71 (Leo Paul S. de Alvarez trans., 1981) (1532) ("[T]here cannot be good laws where there are not good arms.").
35. See Albert O. Hirschman, Exit, Voice, and Loyalty (1970).
36. Scott Gordon, Controlling the State 15 (2009).

248 NOTES

37. As it happens, Hobbes's first published work was the first English translation of Thucydides from the Greek.
38. *The Federalist No. 51* at 298 (James Madison) (Clinton Rossiter ed., 2003).
39. Thomas Hobbes, On the Citizen 156 (Richard Tuck & Michael Silverthorne eds. & trans., 1998) (1647).
40. Ronald Dworkin, Sovereign Virtue 6 (2000).
41. John Rawls, A Theory of Justice 3, 7, 54–55 (1971). See Liam Murphy, Institutions and the Demands of Justice, 27 Phil. & Pub. Aff. 251, 257–64 (1998).
42. Rawls at 29.
43. Leviathan at 114.
44. See Oona A. Hathaway & Scott J. Shapiro, The Internationalists 269–70 (2017).
45. And perhaps as well on a distinctly American outlook toward international law. See generally John F. Witt, The View from the U.S. Leviathan: Histories of International Law in the Hegemon (January 22, 2022).

Chapter 1

1. Hobbes did allow for the existence of a kind of natural law that applied to persons in the state of nature, and also to the state or its governors. See Thomas Hobbes, Leviathan chs. 14, 15, 26, 30 (Richard Tuck ed., 1991) (1651). How exactly Hobbes understood these "laws of nature"—whether they originated from god, reason, morality, or something else; and what their relationship was to civil law—has been a topic of ongoing debate. Against the orthodox view of Hobbes as a legal positivist who recognized only state-made law as genuinely legal, David Dyzenhaus has made the interesting case that natural law for Hobbes was a kind of proto-constitutionalism, imposing legal obligations on the state. David Dyzenhaus, Hobbes on the Authority of Law, in Hobbes and the Law (David Dyzenhaus & Thomas Poole eds., 2012); David Dyzenhaus, Hobbes's Constitutional Theory, in Leviathan (Ian Shapiro ed., 2010); David Dyzenhaus, Hobbes and the Legitimacy of Law, 20 L. & Phil. 461 (2001).
2. As the discussion that follows will make clear, these are not jurisprudential claims about the nature of law or legal obligation, but simply observations about common perceptions and expectations.
3. See, e.g., John Austin, The Province of Jurisprudence Determined 141–43, 254–64 (Wilfrid E. Rumble ed., 1995) (1832).
4. H.L.A. Hart, The Concept of Law (2d ed. 1994).
5. Id. at 3–4.
6. Eric A. Posner, The Perils of Global Legalism 8 (2009).
7. Austin at 141–43, 254–64.
8. Concept of Law, at 66–78. For purposes of this argument, Hart focused on constitutional law to avoid having to invoke "disputable or challengeable types of law," such as international law. Id. at 68. As Hart clearly recognized, however, international law shares the salient feature of limiting what the sovereign state can command.

9. The structural parallels between constitutional and international law have not entirely escaped notice by contemporary commentators. In addition to the sources cited below, this chapter builds upon Christopher A. Whytock, Thinking Beyond the Domestic-International Divide: Toward a Unified Concept of Public Law, 36 Geo. J. Int'l L. 155 (2004).
10. U.N. Charter Arts. 2(4), 24, 25, 51.
11. Jack Goldsmith, Is the U.N. Charter Law?, Lawfare, Apr. 16, 2018.
12. Eric Posner, Has Obama Upheld the Rule of Law?, Slate, Nov. 9, 2015.
13. Thomas Hobbes, Human Nature and de Corpore Politico 103 (J.C.A. Gaskin ed., 2008) (1650).
14. See Leviathan ch. 26; see also Richard Tuck, The Rights of War and Peace 131–32 (2001); Jeremy Waldron, Law and Disagreement 39–41 (1999).
15. See Larry Alexander & Frederick Schauer, On Extrajudicial Constitutional Interpretation, 110 Harv. L. Rev. 1359, 1371 (1997).
16. Concept of Law, at 92.
17. See id. at 94–98.
18. See Louis Henkin, How Nations Behave 22–25 (2d ed. 1979); Hans J. Morgenthau, Politics Among Nations 253–68 (2d ed. 1955); Hart at 214.
19. Monika Hakimi, Making Sense of Customary International Law, 118 U. Mich. L. Rev. 1487, 1493 (2020).
20. U.N. Charter Art. 103.
21. See, e.g., Antonio Cassese, Ex Iniuria Ius Oritur: Are We Moving Towards International Legitimation of Forcible Humanitarian Countermeasures in the World Community?, 10 Eur. J. Int'l. L. 23 (1999); Julie Mertus, Reconsidering the Legality of Humanitarian Intervention: Lessons from Kosovo, 41 Wm. & Mary L. Rev. 1743 (2000). Another way internationalists found of approving the NATO intervention was to argue that it was technically illegal but nonetheless "legitimate." See, e.g., Anthea Roberts, Legality vs. Legitimacy: Can Uses of Force be Illegal but Justified?, in Human Rights, Intervention, and the Use of Force 179 (Philip Alston & Euan MacDonald eds., 2008).
22. See Rebecca Barber, Does the "Responsibility to Protect" Require States to go to War with Russia?, Just Security, March 25, 2022.
23. In theory, the international legal system has a set of meta-rules—rules of non-retroactivity, last-in-time, the priority of *lex specialis*, and normative hierarchy (prioritizing the U.N. Charter or *jus cogens* norms)—that are supposed to help sort out these conflicts. But in practice these meta-rules themselves are often contested and indeterminate, leaving a sea of contradictory norms up for debate. See generally Study Group of the Int'l Law Comm'n, Fragmentation of International Law: Difficulties Arising from the Diversification and Expansion of International Law, U.N. Doc. A/CN.4/L.682 (Apr. 13, 2006) (finalized by Martti Koskenniemi).
24. Chapter 8 explores the rise of global governance institutions in greater depth.
25. See Eyal Benvenisti & George W. Downs, The Empire's New Clothes: Political Economy and the Fragmentation of International Law, 60 Stan. L. Rev. 595 (2007); Martti Koskenniemi & Päivi Leino, Fragmentation of International Law? Postmodern

Anxieties, 15 Leiden J. Int'l L. 553, 562–67 (2002); Anne Peters, The Refinement of International Law: From Fragmentation to Regime Interaction and Politicization, 15 Int'l J. Con. L. 671 (2017).

26. See William W. Burke-White, International Legal Pluralism, 25 Mich. J. Int'l L. 963, 965–68 (2004); Paul Schiff Berman, Global Legal Pluralism, 80 S. Cal. L. Rev. 1155 (2007); Nico Krisch, The Case for Pluralism in Postnational Law.

27. Credit is due to theorists who have inspected constitutional law more closely and noticed that it is unsettled in some of the same ways as international law. See Alec Stone Sweet, The Structure of Constitutional Pluralism, 11 ICON 491 (2014); Daniel Halberstam, Constitutional Heterarchy: The Centrality of Conflict in the European Union and the United States, in Ruling the World? (Jeffrey L. Dunoff & Joel P. Trachtman eds., 2009).

28. On the complexity and uncertainty of the rule of recognition for what counts as constitutional law, see generally The Rule of Recognition and the U.S. Constitution (Matthew Adler & Kenneth Einar Himma eds., 2009).

29. See McCulloch v. Maryland, 17 U.S. 316 (1819). Of course, some constitutions are more prolix and specific than others. At approximately 8000 words (including amendments), the U.S. Constitution is especially concise. Compare, e.g., the South African Constitution, which contains 100,000 words, or the constitution of the state of Alabama, which is close to 400,000.

30. This may be an understatement. See Louis Michael Seidman, Our Unsettled Constitution 11 (2001) ("[C]onstitutional rhetoric provides powerful support for virtually any outcome to any argument.").

31. Joseph Fishkin & William E. Forbath, The Anti-Oligarchy Constitution (2022).

32. Richard Epstein, The Classical Liberal Constitution (2014).

33. Adrian Vermeule, Common Good Constitutionalism (2022).

34. 6 Reg. Deb. 78 (1830); see also Keith E. Whittington, Political Foundations of Judicial Supremacy 1 (2007) (connecting Webster's remarks to judicial review and judicial supremacy).

35. See Alexander & Schauer.

36. See Lawrence G. Sager, Fair Measure: The Legal Status of Underenforced Constitutional Norms, 91 Harv. L. Rev. 1212 (1978); see also Frederick Schauer, Foreword: The Court's Agenda—and the Nation's, 120 Harv. L. Rev. 5 (2006).

37. See generally Keith E. Whittington, Constitutional Construction (1999) (theorizing and describing the "construction" of constitutional meaning through extrajudicial politics); Keith E. Whittington, Extrajudicial Constitutional Interpretation: Three Objections and Responses, 80 N.C. L. Rev. 773 (2002).

38. See Eric A. Posner & Adrian Vermeule, Constitutional Showdowns, 156 U. Pa. L. Rev. 991 (2008).

39. Stephen Griffin, American Constitutionalism 45 (1996).

40. Cooper v. Aaron, 358 U.S. 1, 18 (1958).

41. See Daniel Farber, Lincoln's Constitution 176–92 (2003); Noah Feldman, The Broken Constitution 104–12 (2021).

42. See Farber at 157–63; Feldman at 183–209.

43. See Barry E. Friedman, The Will of the People 129–36 (2009).

44. See id. at 195–236.
45. See Michael J. Klarman, From Jim Crow to Civil Rights 385–421 (2004).
46. See Larry D. Kramer, The People Themselves: Popular Constitutionalism and Judicial Review (2004).
47. See id.; see also Richard H. Fallon, Jr., Judicial Supremacy, Departmentalism, and the Rule of Law in a Populist Age, 96 Tx. L. Rev. 487, 491 (2018) ("Our system is not, never has been, and probably never could be one of pure judicial supremacy.").
48. Fallon at 494.
49. Robert Post & Reva Siegel, Popular Constitutionalism, Departmentalism, and Judicial Supremacy, 92 Calif. L. Rev. 1027, 1041 (2004).
50. Larry D. Kramer, Lecture, "The Interest of the Man": James Madison, Popular Constitutionalism, and the Theory of Deliberative Democracy, 41 Val. U. L. Rev. 697, 750–51 (2006).
51. Id. at 63.
52. Id. at 30.
53. See Sanford Levinson, Constitutional Faith 246–54 (2011) (distinguishing between the "Constitution of Settlement" and the "Constitution of Conversation").
54. Larry Alexander & Lawrence B. Solum, Popular? Constitutionalism?, 118 Harv. L. Rev. 1594, 1611 (2005).
55. See Alec Stone Sweet, Why Europe Rejected American Judicial Review: And Why It May Not Matter, 101 Mich. L. Rev. 2744, 2779 (2003).
56. For versions of these arguments, see, e.g., Paul Schiff Berman, A Pluralist Approach to International Law, 32 Yale J. Int'l L. 301 (2007); Burke-White; Jonathan I. Charney, Is International Law Threatened by Multiple International Tribunals?, 271 Recueil des Cours 101, 347 (1998); Nico Krisch, Beyond Constitutionalism: The Pluralist Structure of Postnational Law (2010); Frederic Megret, International Law as a System of Legal Pluralism, in The Oxford Handbook of Global Legal Pluralism ch. 19 (Paul Schiff Berman ed., 2020).
57. See Seidman.
58. See Frederick Schauer, The Force of Law 1 (2015).
59. Leviathan at 100–101.
60. Leviathan at 117.
61. 1 John Austin, Lectures on Jurisprudence 121, 141–42 (Robert Campbell ed., 1875).
62. H.L.A. Hart, Positivism and the Separation of Law and Morals, 71 Harv. L. Rev. 593, 603 (1958); see also Concept of Law, at 18–25.
63. See Schauer, Force of Law. Oona Hathaway and Scott Shapiro rightly attribute much of the enduring skepticism of international law to the firm hold of a "modern state conception" of law that depends on the existence of states—with their armies, police forces, and monopoly over the use of force—to coerce legal compliance through the threat or imposition of violence. See Oona A. Hathaway & Scott J. Shapiro, Outcasting: Enforcement in Domestic and International Law, 121 Yale L.J. 252 (2011).
64. Hathaway & Shapiro.
65. Hans J. Morgenthau, Politics Among Nations 271 (2d ed. 1955).
66. Morgenthau at 270–71.

67. Henkin, at 47. For a more precise survey of the theory and empirical evidence of international legal compliance, see Beth Simmons, Treaty Compliance and Violation, 13 Ann. Rev. Pol. Sci. 273 (2010).
68. Goldsmith & Posner at 168; Detlev F. Vagts, International Law in the Third Reich, 84 Am. J. Int'l L. 661 (1990).
69. See, e.g., George W. Downs et al., Is the Good News About Compliance Good News About Cooperation?, 50 Int'l Org. 379 (1996); see also Goldsmith & Posner, at 27–28.
70. It also follows from the game-theoretical logic of Hobbes's account of people contracting their way out of the state of nature, transposed to (contracting and other forms of cooperation) among Leviathans. Game-theoretical interpretations of Hobbes include David Gauthier, Morals by Agreement (1986); Jean Hampton, Hobbes and the Social Contract Tradition 132–88 (1986); and Gregory Kavka, Hobbesian Moral and Political Theory (1986).
71. See, e.g., Robert O. Keohane, After Hegemony (1984); Robert O. Keohane & Lisa L. Martin, The Promise of Institutionalist Theory, 20 Int'l Security 39 (1995); Duncan Snidal, The Game Theory of International Politics, in Cooperation Under Anarchy 25 (Kenneth A. Oye ed., 1986); Andrew Guzman, How International Law Works: A Rational Choice Theory (2008).
72. For an overview and many applications of these game-theoretical dynamics, see Goldsmith & Posner.
73. Alexander Wendt, Anarchy Is What States Make of It: The Social Construction of Power Politics, 46 Int'l Org. 391, 412 (1992).
74. See generally John Gerard Ruggie, Constructing the World Polity (1998); Alexander Wendt, Social Theory of International Politics (1999).
75. Henkin at 22.
76. Martha Finnemore, National Interests in International Society 5–6 (1996).
77. Thomas M. Franck, The Power of Legitimacy Among Nations 24 (1990) (emphasis omitted).
78. Harold Hongju Koh, Why Do Nations Obey International Law?, 106 Yale L.J. 2599, 2600 n.3 (1997).
79. See Derek Jinks & Ryan Goodman, Socializing States: Promoting Human Rights Through International Law (2013).
80. Austin recognized the parallel as well and for that reason viewed constitutional law, like international law, as not really law but merely "positive morality." Austin at 141–42.
81. See Richard H. Fallon, Jr., Constitutional Constraints, 97 Calif. L. Rev. 975, 977 (2009) (noting the lack of attention among constitutionalists to constitutional constraints and how they are supposed to work).
82. Mark Tushnet, Taking the Constitution Away from the Courts 95–128 (1999).
83. See Alexander Bickel, The Least Dangerous Branch (1962).
84. Matthew C. Stephenson, "When the Devil Turns": The Political Foundations of Independent Judicial Review, 32 J. Leg. Stud. 59, 60 (2003).
85. Whittington at 11.
86. *The Federalist No. 48* at 305.

87. Letter from James Madison to Thomas Jefferson (Oct. 17, 1788), in Jack N. Rakove, Declaring Rights 160, 161 (1998).
88. *The Federalist No. 51* at 319.
89. Id. at 320–21.
90. See David E. Pozen, Self-Help and the Separation of Powers, 124 Yale L.J. 2 (2014) (recognizing this parallel).
91. See Farber at 158, 192–95.
92. Korematsu v. United States, 323 U.S. 214, 244 (Jackson, J., dissenting).
93. Jack Goldsmith, Law Wars, The New Rambler, November 10, 2015.
94. Posner, Has Obama Upheld the Rule of Law?
95. Eric A. Posner & Adrian Vermeule, The Executive Unbound 15 (2011).
96. Bruce Ackerman, The Decline and Fall of the American Republic 152, 88 (2010). Other observers view these claims as incorrect, or at least unproven. See Trevor W. Morrison, Constitutional Alarmism, 124 Harv. L. Rev. 1688 (2011); Richard H. Pildes, Law and the President 125 Harv. L. Rev. 1381, 1392–1403. The empirical evidence remains indeterminate, perhaps inevitably so. Even with visible examples of presidential demands being blocked by law, there is always the possibility that law-abiding presidents simply do not consider obviously illegal courses of action, giving courts and government lawyers few opportunities to say no. See Curtis A. Bradley & Trevor W. Morrison, Presidential Power, Historical Practice, and Legal Constraint, 113 Colum. L. Rev. 1097, 1150 (2013) ("focusing on the law's impact on actions actually taken by the President or other executive actors threatens to obscure the potentially much broader universe of actions not taken").
97. Louis Michael Seidman, On Constitutional Disobedience ch. 3 (2012) ("The Banality of Constitutional Violation"); David E. Pozen, Constitutional Bad Faith, 129 Harv. L. Rev. 885 (2016).
98. See generally Barry Friedman et al., Judicial Decision-Making 95–164 (2020).
99. Seidman, Constitutional Disobedience, at 66–67, 95–164.
100. Robert A. Dahl, Decision-Making in a Democracy: The Supreme Court as a National Policy-Maker, 6 J. Pub. L. 279, 285 (1957); see also Friedman (documenting the responsiveness of the Court to public opinion throughout constitutional history). There are, of course, numerous complexities here that create room for questioning the scope and reliability of Dahl's thesis. See Richard H. Pildes, Is the Supreme Court a "Majoritarian" Institution?, 2010 Sup. Ct. Rev. 103.
101. This prediction is directed to the national level of politics. In fact, most of the Court's major interventions have been to impose an emerging or consolidated national consensus on local outliers who disagree. See Michael J. Klarman, Rethinking the Civil Rights and Civil Liberties Revolutions, 82 Va. L. Rev. 1, 6 (1996). There is no great puzzle of compliance when state or regional minorities are subject to the will of national majorities, who enjoy political, financial, and military supremacy. The analogy is to powerful states in the international arena coercing weaker ones.
102. See Pozen, Self-Help and the Separation of Powers.
103. See Adam Przeworski, Democracy and the Market 26 (1991).

104. See Rui J.P. de Figueiredo, Jr., & Barry R. Weingast, Self-Enforcing Federalism, 21 J.L. Econ. & Org. 103 (2005).
105. Barry R. Weingast, The Political Foundations of Democracy and the Rule of Law, 91 Am. Pol. Sci. Rev. 245 (1997); Sonia Mittal & Barry R. Weingast, Self-Enforcing Constitutions: With an Application to Democratic Stability in America's First Century, 29 J.L. Econ & Org. 278 (2011).
106. See Russell Hardin, Liberalism, Constitutionalism, and Democracy 82–140 (1999). One illustration: In the early years of the United States, the Anti-Federalists rather quickly came to accept a constitution they had vehemently opposed, in large part because of the calculation that even a bad law was better than lawlessness. See David J. Siemers, Ratifying the Republic, at xiv–xvii (2000) (describing how "[f]ear induced stability" in the early Republic).
107. See David A. Strauss, Common Law, Common Ground, and Jefferson's Principle, 112 Yale L.J. 1717, 1733–37 (2003).
108. See Posner & Vermeule, Constitutional Showdowns.
109. Recent work in law and political science has recognized the parallels between institutionalist approaches to explaining judicial authority in the international and constitutional realms. See, e.g., Clifford James Carruba, A Model of the Endogenous Development of Judicial Institutions in Federal and International Systems, 71 J. Pol. 55 (2009); Jeffrey K. Staton & Will H. Moore, Judicial Power in Domestic and International Politics, 65 Int'l Org. 553 (2011); Shalev Roisman, Constraining States: Constitutional Lessons for International Courts, 55 Va. J. Int'l L. 729 (2015).
110. See Alexander & Schauer at 1377.
111. Madison, Letter to Jefferson, at 162.
112. See David S. Law, A Theory of A Theory of Judicial Power and Judicial Review, 97 Geo. L.J. 723 (2009); Weingast, Political Foundations.
113. See J. Mark Ramseyer, The Puzzling (In)Dependence of Courts: A Comparative Approach, 23 J. Leg. Stud. 721 (1994); Stephenson.
114. See Tom Ginsburg, Judicial Review in New Democracies 21–33 (2003).
115. See Ramseyer at 742–43.
116. Madison, Letter to Jefferson, at 162.
117. Richard H. Fallon, Jr., Law and Legitimacy in the Supreme Court 22 (2018).
118. Id. at 22–23.
119. Dobbs v. Jackson Women's Health Org., 597 U.S. __(2022).
120. Adam Liptak, A Critical Moment for *Roe*, and the Supreme Court's Legitimacy, NY Times, Dec. 4, 2021.
121. See Tom R. Tyler & Gregory Mitchell, Legitimacy and the Empowerment of Discretionary Legal Authority: The United States Supreme Court and Abortion Rights, 43 Duke L.J. 703 (1994).
122. See Richard H. McAdams, A Focal Point Theory of Expressive Law, 86 Va. L. Rev. 1649 (2000).
123. See Tom R. Tyler, Why People Obey the Law (2006); Cass R. Sunstein, Endogenous Preferences, Environmental Law, 22 J. Legal Stud. 217 (1993).
124. See Hampton at 132–88 (identifying and attempting to fill in this crucial gap in Hobbes's theory); see also Jody Kraus, The Limits of Hobbesian Contractarianism ch. 3 (1993) (denying the success of Hampton's solution).

125. John Ferejohn & Lawrence Sager, Commitment and Constitutionalism, 81 Tex. L. Rev. 1929, 1948–49 (2003).
126. See Douglass C. North & Barry R. Weingast, Constitutions and Commitment: The Evolution of Institutions Governing Public Choice in Seventeenth-Century England, 49 J. Econ. Hist. 803 (1989); Barry R. Weingast, The Economic Role of Political Institutions: Market-Preserving Federalism and Economic Development, 11 J.L. Econ. & Org. 1 (1995).
127. McNollGast, The Political Economy of Law (2010); Terry M. Moe, The Politics of Structural Choice, in Organization Theory 116 (Oliver E. Williamson ed., 1990); Kenneth Shepsle, Bureaucratic Drift, Coalitional Drift, and Time Consistency, 8 J.L. Econ. & Org. 111 (1992).
128. See Rachel Brewster, The Domestic Origins of International Agreements, 44 Va. J. Int'l L. 501, 511–24 (2004); see also Tom Ginsburg, Locking in Democracy: Constitutions, Commitment, and International Law, 38 NYU J. Int'l L. & Pol. 707 (2006); Beth A. Simmons & Allison Danner, Credible Commitments and the International Criminal Court, 64 Int'l Org. 225 (2010).
129. This is the self-critical diagnosis of a leading social scientist working in this vein. Weingast, The Economic Role of Political Institutions, at 3; see also Barry R. Weingast, Political Institutions: Rational Choice Perspectives, in A New Handbook of Political Science 133, 167, 175 (Robert E. Goodin & Hans-Dieter Klingemann eds., 1996) (noting that "[m]ost studies of institutions ignore" the question of "what makes institutions resistant to change" by "assuming that institutions are fixed."). For further criticisms along these lines, see William H. Riker, Implications from the Disequilibrium of Majority Rule for the Study of Institutions, 74 Am. Pol. Sci. Rev. 432, 443–44 (1980); John J. Mearsheimer, The False Promise of International Institutions, 19 Int'l Security 5 (1994).

Chapter 2

1. Prime Minister Boris Johnson's Brexit Address, Reuters, Jan. 31, 2020.
2. Quoted in Ali Wyne, Book Review: The Sovereignty Wars by Stewart Patrick, The Rand Blog, May 17, 2018.
3. See Jan-Werner Muller, What Is Populism (2016); Aziz Z. Huq, The People Against the Constitution, 116 Mich. L. Rev. 1123 (2018).
4. In a monarchy, said Hobbes, "the King is the people." Thomas Hobbes, On the Citizen 137 (Richard Tuck & Michael Silverthorne eds. & trans., 1998) (1647).
5. F.H. Hinsley, Sovereignty 158 (2d ed. 1986).
6. This is not to assert that Hobbes himself was influenced by the Peace of Westphalia when writing *Leviathan*. See David Armitage, Modern International Thought 73 (2013) (casting doubt on that possibility). Historians have also come to question the extent to which the Peace of Westphalia itself laid the groundwork for the international system of sovereign states. See Andreas Osiander, Sovereignty, International Relations, and the Westphalian Myth, 55 Int'l Org. 251 (2001).

7. Thomas Hobbes, Leviathan 155 (Richard Tuck ed., 1991) (1651).
8. John Austin, The Province of Jurisprudence Determined 212 (Wilfrid E. Rumble ed., 1995) (1832).
9. H.L.A. Hart, The Concept of Law 220 (2d ed. 1994); see also Janis Grzybowski & Martti Koskenniemi, International Law and Statehood: A Performative View, in The Concept of the State in International Relations 23, 25 (Robert Schuett & Peter M. R. Stirk eds., 2015) ("Twentieth-century international jurisprudence may be summarized as an extensive effort of trying to fit the view that states are sovereign with the view that they are still 'bound' by an international law.").
10. See Louis Henkin, International Law: Politics and Values 27 (1995) ("State consent is the foundation of international law. The principle that law is binding on a state only by its consent remains an axiom of the political system, an implication of state autonomy."). Here is Chief Justice John Marshall explicating the linkage between sovereignty and consent:

> The jurisdiction of the nation within its own territory is necessarily exclusive and absolute. It is susceptible of no limitation not imposed by itself. Any restriction upon it, deriving validity from an external source, would imply a diminution of its sovereignty to the extent of the restriction, and an investment of that sovereignty to the same extent in that power would could impose such restriction.
>
> All exceptions, therefore, to the full and complete power of a nation within its own territories, must be traced up to the consent of the nation itself. They can flow from no other legitimate source.

The Schooner Exchange v. M'Faddon, 11 U.S. (7 Cranch) 116 (1822).
11. Leviathan at 190.
12. Austin at 212.
13. See, e.g., Curtis A. Bradley & Mitu Gulati, Withdrawing from International Custom, 120 Yale L.J. 201 (2010) (recognizing and criticizing this "mandatory view" of CIL).
14. See, e.g., Laurence R. Helfer, Exiting Treaties, 91 Va. L. Rev. 1579 (2005).
15. Kenneth W. Abbott & Duncan Snidal, Hard and Soft Law in International Governance, 54 Int'l Org. 421 (2000).
16. See Ronald Dworkin A New Philosophy for International Law, 41 Phil. & Pub. Aff. 2, 7 (2013) ("International law could not serve the purposes it must serve in the contemporary world—disciplining the threat some states offer to others—unless it escaped the straightjacket of state-by-state consent.").
17. See generally Andreas Follesdal, The Significance of State Consent for the Legitimate Authority of Customary International Law, in The Theory, Practice, and Interpretation of Customary International Law (Panos Merkouris et al. eds., 2022). The International Law Commission has recently rejected consent as a requirement for CIL. See International Law Commission (ILC), Draft Conclusions on Identification of Customary International Law, in Report of the International Law Commission, A/73/10, 70th Sess., Supp. No. 10 at 123 fn. 665, 138–40 (2018).
18. See Restatement (Third) of the Foreign Relations Law of the United States § 102(2) (1987).
19. See ILC Draft Conclusions at 120.

20. Restatement at § 206 cmt. a; see also id. § 102 cmt. d.
21. Henkin at 36.
22. U.N. Charter Arts. 2(6), 27(3).
23. See Ryan Goodman, Human Rights Treaties, Invalid Reservations, and State Consent, 96 Am. J. Int'l L. 531 (2002); see also Tom Ginsburg, Objections to Treaty Reservations: A Comparative Approach to Decentralized Interpretation, in Comparative International Law 231 (Anthea Roberts et al. eds., 2018).
24. See Madeline Morris, High Crimes and Misconceptions: The ICC and Non-Party States, Law & Contemp. Probs., Winter 2001, at 13.
25. See Dapo Akande, The Immunity of Heads of States of Nonparties in the Early Years of the ICC, 112 AJIL Unbound 172 (2018).
26. For more on global governance, see Chapter 8.
27. See Vienna Convention on the Law of Treaties arts. 53, 64, opened for signature May 23, 1969, 1155 U.N.T.S. at 344, 347. On how international law attempts to justify imposing nonconsensual jus cogens norms on states, Andrea Bianchi, Human Rights and the Magic of Jus Cogens, 19(3) Eur. J. Int'l L. 491 (2008); Jens David Ohlin, In Praise of Jus Cogens' Conceptual Incoherence, 63 McGill L.J. 701 (2018).
28. See 2005 World Summit Outcome (resolution adopted by the General Assembly) A/RES/60?1 at 138–39. Int'l Comm'n on Intervention and State Sovereignty, The Responsibility to Protect (2001).
29. See Eyal Benvenisti, Sovereigns as Trustees of Humanity: On the Accountability of States to Foreign Stakeholders, 107 Am. J. Int'l L. 295 (2013); see also Mattias Kumm, The Cosmopolitan Turn in Constitutionalism: An Integrated Conception of Public Law, 20 Ind. J. Glob. L. Stud. 605 (2013).
30. See, e.g., Charles Beitz, The Idea of Human Rights (2019); Allen Buchanan, Justice, Legitimacy, and Self-Determination (2004); David Held, Democracy and the Global Order (1995); Thomas Pogge, World Poverty and Human Rights, Cosmopolitan Responsibilities and Reforms (2d ed. 2008).
31. See W. Michael Reisman, Sovereignty and Human Rights in Contemporary International Law, 84 Am. J. Int'l L. 866 (1990).
32. See Michael Walzer, The Moral Standing of States, 9 Phil. & Pub. Aff. 209 (1980). Even non-democratic states may be understood as serving the collective good of their people, as Hobbes, for one, insisted. See Charles R. Beitz, The Moral Standing of States Revisited, 23 Ethics & Int'l Aff. 325 (2009).
33. See id.
34. Oona A. Hathaway, International Delegation and State Sovereignty, 71 L. & Contemp. Probs. 115, 115 (2008).
35. How Barack Obama is Endangering Our National Sovereignty 2–4 (2010), quoted in Don Herzog, Sovereignty RIP 283 (2020).
36. National Security Adviser John Bolton Remarks to the Federalist Society, Lawfare, Sept. 10, 2018.

37. Jeremy A. Rabkin, Law Without Nations? Why Constitutional Government Requires Sovereign States (2005).
38. Sosa v. Alvarez-Machain, 542 U.S. 692, 749 (2004) (Scalia, J., concurring).
39. Jed Rubenfeld, Unilateralism and Constitutionalism, 79 N.Y.U. L. Rev. 1971, 2020 (2004).
40. Id. at 1993, 2007, 2010.
41. William Blackstone 1 Commentaries 91, 161 (1765). Blackstone did, however, believe in another sense of "constitutional" constraint that could be applied to Parliament, which was the withdrawal of popular support on the grounds that fundamental rights or rules of the system of government had been violated. See John C.P. Goldberg, The Constitutional Status of Tort Law: Due Process and the Right to a Law for the Redress of Wrongs, 115 Yale L.J. 524, 556–58 (2005).
42. Trump v. Hawaii, 138 S. Ct. 2392, 2408 (2018).
43. Kawananakoa v. Polybank, 205 U.S. 340, 353 (1907).
44. See Akhil Reed Amar, Of Sovereignty and Federalism, 96 Yale L.J. 1425 (1987) (arguing that sovereign immunity was superseded by constitutionalism based on popular sovereignty).
45. While popular sovereignty is commonly understood to be the opposite of the Hobbesian kind, vested in the ruling sovereign, the distinction is not nearly so sharp. In Hobbes's telling, sovereignty was originally the creation and possession of a political "people" who mutually consented to collective self-rule. Hobbes's people then proceed to delegate unlimited sovereignty to the government, giving rise to the kind of absolutist authority of the government that we now describe as Hobbesian. See Richard Tuck, The Sleeping Sovereign 86–109 (2015). Subtract the delegation step from Hobbes's theory, however, and what comes before is something very close to popular sovereignty as we have come to understand it, developed in various ways after Hobbes by Rousseau, Locke, and Sieyes, among others. Id. at 109–80.
46. The Declaration of Independence para. 2 (U.S. 1776).
47. Tuck at 181–248; Gordon S. Wood, The Creation of the American Republic: 1776–1787, at 567–92 (1969). A federal structure of government that divides power between nation and state also poses no problem for sovereignty, which remains undivided in the people.
48. Many of the structural provisions of the Constitution and Bill of Rights were originally designed to constrain the self-serving behavior of federal officials and to protect institutions of state and local self-government that would insulate citizens from these officials' potentially despotic reach. That made it relatively easy to conceptualize constitutionalism as a sovereignty-enhancing solution to the problem of representative government. See Akhil Reed Amar, The Bill of Rights: Creation and Reconstruction, at xii–xiii (1998).
49. *The Federalist No. 51* at 320 (James Madison) (Clinton Rossiter ed., 1999).
50. First Inaugural of Abraham Lincoln, Avalon Project (Mar. 4, 1861).
51. Wood at 378 (quoting Webster).
52. See David Singh Grewal & Jedediah Purdy, The Original Theory of Constitutionalism, 127 Yale L.J. 664, 681 (2018).

53. This assumes that the constitutional norms being enforced are identical to the norms that were originally blessed with the people's consent. Contractarian understandings of constitutionalism demand that constitutional interpreters—courts and other political actors—accurately reflect the original understanding of the parties to the constitutional contract, or the original meaning of the constitutional text. If, as is often the case in actual practice, interpreters are deriving constitutional law from nonoriginalist sources and methods, or if originalist sources and methods do not accurately track consent, then it becomes less clear how popular consent can legitimate constitutional practice. See Adam M. Samaha, Dead Hand Arguments and Constitutional Interpretation, 108 Colum. L. Rev. 606, 655 (2008).
54. Here is the version offered by Chief Justice Marshall in *Marbury v. Madison*:

> That the [P]eople have an original right to establish, for their future government, such principles as, in their opinion, shall most conduce to their own happiness, is the basis, on which the whole American fabric has been erected. The exercise of this original right is a very great exertion; nor can it, nor ought it to be frequently repeated. The principles, therefore, so established, are deemed fundamental. And as the authority, from which they proceed, is supreme, and can seldom act, they are designed to be permanent.
>
> 5 U.S. (1 Cranch) 137, 176 (1803).

55. On the Citizen at 99–100.
56. See Tuck.
57. See Grewal & Purdy at 691–96.
58. Wood at 379 (quoting Daniel Webster).
59. Letter from Thomas Jefferson to James Madison (Sept. 6, 1789), in 15 The Papers of Thomas Jefferson 392, 395–96 (Julian P. Boyd & William H. Gaines, Jr., eds., 1958).
60. As David Strauss observes, echoing Jefferson and Webster:

> [I]t would be bizarre if the current Canadian parliament asserted the power to govern the United States on such matters as . . . race discrimination, criminal procedure, and religious freedom. But we have far more in common—demographically, culturally, morally, and in our historical experiences—with Canadians of the 1990s than we do with Americans of the 1780s or 1860s.
>
> David A. Strauss, Common Law Constitutional Interpretation, 63 U. Chi. L. Rev. 877, 880 (1996); see also David A. Strauss, Common Law, Common Ground, and Jefferson's Principle, 2003 Yale L.J. 1717 (2003).

61. See, e.g., Martin Loughlin, Against Constitutionalism (2022); Louis Michael Seidman, On Constitutional Disobedience (2012).
62. See 1 Bruce Ackerman, We the People: Foundations (1991); 2 Bruce Ackerman, We the People: Transformations (1998); 3 Bruce Ackerman, We the People: The Civil Rights Revolution (2018).
63. Larry D. Kramer, Popular Constitutionalism, circa 2004, 92 Calif. L. Rev. 959, 959; see also Larry D. Kramer, The People Themselves (2004); Mark Tushnet, Taking the Constitution Away from the Courts (2000).
64. See United States v. Carolene Products., 304 U.S. 144, 152 n.4 (1938); John Hart Ely, Democracy and Distrust (1980).

260 NOTES

65. See Jon Elster, Ulysses Unbound 88–174 (2000); Stephen Holmes, Passions and Constraint 134–77 (1995).
66. Stephen D. Krasner, Sovereignty: Organized Hypocrisy (1999).
67. See Herzog.
68. Hannah Arendt, On Revolution 16 (1963).
69. This is the overarching thesis of Herzog's tour de force. Herzog.
70. Hart at 66–78 (constitutional law); id. at 220–26 (international law).
71. See generally Richard Tuck, The Rights of War and Peace: Political Thought and the International Order from Grotius to Kant (1999).
72. See Hart at 224 (drawing the connection between consent-based theories of international law and social contract theories of individual political obligation).
73. See also John Stuart Mill, On Liberty 81 (David Bromwich & George Kateb eds., Yale Univ. Press 2003) (1859) ("Over himself, over his own body and mind, the individual is sovereign."). The difficulties with social contractarian accounts of this kind—Hobbes's and Locke's, as well as Rousseau's, Rawls's, and others'—have been extensively vetted. See generally Tom Cristiano, Authority, Stanford Encyclopedia of Philosophy; Fred D'Agostino et al., Contemporary Approaches to the Social Contract, Stanford Encyclopedia of Philosophy.
74. Charles R. Beitz, Political Theory and International Relations 180 (1979).
75. See Walzer; Beitz.
76. See generally William N. Eskridge & Sanford V. Levinson, Constitutional Stupidities, Constitutional Tragedies (1998).
77. Jeremy Waldron, The Rule of International Law, 30 Harv. J. L. & Pub. Pol'y 15, 24 (2006).
78. Id. at 18.
79. On the philosophical difficulties, see, e.g., John A. Simmons, Justification and Legitimacy (2001); Cristiano.

Chapter 3

1. Matthew Gault, Is the U.S. a Failed State?, Vice, June 8, 2020 (quoting Daron Acemoglu).
2. During the pandemic, scholars turned their attention to a heretofore-neglected feature of Hobbes's *Leviathan* frontispiece. Among the few humans not subsumed into the arms and torso of Leviathan are, apparently, two plague doctors, characteristically identifiable by their beaked masks. See Benedict Kingsbury, Hobbes and the Plague Doctors, IILJ Working Paper 2021/4 (forthcoming in International Crisis Narratives (Jean D'Aspremont & Makane Mbengue eds.). Kingsbury credits Francesa Falk, Hobbes' *Leviathan* und die aus dem Blick gefallenen Schnabelmasken, 39 Leviathan 247 (2011) and Thomas Poole, Leviathan in Lockdown, London Review of Books, May 1, 2020, for bringing this feature of the frontispiece to light and connecting it to COVID, respectively.
3. George Packer, We Are Living in a Failed State, The Atlantic, June 2020.

4. See generally Sharon A. Lloyd & Susanne Sreedhar, Hobbes's Moral and Political Philosophy §8, Stanford Encyclopedia of Philosophy, revised Sept. 12, 2022.
5. See Richard H. Pildes, The Age of Political Fragmentation, 4 J. Democracy 146 (2021).
6. Steven Pinker credits the state for much of the historical decline in violence over recent centuries. Steven Pinker, The Better Angels of Our Nature 680–82 (2012).
7. Thomas Hobbes, Leviathan 89 (Richard Tuck ed., 1991) (1651).
8. Charles Tilly, Coercion, Capital, and European States, AD 990–1992 (1992); Charles Tilly, War Making and State Making as Organized Crime, in Bringing the State Back In 169 (Peter B. Evans et al. eds., 1985).
9. The poverty that afflicts much of Africa has been attributed in part to a historical path of development that did not include the continuous warfare and demands for militarization that characterized early modern Europe and hence resulted in weaker states. See Jeffrey Herbst, States and Power in Africa (2000); see also Paul Collier, Wars, Guns, and Votes 182–85 (2009) (considering the possibility that the path to development in contemporary sub-Saharan Africa, following the example of European state-building, might be to encourage greater military rivalry among states).
10. Cf. Barry R. Weingast, The Economic Role of Political Institutions: Market-Preserving Federalism and Economic Development, 11 J. L. Econ. & Org. 1, 1 (1995) ("The fundamental political dilemma of an economic system" is that "[a] government strong enough to protect property rights . . . is also strong enough to confiscate the wealth of its citizens.").
11. This approach reflects a turn away from the prior "Washington Consensus" that a powerful state apparatus was too great a threat to free markets and individual liberty and that the better course was to "privatize, privatize, privatize." See Francis Fukuyama, State-Building 19 (2004) (quoting Milton Friedman).
12. See Fukuyama at 22 (2004).
13. See Kenneth M. Pollack et al., Unfinished Business: An American Strategy for Iraq Moving Forward 6, Saban Center for Middle East Policy at Brookings Analysis Paper No. 22, 2010 ("Washington needs to remain wary of building another Iraqi Frankenstein's monster, as it did to some extent with Saddam [Hussein] himself in the 1980s."). Osama bin Laden and the Taliban in Afghanistan could also be described in this way, as their power was built in significant part through American aid to bin Laden and other mujahideen fighting against the Soviet occupation. See A Bitter Harvest, The Economist, Sept. 15, 2001, at 19.
14. Joseph Bosco, The Historic Opening to China: What Hath Nixon Wrought?, Harvard Law School National Security Journal, Sept. 25, 2015; John J. Mearsheimer, The Inevitable Rivalry, Foreign Affairs, Nov./Dec. 2021.
15. Fukuyama at 19.
16. Cf. David Lake, The Statebuilder's Dilemma (2016). Lake's version of the dilemma stems from the competing imperatives of building a state that serves the interests of the builder and building a state that will be received as legitimate by the subject population.
17. See William I. Hitchcock, The Marshall Plan and the Creation of the West, in 1 The Cambridge History of the Cold War (Melvyn P. Leffler & Odd Arne Westad eds., 2010).

18. U.S. Department of State, Foreign Relations of the United States, The Conference at Quebec 1944, at 128–43 (1944).
19. As Winston Churchill would describe the basic thrust, Germany was to be changed "into a country primarily agricultural and pastoral in its character." See John Dietrich, The Morgenthau Plan 64 (2d ed. 2013).
20. See Michael Beschloss, The Conquerors: Roosevelt, Truman and the Destruction of Hitler's Germany, 1941–1945, at 132 (2003).
21. See James McCallister, No Exit: America and the German Problem, 1943–1954, at 52 (2002).
22. Beschloss at 273.
23. See McAllister at 78–79.
24. How much credit the Marshall Plan deserves for post-war economic growth is a topic of ongoing debate. See Lucrezia Reichlin, The Marshall Plan Reconsidered, in Europe's Postwar Recovery 39, 40–41 (Barry Eichengreen ed., 1995).
25. See Hitchcock at 154–73.
26. See Michael J. Hogan, The Marshall Plan: America, Britain, and the Reconstruction of Western Europe, 1947–1952, at 337–38 (1987). Starting in the mid-1950s, Germany itself would eventually build a new military force under the command structure of NATO. The reborn German military was designed as a strictly defensive force, aimed at deterring a Warsaw Bloc attack. See Jonathan M. House, The European Defense Community, in Rearming Germany 73, 90–91 (James S. Corum ed., 2011).
27. Luke Harding, Kohl Tells of Being Battered by Iron Lady, The Guardian, Nov. 2, 2005.
28. See Medhi Hasan, Angela Merkel's Mania for Austerity is Destroying Europe, New Statesmen (June 20, 2012).
29. See Max Edling, A Revolution in Favor of Government (2003).
30. Edling at 73–81.
31. Stephen Skowronek, Building a New American State 20 (1982).
32. See Jack N. Rakove, Original Meanings: Politics and Ideas in the Making of the Constitution 152 (1996).
33. Saul Cornell, The Other Founders 95 (1999).
34. See Edling at 44.
35. Id. at 110.
36. *The Federalist No. 41* at 255–56 (Clinton Rossiter ed., 1961) (James Madison).
37. Edling at 93 (quoting Oliver Ellsworth).
38. Id.
39. *The Federalist No. 25* (Hamilton).
40. Id.
41. Edling at 93 (quoting Oliver Ellsworth).
42. Edling at 98 (quoting James Madison).
43. See David M. Golove & Daniel J. Hulsebosch, A Civilized Nation: The Early American Constitution, the Law of Nations, and the Pursuit of International Recognition, 85 N.Y.U. L. Rev. 932, 955–57 (2010). For their own part, Federalists saw the Constitution as a step toward recognition and acceptance as a full-fledged member of the Europe-centered society of states. Id. at 935–36.

44. See, e.g., Timothy Besley & Torsten Persson, State Capacity, Conflict, and Development, 78 Econometrica 1 (2010); Jonathan K. Hanson & Rachel Sigman, Leviathan's Latent Dimensions: Measuring State Capacity for Comparative Political Research, 83 J. Pol. 1495 (2021). There is a close relationship between state capacity and what Michael Mann has termed the "infrastructural power" of the state. See Michael Mann, The Autonomous Power of the State: Its Origins, Mechanisms and Results, 25 Eur. J. Soc. 185 (1984).
45. Tilly at 100.
46. See James C. Scott, Seeing Like a State 35 (1998) ("Tax and tithe rolls, property rolls, conscription lists, censuses, and property deeds recognized in law were inconceivable without some means of fixing an individual's identity and linking him or her to a kin group.").
47. See, e.g., Jacob Soll, The Information Master: Jean-Baptiste Colbert's Secret State Intelligence System (2009) (describing the efforts under the reign of Louis XIV, led by his chief minister, Jean-Baptiste Colbert, to strengthen the French monarchy and realize its absolutist ambitions by creating an elaborate system of information gathering and management).
48. See Jack M. Balkin, The Constitution in the National Surveillance State, 93 Minn. L. Rev. 1, 3 (2008); see also Barry Friedman, Lawless Surveillance, 97 N.Y.U. L. Rev. 1143 (2022).
49. Scott at 57 (1998).
50. See Alison Des Forges, "Leave None to Tell the Story": Genocide in Rwanda 8–9, 231–41 (1999).
51. Scott at 78 ("If one reflects briefly on the kind of detailed information on names, addresses, and ethnic backgrounds . . . and the cartographic exactitude required to produce this statistical representation, the contribution of legibility to state capacity is evident.").
52. Scott at 78.
53. Compare Adrian Vermeule's notion of "precautionary constitutionalism" as an approach to dealing with political risks. Adrian Vermeule, The Constitution of Risk 2, 10 (2014). Vermeule defines precautionary constitutionalism as the view that:

[C]onstitutional rules should above all entrench precautions against the risks that official action will result in dictatorship or tyranny, corruption and official self-dealing, violations of the rights of minorities, or other political harms of equivalent severity. On this view, constitutional rulemakers and citizens design and manage political institutions with a view to warding off the worst case. The burden of uncertainty is to be set against official power, out of a suspicion that the capacity and tendency of official power to inflict cruelty, indignity, and other harms are greater than its capacity and tendency to promote human welfare, liberty, or justice.

Id. at 11.
54. The Federalist No. 25 at 167.

55. See Tilly at 102–103; see also Lisa Blaydes & Eric Chaney, The Feudal Revolution and Europe's Rise: Political Divergence of the Christian West and the Muslim World Before 1500 CE, 107 Am. Pol. Sci. Rev. 16, 16–17 (2013).
56. Daron Acemoglu & James Robinson, Why Nations Fail 185–97 (2012); see also John Brewer, The Sinews of Power: War, Money, and the English State, 1688–1783 (1988).
57. See Acemoglu & Robinson at 196 ("Parliament had opposed making the state more effective and better resourced prior to 1688 because it could not control it. After 1688 it was a different story."); see also Douglass C. North & Barry R. Weingast, Constitutions and Commitment: The Evolution of Institutional Governing Public Choice in Seventeenth-Century England, 49 J. Econ. Hist. 803, 817 (1989) ("[I]n exchange for the greater say in government, parliamentary interests agreed to put the government on a sound financial footing... [by] provid[ing] sufficient tax revenue.").
58. North & Weingast at 817.
59. See Edling at 64 (quoting Blackstone).
60. Daron Acemoglu, Institutions, Factor Prices, and Taxation: Virtues of Strong States?, 100 Am. Econ. Rev. 115, 118 (2010).
61. *The Federalist No. 51* at 319.
62. See Cornell at 72–73, 85, 90: Edling at 181–82.
63. Edling at 182 (quoting Federal Farmer).
64. See Rakove at 229–30.
65. Actually, the Bill of Rights as originally conceived and, in part, enacted was as much about bolstering popular political control as it was about protecting discretely enumerated rights. Many of the rights it enumerated were meant to empower majoritarian governance by placing limits on the self-serving behavior of federal officials and by safeguarding institutions of state and local self-government to insulate citizens from these officials' despotic reach. See Akhil Reed Amar, The Bill of Rights: Creation and Reconstruction, at xii–xiii, 3–133 (1998).
66. Edling at 228, quoting John M. Murrin, The Great Inversion, or Court Versus Country: A Comparison of the Revolutionary Settlements in England (1688–1721) and America (1776–1816), in Three British Revolutions 1641, 1688, 1776, at 368, 425 (J.G.A. Pocock ed., 1980).
67. Brian Balough, A Government Out of Sight 112 (2009).
68. Ira Katznelson, Flexible Capacity: The Military and Early American Statebuilding, in Shaped by War and Trade 82, 89 (Ira Katznelson & Martin Shefter eds., 2002).
69. William J. Novak, The Myth of the "Weak" American State, 113 Am. Hist. Rev. 752, 758 (2008).
70. See, e.g., Akhil Reed Amar, America's Constitution: A Biography 64 (2005).
71. Mutual monitoring and checking among the branches might also facilitate ongoing electoral control. See Jide O. Nzelibe & Matthew C. Stephenson, Complementary Constraints: Separation of Powers, Rational Voting, and Constitutional Design, 123 Harv. L. Rev. 617, 626 (2010).
72. Cass R. Sunstein, After the Rights Revolution 15–16 (1993); see also Boumediene v. Bush, 553 U.S. 723, 742 (2008) ("The Framers' inherent distrust of governmental

power was the driving force behind" the constitutional separation of powers, which serves to "secure individual liberty").
73. *The Federalist No. 73* at 442 (Alexander Hamilton).
74. Herbert Croly, Progressive Democracy 40 (1915).
75. See Jerry L. Mashaw, Creating the Administrative Constitution 10 (2012).
76. Jerry L. Mashaw, Recovering American Administrative Law: Federalist Foundations, 1787–1801, 115 Yale L.J. 1256, 1337 (2006).
77. Elena Kagan, Presidential Administration, 114 Harv. L. Rev. 2245, 2246 (2001).
78. Gary Lawson, The Rise and Rise of the Administrative State, 107 Harv. L. Rev. 1231 (1994).
79. This was the phrase used by Trump's chief strategist, Stephen Bannon, to describe the agenda of the Trump administration. See Philip Rucker & Robert Costa, Bannon Vows a Daily Fight for "Deconstruction of the Administrative State," Wash. Post, Feb. 23, 2017.
80. Gundy v. United States, 139 S. Ct. 2116, 2130 (2019).
81. See Nicholas Bagley, The Procedure Fetish, 118 Mich. L. Rev. 345 (2019); Brink Lindsey, State Capacity: What Is It, How We Lost It, and How to Get It Back 5–7, Niskanen Center White Paper, Nov. 2021.
82. The term "imperial presidency" was coined by Arthur Schlesinger, though Schlesinger was using the term in a somewhat different sense. Schlesinger, The Imperial Presidency (1973).
83. 1 The Records of the Federal Convention of 1787, at 66 (Max Farrand ed., 1911) (providing Edmund Randolph's description of the presidency at the Philadelphia Convention).
84. See Eric A. Posner, The Dictator's Handbook, U.S. Edition, in Can It Happen Here? Authoritarianism in America 1 (Cass R. Sunstein ed., 2018); see also Steven Levitsky & Daniel Ziblatt, How a Democracy Dies, The New Republic, Dec. 7, 2017.
85. Richard H. Pildes, Law and the President, 125 Harv. L. Rev. 1381, 1383 (2012).
86. Eric A. Posner & Adrian Vermeule, The Executive Unbound 4 (2010).
87. Id. at 176.
88. Martin S. Flaherty, The Most Dangerous Branch, 105 Yale L.J. 1727, 1731 (2002).
89. See Theodore J. Lowi, The Personal President, at xi (1985). "Plebiscitary" is sometimes used in a different and nearly opposite sense to mean accountable only at election time, but unaccountable to Congress, the press, or the public while actually governing. This was how Schlesinger used the term in *The Imperial Presidency*. See Schlesinger at 255.
90. Jack Goldsmith, Power & Constraint xv (2012).
91. Goldsmith.
92. Bruce Ackerman, The Decline and Fall of the American Republic 6 (2010).
93. Id. at 119–40, 141–79.
94. See id. at 165–74, 152–59; see also Bruce Ackerman, The New Separation of Powers, 113 Harv. L. Rev. 633 (2000).
95. Ackerman, Decline and Fall, at 124.
96. Gregory v. Ashcroft, 501 U.S. 452, 458 (1991) (quoting Atascadero State Hosp. v. Scanlon, 473 U.S. 234, 242 (1985)); see also Andrzej Rapaczynski, From Sovereignty to Process: The Jurisprudence of Federalism After Garcia, 1985 Sup. Ct. Rev. 341, 380 ("Perhaps the most frequently mentioned function of the federal system is the one it

shares ... with the [system of] separation of powers, namely, the protection of the citizen against governmental oppression—the 'tyranny' that the Framers were so concerned about.").
97. *The Federalist No. 51* at 323 (James Madison).
98. See *The Federalist No. 45* at 291 (James Madison); Larry D. Kramer, Putting the Politics Back into the Political Safeguards of Federalism, 100 Colum. L. Rev. 215 (2000); Herbert Wechsler, The Political Safeguards of Federalism: The Role of the States in the Composition and Selection of the National Government, 54 Colum. L. Rev. 543 (1954); Heather K. Gerken, Federalism All the Way Down, 124 Harv. L. Rev. 4 (2010).
99. Fukuyama at 103.
100. See John Gerring et al., An Institutional Theory of Direct and Indirect Rule, 63 World Pol. 377 (2011).
101. See Tilly at 104.
102. See Matthew Lange, Lineages of Despotism and Development: British Colonialism and State Power 21–33 (2009).
103. See J. H. Elliott, Empires of the Atlantic World: Britain and Spain in America, 1492–1830, at 140, 149–52 (2006).
104. Elliott at 149.
105. See William H. Riker, Federalism 3–5 (1964).
106. See Daniel Ziblatt, Structuring the State 2–3 (2006).
107. Id. at 3.
108. See Cornell at 30; Rakove at 148.
109. See Edling at 185–205.
110. Roderick M. Hills, Jr., The Political Economy of Cooperative Federalism: Why State Autonomy Makes Sense and "Dual Sovereignty" Doesn't, 96 Mich. L. Rev. 813, 833 (1998) ("Anti-Federalists—quintessential defenders of state power—wanted the national government to rely exclusively on the state governments to implement national policy."); Saikrishna Bangalore Prakash, Field Office Federalism, 79 Va. L. Rev. 1957, 2005 (1993) ("[T]hose who feared that a gargantuan federal bureaucracy would overpower the states were reassured that existing state officers could carry out federal tasks."); see also *The Federalist No. 27* at 177 (Alexander Hamilton) ("[T]he legislatures, courts, and magistrates, of the respective members will be incorporated into the operations of the national government ... and will be rendered auxiliary to the enforcement of its laws.").
111. See Abbe R. Gluck, Instrastatutory Federalism and Statutory Interpretation: State Implementation of Federal Law in Health Reform and Beyond, 121 Yale L.J. 534, 564 (2011).
112. See Jessica Bulman-Pozen & Heather K. Gerken, Uncooperative Federalism, 118 Yale L.J. 1256 (2009).
113. From this perspective, the Court's invention of "anticommandeering" as a constitutional constraint on the national government's harnessing state implementation and enforcement capacity is perverse. See Wesley J. Campbell, Commandeering and Constitutional Change, 122 Yale L.J. 1104 (2013).

Chapter 4

1. Richard H. Pildes, The Supreme Court 2003 Term—Foreword: The Constitutionalization of Democratic Politics, 118 Harv. L. Rev. 28, 40 (2004).
2. See David Kennedy, Lawfare and Warfare, in The Cambridge Companion to International Law 158 (James Crawford ed., 2012); David Kennedy, Of War and Law 99–164 (2006).
3. See Oona A. Hathaway & Harold Hongju Koh, Foundations of International Law and Politics (2005); International Law and International Relations (Beth A. Simmons & Richard H. Steinberg eds., 2007); Anne-Marie Slaughter Burley, International Law and International Relations Theory: A Dual Agenda, 87 Am. J. Int'l L. 205 (1993); Anne-Marie Slaughter et al., International Law and International Relations Theory: A New Generation of Interdisciplinary Scholarship, 92 Am. J. Int'l L. 367 (1998).
4. See generally Legalization and World Politics (Judith L. Goldstein et al. eds., 2001).
5. See Mark A. Graber, Enumeration and Other Constitutional Strategies for Protecting Rights: The View from 1787/1791, 9 U. Pa. J. Const. L. 357 (2007).
6. Letter from James Madison to Thomas Jefferson (Oct. 17, 1788), in Jack A. Rakove, Declaring Rights: A Brief History with Documents 160, 161–62 (1998). As Madison distinguished these two types of political failures in *The Federalist No. 51*, "It is of great importance in a republic not only to guard the society against the oppression of its rulers, but to guard one part of the society against the injustice of the other part." See *The Federalist No. 51* at 323 (Clinton Rossiter ed., 1961).
7. Madison, Letter to Jefferson, at 162.
8. Id. at 161.
9. *The Federalist No. 57* at 350 (James Madison).
10. *The Federalist No. 10* at 82 (James Madison).
11. In *The Federalist No. 10*, Madison explains:

    Extend the sphere, and you take in a greater variety of parties and interests; you make it less probable that a majority of the whole will have a common motive to invade the rights of other citizens; or if such a common motive exists, it will be more difficult for all who feel it to discover their own strength, and to act in unison with each other.

    The Federalist No. 10 at 83 (James Madison).
12. *The Federalist No. 51* at 270 (James Madison).
13. See *The Federalist No. 51* at 322; see also *The Federalist No. 45* at 290–91.
14. *The Federalist No. 84* at 515 (Alexander Hamilton).
15. James Madison, Speech to the Virginia Constitutional Convention (1829), in Selected Writings of James Madison 355 (Ralph Ketcham ed., 2006).
16. Speech of James Madison at the Constitutional Convention (Aug. 25, 1787), in 10 The Papers of James Madison 157, 157 (Robert A. Rutland et al. eds., 1977).
17. Mark A. Graber, Dred Scott and the Problem of Constitutional Evil 114 (2006).
18. Id. at 126–27.
19. See Jesse T. Carpenter, The South as a Conscious Minority, 1789–1861 at 89–92 (1990).

20. See Graber, Constitutional Evil, at 140–44; Barry R. Weingast, Political Stability and Civil War: Institutions, Commitment, and American Democracy, in Analytic Narratives 148, 153–55 (Robert H. Bates et al. eds., 1998).
21. See Weingast at 156–59.
22. Echoing Madison's Founding-era view, James Randolph declared, "I have no faith in parchment." 42 Annals of Cong. 2361 (1824).
23. Carpenter at 141 (quoting Abel Upshur from the debates of the Virginia Constitutional Convention).
24. John C. Calhoun, A Disquisition on Government and Selections from the Discourse 20 (C. Gordon Post ed., 1953) (1851). On Calhoun's concurrent majority, see generally Carpenter at 77–126; David M. Potter, The South and the Concurrent Majority (1972); James H. Read, Majority Rules Versus Consensus: The Political Thought of John C. Calhoun (2009).
25. See Carpenter at 94–95, 98–99.
26. Martin Luther King, Jr., Give Us the Ballot, Address Delivered at the Prayer Pilgrimage for Freedom (May 17, 1957), in 4 The Papers of Martin Luther King, Jr., 208, 210 (Clayborne Carson et al. eds., 2000).
27. See Mark Tushnet, The Politics of Equality in Constitutional Law: The Equal Protection Clause, Dr. Du Bois, and Charles Hamilton Houston, 74 J. Am. Hist. 884, 888–89 (1987).
28. Michael J. Klarman, The Puzzling Resistance to Political Process Theory, 77 Va. L. Rev. 747, 790–94 (1991)
29. Id. at 797–812.
30. For an overview of empirical studies examining the effects of the Voting Rights Act, see id. at 802–803; Richard H. Pildes, The Politics of Race, 108 Harv. L. Rev. 1359, 1377 (1995) (book review).
31. Reynolds v. Sims, 377 U.S. 533, 566, 562 (1964).
32. Samuel Issacharoff, Polarized Voting and the Political Process: The Transformation of Voting Rights Jurisprudence, 90 Mich. L. Rev. 1833, 1867–68 (1992).
33. Katzenbach v. Morgan, 384 U.S. 641, 652 (1966).
34. See James A. Gardner, Liberty, Community and the Constitutional Structure of Political Influence: A Reconsideration of the Right to Vote, 145 U. Pa. L. Rev. 893 (1997).
35. Lani Guinier, The Triumph of Tokenism: The Voting Rights Act and the Theory of Black Electoral Success, 89 Mich. L. Rev. 1077, 1082 n.14 (1991).
36. See United States v. Carolene Products, 304 U.S. 144, 152 n.4 (1938); John Hart Ely, Democracy and Distrust (1980).
37. See U.S. v. Carolene Prods. Co., 304 U.S. at 153 n.4.
38. See Jane S. Schacter, Ely at the Altar: Political Process Theory Through the Lens of the Marriage Debate, 109 Mich. L. rev. 1363 (2011); Kenji Yoshino, Speak Now 142–54 (2015).
39. Romer v. Evans, 517 U.S. 620, 646 (1996) (Scalia, J., dissenting).
40. Ely at 86.

41. See Sujit Choudhry, Bridging Comparative Politics and Comparative Constitutional Law: Constitutional Design in Divided Societies, in Constitutional Design for Divided Societies 3 (Sujit Choudhry ed., 2008).
42. See Arend Lijphart, Democracy in Plural Societies (1977); Arend Lijphart, Consociational Democracy, 21 World Pol. 207 (1969).
43. See Choudhry at 15–26.
44. See Lijphart, Plural Societies, at 27; see also Read at 196–204. In fact, the constitutional order of the antebellum United States fits the description of consociational democracy. See Graber, Constitutional Evil, at 187–91.
45. See Read at 217; see also Arend Lijphart, Power-Sharing in South Africa (1985).
46. See Christina Murray & Richard Simeon, Recognition Without Empowerment: Minorities in a Democratic South Africa, in Constitutional Design for Divided Societies, at 409, 425.
47. See Ran Hirschl, Towards Juristocracy 90, 90–93 (2004).
48. See id. at 94–95.
49. Albie Sachs, South Africa's Unconstitutional Constitution: The Transition from Power to Lawful Power, 41 St. Louis U. L.J. 1249, 1250 (1997).
50. On the reasons for the ANC's shift, see Heinz Klug, Constitutional Democracy: Law, Globalism, and South Africa's Political Reconstruction 76–77 (2000).
51. S. Afr. Const., 1996, ch. 2, § 7.
52. See Shefali Jha, Rights Versus Representation: Defending Minority Interests in the Constituent Assembly, 38 Econ. & Pol. Wkly. 1579, 1579–80 (2003).
53. See Choudhry, Bridging, at 12. Northern Ireland's Good Friday Agreement of 1998 similarly combined incorporation of the European Convention on Human Rights and the creation of additional rights protections with a consociational political structure that required dual Protestant and Catholic majorities for all "key decisions" and created a diarchical Protestant and Catholic executive. See Read at 204–206.
54. Daron Acemoglu & James A. Robinson, Economic Origins of Dictatorship and Democracy (2006).
55. See id. at 10–14.
56. Hirschl, Juristocracy.
57. Id. at 11.
58. See id. at 89–97.
59. Ronald Dworkin, Taking Rights Seriously, at xi (1977).
60. For a recent survey of the different ways constitutional rights in the United States and other countries are rendered non-absolute, see Jamal Greene, Foreword: Rights as Trumps?, 132 Harv. L. Rev. 28 (2018).
61. See Graber, Enumeration, at 367–68.
62. 3 The Debates in the Several State Conventions on the Adoption of the Federal Constitution as Recommended by the General Convention at Philadelphia 1787, at 626 (Jonathan Elliot ed., 2d ed. 1891).
63. *The Federalist No. 84* (Alexander Hamilton).
64. Ely at 81.

65. Graber, Enumeration, at 368–72. This idea once again came to the fore in constitutional jurisprudence during the Lochner era. Due Process and related rights were understood to protect against "partial" legislation directed at particular classes or toward "private" ends. Laws designed to further the public good were constitutionally unobjectionable—even when these laws interfered with the life, liberty, or property of individuals. See generally Barry Cushman, Rethinking the New Deal Court (1998); Howard Gilman, The Constitution Besieged (1993).
66. S. Afr. Const., 1996, ch. 2, §§ 26–27, 29.
67. The Bill of Rights grants everyone "the right to use the language and to participate in the cultural life of their choice," S. Afr. Const., 1996, ch. 2, § 29, and the right "to receive education in the official language or languages of their choice," id. § 30, and the Constitution establishes a body called the Commission for the Promotion and Protection of the Rights of Cultural, Religious, and Linguistic Communities to help secure these rights. Id. ch. 9, §§ 185–86.
68. See, e.g., Bruce A. Ackerman, Beyond Carolene Products, 98 Harv. L. Rev. 713, 742–46 (1985).
69. John Ferejohn & Lawrence Sager, Commitment and Constitutionalism, 81 Tex. L. Rev. 1929, 1948–49 (2003).
70. Ely at 87–88. Writing in a more critical register, Sanford Levinson bemoans a number of structural features of U.S. democracy (bicameralism, equal state representation in the Senate, the Electoral College) that in his view have become increasingly dysfunctional but that are firmly fixed in place by the constitution and practically impossible to change. Levinson views constitutional rights, in contrast, as readily revisable: "It is always the case that courts are perpetually open to new arguments about rights—whether those of gays and lesbians or of property owners—that reflect the dominant public opinion of the day." Sanford Levinson, Our Undemocratic Constitution 5 (2006).
71. See Sujit Choudhry, After the Rights Revolution: Bills of Rights in the Postconflict State, 6 Ann. Rev. L. & Soc. 301, 311–16 (2010).
72. Donald Horowitz, A Democratic South Africa? Constitutional Engineering in a Divided Society 158–60 (1991).
73. See discussion in Chapter 1, pp. 57–59. One plausible theory of the durability of constitutional provisions distinguishes among different kinds of rights. Adam Chilton and Mila Versteeg hypothesize that rights backed by the political power of organizations, such as freedom of religion or rights to unionization, will be stronger than rights that protect dispersed or disorganized individuals. See Adam Chilton & Mila Versteeg, How Constitutional Rights Matter (2020). Another kind of organizationally backed right highlighted in the Chilton & Versteeg study is the rights of political parties, which would be categorized for present purposes as votes.
74. See Robert E. Goodin, Enfranchising All Affected Interests, And Its Alternatives, 35 Phil. & Pub. Aff. 40 (2007). Democratic Theorists have long puzzled over principled criteria for establishing the appropriate boundaries of the *demos*. See, e.g., Robert A. Dahl, Democracy and Its Critics 193–209 (1989); Frederick G. Whelan, Prologue: Democratic Theory and the Boundary Problem, in Liberal Democracy 13 (J. Roland Pennock & John W. Chapman eds., 1983).
75. Robert A. Dahl, After the Revolution 67 (1990).

76. Goodin at 68.
77. This possibility is considered in the final chapter.
78. See Goodin at 64–65.
79. See Gráinne de Búrca, Developing Democracy Beyond the State, 46 Colum. J. Transnational L., 221, 240–48 (2008).
80. See, e.g., David Cole, Enemy Aliens, 54 Stan. L. Rev. 953, 981 (2002).
81. John Stuart Mill, On Liberty 18 (David Spitz ed., 1975) (1859).
82. See *The Federalist No. 10* at 82–84.
83. Calhoun at 14.
84. See Read at 11–13.
85. Lani Guinier, The Tyranny of the Majority 4, 42–43 (1994).
86. Id. at 107–108, 149.
87. See Read at 162–64, 172–78.
88. See Read at 197. The failure of consociational arrangements in other countries like Yugoslavia (under its 1974 constitution) has, in fact, been blamed on the governance deadlock created by the mutual veto power of uncooperative ethnic groups. Id. at 213.
89. See Hirschl, Looking Sideways, at 434–40; David S. Law, Generic Constitutional Law, 89 Minn. L. Rev. 652, 662–69 (2005).
90. Judith N. Shklar, American Citizenship: The Quest for Inclusion 2–3 (1991); see also Don Herzog, Happy Slaves 219 (1989).
91. See Jeremy Waldron, Participation: The Right of Rights, 98 Proc. Aristotelian Soc. 307, 314 n.20 (1998).
92. See Shklar at 15–17.
93. Heather K. Gerken, Second-Order Diversity, 118 Harv. L. Rev. 1099, 1144 (2005).
94. On republicanism and political participation, see generally Frank I. Michelman, Conceptions of Democracy in American Constitutional Argument: Voting Rights, 41 Fla. L. Rev. 443, 451 (1989); Frank Michelman, Law's Republic, 97 Yale L.J. 1493 (1988); Cass R. Sunstein, Beyond the Republican Revival, 97 Yale L.J. 1539 (1988).
95. See John Stuart Mill, Considerations on Representative Government, in On Liberty and Other Essays 202, 303–24 (John Gray ed., 1991) (1861).
96. See Dahl, Democracy and Its Critics, at 91–93.
97. See, e.g., Ronald Dworkin, Takings Rights Seriously 277 (1977) (grounding rights in the moral imperative that government treat its citizens with "equal concern and respect"); Jeremy Waldron, Introduction to Theories of Rights 1, 11 (Jeremy Waldron ed., 1984) ("Rights have been seen as a basis of protection . . . for [human interests] specifically related to choice, self-determination, agency, and independence.").
98. Karl Marx, On the Jewish Question (1843), reprinted in Nonsense upon Stilts: Bentham, Burke, and Marx on the Rights of Man 137, 147 (Jeremy Waldron ed., 1987).
99. See Jeremy Waldron, Karl Marx's 'On the Jewish Question,' in Nonsense upon Stilts, at 119, 126–29. Marx took a more sanguine view of democratic rights, which are "only exercised in community with other men." Marx at 144; see also Waldron at 129–32 (elaborating Marx's views about democratic politics).

100. Important critiques of rights-based liberalism from a communitarian perspective include Alasdair MacIntyre, After Virtue (2d ed. 1984); Michael J. Sandel, Democracy's Discontent (1996); Michael Walzer, Spheres of Justice (1983); and 2 Charles Taylor, Philosophy and the Human Sciences: Philosophical Papers 187–229 (1985).
101. See generally Mary Ann Glendon, Rights Talk (1991).
102. Heather K. Gerken, Keynote Address: What Election Law Has to Say to Constitutional Law, 44 Ind. L. Rev. 7, 13 (2010).
103. Id. at 10–12.
104. Richard H. Pildes, Ethnic Identity and Democratic Institutions: A Dynamic Perspective, in Constitutional Design for Divided Societies, at 173, 177.
105. See Murray & Simeon at 420.
106. Choudhry, After the Rights Revolution, at 10–11, 16–22.
107. Guinier, Tyranny, at 69.
108. See Anne Phillips, Democracy Versus Rights, APSA 2009 Toronto Meeting Paper (available on SSRN).
109. See Will Kymlicka, Multicultural Citizenship 176–81 (1995).
110. See Donald L. Horowitz, Constitutional Design: Proposals Versus Processes, in The Architecture of Democracy 15, 20–30 (Andrew Reynolds ed., 2002).
111. See Guinier, Tyranny, at 16.
112. This point is emphasized, and empirically corroborated, by Chilton & Versteeg.
113. Within the white elite, fear of the consequences of democratization was most intense among Afrikaner farmers, whose wealth was tied up in land. Financial and industrial elites could more easily escape expropriation by a democratic majority by moving their capital abroad. See Carles Boix, Democracy and Redistribution 12 (2003).
114. See Michael J. Klarman, From Jim Crow to Civil Rights 421–36 (2004).
115. Madison, Letter to Jefferson, at 162. The idea that violations of constitutional rights might mobilize majorities to punish their misbehaving representatives has been recast by contemporary legal theorists and social scientists as an explanation for the efficacy of constitutional law more generally and for the political stability of an independent judiciary. See David S. Law, A Theory of Judicial Power and Judicial Review, 97 Geo. L.J. 723 (2009); Barry R. Weingast, The Political Foundations of Democracy and the Rule of Law, 91 Am. Pol. Sci. Rev. 245 (1997).
116. See William N. Eskridge, Jr., Channeling: Identity-Based Social Movements and Public Law, 150 U. Pa. L. Rev. 419 (2001). On the other hand, the recognition of rights can also be politically disempowering. Judicial recognition of rights can create a backlash against the causes these rights were supposed to benefit. See Michael J. Klarman, How *Brown* Changed Race Relations: The Backlash Thesis, 81 J. Am. Hist. 1 (1994); Robert Post & Reva Siegal, *Roe* Rage: Democratic Constitutionalism and Backlash, 42 Harv. C.R.-C.L. L. Rev. 373 (2007). Even where judicially recognized rights do not create political backlash, they may lead to complacency or demobilization by the beneficiaries. See, e.g., Gerald N. Rosenberg, The Hollow Hope 339 (1991) (presenting evidence that Roe led to the demobilization of the pro-choice movement).

117. See Corey Brettschneider, Democratic Rights (2007).
118. See Alexander Meiklejohn, Free Speech and Its Relation to Self-Government (1948).
119. See Ely ch. 6.
120. See Waldron, Participation, at 330–34. Waldron says that democratic participation "calls upon the very capacities that rights as such connote, and it evinces a form of respect in the resolution of political disagreement which is continuous with the respect that rights as such evoke." Id. at 334.
121. Tushnet, Politics of Equality, at 888–89.
122. Reva B. Siegel, She the People: The Nineteenth Amendment, Sex Equality, Federalism, and the Family, 115 Harv. L. Rev. 947, 1041 (2002).
123. See Albert O. Hirschman, Exit, Voice, and Loyalty (1970).
124. Or, more precisely, fleeing the power of one state or government and substituting a different one. The possibility of feeling *all* state power is a different thing, and one that is barely possible in the modern world. But cf. James C. Scott, The Art of Not Being Governed (2009).
125. It is possible to view at least some types of rights as continuous with, or a special case of, federalism and secession. To the extent rights function to grant individuals or groups autonomy over a certain sphere, they can be understood as delegations of decisionmaking authority in much the same way as decentralized or independent governance arrangements. This is the analogy invoked by H.L.A. Hart's description of right holders as "small-scale sovereign[s]." H.L.A. Hart, Legal Rights, in Essays on Bentham, 162, 183 (1982). A further step in this direction is to recognize that rights protecting individual autonomy against government interference often have the practical effect of empowering nongovernmental groups—families, schools, unions, churches, and the like—to exert more sway over individual choice. In this light, rights switch from one collective decisionmaking process (the traditionally governmental one) to another (which might be described as "private government"). See Roderick M. Hills, Jr., The Constitutional Rights of Private Governments, 78 N.Y.U. L. Rev. 144 (2003).
126. See Hills, Back to the Future, at 983–87.
127. See Read at 95–97.
128. See Kymlicka at 26–33. Lijphart sees federalism and power-sharing in the national government as complementary parts of the consociational design package. See Lijphart, Plural Societies, at 25–47; see also Donald L. Horowitz, Ethnic Groups in Conflict 601–52 (2d ed. 2000) (presenting federalism alongside minority-empowering electoral systems as "substitutab[le]" techniques for managing ethnic conflict); Pildes, Ethnic Identity, at 173–76, 184–85, 198–200 (viewing democratic representation schemes, judicially enforced rights, and federalism as alternative tools for protecting ethnic minorities in constitutional design).
129. See Murray & Simeon at 431–32. While the South African Constitution did create a system of multilevel government, the provinces were not set up as ethnic enclaves or strongly empowered as autonomous decisionmaking bodies. See id. at 432–34.

130. See Read at 96 (describing the views of Calhoun).
131. Michael J. Klarman, How Great Were the "Great" Marshall Court Decisions?, 87 Va. L. Rev. 1111, 1140–44 (2001); Barry R. Weingast, The Economic Role of Political Institutions: Market-Preserving Federalism and Economic Development, 11 J.L. Econ. & Org. 1, 19 (1995).
132. Murray & Simeon at 432.
133. See Alberto Alesina & Enrico Spolare, The Size of Nations 11 (2005).
134. See Weingast, Market-Preserving Federalism.
135. See Heather K. Gerken, The Supreme Court 2009 Term—Foreword: Federalism All the Way Down, 124 Harv. L. Rev. 4, 64 (2010).
136. See Sujit Choudhry & Nathan Hume, Federalism, Secession, and Devolution: From Classical to Post-Conflict Federalism, in Research Handbook on Comparative Constitutional Law 366–67 (Tom Ginsburg & Rosalind Dixon eds., 2010).
137. See Heather K. Gerken, Dissenting by Deciding, 57 Stan. L. Rev. 1745, 1794–95 (2005).
138. See Kymlicka at 181–86; Choudhry & Hume at 367–78.
139. See Roderick M. Hills, Jr., Federalism as Westphalian Liberalism, 75 Fordham L. Rev. 769 (2006).

Chapter 5

1. Scott Gordon, Controlling the State (2002).
2. As it happens, Hobbes's first published work was the first English translation of *The Peloponnesian War*. See Thucydides, The Peloponnesian War: The Complete Hobbes Translation (David Grene ed., 1989).
3. Adam Schiff, Twitter, Feb. 17, 2019. See also Daryl J. Levinson & Richard H. Pildes, Separation of Parties, Not Powers, 119 Harv. L. Rev. 2311 (2006).
4. *The Federalist No. 47* at 298 (James Madison) (Clinton Rossiter ed., 2003).
5. Jon D. Michaels, An Enduring, Evolving Separation of Powers, 115 Colum. L. Rev. 515, 517 (2015).
6. Martin Gilens, Affluence and Influence: Economic Inequality and Political Power in America 81, 1 (2012).
7. See Joseph Fishkin & William E. Forbath, The Anti-Oligarchy Constitution (2022) (arguing that the concentration of economic and political power was once and should again be understood as a constitutional problem, while recognizing that this understanding has gone missing from current constitutional law). For another version of the claim that the corrupting influence of wealth has undermined the American republic, see Lawrence Lessig, Republic, Lost (2011).
8. See Eric A. Posner, Balance-of-Powers Arguments, the Structural Constitution, and the Problem of Executive "Underenforcement," 164 U. Pa. L. Rev. 1677, 1680 (2016).
9. See Jeremy Waldron, Political Theory 55–62 (2016) (lamenting the lack of any explanation in Madison, Montesquieu, or other canonical sources for the danger constitutionally unbalanced power is supposed to present).

10. Thomas Hobbes, Leviathan 70 (Richard Tuck ed., 1991) (1651); see also Richard Tuck, The Rights of War and Peace 230 (crediting Rousseau for recognizing "at the imaginative as well as theoretical heart of Hobbes" a vision of man as "displaying characteristics that were usually encountered only in states, such as a constant and unforgiving striving for power").
11. Leviathan at 90.
12. Kenneth N. Waltz, Theory of International Politics 118 (1979); see also John J. Mearsheimer, The Tragedy of Great Power Politics (2001).
13. Leviathan at 90.
14. See Introduction, p. 5; see also Chapter 6, p. 167. Another way of understanding Hobbes's thinking on this point is to draw a distinction not between states and persons, but between persons in the state of nature and persons in the context of the state. The latter might have different interests and values less conducive to war and aggression, and their states might behave accordingly. See David Singh Grewal, The Domestic Analogy Revisited: Hobbes on International Order, 125 Yale L.J. 618 (2016).
15. Leviathan at 70.
16. For a broad survey, see Gordon, Controlling the State.
17. Gordon at 283.
18. Brutus I, N.Y.J., Oct. 18, 1787, reprinted in 2 The Complete Anti-Federalist 363, 367–68 (Herbert J. Storing ed., 1981).
19. See Akhil Reed Amar, Of Sovereignty and Federalism, 96 Yale L.J. 1425, 1496–97 & n.283 (1987) (identifying in The Federalist Papers the connection between the Framers' thinking about structural constitutionalism and the international balance of powers); see also Morgenthau, Politics Among Nations 191 (drawing the same analogy).
20. *The Federalist No. 51* at 321–22 (James Madison).
21. See Oona A. Hathaway & Scott J. Shapiro, The Internationalists 343 (2017).
22. Robert O. Keohane, Reciprocity in International Relations, 40 Int'l Org. 1, 1 (1986).
23. See, e.g., Robert O. Keohane, After Hegemony (1984); Robert O. Keohane & Lisa L. Martin, The Promise of Institutionalist Theory, 20 Int'l Sec. 39 (1995).
24. See David A. Baldwin, Neoliberalism, Neorealism, and World Politics, in Neorealism and Neoliberalism: The Contemporary Debate 5–6 (David A. Baldwin ed., 1993); Robert Powell, Absolute and Relative Gains in International Relations Theory, 85 Am. Pol. Sci. Rev. 1303 (1991).
25. Andrew Moravcsik, Taking Preferences Seriously: A Liberal Theory of International Politics, 51 Int'l Org. 513 (1997).
26. Id.
27. Guarding against the "aggrandizement" of one branch at the expense of the others has become the primary mission of courts adjudicating separation of powers cases. See Walter Dellinger, The Constitutional Separation of Powers Between the President and Congress, 63 L. & Contemp. Probs. 513, 521 (2000).
28. *The Federalist No. 51* at 321 (James Madison).
29. See Levinson & Pildes.
30. See Jessica Bulman-Pozen, Partisan Federalism, 127 Harv. L. Rev. 1077, 1080 (2014).
31. Id.

32. See generally David Epstein & Sharyn O'Halloran, Delegating Powers 29–33 (1999) (surveying theories of delegation, benign and malign).
33. Eric A. Posner & Adrian Vermeule, Terror in the Balance 47 (2007).
34. See Elena Kagan, Presidential Administration, 114 Harv. L. Rev. 2245, 2309 (2001); Terry M. Moe & William G. Howell, The Presidential Power of Unilateral Action, 15 J.L. Econ. & Org. 132, 138 (1999).
35. On these dynamics, see generally Eric A. Posner & Adrian Vermeule, The Executive Unbound: After the Madisonian Republic (2010).
36. See Jeff D. Colgan & Robert O. Keohane, The Liberal Order Is Rigged, Foreign Affairs, May/June 2017.
37. The Federalist No. 47 at 298 (James Madison).
38. The Federalist No. 10 at 75–79 (James Madison); see also The Federalist No. 51 at 319–20 ("[T]he society itself will be broken into so many parts, interests and classes of citizens, that the rights of individuals, or of the minority, will be in little danger from interested combinations of the majority.").
39. M.J.C. Vile, Constitutionalism and the Separation of Powers 37 (2d ed. 1998).
40. Arend Lijphart, Consociation: The Model and Its Applications in Divided Societies, in Political Cooperation in Divided Societies 166, 168 (Desmond Rea ed., 1982).
41. That distinguished them from Hobbes, who loathed the model of "mixt Monarchy" that divided power among king, lords, and commons and substituted for "one independent Common-wealth . . . three independent Factions," inviting conflict, war, and ruin. Leviathan at 228. See also Skinner, From Humanism to Hobbes 285–86 (2018).
42. Gordon S. Wood, The Creation of the American Republic, 1776–1787, at 606–607 (1969).
43. See The Federalist No. 47 at 298–301 (James Madison).
44. See Jack N. Rakove, Original Meanings 245 (1996).
45. On the fusion of mixed government and separation of functions in the U.S. constitutional design, see W.B. Gwyn, The Meaning of the Separation of Powers (1965); Rakove at 245–56; Vile at 36–40; M. Elizabeth Magill, The Real Separation in Separation of Powers Law, 86 Va. L. Rev. 1127, 1161–67 (2000).
46. See Wood at 604.
47. 4 The Papers of Alexander Hamilton 185–86 (Harold C. Syrett & Jacob E. Cooke eds., 1962).
48. 3 The Debates in the Several State Conventions at 164 (Jonathan Elliot ed., 2d ed. 1891).
49. Letter XI from the Federal Farmer to the Republican (Jan. 10, 1788), reprinted in 2 The Complete Anti-Federalist 287–88 (Herbert J. Storing ed., 1981).
50. The Federalist No. 48 at 306 (James Madison).
51. The Federalist No. 51 at 317–18 (James Madison).
52. Id. at 319.
53. See Wood at 567–87.
54. 1 The Records of the Federal Convention of 1787, at 299 (Max Farrand ed., 1911) (speech of Alexander Hamilton).

55. There were some in the Convention who would have preferred to preserve this role for the Senate. See John Hart Ely, The Apparent Inevitability of Mixed Government, 16 Const. Comment. 283, 284 (1999); see also Amar at 66 (recounting Gouverneur Morris's arguments for a Senate made up of men with "great personal property" and possessing "the aristocratic spirit").
56. See Michael J. Klarman, The Framers' Coup 394 (2016). Antifederalists, for their own part, suspected that the Senate, as well as the presidency, had been designed to ensure that the government would be controlled by the aristocracy. See id. at 363, 367; see also Wood at 516–18.
57. Klarman at 257.
58. Id.
59. Id. at 258.
60. See Mark A. Graber, Dred Scott and the Problem of Constitutional Evil 103 (2006).
61. James C. Calhoun clearly presented the problem: "[But] as each and all the departments—and, of course, the entire government—would be under the control of the numerical majority, it is too clear to require explanation that a mere distribution of its powers among its agents or representatives could do little or nothing to counteract its tendency to oppression and abuse of power." John C. Calhoun, A Disquisition on Government and Selections from the Discourse 27 (C. Gordon Post ed., 1953) (1853).
62. James H. Read, Majority Rule Versus Consensus 199–204 (2009). Nor, in Calhoun's view, was Madison's *The Federalist No. 10* solution of fragmented pluralism likely to prevent the formation of a unified, stable majority faction. Even "[i]f no one interest be strong enough, of itself, to obtain [a majority]," Calhoun explained, "a combination will be formed between those whose interests are most alike—each conceding something to the others, until a sufficient number is obtained to make a majority." Calhoun at 14. In particular, Calhoun believed that political parties would facilitate the organization of majority coalitions and ensure their ability to control the whole of government. See Read at 49–50.
63. Calhoun at 27.
64. See Jonathan S. Gould & David E. Pozen, Structural Biases in Structural Constitutional Law, 97 N.Y.U. L. Rev. 59 (2022).
65. See Eric A. Posner & Cass R. Sunstein, Institutional Flip-Flops, 94 Tex. L. Rev. 485 (2016).
66. For an overview of the debates, see generally Giovanni Sartori, Comparative Constitutional Engineering 83–119 (2d ed. 1997); The Failure of Presidential Democracy (Juan J. Linz & Arturo Valenzuela eds., 1994).
67. *The Federalist No. 51* at 320 (James Madison).
68. See, e.g., Ganesh Sitaraman, The Crisis of the Middle-Class Constitution (2017).
69. See Ganesh Sitaraman, The Puzzling Absence of Economic Power in Constitutional Theory, 101 Cornell L. Rev. 1445, (2016) (pointing to the possibility of capping the wealth of candidates for the House of Representatives).
70. See Daniel Epps & Ganesh Sitaraman, How to Save the Supreme Court, 129 Yale L.J. 148, 193–205 (2019).

71. See Daron Acemoglu & James A. Robinson, Economic Origins of Dictatorship and Democracy 24–25 (2006).
72. An intuitive principle is "that democratic institutions should provide citizens with equal procedural opportunities to influence political decisions (or, more briefly, with equal power over outcomes)." Charles R. Beitz, Political Equality 4 (1989) (emphasis omitted) (describing this view of political equality as "the most widely held," though proceeding to criticize it as too simple). Not all political theorists endorse equality of political power. A competing tradition—running from Plato to Schumpeter to contemporary proponents of bureaucratic expertise and judicial wisdom—calls for allocating political power to those with the most ability to make good decisions. John Stuart Mill, for one, believed that "every one ought to have a voice," but rejected the "totally different proposition" that "every one should have an equal voice," arguing instead that the opinions of intelligent and knowledgeable people should be "entitled to a greater amount of consideration." John Stuart Mill, Considerations on Representative Government 172–174 (2010) (1861); see also Dale E. Miller, The Place of Plural Voting in Mill's Conception of Representative Government, 77 Rev. Pol. 399 (2015). Many of the Framers of the U.S. Constitution were similarly committed to the priority of elite rule. See Klarman at 363, 367.
73. See generally Beitz, Political Equality; Ronald Dworkin, Sovereign Virtue ch. 4 (2000); Anne Phillips, The Politics of Presence 27–38 (1995).
74. See generally Ian Shapiro, Politics Against Domination (2016).
75. Holder v. Hall, 512 U.S. 874, 893 (1994) (Thomas, J., concurring in the judgment) (describing the Voting Rights Act in particular).
76. Adam B. Cox, The Temporal Dimension of Voting Rights, 93 Va. L. Rev. 361, 362 (2007). See generally Samuel Issacharoff & Pamela S. Karlan, Groups, Politics, and the Equal Protection Clause, 58 U. Miami L. Rev. 35, 42 (2003) (elaborating on a "group-disadvantaging conception of political equality").
77. See Samuel Issacharoff & Richard H. Pildes, Politics as Markets: Partisan Lockups of the Democratic Process, 50 Stan. L. Rev. 643, 644–46, 717 (1998).
78. Buckley v. Valeo, 424 U.S. 1, 48–49 (1976) (per curiam).
79. Lani Guinier, The Tyranny of the Majority 42–43 (1994).
80. See James A. Gardner, Liberty, Community and the Constitutional Structure of Political Influence: A Reconsideration of the Right to Vote, 145 U. Pa. L. Rev. 893, 927–29 (1997) ("protective democracy"); Pamela S. Karlan, The Rights to Vote: Some Pessimism About Formalism, 71 Tex. L. Rev. 1705, 1716 (arguing that the Court has given short shrift to "[v]oting as [g]overnance" concerns such as "whether there is a significant lack of responsiveness on the part of elected officials to the particularized needs of the members of the minority group").
81. Nicholas Stephanopoulos, The False Promise of Black Political Representation, The Atlantic, June 11, 2015.
82. See Martin Gilens & Benjamin I. Page, Testing Theories of American Politics: Elites, Interest Groups, and Average Citizens, 12 Persp. on Pol. 564, 565 (2014).
83. Id. at 577.
84. Nicholas O. Stephanopoulos, Elections and Alignment, 114 Colum. L. Rev. 283, 312 (2014).

85. See Nicholas O. Stephanopoulos, Political Powerlessness, 90 N.Y.U. L. Rev. 1527, 1537–42 (2015).
86. See Stephanopoulos, Political Powerlessness, at 1537–42. Of the factors just listed, only the presence or absence of antidiscrimination legislation speaks directly to the power of groups to secure favorable policy outcomes. Yet courts only sometimes view the existence of antidiscrimination laws as evidence of sufficient political power; in other cases these laws are viewed as evidence of an ongoing threat of discrimination against which the group lacks adequate power to protect itself. See Jane S. Schacter, Ely at the Altar: Political Process Theory Through the Lens of the Marriage Debate, 109 Mich. L. Rev. 1363, 1369, 1377, 1381–83 (2011); see also Bertrall L. Ross II & Su Li, Measuring Political Power: Suspect Class Determinations and the Poor, 104 Calif. L. Rev. 323 (2016) (arguing that the enactment of laws benefitting a group does not necessarily speak to the political power of that group, and illustrating that point with empirical evidence that legislators' support for antipoverty legislation does not reflect the political influence of the poor).
87. See Schacter at 1383–90.
88. Romer v. Evans, 517 U.S. 620, 646 (1996) (Scalia, J., dissenting).
89. See Kenji Yoshino, The Paradox of Political Power: Same-Sex Marriage and the Supreme Court, 2012 Utah L. Rev. 527, 539.
90. See David A. Strauss, Discriminatory Intent and the Taming of Brown, 56 U. Chi. L. Rev. 935 (1989); see also Owen M. Fiss, Groups and the Equal Protection Clause, 5 Phil. & Pub. Aff. 107, 129–30, 157–64 (1976); Jack M. Balkin & Reva B. Siegel, Remembering How to Do Equality, in The Constitution in 2020, at 93 (Jack M. Balkin & Reva B. Siegel eds., 2009).

Chapter 6

1. See Hedwig Lee et al., The Demographics of Racial Inequality in the United States, Brookings, July 27, 2020.
2. See Paula England et al., Progress Toward Gender Equality in the United States Has Slowed or Stalled, 117 Proc. Nat'l Acad. Sci. 6990 (2020); Violence Against Women in the United States: Statistics, National Organization for Women.
3. Council on Foreign Relations, The U.S. Inequality Debate, updated April 20, 2022; Gini Coefficient by Country, World Population Review. The comparison between the three richest Americans and the bottom 50% was made by Bernie Sanders in 2019. See Bernie Sanders, Trump Is the Worst Kind of Socialist, Wall St. J., June 26, 2019.
4. See Richard Tuck, The Rights of War and Peace 8–9, 126–41 (1999).
5. Thomas Hobbes, On the Citizen 156 (Richard Tuck & Michael Silverthorne eds. & trans., 1998) (1647).
6. Thomas Hobbes, Leviathan 244 (Richard Tuck, ed., 1991) (1651).
7. For states, in contrast, "the notions of Right and Wrong, Justice and Injustice have there no place. Where there is no common Power there is no Law: where no Law, no Injustice." Leviathan at 90.

280 NOTES

8. Michael Walzer, Just and Unjust Wars 89 (1977).
9. Id. at 58.
10. Id. at 61.
11. Leviathan at 90.
12. David Singh Grewal, The Domestic Analogy Revisited: Hobbes on International Order, 125 Yale L.J. 618, 651 (2016).
13. Charles R. Beitz, Political Theory and International Relations 180 (1979).
14. Walzer at 72.
15. Ronald Dworkin, Sovereign Virtue 6 (2000).
16. John Rawls, A Theory of Justice 7 (1971); see also John Rawls, Political Liberalism 258 (1993) (explaining that the basic structure includes "the political constitution, the legally recognized forms of property, and the organization of the economy" and other major institutional determinants of the life prospects of people in society.
17. Rawls, Theory of Justice, at 54.
18. John Rawls, Political Liberalism 268–69 (1993); see also Liam B. Murphy, Institutions and the Demands of Justice, 27 Phil. & Pub. Aff. 251, 257–58.
19. Rawls, Theory of Justice, at 29.
20. See generally Cass R. Sunstein, The Partial Constitution (1993).
21. See generally Richard H. Fallon, Constitutionally Forbidden Legislative Intent, 130 Harv. L. Rev. 523 (2016).
22. See, e.g., Jedediah Britton-Purdy et al., Building a Law-and-Political-Economy Framework: Beyond the Twentieth-Century Synthesis 129 Yale L.J. 1784, 1806–13 (2020); Robert Hale, Coercion and Distribution in a Supposedly Noncoercive State, 38 Pol. Sci. Q. 470 (1923); Reva Siegel, Why Equal Protection No Longer Protects: The Evolving Forms of Status-Enforcing State Action, 49 Stan. L. Rev. 1111 (1997); David A. Strauss, Discriminatory Intent and the Taming of Brown, 56 U. Chi. L. Rev. 935 (1989).
23. See Louis Michael Seidman & Mark V. Tushnet, Remnants of Belief 27–28, 66–67 (1996); Sunstein, Partial Constitution, at 71–75; Cass R. Sunstein, State Action Is Always Present, 3 Chi. J. Int'l L. 465 (2002).
24. See Ta-Nehisi Coates, The Case for Reparations, The Atlantic, June 2014.
25. See generally Barbara H. Fried, The Progressive Assault on Laissez Faire (1998).
26. See Morris R. Cohen, Property and Sovereignty 13 Cornell L. Rev. 8 (1927).
27. See Cass R. Sunstein, The Second Bill of Rights 17–31 (2004).
28. Id. at 25.
29. Id. at 235–44 (reprinting Roosevelt's address); 9–16.
30. Roosevelt himself did not conceive of his Second Bill as creating judicially enforceable constitutional rights. See id. at 61–66.
31. See id. at 99–105.
32. S. Afr. Const., 1996, ch. 2, Sections 26–27, 29; see also Sunstein, Second Bill, at 216–29.
33. See Sunstein, Second Bill, at 220–23. For a broader survey of judicial enforcement of social welfare rights around the world, see Mila Versteeg, Can Rights Combat Economic Inequality?, 133 Harv. L. Rev. 2017 (2017).
34. Sunstein, Second Bill, at 149–71; see also Frank I. Michelman, Foreword: On Protecting the Poor Through the Fourteenth Amendment, 83 Harv. L. Rev. (1969).

35. See James E. Ryan & Thomas Saunders, Foreword to Symposium on School Finance Litigation: Emerging Trends or Dead Ends?, 22 Yale Law & Pol'y Rev. 463 (2004).
36. Lawrence G. Sager, Justice in Plainclothes 78–81 (2004).
37. See Mark Tushnet, Weak Courts, Strong Rights (2009).
38. See Sager at 84–128; see also Lawrence Sager, Material Rights, Underenforcement, and the Adjudication Thesis, 90 B.U. L. Rev. 579 (2010).
39. This default model of constitutional adjudication has been brought into relief by experimental departures, perhaps most strikingly the ambitious structural reform litigation attempted by courts in the 1970s. See Owen Fiss, Foreword: The Forms of Justice, 93 Harv. L. Rev. 1 (1978) ("The focus of structural reform is not upon particular incidents or transactions, but rather upon the conditions of social life and the role that large-scale organizations play in determining those conditions.").
40. This is a point that has been made about states from an international perspective. See Martha C. Nussbaum, Frontiers of Justice 308 (2006); Michael J. Green, Institutional Responsibility for Global Problems, 30 Phil. Topics 79, 85–86 (2002). Both Nussbaum and Green distinguish individuals from high-capacity "institutions," a category that includes not just states but also, for example, multinational corporations.
41. See Saul Levmore, Waiting for Rescue: An Essay on the Evolution and Incentive Structure of the Law of Affirmative Obligations, 72 Va. L. Rev. 879 (1986).
42. See infra note 23.
43. Cass R. Sunstein & Adrian Vermeule, Is Capital Punishment Morally Required? Acts, Omissions, and Life-Life Tradeoffs, 53 Stan. L. Rev. 703, 709, 722 (2005) (arguing that the "act/omission distinction ... systematically misfires when applied to government, which is a moral agent with distinctive features," and that the "very concept of 'intentional' action, and the moral relevance of intention, are both obscure when government is the pertinent moral agent").
44. See, e.g., Peter Singer, Famine, Affluence, and Morality, 1 Phil. & Pub. Aff. 229 (1972).
45. See Thomas Nagel, Mortal Questions 83 (2012); Thomas Nagel, Autonomy and Deontology, in Consequentialism and Its Critics 142 (Samuel Scheffler ed., 1988); Nussbaum at 308–309; Bernard Williams, A Critique of Utilitarianism, in Utilitarianism: For and Against (J.J.C. Smart & Bernard Williams eds., 1973).
46. See Nagel, Mortal Questions, at 93; see also David Enoch, Intending, Foreseeing, and the State, 13 Legal Theory 1, 23 (2007).
47. For an overview of how tort law has handled these kinds of cases, see Ariel Porat & Eric Posner, Offsetting Benefits, 100 Va. L. Rev. 1165 (2014).
48. This is what is sometimes called the "baselines" critique of constitutional law. For examples, see, e.g., Robert Hale, Unconstitutional Conditions and Constitutional Rights, 35 Colum. L. Rev. 321 (1935); Seidman & Tushnet at 27–28, Sunstein, Partial Constitution, at 351–53.
49. This is what is sometimes called the "framing" critique of constitutional law. See Daryl J. Levinson, Framing Transactions in Constitutional Law, 111 Yale L.J. 1311 (2002); see also id. at 1376–83 (explaining how the framing and baselines critiques fit together).
50. See Stephen R. Perry, On the Relationship Between Corrective and Distributive Justice, in Oxford Essays on Jurisprudence, Fourth Series 237 (Jeremy Horder ed., 2000).

51. See Perry at 261; see also Louis Kaplow & Steven Shavell, Why the Legal System Is Less Efficient Than the Income Tax in Redistributing Income, 23 J. Legal Stud. 797 (2000).
52. Perry at 238–39; Christopher Kutz, Reparations: The Cost of Memory and the Value of Talk, 32 Phil. & Pub. Aff. 277, 299–300 (2004); see also Ronald Dworkin, Law's Empire 310 (1986).
53. G. A. Cohen, Where the Action Is: On the Site of Distributive Justice, 26 Phil. & Pub. Aff. 3 (1997); Murphy; Thomas W. Pogge, On the Site of Distributive Justice: Reflections on Cohen and Murphy, 29 Phil. & Pub. Aff. 137 (2000).
54. Murphy at 253.
55. See id. at 254, 263, 280; Liam Murphy & Thomas Nagel, The Myth of Ownership 71 (2002).
56. This was Bernard Williams's derogatory characterization. See Bernard Williams, Ethics and the Limits of Philosophy 108 (1995).
57. See Robert E. Goodin, Utilitarianism as a Public Philosophy 60–77 (1995).
58. See Samuel Scheffler, Boundaries and Allegiances 149–72 (2001).
59. See Robert Nozick, Anarchy, State, and Utopia 204–13 (1974).
60. Political Liberalism at 268–69.
61. Samuel Scheffler & Veronique Munoz-Darde, The Division of Moral Labour, 79 Proc. Aristotelian Soc'y, 229, 231–34 (2005).
62. Id. at 269.
63. Thomas Nagel, Equality and Partiality 53 (1991).
64. See Goodin at 65–77.
65. See Nagel, Mortal Questions, at 83–86.
66. See Thomas W. Pogge, Realizing Rawls 36–47 (1989).
67. Rawls, Political Liberalism, at 227–30.
68. Nagel, Equality and Partiality, at 87–89.
69. Rawls and Nagel seem to share the belief that constitutional rights require more specificity and agreement than will be typically be possible for principles of justice. See Rawls, Political Liberalism, at 229–30; Nagel, Equality and Partiality, at 88 (arguing that the limited aims of constitutional norms facilitate the kind of consensus that is necessary for stability); see also Lawrence G. Sager, The Why of Constitutional Essentials, 72 Fordham L. Rev. 1421, 1430 (1994) (explicating and embracing Rawls's view).
70. John Rawls, Justice as Fairness, 42–44 (2001).
71. See Rawls, Justice as Fairness, at 150–52. Rawls makes an exception for political participation rights, which he says must be guaranteed their fair value. See id. at 45. He also recognizes a right to a "social minimum providing for the basic needs of all citizens," which is included among the constitutional essentials. See id. at 148–50, 47–48.
72. Something like this "two principles" view of justice is widely shared among egalitarian moral and political philosophers. Even after rejecting the "rights-based, deontological political morality" of libertarianism when it comes to distributive justice in the economic sphere, Nagel continues to endorse traditional rights as a matter of political and constitutional justice. See Murphy & Nagel at 65. Dworkin, too, places distributive justice on a different philosophical track from other issues of political morality, developing a special theory of equality of resources that operates separately from moral assessment of whether government is treating its citizens with equal

concern when it comes to civil liberties and political equality. See Dworkin at 138–47 (liberty), 209–10 (political equality).
73. Jeremy Bentham, The Theory of Legislation 113 (C.K. Ogden ed., Richard Hildreth trans., 1931) (1802).
74. See Pogge at 45–47.
75. Scheffler & Munoz-Darde at 229. Scheffler observes that monists seem to share the libertarian impulse to bring together personal morality and political justice but with the opposite goal of making the obligations of distributive justice play a greater role in personal morality.
76. Rawls excludes a prohibition on race discrimination from the basic liberties under his first principle of justice and instead deals with racial equality as a distributive issue pursuant to the second principle. See Seana Shiffrin, Race, Labor, and the Fair Equality of Opportunity Principle, 72 Fordham L. Rev. 1643 (2004).
77. See Thomas W. Pogge, Three Problems with Contractarian-Consequentialist Ways of Assessing Social Institutions, 1995 Soc. Phil. & Pol'y 241; Vermeuele & Sunstein; Adrian Vermeule, A New Deal for Civil Liberties: An Essay in Honor of Cass Sunstein, 43 Tulsa L. Rev. 921 (2007).
78. See, e.g., Murphy & Nagel at 55 ("Egalitarian liberals simply see no moral similarity between the right to speak one's mind, to practice one's religion, or to act on one's sexual inclinations, and the right to enter into a labor contract or a sale of property unencumbered by a tax bite.").
79. Rawls's view is complicated in this regard. He insists on the lexical priority of the first principle of justice over the second. But within the first principle, Rawls also says that "liberty can be restricted . . . for the sake of liberty," possibly paving the way for a systemic approach to maximizing overall liberty *within* the first principle in pursuit of "the best total system" of liberties. Rawls provides little guidance, however, in how the best total system would trade-off promoting liberty at the level of individual, transactional rights versus more systematically.
80. See T. M. Scanlon, Rights, Goals, and Fairness, 11 Soc. Ethics 81, 81 (1977) ("[R]ights themselves need to be justified somehow, and how other than by appeal to the human interests their recognition promotes and protects?").
81. Thomas Nagel, Concealment and Exposure 34 (2002).
82. Id. at 35; see also Thomas Nagel, The View from Nowhere 175–80 (1986).
83. In at least some versions of the trolley problem, for example, it is not morally permitted to kill one innocent person to save the lives of five others. See generally F.M. Kamm, The Trolley Problem Mysteries (2015); Judith Jarvis Thomson, Killing, Letting Die, and the Trolley Problem, 59 Monist 204 (1976); Judith Jarvis Thomason, The Trolley Problem, 94 Yale L.J. 1395 (1985).
84. Nagel, Mortal Questions, at 82, 84.
85. Again, this is the thrust of Enoch and Sunstein & Vermeule, Is Capital Punishment Morally Required; see also Cass R. Sunstein & Adrian Vermeule, Deterring Murder: A Reply, 55 Stan. L. Rev. 847, 849–52 (2005). But see Adam Omar Hosein, Doing, Allowing, and the State, 33 L. & Phil. 235 (2014).
86. See Nagel, Concealment and Exposure, at 42–48.
87. See id. at 34.

284 NOTES

88. See Murphy at 278–84.
89. Walzer at 58.
90. Id. at 61. This is at the level of moral philosophical justification. As a matter of historical and political explanation, rules of *jus in bello* have been designed in large part to serve the military advantage of powerful states. See Samuel Moyn, Humane (2021); see also John Fabian Witt, Oh, the Humanity, Just Security, Sept. 8, 2021.
91. See Jeff McMahan, Killing in War 79 (2009) (describing this view for the purpose of arguing against it).
92. See Michael Walzer, Political Action: The Problem of Dirty Hands, 2 Phil. & Pub. Aff. 160 (1973). The force of this idea might be connected to Hobbes's insistence that the imperative of self-preservation trumps the demands of morality—a personified principle of morality as applied to the state. See C.A.J. Coady, The Problem of Dirty Hands, Stanford Encyclopedia of Philosophy, revised July 2, 2018. But in the hands of Walzer and others, the idea has gone in the direction of a special kind of political permission that does not have a direct equivalent at the personal level.
93. McMahan at 85. McMahan cites Hobbes as a supporter of this view: "[I]f I wage warre at the Commandment of my Prince, conceiving of the warre to be unjustly undertaken, I doe not therefore doe unjustly, but rather if I refuse to doe it, arrogating to my selfe the knowledge of what is just and unjust, which pertains onely to my Prince."
94. See generally Adil Haque, Law, Morality, and War (2017).
95. McMahan at 79.
96. See, e.g., Beitz at 67–123; David Luban, Just War and Human Rights, 9 Phil. & Pub. Aff. 161 (1980).
97. McMahan at 79.
98. John Rawls, The Law of Peoples 23–35 (1999).
99. Id. at 113–20; see also Samuel Freeman, Justice and the Social Contract 267–69, 305–308 (2007); Michael Blake, Distributive Justice, State Coercion, and Autonomy, 30 Phil. & Pub. Aff. 257 (2001).
100. See, e.g., Pogge, Realizing Rawls, at 247.
101. See, e.g., Charles R. Beitz, Bounded Morality: Justice and the State in World Politics, 33 Int'l Org. 405 (1979); Joshua Cohen & Charles Sabel, Extra Republicam Null Justitia?, 34 Phil. & Pub. Aff. 147 (2006).
102. For a further discussion of this phenomenon, see Chapter 8.
103. Thomas Nagel, The Problem of Global Justice, 33 Phil. & Pub. Aff. 113, 121 (2005).

Chapter 7

1. The precise numbers of deaths are difficult to determine. See David Cortright, A Hard Look at Iraqi Sanctions, The Nation, Dec. 3, 2001 (surveying studies).
2. Here again, estimates of the number of deaths vary. See John G. Heidenrich, The Gulf War: How Many Iraqis Died?, 90 Foreign Pol'y 108 (1993) (estimating military

deaths); Watson Institute, Brown University, Costs of War website (counting civilian deaths). Whether the Iraq war was permissible as a matter of international law remains contested, but the same kinds of human costs follow from military actions that are unambiguously lawful. Cf. David Luban, War as Punishment, 39 Phil. & Pub. Aff. 299 (2011).
3. Carrie Sloan & Johnae Strong, Chicago Has Spent Half a Billion Dollars on Police Brutality Cases—And It's Impoverishing the Victims' Communities, The Nation, Mar. 11, 2016.
4. Thomas Hobbes, Leviathan 114 (Richard Tuck, ed., 1991) (1651).
5. Leviathan at 344. Hobbes offers this release of responsibility for purposes of divine punishment.
6. On Hobbes's theoretical inconsistency here, and how it served his broader purposes, see Don Herzog, Happy Slaves 108 (1989). For an attempt at constructing a coherent Hobbesian theory of citizens' responsibility for the actions of their states, see Sean Fleming, Leviathan on a Leash (2020).
7. See Eric A. Posner & David Weisbach, Climate Change Justice 99–118 (2010).
8. Even when a state is simply forced to comply with international law, those citizens who benefit from noncompliance suffer the costs. Those citizens are in effect punished for the actions of their state. See Liam Murphy, International Responsibility, in The Philosophy of International Law 299, 301–302 (Samantha Besson & John Tasioulas eds., 2010).
9. Oona A. Hathaway & Scott J. Shapiro, The Internationalists 269–70 (2017).
10. The Nuremberg approach of individualizing responsibility has been continued through international criminal law and the establishment of the International Criminal Court. See generally Antonio Cassese et al., Cassese's International Criminal Law (3d ed. 2013); William A. Schabas, An Introduction to the International Criminal Court (5th ed. 2017).
11. Richard A. Posner, The Economics of Justice 193–94 (1981).
12. See A.S. Diamond, The Evolution of Law and Order 108–12 (1951); Oliver Wendell Holmes, The Common Law 6 (Mark DeWolfe Howe ed., 1963) (1881).
13. See Posner at 193–94.
14. See H. D. Lewis, The Non-Moral Notion of Collective Responsibility, in Individual and Collective Responsibility 119, 131 (Peter A. French ed., 1972).
15. Henry Sumner Maine, Ancient Law 121 (Ashley Montagu ed., 1986) (1861). Maine's account of the movement from communalism to individualism—summarized in his famous aphorism about the movement from "status" to "contract," id. at 165, resonates with much of late nineteenth-century legal and social theory. See generally Emile Durkheim, The Division of Labour in Society (W.D. Halls trans., 1984) (1893) (describing developmental path from mechanical to organic solidarity); Ferdinand Tonnies, Community & Society (Charles P. Loomis ed. & trans., 1957) (1887) (describing progression from traditional agrarian Gemeinschaft to modern industrialized Gesellschaft); see also Sally F. Moore, Legal Liability and Evolutionary Interpretation, in The Allocation of Responsibility 51, 56 (Max Gluckman ed., 1972) (tying together Maine and Durkheim with the thematic thread of "the general

movement of legal-historical change ... from an emphasis on legal community and collectivity to an emphasis on legal individuality").
16. See Maine at 122.
17. H.D. Lewis, Collective Responsibility, 23 Phil. 3, 3 (1948).
18. See Antonio Cassese, International Law 241 (2d ed. 2005).
19. See, e.g., Peter A. French, Collective and Corporate Responsibility (1984); Christian List & Phillip Pettit, Group Agency (2011); David Copp, On the Agency of Certain Collective Entities, 30 Midwest Stud. Phil. 194 (2006); Philip Pettit, Responsibility Incorporated, 117 Ethics 171 (2007).
20. See Liam Murphy, International Responsibility for Global Environmental Harm, in Theories of International Responsibility Law 165, 171–74 (Samantha Besson ed., 2022).
21. For a skeptical survey of the progress to date, see Holly Lawford-Smith, Not in Their Name (2019). But the efforts continue. See, e.g., Avia Pasternak, Responsible Citizens, Irresponsible States (2021) (developing the argument that citizens who intentionally participate in their state should be held collectively and equally responsible for rectifying its harms, without further regard for their individual contributions).
22. See Murphy at 306–309; John M. Parrish, Collective Responsibility and the State, 1 Int'l Theory 119 (2009); Anna Stilz, Collective Responsibility and the State, 19 J. Pol. Phil. 190 (2011).
23. Thomas Nagel, The Problem of Global Justice, 33 Phil. & Pub. Aff. 113, 128 (2005).
24. See Chapter 6, p. 192.
25. See Stilz.
26. The individualist challenge might be broadly met by a moral defense of collective responsibility at the level of states or nations. See, e.g., David Miller, National Responsibility and Global Justice (2007).
27. Dennis F. Thompson, Political Ethics and Public Office 40 (1987).
28. See Michael Walzer, Just Unjust Wars 296–303 (1977).
29. Compare the benefits of state sovereignty to the people who live in states, discussed in Chapter 2.
30. See William Ian Miller, Bloodtaking and Peacemaking 179–220 (1990).
31. See Ted Robert Gurr, Historical Trends in Violent Crime: A Critical Review of the Evidence, in 3 Crime and Justice: An Annual Review of Research 295, 313 (Michael Tonry & Norval Morris eds., 1981). On crime in medieval England, see generally John Bellamy, Crime and Public Order in England in the Later Middle Ages (1973).
32. Stephen C. Yeazell, From Medieval Group Litigation to the Modern Class Action 83 (1997); 1 Sir Frederick Pollock & Frederic William Maitland, The History of English Law 558 (2d ed. 1968); William Alfred Morris, The Frankpledge System (1910).
33. See Hathaway & Shapiro at 371–80.
34. Stilz at 206.
35. One indication of Hussein's ability to insulate himself and his close supporters from the effects of economic sanctions was the luxury sportscar collection of his elder son, Uday, discovered by American soldiers after the U.S. invasion in 2003. See Hathaway & Shapiro at 387–88.

36. See Daniel W. Drezner, Sanctions Sometimes Smart: Targeted Sanctions in Theory and Practice, 13 Int'l Stud. Rev. 96, 99 (2011).
37. See Hathaway & Shapiro at 388–90.
38. Doug Palmer & Adam Behsudi, Trade Wars: Tariffs on Bourbon, Harleys, and Blue Jeans, Politico, March 2, 2018.
39. See U.S. Dep't of the Treasury, Press Release: Treasury Sanctions Kremlin Elites, Leaders, Oligarchs, and Family for Enabling Putin's War Against Ukraine, March 11, 2022.
40. The comparison between state responsibility in international law and corporate liability in domestic law has been drawn by Eric Posner and Alan Sykes. See Eric A. Posner & Alan O. Sykes, Economic Foundations of International Law, 113–21 (2013).
41. The personification of corporations has a long history. Blackstone described "bodies corporate" and "bodies politic" alike as "artificial persons." 1 Blackstone's Commentaries on the Laws of England ch. 18, at 455 (Oxford 1st ed., available online through the Avalon Project, Yale Law School). On the intellectual history of corporate personality in law, see Morton J. Horowitz, Santa Clara Revisited: The Development of Corporate Theory, 88 W. Va. L. Rev. 173 (1986); Gregory A. Mark, The Personification of the Business Corporation in American Law, 54 U. Chi. L. Rev. 1441 (1987). On the psychology of personifying and punishing corporations and other collective entities, see Tom R. Tyler & Avital Mentovich, Punishing Collective Entities, 19 J. L. & Pol'y 203 (2010); Steven J. Sherman & Elise J. Percy, The Psychology of Collective Responsibility: When and Why Collective Entities Are Likely to Be Held Responsible for the Misdeeds of Individual Members, 19 J. L. & Pol'y 137 (2010).
42. See Daniel R. Fischel & Frank H. Easterbrook, The Economic Structure of Corporate Law 12 ("More often than not a reference to the corporation as an entity will hide the essence of the transaction" as it bears on different groups of corporate stakeholders); see also John Dewey, The Historical Background of Corporate Legal Personality, 35 Yale L.J. 655, 673 (1926) (describing corporate personality as a fiction that distracts attention from "the concrete facts and relations involved").
43. See John C. Coffee, Jr., "No Soul to Damn: No Body to Kick": An Unscandalized Inquiry into the Problem of Corporate Punishment, 79 Mich. L. Rev. 386, (1981).
44. Corporations can, however, be incapacitated, by prohibiting their participation in certain lines of business or entire industries, or permanently divesting them of all assets. See W. Robert Thomas, Incapacitating Criminal Corporations, 72 Vand. L. Rev. 905 (2019). As we saw in Chapter 3, states, too, can be incapacitated.
45. Coffee at 387.
46. Albert W. Alschuler, Two Ways to Think about the Punishment of Corporations, 46 Am. Crim. L. Rev. 1359, 1372 (2009).
47. See, e.g., Peter A. French, The Corporation as a Moral Person, in Collective Responsibility: Five Decades of Debate in Theoretical and Applied Ethics 133 (Larry May & Stacey Hoffman eds., 1991).
48. See Christopher Kutz, Complicity 236–53 (2000).
49. See Stilz at 196. But cf. Miller, National Responsibility, at 111–34 (arguing for collective national responsibility on the basis of members' shared purpose and the cooperative benefits that come with membership).

50. See Henry Hansmann, The Ownership of Enterprise 57–62 (1996).
51. See generally Jennifer Arlen, Corporate Crime and Its Control, in 1 The New Palgrave Dictionary of Economics and the Law; V. S. Khanna, Corporate Criminal Liability: What Purpose Does It Serve?, 109 Harv. L. Rev. 1477 (1996); Reinier H. Kraakman, Corporate Liability Strategies and the Costs of Legal Controls, 93 Yale L.J. 857 (1984); A. Mitchell Polinsky & Steven Shavell, Should Employees Be Subject to Fines and Imprisonment Given the Existence of Corporate Liability?, 13 Int'l Rev. L. & Econ. 239 (1993).
52. See Alschuler at 1376–82.
53. To their credit, however, constitutionalists have paid a great deal of attention—much more than their internationalist counterparts—to the broader questions of how to justify collective, intergenerational responsibility for legal compliance. This is the problem of reconciling constitutional constraints with popular sovereignty that has been a core concern of constitutional theory since its inception and is the topic of Chapter 2.
54. For a deft elaboration of this point in the context of the constitutional law of policing, see Alice Ristroph, Covenants for the Sword, 61 U. Toronto L.J. 657 (2011).
55. Directing constitutional litigation against individual officers was, among other things, a way of solving the perceived problem of sovereign immunity—based on the Hobbesian doctrine that states themselves could not be sued. See id. at 684; see also Chapter 2, pp. 68–69.
56. See Peter H. Schuck, Suing Government 68 (1983).
57. See Joanna C. Schwartz, How Governments Pay: Lawsuits, Budgets, and Police Reforms, 63 UCLA L. Rev. 1144 (2016).
58. Armstrong v. United States, 364 U.S. 40, 49 (196).
59. For a survey of the arguments on both sides, see Eric A. Posner & Adrian Vermeule, Reparations for Slavery and Other Historical Injustices, 103 Colum. L. Rev. 689 (2003).
60. See Vicki Been, Lucas v. The Green Machine: Using the Takings Clause to Promote More Efficient Regulations?, in Property Stories 221, 250–51 (Gerald Korngold & Andrew P. Morriss eds., 2004).
61. See Daniel A. Farber, Public Choice and Just Compensation, 9 Const. Comm. 279, 291 (1992) (suggesting that concerns about government over-taking and over-regulation might be better met by prohibiting, as opposed to mandating, compensation).
62. Richard A. Posner, Economic Analysis of Law 64 (5th ed. 1998).
63. Michael A. Heller & James E. Krier, Deterrence and Distribution in the Law of Takings, 112 Harv. L. Rev. 997, 999 (1999); see also Frank I. Michelman, Property, Utility, and Fairness: Comments on the Ethical Foundations of "Just Compensation" Law, 80 Harv. L. Rev. 1165, 1218 (1967).
64. This assumes that officials cannot just embezzle the money and take it for themselves. As discussed below, in deeply corrupt systems of government, where money in the treasury is treated by officials or leaders as their personal property, personified models of government behavior become depressingly accurate.

65. Richard H. Fallon, Jr., & Daniel J. Meltzer, New Law, Non-Retroactivity, and Constitutional Remedies, 104 Harv. L. Rev. 1731, 1788 (1991).
66. See James Forman, Jr., Locking Up Our Own (2017).
67. Of course, money cannot fully compensate for the costs of injuries and death, or the dignitary harms of discrimination and harassment. It is an open question how much victims and their allies will be placated by compensation payments.
68. Another possibility is that the immediate costs will be covered by private insurers (in exchange, of course, for premiums that will ultimately be paid by taxpayers and defunded beneficiaries). There is some evidence that insurers exert effective regulatory influence over the police agencies they insure, reducing the risk of misconduct. See John Rappaport, How Private Insurers Regulate Public Police, 130 Harv. L. Rev. 1539 (2017).
69. See Geoffrey Brennan & James M. Buchanan, The Power to Tax (1980).
70. Mancur Olson, Dictatorship, Democracy, and Development, 87 Am. Pol. Sci. Rev. 567 (1993).
71. Sinclair Davidson & Jason Potts, The Stationary Bandit Model of Intellectual Property, 37 Cato J. 69, 70 (2017).
72. See generally Charles Tilly, War Making and State Making as Organized Crime, in Bringing the State Back In 169 (Peter B. Evans et al. eds., 1985).
73. See Hathaway & Shapiro at 338–45.
74. Id. at 345.
75. See id. at 336–51; see also Alberto Alesina & Enrico Spolare, The Size of Nations 175–201 (2005).
76. See Alesina & Spolare at 1.
77. Corruption aside, for much of American history government officials were legally authorized to collect money in exchange for performing their public duties. That practice disappeared only in the twentieth century, when fixed salaries eliminated any profit motive from government work. See Nicholas R. Parrillo, Against the Profit Motive (2013).
78. A partial exception to this generalization is the compensation of government officials and employees themselves. Writing in the Jacksonian era of rampant patronage, John C. Calhoun sometimes veered from his general view of competing interests in society to fulminate about the independent motivations of the "spoilsmen" in government who represented no interest but their own. Calhoun's political objections to the Tariff of Abominations and his theoretical writings about the conflict between "tax-payers and tax-consumers" combined claims of distributive unfairness among sections and economic interests with complaints that the tax-consumers included government "spoilsmen." See William W. Freehling, Spoilsmen and Interests in the Thought and Career of John C. Calhoun, 52 J. Am. Hist. 25 (1965).
79. See Tim Wu, The Curse of Bigness: Antitrust in the New Gilded Age (2018) (echoing a phrase coined by Louis Brandeis).
80. See, e.g., Oliver Williamson, Markets and Hierarchies (1975); Ronald H. Coase, The Nature of the Firm, 4 Econometrica 386 (1937).

81. See, e.g., Michael C. Jensen, Agency Costs of Free Cash Flow, Corporate Finance, and Takeovers, 76 Am. Econ. Rev. 323 (1986).
82. Recall the discussion in Chapter 3, pp. 102–4.
83. Gary S. Lawson, The Rise and Rise of the Administrative State, 107 Harv. L. Rev. 1231 (1994).
84. Steven G. Calabresi, The Era of Big Government Is Over, 50 Stan. L. Rev. 1015, 1053 (1998).
85. See Cass R. Sunstein & Adrian Vermeule, Law & Leviathan 19–37 (2020) (offering a similar description of critical perspectives on the administrative state).
86. See William A. Niskanen, Jr., Bureaucracy and Representative Government 36–42 (1971).
87. James Q. Wilson, Bureaucracy 118 (1989).
88. See Kenneth A. Shepsle & Mark S. Bonchek, Analyzing Politics 353–55 (1997).
89. See id. at 347–48; Anthony Downs, Inside Bureaucracy 26–84 (1989).
90. See Wilson at 187–88.
91. See, e.g., Michael S. Greve, Real Federalism: Why It Matters, How It Could Happen 3 (1999).
92. See Michael W. McConnell, Federalism: Evaluating the Founders' Design, 54 U. Chi. L. Rev. 1484, 1499; Barry R. Weingast, The Economic Role of Political Institutions: Market-Preserving Federalism and Economic Development, 11 J.L. Econ. & Org. 1 (1995).
93. See, e.g., Dani Rodrik, Has Globalization Gone Too Far? (1997). For a more skeptical take, see Daniel W. Drezner, Bottom Feeders, 121 Foreign Pol'y 64 (2000).
94. See Charles M. Tiebout, A Pure Theory of Local Expenditures, 64 J. Pol. Econ. 416 (1956).
95. See Ilya Somin, Free to Move: Foot Voting, Migration, and Political Freedom (2020).
96. Tiebout's original model was content to assume away supply-side incentives. Focusing on demand-side sorting as a mechanism for revealing preferences for public goods, the model simply assumes that each jurisdiction has an optimal size at which the average cost of providing public goods is minimized, and that jurisdictions below the optimal size will seek to attract residents while jurisdictions above the optimal size will seek to expel residents. See Tiebout at 419.
97. McConnell at 1499; see also, e.g., William W. Bratton & Joseph A. McCahery, The New Economics of Jurisdictional Competition: Devolutionary Federalism in a Second-Best World, 86 Geo. L.J. 201, 235–37 (1997); Epple & Allan Zelenitz, The Implications of Competition Among Jurisdictions: Does Tiebout Need Politics?, 89 J. Pol. Econ. 1197 (1981) (modeling governments as seeking to maximize tax revenues); Caroline M. Hoxby, School Choice and School Productivity: Could School Choice Be a Tide That Lifts All Boats?, in The Economics of School Choice 287, 301–302 (Caroline M. Hoxby ed., 2003) (developing a model of school competition based on budget-maximizing government officials).
98. See Clayton P. Gillette, Local Redistribution and Local Democracy (2011).
99. See, e.g., Paul E. Peterson, City Limits 131–49 (1981).

100. See John E. Chubb, How Relevant Is Competition to Government Policymaking?, in Competition Among States and Local Governments 57, 60–62 (Daphne A. Kenyon & John Kincaid eds., 1991); Jonathan Rodden & Susan Rose-Ackerman, Does Federalism Preserve Markets?, 83 Va. L. Rev. 1521, 1532–43 (1997).
101. See Richard L. Revesz, Rehabilitating Interstate Competition: Rethinking the "Race-to-the-Bottom" Rationale for Federal Environmental Regulation, 67 N.Y.U. L. Rev. 1210 (1992). The literature on globalization has not been as clear on the conceptual shortcomings of supply-side race to the bottom arguments, but empirical evidence has been adduced to cast doubt. See Drezner.
102. See Daniel N. Shaviro, Can Tax Cuts Increase the Size of Government?, 18 Can. J. L. & Juris. 1 (2005) (demonstrating that dollar flows through taxing and spending cannot be a meaningful measure of the size of government).
103. Mark Kelman, Strategy or Principle: The Choice Between Regulation and Taxation (1999).
104. See Desmond King & Robert C. Lieberman, Ironies of State-Building: A Comparative Perspective on the American State, 61 World Pol. 547, 547–48 (2009).
105. More careful measures of the size of the national government do count, for example, the 12 million workers in state and local governments and the private sector who are paid to administer federal policies and programs, on top of the two million official federal government non-military employees, as part of that bigness. See John J. DiIulio, Jr., Ten Questions and Answers About America's "Big Government," Brookings, Feb. 13, 2017.
106. See Brian Balogh, A Government Out of Sight (2009); Suzanne Mettler, The Submerged State (2011).
107. Liam Murphy & Thomas Nagel, The Myth of Ownership 31, 16 (2002).

Chapter 8

1. Jack Goldsmith & Tim Wu, Who Controls the Internet? 25 (2006).
2. Id. at ix.
3. Or perhaps the state will take a different form. See, e.g., Philip Bobbitt, The Shield of Achilles (2002) (describing transformations in the nature of the state resulting from strategic and technological shifts).
4. See Chapter 7, p. 215.
5. Thomas Hobbes, Leviathan 230 (Richard Tuck ed., 1991) (1651).
6. A.V. Dicey, Combination Laws as Illustrating the Relation Between Law and Opinion in England During the Nineteenth Century, 17 Harv. L. Rev. 511, 513 (1904).
7. Paul Vinogradoff, Juridical Persons, 24 Colum. L. Rev. 594, 595 (1924).
8. See Morton J. Horwitz, Santa Clara Revisited: The Development of Corporate Theory 88 W. Va. L. Rev. 173, 180 (1985).
9. See Gerald E. Frug, The City as a Legal Concept, 93 Harv. L. Rev. 1057 (1980).
10. See Nikolas Bowie, Corporate Personhood v. Corporate Statehood, 132 Harv. L. Rev. 2009 (2019).

11. Id. at 2016.
12. Frug at 1095.
13. Bowie at 2013.
14. See Nina Totenberg, When Did Companies Become People?, NPR morning Edition, July 28, 2014.
15. See Adam Winkler, We the Corporation (2018).
16. See Reinier Kraakman et al., The Anatomy of Corporate Law 23–28 (2004).
17. See Bowie at 2014.
18. Morris Cohen, Property and Sovereignty, 13 Cornell L.J. 8 (1927).
19. Quoted in Warren J. Samuels, Essays in the History of Heterodox Political Economy 184 (1992).
20. Joseph Fishkin & William E. Forbath, The Anti-Oligarchy Constitution 140 (2022).
21. Louis K. Liggett Co. v. Lee, 288 U.S. 517, 565 (1933) (Brandeis, J., dissenting). This warning would later be driven home for the New Dealers by the role of German industrialists in overthrowing the Weimar Republic and bringing the Nazis to power. See Ganesh Sitaraman, Unchecked Power, The New Republic, Nov. 29, 2018.
22. See generally K. Sabeel Raman, Democracy Against Domination 64–68, 80–96 (2016).
23. K. Sabeel Rahman, Artificial Sovereigns: A Quasi-Constitutional Moment for Tech?, LPE Blog, June 15, 2018.
24. See Barbara H. Fried, The Progressive Assault on Laissez Faire 29–107 (2001). Another source of rights protection—and another approach to blurring the boundary between public and private—was the Progressive Era innovation of public utilities regulation. Railroads, energy producers, telecommunications companies, and other businesses that monopolized essential infrastructure would be regulated as public utilities or common carriers, subject to special legal regimes requiring nondiscrimination and fair treatment. The quasi-public status of these entities justified the imposition of quasi-constitutional rights. Id. at 160–204; K. Sabeel Rahman, The New Utilities: Private Power, Social Infrastructure, and the Revival of the Public Utility Concept, 39 Cardozo L. Rev. 1621 (2018).
25. Bowie at 2037; see also Fishkin & Forbath at 197–210.
26. Ganesh Sitaraman, The Crisis of the Middle-Class Constitution 179–80 (2017).
27. Cynthia Estlund, Regoverning the Workplace: From Self-Regulation to Co-Regulation 28–29 (2010).
28. See Fishkin & Forbath at 212–30.
29. 21 Cong. Rec. 2461 (1890) (statement of Sen. Sherman).
30. See Tim Wu, The Curse of Bigness 33–44 (2018).
31. See Sitaraman, Middle-Class Constitution, at 186; see also Fishkin & Forbath at 284–87.
32. See id. at 174.
33. James McCauley Landis, The Administrative Process 46 (1938).
34. Id. at 11.
35. See Adrian Vermeule, Bureaucracy and Distrust: Landis, Jaffe, and Kagan on the Administrative State, 130 Harv. L. Rev. 2463, 2467–70 (describing Landis's theory

of administrative power as driven by the need to balance corporate power); see also Fishkin & Forbath at 312 (describing FDR's goal of "constitut[ing] the federal government as a countervailing power to regulate and constrain[] giant firms to work for the public good").

36. In the view of some observers, the right metaphorical monster for Big Tech and other multinational corporations is not the territorial and hierarchical Leviathan but the mobile, many-tentacled Kraken. See Robert Fredona & Sophus A. Reinert, Leviathan and Kraken: States, Corporations, and Political Economy, 59 Hist. & Theory 167 (2020).
37. Rahman, Artificial Sovereigns.
38. Quoted in Kate Klonick, The New Governors: The People, Rules, and Processes Governing Online Speech, 131 Harv. L. Rev. 1598, 1599 (2018).
39. See Kristen E. Eichensehr, Digital Switzerlands, 167 U. Pa. L. Rev. 665, 685–87 (2019).
40. See Alexis Wichowski, The U.S. Can't Regulate Big Tech Companies When They Act Like Nations, Wash. Post, Oct. 29, 2020.
41. Adam Satariano, The World's First Ambassador to the Tech Industry, N.Y. Times, Sept. 3, 2019.
42. Frank Pasquale, From Territorial to Functional Sovereignty, LPE Blog, Dec. 6, 2017.
43. See Jed Rubenfeld, Are Facebook and Google State Actors?, Lawfare, Nov. 4, 2019.
44. On the general prospects for holding corporations liable under international human rights law, see Steven R. Ratner, Corporations and Human Rights: A Theory of Legal Responsibility, 111 Yale L.J. 443 (2001).
45. See Elizabeth Culliford, Rohingya Refugees Sue Facebook for $150 Billion over Myanmar Violence, Reuters, Dec. 8, 2021.
46. Kate Klonick, The Making of Facebook's Supreme Court, The New Yorker, Feb. 12, 2021.
47. Id.
48. Id.
49. Kate Klonick, The Facebook Oversight Board: Creating an Independent Institution to Adjudicate Online Free Expression, 129 Yale L.J. 2418, 2458 (2020). Reformers have also proposed other mechanisms of representation, such as juries of ordinary citizens empowered to determine whether political advertisements are false or misleading. See Jonathan Zittrain, A Jury of Random People Can Do Wonders for Facebook, The Atlantic, Nov. 14, 2019.
50. Evelyn Douek, Somebody Has to Do It, The Atlantic, May 6, 2021.
51. Leviathan at 190.
52. Sitaraman, Unchecked Power.
53. Rahman.
54. Sitaraman, Unchecked Power.
55. See Rahman.
56. Id.
57. Hedley Bull, The Anarchical Society 46 (1977).
58. Alexander Wendt, Why a World State Is Inevitable, 9 Eur. J. Int'l Rel. 491, 491 (2003).

59. Immanuel Kant, Toward Perpetual Peace, in Toward Perpetual Peace and Other Writings on Politics, Peace, and History 67, 91–92 (David L. Colclasure trans. & Pauline Kleingeld ed., 2008).
60. Though not all. See Wendt.
61. For an overview, see Catherine Lu, World Government, The Stanford Encyclopedia of Philosophy, revised Jan. 5, 2021.
62. See Thomas Pogge, Kant's Vision of a Just World Order, in The Blackwell Guide to Kant's Ethics 196, 205–206 (Thomas E. Hill ed., 2009); see also William E. Scheuerman, Cosmopolitanism and the World State, 40 Rev. Int'l Stud. 419 (2014) (describing cosmopolitan visions of a world state that are, in fact, quite statist, if more along the lines of the United States or Switzerland than Hobbesian centralization and absolutism).
63. See, e.g., The Worlds of European Constitutionalism (Grainne de Burca & J.H.H. Weiler eds., 2012); Jurgen Habermas, Democracy in Europe: Why the Development of the EU into a Transnational Democracy Is Necessary and How It Is Possible, 21 Eur. L.J. 546 (2015); Dieter Grimm, Sovereignty in Europe, in The Constitution of European Democracy 39 (Dieter Grimm ed., 2017); Mattias Kumm, Beyond Golf Clubs and the Judicialization of Politics: Why Europe Has a Constitution Properly So Called, 54 Am. J. Comp. L. Supp. 505 (2006); Eric Stein, Lawyers, Judges, and the Making of a Transnational Constitution, 75 Am. J. Int'l L. 1 (1981); Neil Walker, Late Sovereignty in the European Union, in Sovereignty in Transition 3 (Neil Walker ed. 2003); J.H.H. Weiler, The Transformation of Europe, 100 Yale L.J. 2403 (1991).
64. See generally Jose E. Alvarez, International Organizations as Law-Makers (2006); The Oxford Handbook of International Organizations (Jacob Katz Cogan et al. eds., 2016).
65. See Joshua Cohen & Charles F. Sabel, Global Democracy, 37 N.Y.U. J. Int'l L. & Pol. 763, 764–66 (2005).
66. See, e.g., Jan Klabbers et al., The Constitutionalization of International Law (2009); Ruling the World? Constitutionalism, International Law, and Global Governance (Jeffrey L. Dunoff & Joel P. Trachtman eds., 2009); Mattias Kumm et al., How Large Is the World of Global Constitutionalism?, 3 Global Const. 1 (2014). Parallel perspectives that do not use the terminology of "constitutionalism" include Eyal Benevisti, The Law of Global Governance (2014); Armin von Bogdandy et al., From Public International to International Public Law, 28 Eur. J. Int'l L. 115 (2017); Benedict Kingsbury et al., The Emergence of Global Administrative Law, 68 L. & Contemp. Probs. 15 (2005). Different analytic frameworks have been proposed for more precisely understanding what a "constitution" should mean in the global context. See, e.g., G. John Ikenberry, After Victory (2001); Kumm, Why Europe Has a Constitution; Alec Stone, What Is a Supranational Constitution? An Essay in International Relations Theory, 56 Rev. of Pol. 441 (1994).
67. On the WTO, see Deborah Cass, The Constitutionalization of the World Trade Organization (2005); John H. Jackson, The World Trade Organization: Constitution and Jurisprudence (1998); John O. McGinnis & Mark L. Movesian, The World Trade Constitution, 114 Harv. L. Rev. 511 (2000). On the UN, see Bardo Fassbender, The

United Nations Charter as the Constitution of the International Community (2009); Michael W. Doyle, The UN Charter—A Global Constitution?, in Ruling the World 113; Jurgen Habermas, Does the Constitutionalization of International Law Still Have A Chance?, in The Divided West (Ciaran Cronin ed., 2006).

68. Klabbers et al. at 53.
69. See Alec Stone Sweet, The Structure of Constitutional Pluralism, 11 ICON 491 (2014); Daniel Halberstam, Constitutional Heterarchy: The Centrality of Conflict in the European Union and the United States, in Ruling the World?, in Dunoff & Trachtman 326.
70. See Peter J. Spiro, The New Sovereigntists: American Exceptionalism and Its False Prophets, For. Aff., Nov./Dec. 2000; Michael Goodhart & Stacy B. Taninchev, The New Sovereigntist Challenge for Global Governance: Democracy Without Sovereignty, 55 Int'l Stud. Q. 1047 (2011).
71. See Eric A. Posner, The Perils of Global Legalism 109 (2009).
72. See Robert O. Keohane et al., Democracy-Enhancing Multilateralism, 63 Int'l Org. 1 (2009).
73. See Andrew Moravcsik, Is There a "Democratic Deficit" in World Politics? A Framework for Analysis, 39 Gov't & Opposition 336 (2004); see also Allen Buchanan & Robert O. Keohane, The Legitimacy of Global Governance Institutions, 20 Ethics & Int'l Aff. 405 (2006) (outlining conditions under which global governance could be in the service of democratic sovereignty).
74. See David Held, Democracy and the Global Order (1995); Cosmopolitan Democracy: An Agenda for a New World Order (Daniele Archibugi & David Held eds., 1995); see also Richard Falk & Andrew Strauss, Towards Global Parliament, Foreign Aff., Feb. 2001.
75. Richard B. Stewart, Remedying Disregard in Global Regulatory Governance: Accountability, Participation, and Responsiveness, 108 Am. J. Int'l L. 211 (2014).
76. See, e.g., Alfred C. Aman, Jr., The Democracy Deficit: Taming Globalization Through Law Reform 54 (2004); Gráinne de Búrca, Developing Democracy Beyond the State, 46 Colum. J. Transnational L. 221, 221–36 (2008); Stewart, Disregard.
77. See, e.g., Michael Zurn & Monika Heupel, Protecting the Individual from International Authority: Human Rights in International Organizations (2017).
78. Joined Cases C-402/05 P & C-415/05 P, Kadi & Al Barakaat Int'l Found. v. Council of the European Union, 2008 E.C.R. I-6351; see also Joined Cases C-584/10 P, C-593/10 P & C-595/10 P, Comm'n v. Kadi, EU:C:2013:518 (Grand Chamber) (E.C.J.).
79. See Gráinne de Búrca, The European Court of Justice and the International Legal Order After Kadi, 51 Harv. Int'l L.J. 1, 9–11 (2010).
80. See Stephen C. Sieberson, The Proposed European Union Constitution: Will It Eliminate the EU's Democratic Deficit?, 10 Colum. J. Eur. L. 173, 188–203 (2004); Weiler, Transformation of Europe, at 2466–74. But see Andrew Moravcsik, In Defence of the "Democratic Deficit": Reassessing Legitimacy in the European Union, 40 J. Common Mkt. Studs. 603 (2002) (emphasizing the democratic advantages of governance by institutions not directly accountable to their constituents).

81. See Bundesverfassungsgericht [BVerG] [Federal Constitutional Court] May 29, 1974, 37 ENTSCHEIDUNGEN DES BUNDESVERFASSUNGSGERICHTS [BVERFGE] 271, 1974 (*Solange I*).
82. See Bundesverfassungsgericht [BVerG] [Federal Constitutional Court] Oct. 22, 1986, 73 ENTSCHEIDUNGEN DES BUNDESVERFASSUNGSGERICHTS [BVERFGE] 339, 1987 (*Solange II*).
83. See Wojciech Sadurski, "Solange, Chapter 3": Constitutional Courts in Central Europe—Democracy—European Union, 14 Eur. L.J. 1 (2008).
84. See Kingsbury et al. at 48–51.
85. See Aman at 81–82, 86.
86. See Jurgen Habermas, The Constitutionalization of International Law and the Legitimation Problems of a Constitution for World Society, 15 Constellations 444, 451 (2008) (calling for the development of a "functional global public sphere").
87. Eyal Benvenisti & George W. Downs, Toward Global Checks and Balances, 20 Const. Pol. Econ. 366, 375 (2009); see also Anne-Marie Slaughter, A New World Order 253–55 (2005).
88. Jeff D. Colgan & Robert O. Keohane, The Liberal Order Is Rigged, For. Aff., May/June 2017; see also Quinn Slobodian, Globalists (2020).
89. Ruth W. Grant & Robert O. Keohane, Accountability and Abuses of Power in World Politics, 99 Am. Pol. Sci. Rev. 29, 29 (2005).
90. See Andrew Guzman, International Organizations and the Frankenstein Problem, 24 Eur. J. Int'l L. 999 (2013).

Index

For the benefit of digital users, indexed terms that span two pages (e.g., 52–53) may, on occasion, appear on only one of those pages.

absolutism, 60, 68–69, 75, 84, 98–99, 232, 237, 258, 263
Ackerman, Bruce, 106
Adams, John, 152–53
Administrative Procedure Act, 103–4
administrative state, 101
affirmative action, 33, 133, 186
Afghanistan, 11, 84–85, 87
African National Congress (ANC), 121–23, 136–37
Amazon, 233, 235–36
antebellum Southerners, 135–37
antidiscrimination rights, 118–19, 135, 160, 185–86, 279
Anti-Federalists, 11, 90, 114, 152 *See also* Federalists
antitrust law, 28, 96, 232–33
Arendt, Hannah, 75
Aristotle, 150
armed conflict, 3, 112 *See also* warfare
Articles of Confederation, 90, 95, 237–38
Austin, John, 24–25, 61–62
authoritarianism, 44–45, 60, 79, 85, 105, 202–3
authoritative tribunals, 33–34

Bagehot, Walter, 3–4
balancing power, 4–5, 8–9, 11–13, 130–31, 139–41, 143, 148, 157–62, 188–89, 233–35, *See also* consociational democracy; realism
Beitz, Charles, 77
Big Government, 16–17, 84, 101, 104, 195, 213, 215, 221–22, 233
Big Tech, 17, 215, 227–28, 233–36, 293
Bill of Rights, 70, 98–99, 114–15, 135–36, 264, 267, 270

Blackstone, William, 68–69
Bolton, John, 66–67
Brexit, 60, 66–67
British constitutionalism, 68–69
Brown v. Board of Education, 118, 126
Buchanan, James, 213

Calhoun, John C., 117, 120–21, 129, 153–54, 289
China, 83, 85, 87–88
Civil Rights Act (1866), 135
Civil Rights Act (1964), 134–35
Civil Rights Commission, 118
civil rights for Black people, 117
Clay, Lucius, 89
coercive force, 7–8, 23, 39, 213, 230–31, 237–38
collective action, 24, 174, 192–93, 236–37, 239–41
collective responsibility, 15–16, 195, 200–6, 286
collective sanctions, 16, 195, 200, 204–6, 208–9, 212, 229
consent theory, 62–63
consociational democracy, 120–21, 130, 150, 156, 269
constitutional adjudication, 168–69, 281
constitutional justice, 168
constitutional responsibility, 169–70, 173–74, 205
constitutional rights
 justice and, 168, 182–84, 282
 libertarianism and, 184, 188–89
 structure of, 113
 violations of, 165–66, 183
constitutional showdowns, 34–35
Constitution of India (1950), 121–22

cooperative federalism, 106–7, 110, 223
corporations
  corporate law, 203–6, 230
  corporate Leviathans, 215, 228
  corporate liability, 203
  multinational corporations, 218–19, 234, 241, 244
corrective justice, 14, 172–73, 178–79, 182
cosmopolitan democracy, 242
countermajoritarianism, 11–12, 111, 114, 130–31
counterterrorism, 8, 27
courts
  constitutional courts, 8–9, 31, 33, 38, 60, 121, 243
  European Court of Justice, 242–43
  Federal Constitutional Court of Germany, 243
  International Criminal Court, 57–58, 64–65, 238
  international tribunals, 30, 58–60, 93, 240
  judicial review, 154, 156, 159–60
  US Supreme Court, 34–36, 46, 49–50
COVID pandemic, 83, 85, 95–96, 147–48
customary international law (CIL), 29, 63–64

Dahl, Robert, 49–50, 128
Dayton Peace Accords, 121–22
decentralized governance, 112–13, 135–36, 146
De Klerk, F.W., 120–21, 129
democracy
  consociational democracy, 120–21, 130, 150, 156, 269
  cosmopolitan democracy, 242
  democratic power, 130–31, 151–62, 157, 188–89, 233–35
  democratization, 122–23, 127, 272
  enfranchisement, 118, 122, 127, 131, 135, 137
  Fifthteenth Amendment, 118
  gerrymandering, 34, 37, 133
  industrial democracy, 232–35
  introduction to, 3, 11–12, 14–15
  representative democracy, 57–59, 93, 242–43
  rights and votes under, 127
  state building/unbuilding, 84–85, 87–90, 93, 105
  statutory law of, 158
  voting rights, 11–12, 117, 125, 183
deontological reasoning, 187–88
Dicey, A. V., 228
distributive justice, 178–79, 183, 188–91, 282–83
divided societies, 120–22, 127, 137
division of moral labor, 15, 179–80, 182
domestic analogy, 4–5, 191
domestic legal systems, 1, 8, 23–25, 30–31, 55–56, 121–22
Dred Scott decision, 35
Dworkin, Ronald, 15, 167–68

East India Company, 228–29
economic power, 11–12, 87, 158–59, 214–15, 231, 233, 235–36
Electoral College, 77–78, 106–7, 115–16, 127
empire-building, 16–17, 213, 229, 233
environmental regulation, 145–46, 154, 177–78, 209–11, 218, 224
European Convention on Human Rights, 121–22, 243
European Court of Justice (ECJ), 242–43
European Union, 30–31, 74, 88, 93, 99, 143–44, 237–44

Facebook, 234–36
failed states, 37, 84–85, 87
Federal Constitutional Court of Germany, 243
federalism
  balancing power under, 143, 145–47, 154
  cooperative federalism, 106–7, 110, 223
  economic markets and, 218
  federation/confederation, 237–38
  legal order and, 58
  repeat-play cooperation, 51
  rights and votes, 135–38, 273
  in state-building, 106
  state building/unbuilding, 11, 90, 106

Federalist No. 10 (Madison), 149–50, 158–59, 161, 267
Federalist No. 51 (Madison), 149–50, 161
Federalists, 52, 90, 97, 100–2, 114–16, 152–53, *See also* Anti-Federalists
Fifthteenth Amendment (US Constitution), 118
Fourteenth Amendment (US Constitution), 135
freedom of speech, 84, 178, 229–30, 234
free trade, 57–58, 214, 218–19, 239–41
Friedman, Milton, 87–88

gender discrimination/equality, 174–75, 184, 186
German Basic Law, 243
Germany, 88
Gilded Age, 165, 215, 234
global constitutionalism, 239, 241–42
global governance, 17, 236
globalization, 160, 218–20, 227, 244, 291
Glorious Revolution (1688), 98–99
Goldsmith, Jack, 26, 105–6
Goodin, Robert, 128
Google, 233–34, 236
group punishment, 14, 194, 197
Guinier, Lani, 133
gunman writ large, 8, 40, 54–55

Hamilton, Alexander, 97–98, 115, 151
Hart, H. L. A., 24–25, 28, 62, 75–76
Hathaway, Oona, 50
Henkin, Louis, 41
Henry, Patrick, 152
Hirschman, Albert O., 135
Hitler, Adolf, 41
Hobbes, Thomas, 2, 7, 9, 27–28, 42, 68–69, 71
  absolutism, 60, 68–69, 75, 84, 98–99, 232, 237, 258, 263
  balancing power, 12–13, 139, 141–42
  collective responsibility, 195–96, 198
  corporations, corporate state, 228, 230–31
  global Leviathan, 236–37
  law for states, 6–8, 23–27, 235
  legal enforcement, 39
  legal settlement, 27–28, 38–39
  separation of powers, 276
  sovereignty and, 9–10, 61–63, 67–69, 71–72, 76–77
  state as Leviathan, 2, 4, 10–11, 79, 85–86
  state building, 84–86
  state of nature, 56–59, 86, 224
  states as persons, 4–5, 14–15, 166–68
  statism and justice, 191–92
Holmes, Oliver Wendell, 68–69
Holocaust, 198
Horowitz, Donald, 127
humanitarian interventions, 26, 29–30, 65, 77, 145–46, 191
human rights, 65–67, 75, 77, 181
Hussein, Saddam, 194, 202–3, 212

immigration, 29–30, 60, 145–48, 154, 241
impeachment, 34–35, 139–40
imperial presidency, 101
individualism, 133, 196–99, 285–86
industrial democracy, 232–35
institutionalists/institutionalism, 8–9, 13, 18–19, 42–44, 50–54, 144, 254
interjurisdictional competition, 218
international cooperation, 40, 42–43, 60, 66–67, 143–44, 147, 215
International Criminal Court, 57–58, 64–65, 238
international humanitarian law, 5–6
international institutionalists/institutionalism, 8–9, 50–51, 239–42, 244
International Monetary Fund, 87, 238
international tribunals, 30, 58–60, 93, 240
Iraq, 11, 26, 84–85, 87

Jackson, Robert, 48
Japanese Americans, 48
Jefferson, Thomas, 100–1, 114
Jim Crow South, 33, 119–20, 160–61, 169–70
Johnson, Boris, 60
judicial review, 154, 156, 159–60
judicial supremacy, 35–36, 46, 49–50, 52
jus ad bellum, 190
jus in bello, 190, 284
just compensation for takings, 207

justice
  constitutional justice, 168
  constitutional rights and, 168, 182–84, 282
  corrective justice, 14, 172–73, 178–79, 182
  distributive justice, 178–79, 183, 188–91, 282–83
  global justice, 191–92
  Rawls, theory of, 15, 168, 180–83, 191, 283
  systemic justice, 181–82, 186, 188–89
just war, 5–6, 14, 167, 190–91

Kant, Immanuel, 237
King, Martin Luther, 117–19, 126
Kissinger, Henry, 12–13
Korematsu v. United States, 48
Kramer, Larry, 36

lawfare, 112
League of Nations, 66–67
legal enforcement
  centralized enforcement, 24–25, 26, 40–41, 47–48, 61–62
  challenges of, 8
  decentralized enforcement, 8–9
  parchment barriers, 8–9, 13, 47–48, 52, 57, 97–98, 114, 126–27
legal order/settlement, 8, 27–28, 30–31, 33, 37–39, 54, 239
legitimacy, 8–9, 53–56, 70–71, 84, 130–31, 157–58, 172, 243
Leviathan, frontispiece, 2, 260
liberal internationalists, 4–5
liberalism, 11–12, 144–45, 272
liberal rights, 60, 131–33, 185
libertarianism, 184–85, 224, 282–83
Lincoln, Abraham, 48–49, 69–70

Madison, James
  balancing power, 139–40, 142–43, 149–50, 152–53, 156
  capacity and control, 100
  constitutionalists and, 47–48, 52–54, 57
  constitutional theory, 122
  democratic representation, 119
  Federalist No. 10, 149–50, 158–59, 161, 267
  Federalist No. 51, 149–50, 161

  model of pluralist politics, 129
  opposed to a bill of rights, 124–25
  rights and votes, 114
  right to own slaves, 115–16, 134–35
  sovereignty and, 69–70
Magna Carta, 98–99
Maine, Henry Sumner, 197
Mandela, Nelson, 121
Marshall, John, 31–32, 256, 259
Marshall Plan, 11, 88, 99
Marx, Karl, 131–33
Mashaw, Jerry, 103
Merkel, Angela, 89–90
military power, 86–87, 95, 214
Mill, John Stuart, 129, 131, 278
Missouri Compromise, 115–16
mixed government, 150–54, 156–57
monopolies, 2–3, 7–8, 23, 39, 86, 97, 114–15, 213, 215, 218, 230–33, 237–38, 292
moral dualism *vs.* monism, 73, 180
Morgenthau, Hans, 40–41
Morgenthau, Henry, Jr., 11, 88
Morgenthau Plan, 88–89, 95
multilateral treaty arrangements, 29, 238

Nagel, Thomas, 186–88, 192
Nazi Germany, 41, 89–90
New Deal, 33, 35, 52, 102–5, 170–72, 232–33
Nuremberg Tribunal, 196–97, 199–200, 212, 285

Obama, Barack, 8, 27
online platforms, 34
opinio juris, 10, 23–25, 29, 37, 39–42, 62–63, 65, 165–66, 199, 248
originalism, 18–19, 32, 70–74, 104, 216, 259
outsourcing, 107–8, 110, 223

pacta sunt servanda, 63–64
parchment barriers, 8–9, 13, 47–48, 52, 57, 97–98, 114, 126–27
Peace of Westphalia (1648), 61, 255
Perpetual Peace (Kant), 237
Plato, 150
police violence, 96, 194–95, 206–7
political process theory, 119–20, 126, 129, 160–61

INDEX

popular constitutionalism, 38–39, 45–46, 72–73
popular sovereignty, 60, 66–67, 69, 130–31, 258, 288
populism, 9–10, 60, 79, 149, 241, 244
positivism, 24–25, 28, 39–40
presidential powers, 11, 37, 104–6, 147–48, 155
Progressive Era, 109–10, 147, 231–32, 292
property rights, 57–58, 86–87, 94, 121, 127, 137, 170, 177–78, 186, 188–89, 261
Putin, Vladimir, 202–3

qualified immunity, 206–7

Rabkin, Jeremy, 67
racial discrimination and equality, 33, 35, 118–20, 130, 132, 134–35, 159–61, 169–70, 178, 186, 207–8, 259, 283
Rawls, John, 15, 168, 179–83, 191, 283
Reagan, Ronald, 102
realism, 13, 42, 48, 50, 53, 142–45
Reconstruction Amendments, 118
responsibility to protect, 29–30
rights. *See also* constitutional rights
    antidiscrimination rights, 118–19, 135, 160, 185–86, 279
    civil rights for Black people, 117
    human rights, 65–67, 75, 77
    individual rights, 125, 158–59, 178, 182, 185–88
    liberal rights, 60, 131–33, 185
    minority rights, 114–15, 117
    polyethnic rights, 133
    property rights, 57–58, 86–87, 94, 121, 127, 137, 170, 177–78, 186, 188–89, 261
    relation to political justice, 183
    statutory rights, 134–35
    voting rights, 11–12, 117, 125, 183
rights of man, 131–32
Roman Republic, 150
Roosevelt, Franklin D., 33, 88, 170–71
Rubenfeld, Jed, 67
Rwandan genocide, 149

Scheffler, Samuel, 181
Scott, James C., 94
secession, 12, 34–35, 112–13, 135–38, 273

Second Bill of Rights, 170–71
self-determination, 66, 76–79, 135–36, 232, 241
self-government, 6, 9–10, 66–67, 74, 77–78
separation of powers, 58, 101, 151
Shapiro, Scott, 40
Skinner, Quentin, 2
Smith, Adam, 214
South African Constitution, 120–23, 125, 134, 171
sovereignty/sovereign states
    popular sovereignty, 60, 66–67, 69, 130–31, 258, 288
    self-government and, 6, 9–10, 66–67, 74, 77–78
state capacity, 94–96, 98–99, 102–3, 106–10, 233
Stephanopoulos, Nick, 159

terrorism, 27, 33, 42, 48–49, 84–85, 92–93, 97, 129, 194, 227, 242 *See also* counterterrorism
Thatcher, Margaret, 89–90
Tilly, Charles, 86–87
totalitarianism, 85–86, 105
Trump, Donald, 60, 66–69, 105, 139–40, 235

UN Charter, 26, 29–30, 42, 63–65, 238–39, 242
United Nations (UN), 60, 238, 240
US Supreme Court, 34–36, 46, 49–50
utilitarianism, 180–82

Waldron, Jeremy, 78, 135
Waltzer, Michael, 166–67
warfare, 3, 86–87, 214, 261
Washington Consensus, 87–88, 261
Weber, Max, 2–3
Webster, Noah, 70, 72
Westphalian order, 17, 61, 66, 138, 148–49, 156, 227
Wood, Gordon, 151
World Bank, 87, 238
world government, 4–5, 128, 237, 239, 242
World Trade Organization (WTO), 29–31, 37–38, 58, 112, 238–39

Zuckerberg, Mark, 235